Getting It Right in Afghanistan

Getting It RIGHT in
Afghanistan

SCOTT SMITH
MOEED YUSUF
COLIN COOKMAN
Editors

UNITED STATES INSTITUTE OF PEACE PRESS
Washington, DC

The views expressed in this book are those of the authors alone. They do not necessarily reflect the views of the United States Institute of Peace.

UNITED STATES INSTITUTE OF PEACE
2301 Constitution Avenue, NW
Washington, DC 20037
www.usip.org

First published 2013

To request permission to photocopy or reprint materials for course use, contact the Copyright Clearance Center at www.copyright.com. For print, electronic media, and all other subsidiary rights e-mail permissions@usip.org

Printed in the United States of America

The paper used in this publication meets the minimum requirements of American National Standards for Information Science—Permanence of Paper for Printed Library Materials, ANSI Z39.48-1984.

Library of Congress Cataloging-in-Publication Data

Getting it right in Afghanistan / Scott Smith, Moeed Yusuf, and
    Colin Cookman, editors.
      pages cm
    Includes bibliographical references.
    USN 978-1-60127-182-2 (pbk. : alk. paper)
    1. Peace-building—Afghanistan.   2. Nation building—Afghanistan.
3. Afghanistan—Politics and government—2001.   4. Afghan War,
2001—Peace.   5. Taliban.   6. Afghanistan—Foreign relations—
Pakistan.   7. Pakistan—Foreign relations—Afghanistan.   I. Smith,
Scott Seward, 1969– editor.   II. Yusuf, Moeed, editor.   III. Cookman,
Coln, editor.
    JZ5584.A33G47 2013
    958.104'71—dc26

                                                    2013028981

Perhaps there can be such a thing as 'victory' in a battle, whereas in war there can be only the achievement or nonachievement of our objectives. In the old days, wartime objectives were generally limited and practical ones, and it was common to measure the success of your military operations by the extent to which they brought you closer to your objectives. But where your objectives are moral and ideological ones and run to changing the attitudes and traditions of an entire people or the personality of a regime, then victory is probably something not to be achieved entirely by military means or indeed in any short space of time at all; and perhaps that is the source of our confusion.

—George Kennan

CONTENTS

CONTENTS

Afghanistan

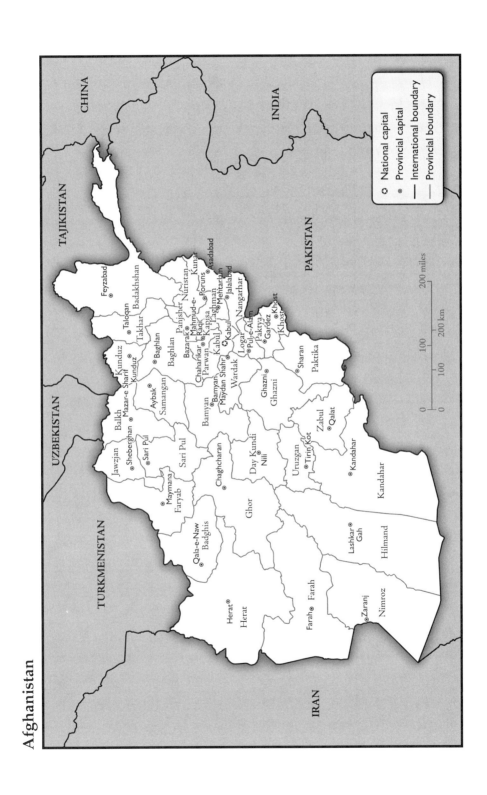

CHINA

INDIA

TAJIKISTAN

PAKISTAN

UZBEKISTAN

TURKMENISTAN

IRAN

National capital
Provincial capital
International boundary
Provincial boundary

200 miles
200 km
100
100
0
0

Feyzabad

Badakhshan

Taloqan

Takhar

Kunduz
Kunduz

Nuristan

Panjsher
Baghlan
Mahmud-e-
Raqic
Kapisa
Asadabad
Poruns
Kunar
Laghman
Mehtarlam
Jalalabad
Nangarhar

Mazar-e Sharif

Aybak
Samangan

Balkh

Bazarak

Chaharikar
Parwan
Kabul
Kabul
Wardak
Logar
Pul-e-Alam
Paktya
Gardez
Khost
Khost

Jawzjan

Sheberghan

Sari Pul
Sari Pul

Bamyan
Maydan Shahr
Bamyan

Ghazni
Ghazni

Sharan
Paktika

Maymana
Faryab

Chaghcharan

Day Kundi
Nili

Uruzgan
Tirin Kot
Zabul
Qalat

Kandahar

Qala-e-Naw
Badghis

Ghor

Kandahar

Herat
Herat

Farah
Farah

Lashkar-e
Gah
Hilmand

Zaranj
Nimroz

Introduction

In recent history, no formerly neglected country has received so much sudden attention and resources as Afghanistan did beginning in 2001. A central but forgotten feature of the effort to reestablish Afghanistan's political order on the pattern of a modern democratic state, however, was many policymakers' ignorance about the country they were trying to change. This ignorance was the result of a decade-long indifference to Afghanistan following the Soviet Union's withdrawal in 1989 by much of the international community. But there were also gaps in Afghans' own understanding of their country, both among those who endured the civil war from 1992 to 2001 and among exiles—a false familiarity that has never really been acknowledged. During the civil war, many Afghans in Afghanistan became concerned with their faction rather than the nation, measuring success by the holding of terrain or the weakening of rivals. The well-being of civilians, the ultimate objective of political order, was mostly addressed by humanitarian agencies. Returning expatriates, meanwhile, spoke their own language and the languages of major donors but had lost touch with their country during their decades of exile. Their perspective was urban while most of the Afghan population in the country was rural. Many of the problems facing the country emerged from this disconnect.

Restoring political order and providing for the well-being of the population became Afghanistan's central problem after 2001, and few of those responsible for addressing it were well equipped to do so. The decade that followed saw policymakers adjusting constantly to the many "sources of confusion," as George Kennan might have put it,[1] that Afghans and international actors confronted as they sought and failed in frustration to establish a lasting political order. A concerted resistance to the premises of that new order further complicated the situation. An insurgency rose from what had been a defeated and discredited Taliban government. What many began to refer to as the "neo-Taliban" regrouped in Pakistan, struck with increasing effectiveness at the weak points of the post-2001 Afghan government, and began to expand beyond its traditional strongholds. In 2006, the number of security incidents recorded by the United Nations (UN) and the North Atlantic Treaty Organization (NATO)–sponsored International Security Assistance Force (ISAF) spiked. Optimistic observers, including much of ISAF's leadership, were reluctant at first to acknowledge that this was the onset of a sustained insurgency. They avoided the term *insurgency* itself, replacing it with a more innocuous lexicon of *anti-government elements* or *the armed opposition*. Only when the counterinsurgency doctrine in Iraq apparently succeeded could the unrest in Afghanistan be labeled for what it had become.

Such was the situation facing the Obama administration when it took office in January 2009. It adopted a number of consequential decisions in an effort to impose its own pattern on the Afghan conflict, the intractability of which was by then not in question. The administration first decided to link U.S. efforts to achieve stability in Afghanistan to its policy in Pakistan by creating the Office of the Special Representative for Afghanistan and Pakistan in the State Department, appointing an experienced diplomat, Richard Holbrooke, as its head. It next decided to agree to a surge in military and civilian support to the Afghan government in December 2009, including increasing U.S. military forces in Afghanistan to approximately one hundred thousand troops. Its third major decision was the simultaneous announcement in December 2009 that U.S. combat operations in Afghanistan would cease at the end of 2014, when Afghan troops would take the lead for security of their own country. This led to an agreement on a formal transition process among ISAF troop-contributing countries and the Afghan government at the NATO summit in Lisbon in November 2010.[2]

Despite some tactical successes in suppressing Taliban activities in several key southern districts and boosting the quantity of trained Afghan soldiers and police, the peak investment of American military and financial assistance during the surge did not alter the underlying parameters of Afghanistan's conflict. With multiple competing strategic priorities in the international community, the United States' time-bound commitment to high-intensity intervention in Afghanistan ultimately required a readjustment of expectations and a willingness to compromise. Over the past two years, the United States signaled that it would make concessions to the armed opposition for the sake of stability. In February 2011, the United States relaxed its preconditions for engaging in talks with the Taliban—a renunciation of violence, separation from al-Qaeda, and a pledge to accept the Afghan constitution—in an effort to advance the possibility of negotiating an end to the conflict.[3]

Attempts at a political settlement in Afghanistan have progressed in fits and starts. A breakthrough seemed possible when diplomats from the United States, through German channels, conducted quiet meetings with senior Taliban representatives beginning in late 2010.[4] By early 2012, the talks were reported to have neared an agreement on an initial series of confidence-building measures, including an exchange of prisoners followed by the opening of a Taliban political office in Qatar, through which more formal diplomatic discussions might proceed.[5] Negotiations broke down by March 2012, however, as Taliban officials publicly accused the United States of failing to follow through on an understanding to release five senior commanders from the U.S. prison at Guantanamo Bay, Cuba.[6] U.S. officials in turn indicated that the Taliban leadership—which faced dissension from some field commanders after reports of U.S. talks became public—had balked at following through on pledges to publicly renounce al-Qaeda and other forms of international terrorism.[7]

The stall in negotiations coincided with serious disruptions in both the U.S.-Pakistan and Pakistan-Afghanistan bilateral relationships. After U.S.-Pakistan relations appeared to reach their nadir in 2011, amid tensions over covert U.S. action in Pakistani territory and a cross-border clash in November 2011 that resulted in the accidental death of twenty-four Pakistani soldiers, U.S. and UK policymakers moved in 2012 to repair regional ties. Trilateral talks on Afghan peace and reconciliation resumed in Islamabad in September 2012, and in November, Afghan High Peace Council Chairman Salahuddin Rabbani made a long-delayed visit to Pakistan, his first trip to the country since taking over the office after the assassination of his father, former president Jalaluddin Rabbani, the year before.[8] Discussions between the High Peace Council delegation and Pakistani leaders led to the release of a dozen mid-level Taliban detainees held by Pakistan. A visit by Afghanistan's foreign minister, Zalmay Rassoul, followed shortly after, during which both sides agreed to the "release of more prisoners, facilitating contacts and urging the Taliban to renounce ties to al-Qaeda."[9]

But tensions between Afghan and Pakistani leaders remain unresolved.[10] As Barnett Rubin and Abubakar Siddique highlighted in 2006 (see chapter 6), fundamental disagreements over the demarcation of the Durand Line separating the two countries continue to hamper agreement on other issues. Disputes over cross-border insurgent attacks and military responses have escalated in seasonal cycles for years since 2010. Afghan leaders accuse the Pakistani military of border incursions and indiscriminate artillery attacks that have resulted in civilian casualties. Pakistani officials complain that Afghan and NATO forces have not sufficiently confronted Pakistani Taliban groups reportedly based in remote parts of eastern Afghanistan.

Since 2011, when the United States dropped its preconditions for talks with the Taliban, significant efforts have been made. These efforts culminated in the long-delayed announcement in June 2013 that a Taliban "political bureau" would be opened in Qatar, a development that the United States, Pakistan, and the Afghan High Peace Council initially backed. These efforts broke down almost immediately, however, when President Karzai accused the Taliban of seeking to present the office as an embassy. While efforts at reconciliation are likely to intensify, given that time is running out and there is little hope in forward movement on this subset of political reconciliation, one can at best be cautiously optimistic. As the time of this writing, the core intra-Afghan conflict remains stalled, with all parties adjusting their strategies to face the final year of significant international involvement.

*

In 2001, policymakers' lack of understanding of Afghanistan undermined their good intentions. Policymakers operating in the endgame period for large-scale direct international investments in Afghanistan do not have the same excuse. There is a wealth of data and analysis available, supported by many information-sharing networks that have developed between Afghans and internationals. A great deal has been learned at a great cost, and the priority now must be to use that knowledge to ensure an outcome in Afghanistan that addresses the question of restoring a sustainable political order.

Since beginning its Afghanistan program in 2002, one of United States Institute of Peace (USIP)'s priorities has been to contribute to the policy formulation process and a better general understanding of Afghanistan by providing accurate, clear, and timely analyses of the conflict. The twelve articles in this volume are a small selection of the more than one hundred publications on Afghanistan and Pakistan that USIP produced between 2005 and 2013 (sixty-eight on Afghanistan and thirty-six on Pakistan). In some ways, these pieces anticipated much of current U.S. policy, including the focus on regional dynamics and the challenges of implementing a reconciliation process that can accommodate the diverse interests of Afghanistan's conflict parties and their neighbors and shift competition to political rather than armed processes. The essays converge around the theme of a political settlement to the Afghan conflict, addressing the sources of the conflict; the roles of Afghanistan's most critical neighbor, Pakistan, and the broader region; and the process of negotiation toward a final settlement. All of the articles continue to be relevant to policymakers. Relevance is not necessarily synonymous with freshness. In some cases, it is the opposite, in that the historical depth of the piece makes it important; understanding the sources and drivers of the insurgency or the border conflicts between Afghanistan and Pakistan is essential to fashioning a political settlement that insurgents and other actors might accept.

This volume is divided into three sections. The first section focuses on the internal political dynamics of Afghanistan and the views of Afghan political actors regarding a peace process. Minna Jarvenpaa assesses the vulnerabilities of the U.S. and NATO transition strategy, arguing for the international community in Afghanistan to prioritize a sustainable political settlement. Hamish

Nixon explores the peace process as Afghans experience and understand it, emphasizing how the Afghan government's legitimacy crisis contributes to the conflict. Noah Coburn looks closely at the local disputes that underpin larger conflicts and reviews their lessons for a more comprehensive dispute resolution processes. Matt Waldman explores the insurgency's diverse and overlapping motivations as well as confidence-building measures through which the Taliban might be engaged.

The second section focuses on the roles of Afghanistan's neighbors in shaping the country's internal politics. Marvin Weinbaum comprehensively surveys Afghanistan's long history of external intervention by its neighbors, while Barnett Rubin and Abubakar Siddique focus specifically on the still-disputed Afghan and Pakistani border. The fundamental dynamics of these relationships have not changed since these chapters were published as reports, which is partly why cross-border conflicts continue. Moeed Yusuf, Huma Yusuf, and Salman Zaidi assess the evolving views toward Afghanistan among Pakistan's military and civilian foreign policy elite. They find that the Pakistani state's objectives are defined by a desire for a relatively stable Afghan government that is not hostile to Pakistani regional interests—in other words, not overly sympathetic to India. This mindset, which is supportive of an intra-Afghan reconciliation process, is increasingly visible in Islamabad's rhetoric and policy decisions.[11] But Sunil Dasgupta sees a "New Delhi consensus" favoring continued Indian strategic engagement in Afghanistan, albeit with little support for direct military intervention. Together the chapters underscore the importance of broader regional security dynamics between Pakistan and India in setting the conditions for Afghanistan's internal settlement.

The third section focuses on efforts to implement a peace and reconciliation process for Afghanistan. Mohammad Masoom Stanekzai outlines a framework for the Afghan government to engage in peace talks; his findings informed the creation of the Afghan High Peace Council, whose secretariat he now heads. Deedee Derksen cautions that reintegration efforts targeted at low-level combatants in Afghanistan will have only limited success without corresponding high-level leadership engagement. Lisa Schirch emphasizes the need for an inclusive consultation that accounts for stakeholders at the international, national, and local levels, involving civil society as well as official government actors to legitimize any new political consensus. Finally, Hamish Nixon and Caroline Hartzell focus on the potential structure of a peace process and the institutional options through which current actors to the conflict could satisfy their political objectives without resorting to violence.

*

The chapters in this volume span the period between 2006 and 2012, when the rise of the Taliban-led insurgency became undeniable and when a consensus was reached that it could not be defeated militarily, and therefore political accommodation was necessary.

The chapters convey the complexity and challenge of translating diplomatic processes into an enduring and stable political consensus. Previously scuttled efforts at prisoner exchanges may yet be the beginnings of a confidence-building process between the insurgency and the government, but the current format for talks—still fragmented and secretive—offers limited input for other political actors in Afghan society and raises suspicions. Afghan political opposition and civil society groups who feel that they are not sufficiently represented on the High Peace Council fear that the government and the Taliban will not consider their interests. Nor is Taliban cohesion assured in the event of accommodation with the Karzai government.

Structuring a process is made difficult by the ongoing confusion among actors, mediators, and facilitators. The United States sees itself as mediating an intra-Afghan dialogue—its stated policy is to "help Afghans talk to Afghans."[12] The Taliban, however, sees the United States as the main party to the conflict. It has to date consistently rejected direct talks with the Afghan government, which it views as illegitimate and impotent, especially when it comes to securing the Taliban's main demand that international forces depart. Pakistan must at some point be a party to the talks, given that peace depends on ensuring certain Pakistan interests, and the country has signaled interest in facilitating negotiations. But its role remains controversial, especially among some in the Afghan government who accuse Pakistan of supporting the insurgency to destabilize Afghanistan. The Afghan government sees itself as leading negotiations as part of a general political settlement in which it has the most to lose and to gain, but it alone cannot guarantee the withdrawal of U.S. forces, nor can it compel the Taliban to engage. Finally, a number of groups within the government are reticent to engage with the Taliban due to long-standing historical rivalries.

The approach of the 2014 transition can impel U.S. policymakers, Afghan leaders, and regional neighbors to reach a settlement. The United States and its NATO partners have pledged to continue support for Afghanistan past the transition deadline; at the same time, the Afghan government must prepare to take on much more responsibility for the security of its citizens. The Afghan presidential elections in 2014 have increased political activity in the country but also have increased uncertainty about the composition of the future Afghan government and its willingness to share power with rival constituencies. Efforts to establish talks have been undermined by setbacks, as negotiators have struggled to identify interlocutors who can speak with authority for their divided constituencies and the various conflict actors have competed among one another to control the basic shape of even preliminary talks. Domestic political considerations in Afghanistan, its neighboring countries, and the United States have been yet another complicating factor. The fluidity of the current situation offers possible breakthroughs but also poses risks of deadlock, fragmentation, and continued cycles of mistrust and conflict.

In many ways, 2014 brings us back to 2001 and the challenge of structuring a political system that can accommodate the diverse array of internal and external interest groups at play in Afghanistan. However, a key difference, as noted above, is that a great deal has been learned in the intervening years. This volume offers clear analysis of the many factors that are likely to complicate a negotiation to end Afghanistan's conflict. But the costs of another decade of conflict—to Afghanistan, its people, its neighbors, and even the United States—will be severe. In the short time remaining before the December 2014 transition deadline, the knowledge gained must be put to good use.

Notes

1. See George F. Kennan, *American Diplomacy, Expanded Edition* (Chicago: University of Chicago Press, 1984), 102.
2. North Atlantic Treaty Organization, "Chicago Summit Declaration on Afghanistan," May 21, 2012, available at http://www.nato.int/cps/en/natolive/official_texts_87595.htm (accessed June 18, 2013).
3. See remarks by Secretary Hillary Clinton in February 2011, in which the previous preconditions were instead identified as "necessary outcomes." U.S. Department of State, "Remarks at the Launch of the Asia Society's Series of Richard C. Holbrooke Memorial Addresses," February 18, 2011, available at http://www.state.gov/secretary/rm/2011/02/156815.htm (accessed June 18, 2013).
4. Christoph Reuter, Gregor Peter Schmitz, and Holger Stark, "Talking to the Enemy: How German Diplomats Opened Channel to Taliban," *Der Spiegel*, January 10, 2012, available at http://www.spiegel.de/international/world/talking-to-the-enemy-how-german-diplomats-opened-channel-to-taliban-a-808068.html (accessed June 18, 2013).
5. Matthew Rosenberg, "Taliban Opening Qatar Office, and Maybe Door to Talks," *New York Times*, January 3, 2012, available at http://www.nytimes.com/2012/01/04/world/asia/taliban-to-open-qatar-office-in-step-toward-peace-talks.html?pagewanted=all (accessed June 18, 2013).
6. *Al Jazeera English*, "Afghan Taliban Suspend Peace Talks with US," March 16, 2012, available at http://www.aljazeera.com/news/asia/2012/03/201231512748620425.html (accessed June 18, 2013).
7. Anand Gopal, "Serious Leadership Rifts Emerge in Afghan Taliban," *CTC Sentinel*, no. 11–12, Combating Terrorism Center at West Point, November 28, 2012, available at http://www.ctc.usma.edu/posts/serious-leadership-rifts-emerge-in-afghan-taliban (accessed June 18, 2013); Karen DeYoung, "As U.S.-Taliban Talks Stall, Hope for Political Solution Dims," *Washington Post*, May 9, 2012, available at http://www.washingtonpost.com/world/national-security/as-us-taliban-talks-stall-hope-for-political-solution-dims/2012/05/09/gIQArTLMCU_story.html (accessed June 18, 2013).
8. Rod Nordland, "More Taliban Prisoners May Be Released," *New York Times*, November 17, 2012, available at www.nytimes.com/2012/11/18/world/asia/taliban-leaders-among-prisoners-freed-in-pakistan.html (accessed June 18, 2013).
9. *Agence France-Presse*, "Pakistan Agrees Release of More Taliban Prisoners," November 30, 2012, available at http://dawn.com/2012/11/30/pakistan-agrees-release-of-more-taliban-prisoners/ (accessed June 18, 2013).

10. Sharif Amiry, "Afghan Govt Repeats Claims of Pakistan's 'Unacceptable' Demands," *TOLO News*, March 30, 2013, available at http://tolonews.com/en/afghanistan/9958-afghan-govt-repeats-claim-of-pakistans-unacceptable-demands (accessed June 18, 2013).

11. Matthieu Aikins, "Pakistan's Charm Offensive," *Foreign Policy*, September 13, 2012, available at http://www.foreignpolicy.com/articles/2012/09/13/pakistans_charm_offensive (accessed June 18, 2013); Jon Boone, "Pakistan 'Walking the Talk' on Peace in Afghanistan," *The Guardian*, December 1, 2012, available at http://www.guardian.co.uk/world/2012/nov/30/pakistan-walking-walk-afghanistan-peace (accessed June 18, 2013).

12. See remarks by Ambassador Marc Grossman, "Prospects for Peace in Afghanistan," U.S. Institute of Peace, April 10, 2012, video available at http://www.usip.org/events/prospects-peace-in-afghanistan-0 (accessed June 24, 2013).

1

Making Peace in Afghanistan
The Missing Political Strategy

Minna Jarvenpaa

Published in February 2011—coinciding with Secretary Hillary Clinton's Asia Society speech, in which she signaled that the United States was dropping its preconditions for talks with the Taliban—Jarvenpaa argues that the presence of international troops has strengthened the insurgency, that a mediator appointed by the international community would need to lead negotiations, and that any reconciliation process should be inclusive of all Afghans.

Jarvenpaa's central point is that, given the insurgency's resilience, the role of external actors in fueling it, and the unwillingness of President Hamid Karzai and Afghan political elites to make genuine reforms, "the international community's main investment should be in facilitating a sustainable political settlement"—not "a deal with Pakistan or the Taliban" but a definition of a state that all Afghans can support. A broad-based public consultation could establish the parameters of such a state before serious negotiations with the Taliban.

From the details of a policy of negotiation and reconciliation, Jarvenpaa teases out a number of dilemmas and internal contradictions that continue to affect the process today and that have not yet been adequately discussed. These include the needs for popular buy-in to the negotiated outcome, for confidentiality during the negotiation process, and for countries in the region to accept the outcome of the peace process, as well as acknowledge their own contributions to the conflict. A government in Afghanistan must be based on some norms of justice, even as an agreement with the Taliban will inevitably require some form of immunity for past actions, as well as bring into power figures who bear responsibility for much of Afghanistan's recent tragedy.

Originally published as Minna Jarvenpaa, "Making Peace in Afghanistan: The Missing Political Strategy," Special Report 267 (Washington, DC: USIP, 2011).

Every year since 2001, Western leaders have announced a last push or critical event that will turn around the situation in Afghanistan. Each time the underlying assumption is that, with increased resources and the right plan, the weaknesses of the Afghan state can be tackled and stability achieved. Yet despite the latest—and massive—military surge and accompanying "civilian uplift,"[1] the political and security situation has continued to deteriorate. The Taliban have expanded their reach across the country from their strongholds in the south and southeast[2] while the Afghan public increasingly views the government of President Hamid Karzai as corrupt.[3] Even under a reform-minded leadership, a self-sufficient central state that could provide security and justice for the people of Afghanistan would take decades to build up. Within the 2014 Lisbon transition timeline, without basic political stability and in an environment dominated by an increasingly self-serving elite, it is practically out of reach.

In the current Afghan context, reports of preliminary contacts between the Afghan government and the Taliban have become a cause for optimism. A political settlement is needed, but at the same time, an exclusive deal between Karzai and the Taliban would be divisive, alienating civil society, minority groups, and other constituencies. If the international community wants to reduce its role by 2014 without further destabilizing Afghanistan, it will need to work out a political strategy to ensure that it does not become the guarantor of a deal that splits the country—or that sets the stage for renewed civil war.

A Reality Check

The *inteqal* or transition process endorsed at the North Atlantic Treaty Organization (NATO) Lisbon summit in November 2010 consists of a familiar menu of counterinsurgency and state-building strategies,[4] and the year-end review of the Obama strategy recommended no major adjustments.[5] International forces in Afghanistan will continue to rely on a mix of military operations to capture and kill insurgents, training and mentoring programs to hand control of security to Afghan forces by the end of 2014, and an assortment of governance and development efforts aimed at generating popular trust in the Afghan government, particularly in the south and east. Meanwhile, the government itself is increasingly unpopular.[6] The Taliban have a safe haven in Pakistan and a growing base of fighters[7] disgruntled with the Karzai government and resentful of the presence of foreign troops.[8]

Missing is a feasible political strategy. Developing one will require a reevaluation of current assumptions, including consideration of the following three propositions: first, that the insurgency shows no signs of subsiding; second, that external resources are fueling conflict through a war and aid economy; and third, that Karzai and Afghan political elites lack genuine commitment to reform, calling into question the international community's state-building and counterinsurgency approach.

Proposition 1: The Insurgency Shows No Signs of Subsiding

The assumption that escalating coalition military operations will force the insurgents to the negotiating table should be treated with caution. So far, the evidence from the field suggests that the military surge has not only intensified the conflict, but also expanded it geographically.[9] The insurgency continues to enjoy access to safe havens and support in Pakistan despite stepped-up drone strikes across the border.

According to NATO estimates, insurgent numbers have swelled in the five years since 2005, from a few thousand fighters to as many as 35,000. The outrage that many Afghans feel over the actions of foreign troops—including night raids, civilian casualties, and detention—and the predatory nature of their own government continue to swell Taliban ranks.[10] For their part, the Taliban target government officials, policemen, aid workers, development contractors, and tribal elders in assassinations and assaults; Taliban fighters also lay roadside bombs that kill Afghan civilians. Despite such brutality, the insurgency is gaining momentum far beyond the south and southeast, and beginning to enlist non-Pashtun fighters.[11] The map of Afghan government access to districts across the country is steadily diminishing. Many previously stable areas in the north (including Badghis and Faryab provinces), northeast (Kunduz, Baghlan, and Takhar), and central Afghanistan (Kapisa) have become key infiltration routes. The Taliban have delivered night letters—threatening notes left on doorsteps under cover of darkness—even in the central highland region of Hazarajat, until now one of the most stable parts of the country.

On the government side, even the best Afghan army and police units are barely capable of operating on their own and often lack the will to challenge the insurgency.[12] Tribes that have been enlisted to provide security against the Taliban have ended up fighting internally, as in the case of the Shinwari tribe in Nangarhar.[13] Local power brokers use their links to the international military to settle personal scores by branding their competitors as Taliban, turning potential allies into insurgents.

International Security Assistance Force (ISAF) casualties are at their highest ever, up 20 percent since 2009 and fourfold since 2005.[14] The NATO-led coalition has captured or killed hundreds of mid-level insurgent commanders in raids over the last year, but this has not reduced violence; it appears only to have fragmented the Taliban and made local units more autonomous. Experienced analysts have suggested that new commanders tend to be more radical, less prone to compromise, and more committed to jihad against the foreign occupation. They may also be less responsive to direction from Mullah Omar.[15]

The ongoing intergenerational transfer of power within the Haqqani network, from Jalaluddin Haqqani to his son Sirajuddin, could have a similar effect in southeastern Afghanistan, as Sirajuddin is involved in a more violent strand of the network, with less respect for traditional authority.[16] At a strategic level such fragmentation could undermine the ability of the insurgent leadership to deliver on a political deal.

Proposition 2: External Resources Are Fueling Conflict

Allocating additional money for development programs—with pressure to spend it fast in pursuit of security objectives—and supplying international military bases across Afghanistan has unintentionally produced a war and aid economy. Donor programs delivered in an environment of state weakness, warlordism, racketeering, and rent seeking create conflict and popular disappointment, rather than winning hearts and minds.[17]

Among contractors, client networks, villages, and tribes, competition for development projects is intense; for Afghan political elites, the conflict has become a lucrative enterprise, and with hundreds of millions of dollars hanging in the balance, there is little economic incentive for political power brokers to end it. Those in power control the mechanisms of government for their personal gain, and instead of promoting stability and good governance, they reap rewards from the development and military contracts that follow the fighting. The construction, trucking, and private security contracts that come with the presence of international military forces thus are plagued by extortion and clientelism. Often a single network or actor becomes dominant. Matiullah Khan controls all the highway security contracts in Uruzgan, while the president's brother Ahmed Wali Karzai towers over private security, real estate, and contracting in Kandahar.[18] A U.S. Senate inquiry links U.S.-paid private security contractors to murder, kidnapping, and bribery, as well as to the Taliban.[19]

Proposition 3: Karzai and Afghan Political Elites
Lack Genuine Commitment to Reform

A lack of real commitment to reform among Afghan leadership calls into question the international community's entire state-building approach. Technical and financial support to institutions cannot substitute for political will.

Karzai has not held to his expressed commitments to cleaner government. Instead, the state has been captured and manipulated by various factions and powerful business and political figures, with a confusion of institutions with private interests. Less than a month after anticorruption undertakings made at the Kabul Conference, Karzai intervened personally to release an aide who had been arrested in connection with an investigation into a *hawala* money transfer business, through which billions of dollars were leaving Afghanistan. He also dismissed the deputy attorney general, Fazel Ahmed Faqiryar, who had authorized the arrest, and took more direct control of the task force that was carrying out the investigation.[20] The government has rejected offers for a transparent audit of Kabul Bank after a bailout of several hundred million dollars.[21] Shareholders include another of the president's brothers, Mahmood Karzai, and a brother of the vice president, Haseen Fahim.[22] Chief executive Khalilullah Fruzi was senior financial advisor to Hamid Karzai's 2009 reelection campaign.[23]

Most reforms remain at the level of empty policy debates and government appointments are bought, sold, and distributed to family and close allies to ensure the loyalty of critical appointees.[24] This includes senior police and customs officer posts, as well as local government offices. While important freedoms and progress have been achieved since the end of Taliban rule, abuses by police and other local government officials have eroded public trust. The social breakdown and lawlessness that preceded the Taliban takeover is being repeated in many parts of Afghanistan, enabling a comeback in some provinces. In Wardak, the Taliban have set up a parallel administration across the province and people look to the shadow governor, district chiefs, and judges for administration and justice. Unlike official government courts, Taliban courts are known for swift decisions, harsh punishments, and not soliciting bribes.[25]

For its part, the international community has become hostage to its own rhetoric of Afghanization and an Afghan lead, and is unwilling or unable—despite a massive financial and military commitment to Afghanistan—to pressure the government to deliver what it has promised. Although few believe Karzai to be a reliable partner,[26] placating him has become a central plank of the international strategy. Karzai still feels betrayed over the 2009 elections, in which foreigners supported the exclusion of more than one million fraudulent votes, denying him a first-round victory. He has delayed inauguration of the newly-elected Parliament, bringing the country to the brink of constitutional crisis. Karzai also has become a vocal critic of the NATO-led military effort.[27] This leaves the international community in a conundrum. Karzai is the elected leader, with a mandate until 2014, and no obvious political alternative. Yet with Karzai as a partner, a counterinsurgency approach, which relies on the government winning the trust of the Afghan people, is unlikely to succeed. The only option for a responsible withdrawal of foreign troops—one that does not leave behind the poisoned seeds of renewed civil war—is a negotiated peace settlement that has broad-based support.

Toward a Sustainable Political Settlement

Based on the above propositions, the international community's main investment should be in facilitating a sustainable political settlement. A peace deal will take time to conclude—perhaps several years. That talks will not be a quick fix, however, should not take away from the urgency of laying out a framework for a political process. There are at least three levels at which solutions need to be sought: internally, among Afghans; with the Taliban; and with regional stakeholders to undergird any deal that emerges. The following sections consider the elements that can contribute to a sustainable settlement and a role for the international community.

Opening Up the Political Space

A sustainable political settlement for Afghanistan is not only about doing a deal with the Taliban or with Pakistan. It is about defining a state that Afghans are willing to support. While the actual negotiations should be kept quiet, there needs to be a broad-based consultation of Afghans to establish the parameters of an acceptable settlement.

Grievances that are fuelling the insurgency—such as corruption, injustice, warlordism, and marginalization of various tribal and ethnic groups, political actors, economic and business elites, and civil society—are costing the government support. Women's groups, human rights advocates, and ethnic minorities are concerned that the discrimination and abuse that Afghans experienced under the Taliban regime of the 1990s will return.[28] A number of prominent ethnic leaders and senior army commanders are also staunch opponents of negotiating with the insurgents and of giving Pakistan a role in Afghanistan's security.[29] All these groups need to be sufficiently involved in the process to be able to seek and receive guarantees. Given research findings that a quarter of all civil war settlements collapse within five years,[30] it is important to reach a political settlement that is widely accepted across all segments of society.

Rather than diplomats determining red lines for negotiations on human rights and women's rights issues, the Afghan public should have a voice in establishing the parameters of an acceptable settlement ahead of any negotiations with the Taliban. A broad-based consultation that engages Afghans across the country in a debate over the future of their state could, in itself, create political pressure for upholding core principles. The peace *jirga* was an exercise for Karzai to seek a mandate from his own base, and had merit as such, but it was not the nationwide consultation it was sold as. Karzai-appointed governors carefully orchestrated the list of invitees, and major Hazara, Tajik, and Uzbek leaders stayed away, as did those affiliated with the Taliban.[31]

Ideally, a carefully balanced and representative government-appointed group would carry out the consultation, along the model of the selection committee for the 2003 constitutional *loya jirga*. In the absence of such an initiative by the government, donors could support alternative methods of bringing Afghans from all thirty-four provinces into the debate. One possibility would be funding televised debates and radio call-in programs. This would give Afghans a voice and begin building up a constituency for a peace settlement.

Talks with the Taliban

President Karzai has been preparing the ground for talks with the "upset brothers," as he calls the insurgency, activating backchannels at various levels, mainly through family connections.[32] Enticements to come over to the government side include a reintegration decree that offers amnesty to Taliban fighters who want to leave the battlefield, on condition that they accept the Afghan constitution and break ties with al-Qaeda and other terrorist groups. The peace *jirga* in June 2010 resulted in proposals for the release of Taliban prisoners and for the lifting of UN sanctions on blacklisted individuals. In September, Karzai announced the creation of a seventy-member High Peace Council as the formal interface for talks with the Taliban. Other political signals have been the replacement of the Tajik intelligence chief Amrullah Saleh with Rahmatullah Nabil, who is Pashtun, as well as the promotion of two Pashtun generals to the crucial posts of chief and deputy chief of staff of the army, both replacing Tajiks.

The political intention to reintegrate Taliban fighters and persuade them to swap allegiances has been translated into the complex and costly Afghanistan Peace and Reintegration Program, launched at the Kabul conference in July 2010. The program, underwritten by $250 million in international pledges, is built on the assumption that lower-ranking fighters join the Taliban to earn an income and can be persuaded to switch sides with promises of work and development projects for their communities. So far there have been few takers, perhaps because the program fails to respond to the political grievances that fuel the insurgency and does not offer credible security guarantees to Taliban who choose to reintegrate. Those who have joined the reintegration program—a few hundred to date—are predominantly former Jamiat fighters and bandits from Herat, Badghis, and the northeast, rather than actual Taliban.[33] In the absence of a broader peace process, the program is likely to continue to lack appeal.[34]

None of the above activity means that a peace deal between Karzai and the Taliban is imminent. There are three main flaws in the preparations undertaken so far. The first is the perception that Karzai is giving in too easily to demands by the Taliban and Pakistan; this is alienating to much of the rest of Afghanistan, especially to non-Pashtuns in northern and central Afghanistan. At worst, an exclusively negotiated Karzai-Taliban deal could lead to the collapse of the government, with non-Pashtun ministers and much of the army walking out.

The second concern is that, despite a flurry of press reports about contacts between the government and the insurgency, the Taliban may not be ready to talk just yet. It is likely that some elements of the movement are tired and looking for an exit. It is also possible that a part of the Quetta Shura is interested in power sharing. However, it is not clear that the contacts that have been reported since September 2010 amount to substantial preliminaries for negotiations. Presumed high-level discussions with Mullah Akhtar Muhammad Mansour, the Taliban second-in-command, facilitated by NATO, turned out to be a sham.[35] Channels have always existed between the insurgents and government to discuss prisoner releases and other deals, but it does not appear that the Quetta Shura has authorized broader political discussions.

The third concern is that much of the activity from Karzai's side is symbolic and appears aimed at fragmenting the insurgency and making a closed deal that allows him to stay in power. The High Peace Council includes many unlikely peace negotiators, and it remains to be seen whether the former Taliban represented on the council can provide a meaningful conduit for talks. Its membership is heavily weighted toward the same factional leaders who have been fighting the wars of the past thirty years and whose lawless rule paved the way for the Taliban to come to power in the 1990s.[36] They are where the armed power, increasingly coupled with economic and political power, of Afghanistan lies, and the leaders have little incentive to share that power. The Taliban have publicly responded by characterizing the High Peace Council as impractical and doomed to fail.[37]

The more Karzai moves toward a genuine national peace settlement, the more power he would have to give, both to the Taliban and to the political opposition, Pashtun and non-Pashtun. At the time of this writing, Western support is shielding Karzai's government and personal networks from having to share power and propping up a false political equilibrium. This has prevented Karzai from having to reach for deals that he would otherwise be compelled to strike. However, as ISAF contributing nations are increasingly looking for the exit, the pressure to satisfy various constituencies will grow.

Exploratory dialogue about a peace settlement has also started between Karzai and Pakistan's army and intelligence chiefs as Pakistan seeks to secure its interests and the loyalty of a future Afghan state.[38] Pakistan has an undeniable role in any future negotiations. Inter-Services Intelligence (ISI), Pakistan's intelligence agency, has deep links into the insurgency, including both the Taliban and Haqqani networks, and may even participate in meetings of the Quetta Shura, the Taliban leadership council.[39] Yet this influence should not be exaggerated; the Afghan Taliban are increasingly driven by indigenous factors and it seems unlikely that Pakistan would have sufficient control to shut down the insurgency even if it wanted to. Together with the problem of Taliban leadership fragmentation due to the killing and capturing of mid-level commanders by international military forces, it is hard to envisage an early or smooth negotiating process. Still, enlisting the unambiguous and firm support of Pakistan is critical to any sustainable political settlement.

Agenda for Talks

Despite the challenges, talks are needed to end the insurgency. Even if, at present, prospects for a settlement are still remote, groundwork to prepare a political process should begin in earnest. The Afghan government has yet to develop its negotiating position beyond calling on the insurgency to respect the constitution and lay down arms. For the international community, the key requirement will be for the Taliban to sever all links to al-Qaeda. As for the insurgency, an eventual negotiation would need to address a wide range of motivations, among them the presence and actions of foreign forces, including night raids, civilian casualties, and detentions; the desire for a more rigorous application of sharia law by the state; the predatory nature of the government, especially the bribe-taking prevalent in the police and justice institutions; perceived ethnic or tribal bias in the distribution of gains from reconstruction activities; and economic vulnerability, which may motivate lower-level fighters.[40]

Both the Afghan government and the Taliban have yet to develop a positive vision of their long-term aspirations for Afghanistan. The Taliban platform does not go much beyond the slogan of forcing out foreign troops along with what they consider to be the puppet government of Karzai, while the Afghan government is inclined to see the root causes of the conflict as exogenous to itself, blaming Pakistan, the United States, and other international players. The government's mindset needs to shift. In reality it is the significant deficit in governance that continues to undermine the emergence of a credible Afghan state and, in turn, loyalty of Afghans to it. Without addressing the grievances that have enabled the insurgency to step up its recruitment, it will be insufficient to entice low-level Taliban from their leadership through the reintegration program.

Some of the issues that the Taliban would look for on the agenda would include foreign troop withdrawals; an expanded role of Islam in national life; power sharing at the provincial and local levels; the release of detainees; and a say in civil service, police, and justice appointments.[41] For the time being, the option of altering the Afghan constitution has been taken off the table; casualties of a more conservatively drafted constitution might include the rights enshrined for women, the role of the Afghan Independent Human Rights Commission, and the freedom of the press. That said, it may be possible to give sharia a more prominent role in law making without bargaining away fundamental freedoms. Similarly, the powers of governors and provincial councils could be enhanced without altering the constitution. Beyond severing ties to al-Qaeda, the principal red lines for any negotiated solution should come not from foreigners but from Afghan constituencies, including civil society actors, that are informed of and included in the process.

Capacity to Negotiate

Groundwork to prepare a political process will need to address key questions about who specifically would be negotiating and the preparedness of the various parties to engage in a long and complex political negotiation. Setting up the High Peace Council does not seem like the real answer from the Karzai administration's side. It is too unwieldy to be more than a formality. The insurgency also lacks the capacity and political structure needed for peace talks. There is a role for diplomats to advocate for a realistic negotiating team that includes legitimate representatives of Afghanistan's various ethnic, social, and political groups, including women, as well as to build up the capacity of such a team to engage in talks. There may also be a role for a regional actor to support the development of insurgent capacity for talks. Karzai has suggested a possible role for Turkey in providing an office that Taliban negotiators can use.[42]

The next stage of preparations should focus on the issues of capacity to engage in peace talks, as well as identifying the interests of the main players.[43] All the main insurgent groups will need to be accepted as interlocutors, along with all key political groupings. The challenge is to ensure that all Afghans who need to be included are included and that underlying principles are adhered to. Genuine political debate about acceptable compromises is needed. Otherwise there is a real danger that women, human rights, and media freedoms become victims of botched negotiations, and that a just peace remains elusive. Other core principles that need safeguarding include a commitment to a functioning Afghan state that fulfills its constitutional obligations toward its citizens as well as its international obligations, maintains normalized relations with regional neighbors and globally, and undertakes not to harbor terrorists. Many of these issues can best be explored through informal contacts, so that all parties can prepare their constituencies ahead of formal negotiations.

Regional Talks

A peace settlement among Afghans would need to be underpinned by a carefully designed regional framework for stabilizing Afghanistan. Neighboring countries could pull Afghanistan apart in a proxy war, such as that seen in the 1990s, or contribute to its stability. The key question is whether it is possible to overcome the mutual distrust among regional actors in favor of even minimally coordinated regional engagement. A stable Afghanistan is ultimately in the interests of all of its neighbors, although each may have its own view of what stability means and may be tempted to fall back on cultivating old client relationships. The thorniest issue in designing a regional strategy is finding a way to move Pakistan and India away from their confrontational positions over Afghanistan.[44]

China has a clear strategic and economic interest in an Afghanistan that is safe for natural-resource extraction and able to tackle Islamist extremism. It may be able to exert constructive pressure based on its close ties with Pakistan. Russia and the Central Asian countries on Afghanistan's northern border are concerned about spillover effects, with a particular concern for links to the latent conflicts in the Ferghana Valley. At the same time, while Russia does not want the Taliban in power in Kabul or elsewhere, it cannot help but savor the prospect of the United States also failing in Afghanistan. It may find it difficult to resist cultivating local allies based on former Northern Alliance and Communist commander networks, which could make a national-level political settlement harder to achieve.

Iran has ambitions to be a regional heavyweight and views Afghanistan largely through the lens of its relations with the United States. Despite a relatively small investment, it wants to maximize its influence over a future Afghanistan and minimize the influence of its enemies, particularly the United States and Saudi Arabia. In line with the former, it is supporting all sides: providing financial support to Karzai's and Abdullah Abdullah's election campaigns and maintaining links to the Northern Alliance and small groups of the insurgency that have been trained in Iran. Iran would not want to see a Taliban government in Kabul, but it wants to keep the United States embroiled in the south; it may be positioning itself to be a spoiler to a peace process. Gaining Iran's support for a political settlement might require assurances that there would not be permanent U.S. military bases in Afghanistan. Yet in the short term Iran may have rather mixed feelings about the U.S. presence in Afghanistan. Hasty troop withdrawal would likely result in an internal shakeout in Afghanistan and, thus, increased instability in Iran's neighborhood. Iran would also lose the leverage it has in being able to hurt U.S. troops, and therefore view itself as more vulnerable to U.S. attacks against its nuclear assets.[45]

While Iran's interest in Afghanistan is limited to ensuring that it is not Taliban dominated or a Western satellite, India and Pakistan are using Afghanistan as a battleground in their broader conflict. India is increasingly assertive in its diplomacy and wants to reduce Pakistan's ability to determine events in Afghanistan. Its financial investment in infrastructure and development and its large diplomatic presence, including four consulates in addition to an embassy, signals its intention to stay a long time. India has also been keen to accelerate the development of Iran's Chabahar port, which will give it access to Afghanistan and Central Asia without needing to go through Pakistan. It has already built the Zaranj-Delaram road through Afghanistan's Nimruz province to connect to Chabahar.[46] The July 2011 date for the beginning of U.S. withdrawal has led to hard-line debate in the Indian strategic community over a backup security plan, with some suggesting the reestablishment of links with Northern Alliance commanders.

Pakistan has been positioning itself as a main broker in talks with the Taliban. Diplomacy between Karzai and Islamabad intensified in 2010, with multiple visits to Kabul by General Kayani and intelligence chief Shuja Pasha. Pakistan envisions an Afghanistan without an Indian presence and with an Afghan government that is not pro-Indian, and will seek to use the insurgency to pressure the government into a deal that offers it a pivotal role in shaping Afghan politics in exchange for closing down sanctuaries. However, Pakistan's ability to control the insurgency is often overstated, and the Taliban's dislike for the ISI is understated. Also, Pakistan recognizes that it is interested in a stable and therefore ethnically balanced government structure in Kabul, and the context for Taliban rule no longer exists.[47]

Given the distrust among the states in the region, it is difficult to conceive of a formal multilateral negotiating process that could deliver a regional consensus, at least not without a preparatory round of bilateral dialogues and deals. To start with, basic principles should be agreed upon to raise the level of confidence between Afghanistan and its neighbors. At their simplest, these principles should include respect for sovereignty and territorial integrity, commitment to the principle of noninterference in the internal affairs of neighbors, and prevention of the use of Afghanistan's territory for hostile activities against its neighbors. Some observers have called for unblocking progress on Kashmir to allow for a solution on Afghanistan to be developed. This would substitute one Gordian knot for another, but even some incremental movement or confidence building measures between India and Pakistan would clearly help.

International Role in Talks

So far, the international community has distanced itself from the anticipated political process by stressing that talks with the insurgency will be conducted under an Afghan government lead. This is partly due to incomplete policy formulation within the United States, where there continues to be nervousness about talking to the Taliban. However, ultimately the countries with troops on the ground will need to engage in peace talks. Neither Karzai nor the newly established High Peace Council has control over many of the issues at stake. With U.S. troops leading the anti-Taliban fight, there are guarantees that only the United States can offer. Similarly, the Afghan government can request the United Nations to review the Resolution 1267 terrorist sanctions list, but will have little control over action that is taken. Negotiations can only be successful if all major players take part.

For talks to be meaningful, the international community will need to facilitate them—not to determine the specific shape of a political settlement, but to help structure the process so that what emerges is sustainable. Despite the recent hype, as mentioned above, a political settlement could take years to conclude and there should be no rush to begin formal negotiations. This does not detract from the urgency of undertaking informal preparations. A mediator or team of mediators and analysts, with at least a minimal mandate, could begin to identify the various stakeholders and analyze their interests, through engaging regional actors and the range of Afghan constituencies, with a view to proposing a structure and format for multilevel negotiations. Such a mediator could also explore ideas for a range of incremental and reciprocal confidence-building measures.

Further down the line a more formal process will be required. Given the Afghan government's testiness about foreign involvement, it will eventually take the United States, as the most powerful actor, to broker agreement over a mediator. The United States itself cannot play this role for lack of impartiality, but whoever is appointed must have U.S. support at the highest level. Successful negotiations will require an exceptionally knowledgeable mediator with a clear plan and the ability to maintain support and coherence among the international actors, as well as sufficient authority to conduct regional diplomacy and bring the parties to a peace conference. This could be a role for a UN mandated envoy, although not for the UN Assistance Mission in Afghanistan; its reputation for impartiality has been weakened among Afghans due to its mandate requiring a close relationship with the Afghan government and its handling of the 2009 elections.

If the end to the conflict in Afghanistan requires a peace settlement, it also follows that the international military forces should orient their strategy to support agreed-upon political ends, rather than vice versa. Within U.S. military and political circles, some argue that intensified capturing and killing of insurgents is driving the Taliban to the negotiating table. Most analysts who have spent longer periods of time in Afghanistan tend to disagree.[48] A less combat-oriented international military posture across the country, covering not only the planned transition of security responsibilities from NATO to Afghan security forces in more benign districts, could create the political space for genuine negotiations. A first step toward talks could be agreeing to a reciprocal and incremental set of confidence-building measures. These might include deescalating hostilities or localized cease-fires, prisoner releases, and delisting insurgents from target lists and the UN sanctions list.

Talks will not result in peace overnight. Crafting a political deal that parties to the conflict accept and regional neighbors endorse will take time and a sustained commitment of foreign troops to back it up. This has consequences for the speed of troop withdrawals. Even Afghans living in Kandahar who have no fondness for foreign troops worry that an ill-considered rush to the exits would make matters even worse.[49] At best, skillful and patient diplomacy leading to a political settlement might result in a tenuous peace that can be consolidated over time. The requirement of maintaining a military presence to underwrite a peace deal should be considered early on to maintain confidence in the process.

Conclusion

The politics of a potential grand bargain between Karzai and the Taliban, underwritten by Pakistan, are divisive. Leaders of the Hazara, Tajik, and Uzbek communities are opposed, as are many Pashtuns—at least without further clarification of what the end goals and their roles in the process are. To be sustainable, a political settlement must be acceptable to a broad range of Afghan constituencies. It must also be supported by regional actors, including those who are backing various factions within Afghanistan. Such a settlement may be years away, but the way ahead needs to be prepared urgently. This means designing a negotiation with a genuine consultation process to give Afghans a say in the kind of state they are willing to support, facilitated by an international mediator to keep talks on track and ensure a decent outcome.

The international community must not become the guarantor of a deal that results in deeper internal conflicts and greater regional instability, under the slogan of Afghanization and an Afghan lead. There are significant security interests at stake, as well as a moral obligation not to leave behind a country that is worse off now than it was before the international intervention began. An exit of NATO combat troops by 2014 is only feasible if the NATO-led military effort falls firmly behind a peace process; before that can happen, however, a political strategy for the country, missing up to now, must be developed.

Notes

1. The White House, Office of the Press Secretary, "Remarks by the President on a New Strategy for Afghanistan and Pakistan," March 27, 2009.
2. Antonio Giustozzi, *Negotiating with the Taliban: Issues and Prospects* (New York: The Century Foundation, 2010).
3. United Nations Office on Drugs and Crime (UNODC), *Corruption in Afghanistan: Bribery as Reported by the Victims* (New York: UNODC, 2010); The Asia Foundation, *Afghanistan in 2010: A Survey of the Afghan People* (San Francisco: The Asia Foundation, 2010).
4. Afghan Government and NATO/ISAF, "*Inteqal:* Strengthening Afghan Sovereignty through International Partnership," joint paper presented to the Kabul Conference, July 20, 2010.
5. The White House, Office of the Press Secretary, "Overview of the Afghanistan and Pakistan Annual Review," December 16, 2010.
6. Julie Ray and Rajesh Srinivasan, "Afghans' Approval of Their Leadership Falls to 33 Percent: Majority Disapprove of Karzai for the First Time," Gallup, July 23, 2010.
7. Matt Waldman, *Dangerous Liaisons with the Afghan Taliban: The Feasibility and Risks of Negotiations* (Washington, D.C.: U.S. Institute of Peace, 2010); Giustozzi, Negotiating with the Taliban.

8. The International Council on Security and Development (ICOS), *Afghanistan: The Relationship Gap* (London: ICOS, 2010); Sarah Ladbury with Cooperation for Peace and Unity in Kabul, "Testing Hypotheses on Radicalisation in Afghanistan: Why Do Men Join the Taliban and Hizb-i Islami? How Much Do Local Communities Support Them?" Independent report for the Department for International Development, London, August 2009.

9. Ernesto Londono, "Red Cross Offers Bleak Assessment of Afghan War," *The Washington Post,* December 15, 2010.

10. Erica Gaston and Jonathan Horowitz, *The Trust Deficit: The Impact of Local Perceptions on Policy in Afghanistan* (New York: Open Society Foundations, October 2010); Thomas Ruttig, "The Other Side—Dimensions of the Afghan Insurgency: Causes, Actors, and Approaches to 'Talks,' " Afghanistan Analysts Network, July 2009.

11. Antonio Giustozzi and Christoph Reuter, "The Northern Front: The Afghan Insurgency Spreading Beyond the Pashtuns," Afghanistan Analysts Network, March 2010.

12. Department of Defense (DOD), *Report on Progress Toward Security and Stability in Afghanistan,* DOD Report to Congress, November 2010.

13. Josh Partlow, "U.S. Military Runs into Afghan Tribal Politics after Deal with Pashtuns," *The Washington Post,* May 10, 2010.

14. iCasualties.org, "Coalition Military Fatalities by Year and Month," December 2010, available at iCasualties.org (accessed January 17, 2011).

15. Felix Kuehn and Alex Strick van Linschoten, "Who Are the Taliban?" Presented at workshop, "Anticipating a Political Process in Afghanistan: How Should the International Community Respond?," Washington, D.C., June 24–25, 2010; Thomas Ruttig, "A Back Somersault in the U.S. Strategy: Lower Aims, Higher Risks," (blog), Afghanistan Analysts Network, October 16, 2010, http://aan-afghanistan.com/ (accessed January 17, 2011).

16. Tom Gregg, "Talk to the Haqqanis, Before It's Too Late," AfPak Channel, September 22, 2010; Thomas Ruttig, "Splitting the Haqqanis with NATO Reconciliation Air?" Blog, Afghanistan Analysts Network, November 1, 2010.

17. "Winning 'Hearts and Minds' in Afghanistan: Assessing the Effectiveness of Development Aid in COIN Operations," report on Wilton Park Conference 1022, March 11–14, 2010; Andrew Wilder, Hearing on U.S. Aid to Pakistan: Planning and Accountability, Testimony to House Committee on Oversight and Government Reform, Subcommittee on National Security and Foreign Affairs, December 9, 2009.

18. Rep. John F. Tierney, Chair, U.S. House of Representatives, Committee on Oversight and Government Reform, Subcommittee on National Security and Foreign Affairs, "Warlord, Inc.: Extortion and Corruption Along the U.S. Supply Chain in Afghanistan," June 2010; Bette Dam, "The Story of 'M': U.S.-Dutch Shouting Matches in Uruzgan," (guest blog), Afghanistan Analysts Network, June 10, 2010, aan-afghanistan.com (accessed January 17, 2011); Carl Forsberg, "Politics and Power in Kandahar," Afghanistan Report 5, Institute for the Study of War, Washington, D.C., April 2010; Kate Clark, "WikiLeaks and the Paktia Governor," (blog) Afghanistan Analysts Network, December 6, 2010.

19. U.S. Senate, Committee on Armed Services, Inquiry into the Role and Oversight of Private Security Contractors in Afghanistan, September 28, 2010.

20. Rod Nordland, "Antigraft Units, Backed by U.S., Draw Karzai's Ire," *The New York Times,* August 6, 2010; Adam Entous, "American Concerns over Karzai Deepen," *Wall Street Journal,* August 30, 2010.

21. Matthew Rosenberg, "Afghanistan Rejects U.S. Aid for Bank Audits," *Wall Street Journal,* November 27, 2010.

22. Dexter Filkins, "Depositors Panic Over Bank Crisis in Afghanistan," *The New York Times,* September 2, 2010.

23. Andrew Higgins, "Banker Feeds Crony Capitalism in Afghanistan," *The Financial Times,* February 22, 2010.

24. For a discussion of patronage in appointments, see Martine van Bijlert, "Between Discipline and Discretion: Policies Surrounding Senior Subnational Appointments," Afghanistan Research and Evaluation Unit, May 2009.

25. Qayum Babak, "Taleban Justice 'Fairer' than State Courts," *Institute for War and Peace Reporting*, no. 369, August 17, 2010; Julius Cavendish, "'If You Have a Problem, the Taliban Solves It. In the Government Offices There Is Only Corruption and Bribery'," *The Herald*, January 3, 2009.

26. Cables leaked from the U.S. State Department have depicted Karzai variously as "not an adequate strategic partner," "erratic," "indecisive and unprepared," and "a paranoid and weak individual unfamiliar with the basics of nation-building." See Peter Baker, "Obama in Unannounced Afghan Visit," *New York Times*, December 3, 2010; Karen DeYoung, "Leaked Afghan Cables Show U.S. Frustration with Leader," *Washington Post*, December 3, 2010.

27. Ahmed Rashid, "Karzai Turns Against Western Allies," *BBC Viewpoint*, November 20, 2010.

28. Coordination Group on Transitional Justice in Afghanistan to participants at the London Conference, "Do Not Sacrifice the Victims: Justice, a Prerequisite for Lasting Peace," Afghanistan Watch, January 23, 2010, www.watchafghanistan.org (accessed January 17, 2011); Human Rights Watch, *The 'Ten-Dollar Talib' and Women's Rights: Afghan Women and the Risks of Reintegration and Reconciliation* (New York: Human Rights Watch, 2010).

29. International Crisis Group, "A Force in Fragments: Reconstituting the Afghan National Army," Asia Report no. 190, May 12, 2010.

30. Astri Suhrke and Ingrid Samset, "What's in a Figure? Estimating Recurrence of Civil War," *International Peacekeeping*, vol. 14, no. 2 (May 2007), 195–203.

31. Kate Clark, "The Afghan Jungle's Big Beasts and 'Lively Debate,'" (blog), Afghanistan Analysts Network, June 4, 2010, aan-afghanistan.com (accessed January 17, 2011); Clark, "Who's Come to Town . . . and Who's Staying Away," (blog), Afghanistan Analysts Network, June 2, 2010.

32. On Qayum Karzai's role, see Abubakar Siddique and Ron Synovitz, "Pursuit of Elusive Peace Could Drive Afghan Government, Taliban to the Table," Radio Free Europe Radio Liberty, October 10, 2008; Talatbek Masadykov, Antonio Giustozzi, and James Page, "Negotiating with the Taliban: Toward a Solution for the Afghan Conflict," Working Paper no. 66, series 2, Crisis States Research Centre, January 2010.

33. Antonio Giustozzi, personal communication, December 6, 2010.

34. Christian Aid, Open Society Foundations, and Oxford Research Group, "Piecemeal or Peace Deal? NATO, Peace Talks, and a Political Settlement in Afghanistan," presented at NATO Heads of Government Summit, Lisbon, November 19–20, 2010.

35. Dexter Filkins and Carlotta Gall, "Taliban Leader in Secret Talks Was an Impostor," *New York Times*, November 22, 2010.

36. Martine van Bijlert, "Warlords' Peace Council," (blog), Afghanistan Analysts Network, September 28, 2010, aan-afghanistan.com (accessed January 17, 2011).

37. "Reaction of the Islamic Emirate to the Announcement of High Peace Council by Karzai," *Afghan Islamic Press*, September 29, 2010.

38. Declan Walsh and Jon Boone, "Afghanistan in Turmoil after Peace Talk Rumours," *The Guardian*, June 28, 2010.

39. Matt Waldman, "The Sun in the Sky: The Relationship between Pakistan's ISI and Afghan Insurgents," Crisis States Research Centre, Discussion Paper no. 18, June 2010.

40. Ruttig, "The Other Side"; Waldman, *Dangerous Liaisons*.

41. Michael Semple, "We Need to Offer the Taliban More Than Just Money," *Financial Times*, February 5, 2010.

42. Simon Cameron-Moore, "Karzai Warms to Idea of Talking to Taliban in Turkey," *Reuters*, December 24, 2010.

43. Some informal work to this end is already ongoing under the auspices of the U.S. Institute for Peace and the Peace Research Institute Oslo; other informal processes have been initiated on a regional basis.

44. This section draws on findings from the workshop "Anticipating a Political Process in Afghanistan: How Should the International Community Respond?" hosted by USIP in Washington D.C., June 24–25, 2010. The author is grateful to the participating experts for their insights.

45. Karim Sadjadpour, "Iran" in *Is a Regional Strategy Viable in Afghanistan?* Ashley Tellis and Aroop Mukharji, ed. (Washington, D.C.: Carnegie Endowment for International Peace, 2010).

46. Gautam Mukhopadyaya, "India" in *Is a Regional Strategy Viable?* Tellis and Mukharji, eds.

47. Frédéric Grare, "Pakistan" in *Is a Regional Strategy Viable?* Tellis and Mukharji, eds.; Rajan Menon, "Pakistan's Dual Policy on Taliban," *Los Angeles Times,* June 30, 2010.

48. "An Open Letter to President Obama," www.afghanistancalltoreason.com.

49. Kuehn and Strick van Linschoten, "Who Are the Taliban?"

2

Afghan Perspectives on Achieving Durable Peace

Hamish Nixon

I n this chapter, Nixon questions the effectiveness of the U.S. policy of endorsing an *"Afghan-led" strategy toward negotiations to end the conflict. He argues that the "United States must engage directly in negotiating a peace settlement" because the United States has decisive influence over one the Taliban's key demands: the withdrawal of international forces.*

Nixon further identifies domestic dissatisfaction with the ruling Afghan government coalition as a principal factor in the worsening conflict, despite the consistent injection of forces and resources designed to end it:

> The poor quality and predatory behavior of the Afghan government is almost universally acknowledged as a driver of the conflict, and a core issue that a peace process must confront. There is a crosscutting perception that the benefits of government are captured and divided among a small elite who are appointed through political deals based on their past roles and who act with a combination of ethnic, factional, economic, and criminal motivations. Both regime insiders and outsiders believe that this system generates interests in continuing the conflict that may challenge a peace process.

Nixon concludes that the international community's simultaneous transition and reconciliation policies are premised on contradictory assumptions. Transition assumes an Afghan state with a security apparatus that can eventually subdue the insurgency, whereas reconciliation assumes that the insurgency cannot be subdued and thus accommodation with it is necessary. "Regardless of the mechanism," Nixon writes, "the current 'transition' strategy of very large national and international forces and expanding local defense initiatives may need reexamination during a settlement process."

Originally published as Hamish Nixon, "Afghan Perspectives on Achieving Durable Peace," Peace Brief 94 (Washington, DC: USIP, 2011).

A final point is that insurgent political demands are extremely vague, as is their critique of the current Afghan state. Since 2011, when this piece was published, insurgents have not greatly clarified their demands, despite the increased opportunities the Taliban has had to articulate its goals to the international community. There is a danger in overanalyzing what we think the Taliban wants; instead we should listen carefully to what its leaders actually say, even as the signals they send continue to be weak.

Introduction

While momentum in pursuit of a peace settlement for Afghanistan increases, ambiguities remain in the U.S. strategy, and there are questions about the ability of the Afghan government to successfully lead a process and the insurgents' interest in one. A burgeoning body of commentary focuses on international and U.S. strategy, but to be durable a settlement will need to incorporate political agreements that take into account the views of a range of Afghan stakeholders.

This report reviews findings from 122 interviews with Afghan leaders in political, military, economic and social arenas about the conflict and the issues that a peace process must address. This work represents part of a project by three leading international institutions to identify and clarify realistic options for Afghanistan to achieve durable peace. Ongoing work analyzes the issues framed by Afghan stakeholders more deeply and draws on comparative experience.

Understandings of the Conflict

Afghan stakeholders have diverse views of the conflict, but several prominent themes have implications for crafting a successful peace process. While the conflict is driven by external and internal factors—including longstanding issues of regional politics and factional competition—grievances resulting from the presence and actions of NATO troops and the deep legitimacy problems of the Afghan government have become increasingly important. Afghans across different groups perceive the United States as a party to the conflict with its own interests. They identify a contradiction between the U.S. and International Security Assistance Force (ISAF) claim that they are not fighting for themselves but supporting the Afghan government on one side, and the government's apparent eagerness for a peace settlement on the other. For many Afghans, including but by no means limited to the Taliban, this contradiction calls into question the effectiveness of the U.S. emphasis on an "Afghan-led" reconciliation strategy. In addition, ambiguity over the "withdrawal" timetable and divergent signals from different U.S. officials and agencies on the objective of "reintegration" of lower level fighters, indicate the need for further clarification of U.S. policy. The result is lingering distrust of U.S. claims to support a political solution, and skepticism about the viability of an "Afghan-led" peace process.

The poor quality and predatory behavior of the Afghan government is almost universally acknowledged as a driver of the conflict, and a core issue that a peace process must confront. There is a crosscutting perception that the benefits of government are captured and divided among a small elite who are appointed through political deals based on their past roles and who act with a combination of ethnic, factional, economic and criminal motivations. Both regime insiders and outsiders believe that this system generates interests in continuing the conflict that may challenge a peace process.

The lack of transparency and the illegitimate manner through which some have gained power allow leaders of all ethnic groups to stoke perceptions that others are benefitting disproportionately. Such perceptions exist across all groups, feeding increasingly ethnic and "negative-sum" politics. The 2010 National Assembly elections and the discourse of "political reconciliation" of the government have heightened these ethnic readings, deepening cleavages that the Taliban exploit and exacerbating the potential for ethnic conflict.

The Military Dimension of a Peace Process

The U.S. must engage directly in negotiating a peace settlement because it has control over a central issue that such a settlement must address: the withdrawal of most or all NATO forces in return for the Taliban's agreement to cease violence and prevent terrorist activities. While some Afghan leaders see negotiation as undesirable and military action as the only option until the Taliban are significantly weakened or defeated, many believe that elaborating a clear framework for NATO withdrawal or changes to military posture linked to steps by the Taliban on the prevention of terrorism may offer possibilities within a peace process. Even some leaders of vulnerable groups such as minorities and women with the greatest concern over a deal with the Taliban acknowledge the need for NATO withdrawal to bring peace.

Evidence on the Taliban suggests that full withdrawal of international forces may not be necessary for a process to begin. Ex-Taliban and Hezb-e Islami leaders suggest that changes to operational patterns, ceasing aerial attacks, legal recognition and timetables for changes to military posture could form part of a settlement. For their part, several operational insurgent commanders in both the north and the south suggest that two interrelated conditions—an agreement on NATO withdrawal and a ceasefire order from Taliban leader Mullah Omar—would be necessary for a decision to cease fighting, and that they would welcome such an order. One agreed to stop fighting in return for local limits on NATO operations. The implication is that the Taliban precondition of withdrawal of foreign forces may be an opening position for peace negotiations. The challenge will be to leverage the presence of NATO forces by linking the possibility of a structured drawdown to necessary steps by insurgents. At the same time, to balance Pakistani interests with Taliban autonomy, the U.S. should support and participate in channels with both.

Views on reintegration and the Afghanistan Peace and Reconciliation Program (APRP) vary from suspicions that it is a patronage device to doubts about its impact due to the Afghan government's inability to provide security and address the presence of foreign forces. At the same time, there are concerns about the morale of Afghan security forces while reconciliation initiatives are ongoing. A peace process will likely entail discussion of the composition and future of the Afghan National Security Forces, and will require a framework of demobilization or integration that can satisfy the concerns of large groups of insurgents while not provoking remilitarization by others. Regardless of the mechanism, the current "transition" strategy of very large national armed forces and expanding local defense initiatives may need re-examination during a settlement process. Discussions of any longer-term U.S. presence will also have to carefully consider the aims of a peace process, perhaps through monitoring of the prevention of terrorism or guaranteeing the provisions of a settlement.

The Political Dimension of a Peace Process

The conflict in Afghanistan is seen not only as a struggle for power and resources—it is also a legitimacy crisis stemming from a system of power and patronage. These viewpoints are often expressed in terms of the lack of any system to appoint "worthy" individuals into government positions through some legitimate criteria.

From this perspective, a settlement must address reform to be sustainable. Most suggestions focus less on large-scale institutional restructuring of the state than on balancing an over-centralized presidency and increasing the legitimacy of appointments. While different criteria for leadership appear—experience and skills, national feeling, or moral and religious virtue—a recurrent theme among diverse interviewees is that when political deals and opaque reasons determine appointments, the nation suffers. As expected, there are constituencies for decentralization and a parliamentary system of government within minority ethnic parties and the political opposition, but these also emphasize incremental reform such as stronger roles for local councils and election of governors, or a more effective parliament.

Taliban reform proposals are vague and focus on the alleged un-Islamic character of the state, and tend to suggest interest in "reform" rather than just participation in an illegitimate system of power-sharing. Justice and defense institutions are mentioned, including changes to the model of the security forces from large paid forces coupled with militias to a conscript-based army. One ex-Taliban official said that the Taliban view of an Islamic regime can correspond to a presidential system, but needs a mode of consultation or guardianship to protect the Islamic nature of the system.

Most stakeholders believe that constitutional reform should not be a barrier to peace, but also that it is not the most pressing issue. The Taliban themselves have not publicly identified detailed demands regarding the constitution, and some former Taliban officials predictably underplay their views on constitutional change before a foreign audience. Analysts suspect they may wish to create new institutions and alter certain provisions in ways that would risk human and women's rights, but may agree to more modest and non-constitutional adjustments to institutions such as the Ministry of Haj or educational curricula. Some ex-Taliban suggest that articles of the constitution that enshrine both Islamic and human rights could be preserved to build confidence.

This implies that a negotiation might occur between those favoring local devolution as an opening for Taliban inclusion, and the Taliban interest in changes to national structures. It also suggests that a settlement might not involve a radical restructuring of the state. A range of actors may find common ground in their diagnosis of lack of balance in the presidential system and corruption, suggesting a negotiating agenda around oversight and procedures to address how people receive power and privileges. An early step might be to clarify the crucial elements of the constitution, and consider the process for amendments among other political arrangements on the negotiating agenda.

There is a tension between reform and using political appointments to accommodate power-sharing demands. To manage this tension, the intra-Afghan peace process could be oriented towards broader inclusion of non-combatants, and identification of cross-cutting interests, while balancing the secrecy required to avoid getting bogged down. Exploring multitrack diplomacy, civilian commissions, ombudspersons, national dialogues and other means of inclusion should be a priority. The High Peace Council is widely seen as unsuited to mediate an intra-Afghan process, nor is it likely to be empowered as a government delegation, and may best play a role advising and generating proposals.

Getting to a Settlement

Specific mediation and logistical arrangements seem less important to stakeholders than are their mutual acceptance by the parties, in keeping with Afghan customary practice. Elections are still quite widely considered a necessary mechanism—including by some operational Taliban—for transitioning from interim to long-term arrangements, though there are problems with the electoral system and indirect methods such as that used in the Emergency Loya Jirga also enjoy legitimacy.

These findings raise questions for combatants and interested third parties to consider in identifying what kind of peace processes might succeed. These questions also point to where further research, discussion, and the experience of other conflicts could help.

- How can the U.S., the Afghan government, and the Taliban develop and communicate military proposals and counter-proposals about withdrawal and short and long-term measures to prevent terrorism?
- How can a negotiation encourage independent Taliban decision-making on Afghan issues, while balancing the interests of Pakistan?
- What are workable options for interim and longer-term arrangements in the security sector that will be acceptable to different parties?
- What scenarios for international support—whether financial, monitoring, verification or enforcement—are possible?
- What methods of promoting inclusion of non-combatants, women, minorities and vulnerable groups will neither compromise negotiating progress nor cause the marginalization of these groups?
- How should the peace process manage the transition from interim measures to a longer-term consensus on reform, possibly including constitutional change?

Any understanding of the conflict in Afghanistan will form only one part of a multifaceted story. Yet, a peace process must necessarily reduce these complexities to a discrete set of issues, agreements and assurances. To succeed, and to be durable, it must take into account the diversity and depth of Afghan views on what will bring peace to their country.

Sources

More detailed discussion of the research project and findings can be found in Hamish Nixon, *Achieving Durable Peace: Afghan Perspectives on a Peace Process*, PRIO paper (Peace Research Institute Oslo/United States Institute of Peace/ Chr. Michelsen Institute: Oslo, May 2011). The paper is available for download at http://www.prio.no/News/NewsItem/?oid=651456 or at http://www.prio. no/Research-and-Publications/.

3

The Politics of Dispute Resolution and Continued Instability in Afghanistan

Noah Coburn

Assessments of the situation in Afghanistan frequently cite local grievances among the drivers of conflict—those the Afghan government addresses either unfairly or not at all. In this chapter, written in 2011, Coburn hones in on these local conflicts in granular detail and examines the strengths and weaknesses of the mechanisms available to solve them.

Put simply, Afghanistan has more conflicts than it has the capacity to solve them, despite the significant resources devoted to the justice sector. Coburn identifies the variety of venues—official, traditional, and religious—available to Afghans to resolve disputes. Focusing on the presumed dichotomy between formal and informal dispute resolution mechanisms, he argues that, rather than opposing each other, they often work together, sometimes even handling different aspects of the same dispute.

As Coburn writes, "While most local disputes in the areas researched do not have their roots in the insurgency, the instability they create and the ability of the Taliban and other government actors to manipulate the situation ultimately have a deep impact on the political and security contexts of the ongoing insurgency." Coburn does not deal explicitly with the connection between the rise of the insurgency and the inability of the government to provide justice—a connection hinted at in chapter 2—but his discussion of local-level dispute resolution shines some light on this question from below.

Coburn delves into how local justice does and does not function in Afghanistan, deploying examples from field research to demonstrate the links between formal and informal systems as well as between dispute resolution and local power struggles. Even

Originally published as Noah Coburn, "The Politics of Dispute Resolution and Continued Instability in Afghanistan," Special Report 285 (Washington, DC: USIP, 2011).

if the government's failure to ensure justice has allowed the insurgency to expand, international efforts to improve local justice by working with traditional mechanisms will not necessarily work. Their legitimacy is rooted in their local authenticity.

Introduction

As the international community increasingly talks about transfer of governance and security responsibility to Afghans and about the sustainability of both, it is important to have an accurate understanding of disputes that drive local instability. While most local disputes in the areas researched do not have their roots in the insurgency, the instability they create and the ability of the Taliban and other government actors to manipulate the situation ultimately have a deep impact on the political and security contexts of the ongoing insurgency. A broad understanding of the disputes, that are the roots of local instability, will undoubtedly lead to a better understanding of the instability on a more national level across Afghanistan.[1]

This report describes trends in local disputes in Afghanistan based on pilot projects and research conducted by the United States Institute of Peace (USIP) throughout Afghanistan in 2009 and 2010. It draws on qualitative and quantitative data describing ways in which communities tend to address these disputes and some of the shortcomings of these mechanisms. USIP has been working on informal justice in Afghanistan since 2002, and in 2009 began a series of pilot projects aimed at testing linkages between the formal and informal sectors. The Institute's Traditional Dispute Resolution project relied on local implementing partners to analyze and encourage linkages between the formal and informal justice sectors in thirteen districts in Helmand, Nimroz, Uruzgun, Herat, Paktya, Nangarhar, Kunduz, and Takhar provinces. These partners, which included The Liaison Office (TLO), Cooperation for Peace and Unity, and the Norwegian Refugee Council, gathered data on local disputes while testing various approaches that encouraged cooperation between the formal and informal actors. The work of these implementers focused on disputes at the village and district levels—first, attempting to understand how disputes were being resolved within the communities and then testing various ways of strengthening the linkages between the formal and informal justice sectors.[2]

The district-level data demonstrate the range of issues involved in local disputes and local dispute resolution. USIP's research shows that dispute resolution is currently taking place in Afghanistan using an ad hoc array of government officials, and local leaders, who often resolve low-level disputes based on community consensus. However, these community-based mechanisms have often been undermined by corrupt officials, local strongmen, and general instability. Arms and access to illicit funds from sources such as the opium trade allow strongmen to manipulate local political structures without being responsive to community needs as leaders have been in the past.

USIP researchers also conducted additional research in the provinces of Parwan and Kabul, particularly focusing within the Kabul court system on how the formal court system takes advantage of informal mechanisms. This research demonstrates the deep reliance that the formal sector continues to have on local leaders—even in the most urban parts of the country.

On a provincial level, USIP created Dispute Resolution Councils (DRCs) that bring tribal leaders and government officials together to resolve disputes in Nangarhar and Kunar. These are usually larger in scale than USIP's village and district level work and often involve multiple tribes. Cases from these provinces demonstrate some of the challenges created by local instability and tensions between local groups and the international military. They also suggest that networks of legitimate, local leaders can do much to contribute to local stability when they are relied upon to help facilitate dispute resolution.

Taken together, USIP's interrelated case studies on dispute resolution at district and provincial levels and in urban court systems paint a holistic picture of the dispute-resolution landscape in Afghanistan and help to identify broader trends. Other reports tend to focus on specific regions, which means they occasionally miss some of the significance of deeper, countrywide trends[3] or only focus on narrow issue areas, such as land disputes.[4] Instead, the USIP work described here conceptualizes the entire spectrum of local disputes and the ways in which various types of disputes fuel each other. It does not attempt to provide a precise analysis of local conflicts in Afghanistan; rather, it points to some trends drawn from both quantitative and qualitative studies to better inform programs going forward.[5]

Sources of Local Conflict

Dispute types vary widely in Afghanistan, but a few types—including land, water, family, and criminal disputes—tend to predominate in the districts where USIP worked. Many disputes fall into more than one of these categories. For example, in one major dispute in which USIP's DRC was involved in Nangarhar, a disagreement over the inheritance of land between an uncle and a nephew led to a feud in which four family members were killed. By the time the dispute was brought to the DRC, the most salient issue had become the murder of the family members, making it simultaneously a dispute over land, inheritance, and murder.

In almost all areas where data were collected, however, land disputes were the most prevalent. In 120 cases considered by DRCs in Nangarhar and Kunar, for example, 55 percent involved land issues. The importance of land issues is found in cases brought to the courts as well, and out of 48 cases studied from the fourth district of Kabul's primary civil court, 39 involved land-related issues (81 percent). Returning refugees, local strongmen grabbing both private and government land, unclear boundary markers, and poorly maintained, conflicting records all exacerbate this situation.[6]

Dispute types also vary over time. Several of those interviewed in Qara Bagh, in Kabul Province, for example, noted that during the civil war and the Taliban periods there were significantly more disputes over criminal matters, such as robbery. Now, though, people are more concerned with civil cases, particularly those involving land and the distribution of development aid. Interestingly, several respondents argued that the decrease in criminal issues was not due to an increase in the rule of law. Instead, they said, it was because so many resources were pouring into the country that local strongmen were spending more time working on securing these funds than trying to secure resources by fighting against each other.

Certain types of disputes tend to remain more localized, while others have the tendency to spiral upward and involve an increasing number of actors, creating wider tension. Since they involve issues of honor and privacy, for example, there is great pressure to resolve family disputes within the family—particularly disputes involving marriage, divorce, or inheritance. This is true of cases involving women and marriage, and those involving inheritance, where there is an added desire to keep the dispute out of sight from government authorities, who might attempt to extract a share of the money. As a result, the director of Women's Affairs in Paktya pointed out to a TLO researcher that it had been years since the last divorce case in the formal justice system in Paktya.[7] Thus it is not surprising that field-research data demonstrate a higher percentage of family cases being resolved at the village level versus at district or provincial levels. In cases collected by TLO among elders in Jalalabad city and the district of Bati Kot, the ratio of land to family disputes was almost 1 to 1 (45 to 41), while in cases registered by the DRC in Nangarhar and Kunar the ratio was 5 to 1 (55 percent of cases involved land, 11 percent involved family issues).

Actors in Local Dispute Resolution

An array of mechanisms is currently being used across the country to address the range of disputes in local communities in Afghanistan. These mechanisms include *jirgas*, gatherings of elders that are used primarily in Pashtun areas and are generally formed temporarily to solve a specific case. Each community also typically has more-permanent councils of elders, called *shuras*, which can range from local mosque *shuras* to district- and provincial-level *shuras*.[8] In addition, a range of respected individuals, including religious and tribal leaders, may act as mediators in a given case. Mediators may also include government officials, such as the district governor or district police chief, if they happen to have local legitimacy. Finally, government bodies like the Ministry of Justice Huqooq Department (civil affairs department) can serve as mediators or as referring agents to one of the above sources of dispute-resolution authority.

Each of these mechanisms is historical, in the sense that they have long been a means for local communities to maintain their autonomy from the Afghan state whose influence generally did not extend far beyond major cities. But they are simultaneously modern in their ability to adapt to current circumstances, such as the presence of large amounts of development aid and coalition forces. In particular, dispute-resolution mechanisms do not break down neatly into formal and informal categories. Tribal elders, for example, may work with local government officials to bring NGO funds to certain communities.

In some areas the range of forums is greater than in others. For example, in urban Jalalabad, each mosque and *nahia*, or neighborhood, generally has a *shura* to resolve neighborhood disputes involving land or family issues. In addition, there are development shuras set up by NGOs distributing aid as well as other *tejarati* (commercial) councils. Tejarati councils of merchants were originally set up under the Soviets, but they continue to be key players in organizing commerce in urban areas and resolving disputes between businesses. Other shuras are not geographically bound and may represent a specific tribe or ethnic group. Within the formal system in Jalalabad, the police are occasionally involved in the resolution of cases that do not get brought into the court system. Even within the court system, confusion and a lack of transparency sometimes mean that it is not always clear to participants which court should be involved in the resolution of a case.

The end result of this diverse dispute-resolution landscape is that urban residents can and do "forum shop," taking their cases into one system or another based upon the case and their personal relationships with those that sit on cases. In one sense, this means access to justice forums in Jalalabad is better than in other parts of the country. At the same time, though, this system sometimes weakens dispute-resolution mechanisms since disputants can undermine each other by seeking different venues. In some cases, such an array of mechanisms may allow disputants to approach the body they feel most comfortable with, increasing access to justice for women, who might not be as likely to approach the formal system. At the same time, however, the personal connections of disputants to influential figures, such as commanders, and their ability to bring these figures into the process can decrease the likelihood that the dispute will be resolved justly.

Informal dispute resolution often relies on bodies of elders whose collective reputations give the resolution legitimacy and create collective social pressure on the community to respect the decision. Individuals can also be respected as dispute resolvers on their own, particularly in lower-level cases and cases involving close family members. Government officials, including judges, prosecutors, members of the Huqooq Department, and district governors are also involved in the resolution of some cases. In many areas, the district governor is also a key figure in shaping the political and security conditions in an area, in turn, shaping the context in which local disputes take place. In two districts north of Kabul, district governors often sit in on district *shura* meetings, although their influence on these *shuras* varies. Many of those interviewed pointed out that one district governor was particularly weak and followed the ruling of the *shura* on most cases. They compared him with his predecessor who, they claimed, determined the composition of the *shura* and shaped its rulings. In each district, however, it was clear that the district governor was making decisions with at least some consultation with the district *shura*.

Notably, judicial officials usually have significantly less influence than the district governor's office over local disputes. The situation in Injil in Herat Province is typical, where the one judge and one prosecutor have tiny, barely furnished rooms in the district governor's compound, while the district governor welcomes guests in his sprawling office. In such a setting it was clear that the majority of local concerns went first to the district governor's office, and only when he saw fit did he send them to the prosecutor next door.

Even in areas close to Kabul, where one would expect formal institutions to have more power, the judiciary has limited influence. In one district, only an hour outside of Kabul, for example, there is one prosecutor and no judge. When interviewed by a USIP researcher, the prosecutor stated that he had only dealt with one case in the past twelve months and that he wished to be transferred back to Kabul since there was no work for him at his current post.

In addition to the informal and formal venues, in much of the country the Taliban have set up a shadow government, whose rules are being observed in an increasing number of provinces. Due to the insecurity in these areas, no systematic research has been done on these courts. However, discussions with individuals living in these areas suggest that the Taliban system rarely exists in isolation from other forms of dispute resolution. As a result, district governors in insurgent areas often have contact with the Taliban justice system. Based upon informal surveys conducted by TLO, district governors were in contact with their Taliban counterparts or other members of the Taliban shadow government in three out of the five districts surveyed in Nangarhar and Paktya.[9]

Based upon anecdotal evidence from the districts in which USIP is currently working, the Taliban justice system itself primarily takes two forms: roaming judges and local elders. Often educated in or imported from Pakistan, roaming judges travel to different areas to resolve cases; the verdicts in those cases are then enforced by local Taliban commanders. Of the districts where USIP worked, it is only in Helmand where roaming judges are at the center of dispute resolution. More common appears to be the co-option of local elders by the Taliban, who essentially demand that these elders resolve certain cases using the Taliban interpretation of *shariah* (Islamic law). The Taliban then leave the elders to resolve other cases as they see fit, leaving a system that resembles the informal system in other less Taliban-influenced parts of the country.[10]

Strategic Choices in Resolving Cases

In most cases, local actors in Afghanistan are faced with a series of options about who to take their dispute to and how best to approach a resolution that favors their side. Should the dispute be kept within the family? Should the disputant first approach an elder from the family or a local religious figure? If the disputant plans to use state institutions, which of the local officials will be most likely to resolve the case effectively with a minimum paid in bribes? These are not always simple questions and the disputant must weigh the costs and benefits of their potential approaches. The disputant must also contend with significant social and political pressure from opponents and allies to approach the case in a specific manner.

Furthermore, while informants may even describe the justice system as divided between formal and informal, a deeper examination of the role different actors play in successfully resolved disputes often reveals a more complicated picture. For example, district governors and other officials frequently sit on *shuras*, on which they have no official capacity. But the fact that they are employed by the government ensures that others on the *shura* afford them more respect. Thus authority does not reside solely in the informal or formal systems.

Cases are rarely confined to one venue and routinely move between bodies. So, for example, in Qara Bagh, when two brothers fought over their inheritance from their father, one of the men brought the case to the primary court in Qara Bagh. Since the dispute was primarily over land, the court investigated briefly and then referred the case to the district shura, which had local knowledge about land issues. Since the amount of land in question was not significant and since it was a family issue, the district *shura* referred the case to a village *shura* composed of four elders. Once these elders had divided the land, the resolution was then brought back to the district *shura*, which formally approved it (see diagram 1).

While the drawback to this approach was that the process took more than a year to resolve, the resolution to the dispute gained legitimacy and enforceability because both formal and informal bodies were included. The outcome was that both men accepted less than they had originally demanded. If the

Diagram 1. Path of a Land Dispute in Qara Bagh

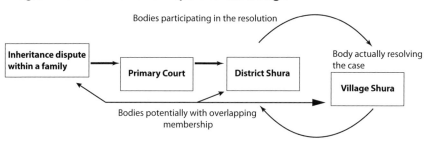

four elders on the village *shura* had simply resolved the dispute initially, there would have been less social pressure for all members of the community to adhere to the result. And the involvement of stronger, district-level actors who reconfirmed the resolution added more political weight to the decision than if the process had remained strictly at the village level. In this case, the movement of the case between bodies gave their resolution more legitimacy and ensured that the most knowledgeable figures about the land in question actually resolved the dispute.

Analysis of hundreds of cases recorded by USIP partners indicates that the path a case takes is significantly influenced by the details of the case and the relationship between those involved in the dispute. However, there are some patterns in the study areas. In both Nangarhar and Paktya, for example, it is common for cases to move from the formal to the informal sides of the dispute-resolution spectrum. In Paktya, this is even true for major criminal cases, with the district governor and prosecutor both claiming that the local preference for the use of jirgas led to this practice. Other informants claimed it was because the prosecutor was overburdened and lazy.[11]

Even within the court system, there is a significant reliance on informal mechanisms. Judges will often send cases out to groups of informal reconcilers, often related to the families of the disputants, to determine compensation. The reconcilers will reach a decision, which is then recorded and certified by the judge—in most cases, with minimal review. In one typical case in a northern suburb of Kabul, there was a dispute over land ownership after one man found another living on land that he owned. The man living on the land claimed he had purchased the land from a third man, but had been given no title. When the case went to court, the judge suggested that the men refer the case to a group of local elders. The elders decided that the man living on the property should pay the man who owned the property some 600,000 Afs, which was less than the value of the property but enough to compensate the owner. Once the decision was reached, the men brought the case back to the court and the judge stamped it (see diagram 2).

Diagram 2. Dispute Resolved Officially by the Kabul Court

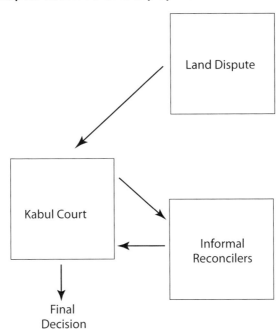

Such cases are common in the Kabul courts; over the course of four months in one primary court, for example, 11 of 27 civil cases and 7 of 23 criminal cases involved such mediation.[12] For criminal cases at the court covering the same *nahias*, informal intervention was most common in robbery cases, but it also occurred in more serious cases. In some cases, other informal actors, such as religious leaders, would also become involved in court proceedings as character witnesses.

In serious criminal cases, particularly murder cases, the court also distinguishes between *haq-ullah* and *haq-ulabd*, or the rights of God and the rights of the community—a distinction outlined in the Quran. The rights of the community apply to the so-called "forgivable" offenses—usually lower-level offenses, such as theft, that can be dealt with by the local community. The rights of God apply to serious offenses, such as murder, that require punishment carried out by the state.

In practice, there is some flexibility in this division even within the courts. In one case that blended both formal and informal elements, an Australian contractor was found guilty in Kabul court of murdering an Afghan colleague. After the verdict was handed down, the judge recommended that the victim's kin and the guilty man reconcile the civil aspect of the case. Since the victim's heirs were minors and the Australian contractor had no kin in Afghanistan, both groups used proxies. A distant relative of the victim and a couple of the Australian's colleagues met to informally determine compensation for the victim's family. The group determined that the contractor should pay the family 460,000 Afs, or approximately US$100,000. Once this *haq-ulabd* aspect of the case had been addressed, the judge reduced the contractor's sentence from death to imprisonment. Thus, while the civil and criminal, and informal and formal aspects of this case were conceptually distinct, the resolution of the civil aspect impacted the final sentence. This case also demonstrates that informal mechanisms are so flexible that they not only often enter court proceedings but even adapt to the international presence in the country.

USIP's research across thirteen districts in Afghanistan demonstrates that communities generally choose mechanisms that will resolve disputes quickly and at the lowest level. In part, this is the result of a high number of local councils and other bodies, but it also reflects the general understanding that escalation of conflict invariably increases the cost of resolution. Of 200 cases reported by TLO in both rural and urban Nangarhar, 72 involved a village-level *shura*, whereas only 21 involved a district *shura*. Disputants consider involving the formal judicial system even more costly, and of the same 200 recorded cases in Nangarhar, only 2 involved the court system. In other districts in Kabul, informants estimated that some 70 percent of cases are resolved at the village level, while only 30 percent eventually involve the district *shura*.

The choice of forum also affects the type of resolution a party can expect. Resolutions of cases brought before local elders often emphasize long-term stability and restorative justice more than individual rights. In a case in Mohmand Dara, for example, a woman was engaged to a man who died while fighting for the Afghan National Army. The family of the man wanted the woman to marry his brother instead. But, since the brother already had a wife, the woman and her family refused, threatening to retaliate with violence. The case was eventually brought before a group of local elders. These men determined that the family of the woman had to return the bride-price to the brother of the dead man. The woman's family also had to promise that she would not marry anyone in the dead man's tribe or within her own tribe. This resolution ensured that whatever political alliances were formed by the future marriage would be less likely to revive the enmity between the two groups.

At times, attempts to eliminate the potential of a return to conflict were more extreme. In several cases involving USIP's DRCs, communities acknowledged that the fear of increased bloodshed led them to involve both government officials and local elders in an attempt to make the resolution of the cases as final as possible. In the resolution of the murder involving the uncle and nephew described above, all parties signed a pact stating that anyone violating the agreement would have their homes burned down and their properties looted.

Challenges to Resolving Localized Disputes

Many have written extensively on the issues surrounding the court system in Afghanistan, often claiming that it is slow and corrupt and that its decisions are rarely enforced.[13] The ineffectiveness of state-justice mechanisms is not isolated from other challenges to resolving local conflicts, however. Indeed, bad governance not only hurts the formal sector, but it undermines the effectiveness of informal actors as well. Corrupt officials, for example, can hinder the dispute-resolution process among community leaders by attempting to undermine decisions by informal bodies. In one case in a town north of Kabul, officials working for the municipality had taken land from an individual six years earlier. The owner of the land, with the support of local elders, went to the Huqooq Department office, where he was given a letter stating that the municipality should return the land to him. Municipal officials refused to do so. The owner went to the primary court where he was similarly successful in winning the case. But the town still refused to turn over the land, and the court had no means for enforcing its decision. Outcomes like this delegitimize the state institutions that are not complying with the law. Such outcomes also cause the informal actors that broker the agreements to lose social capital; no longer are they considered to be individuals who can successfully resolve disputes within the community.

In an ideal setting, informal mechanisms present effective alternatives to a slow and corrupt state court system—yet many Afghans complain that the informal system has also been corrupted. It is clear that the current economic and security contexts have both increased the number of disputes and made resolving them more difficult. The insurgency, uncertain economic times, and also funds from NGOs and coalition forces have promoted the types of instability that make both state and informal mechanisms less effective. Under these unstable and economically volatile conditions, it is clear that there are certain circumstances where informal mechanisms are more effective than they are in other more stable areas.

Family disputes, for example, are often resolved quickly and quietly at the local level—often by close kin. However, when family disputes involve more than one family, they are more likely to become public because the honor of both families is involved. This appears to be even more likely when families are distantly related or from different communities. A case in point is that of the aforementioned woman who did not want to marry the brother of her deceased fiancé. Even in such cases, in which local elders convene to resolve disputes between families, disputants and their kin still attempt to keep the matter as private as possible. In one case where a woman ran away from a tyrannical mother-in-law, a local elder from a different family described how he had been brought in to help. He spoke with each woman from behind a curtain in order to encourage them to resolve their differences. In his description of the case, he made it clear that he emphasized to each woman the importance of resolving the dispute in order to minimize the damage already done to their family's honor. In cases like this, the greater the social distance between the actors, the less likely that the dispute will be resolved locally.

Similarly, when land-related issues are involved, the number of parties in a case generally relates to the social distance between the disputants. Thus, two disputants who are closely related to each other or are from the same tribe are more likely to resolve a case among themselves or use relatives as mediators than are disputants who are not related. A comparison of land disputes in the districts of Istalif and Qara Bagh brings this point into focus. In Istalif, which is fairly ethnically homogenous and where most groups are at least distantly related to each other, land disputes are rarely brought before the district council. On the other hand, in Qara Bagh, which is larger and more ethnically diverse, it is common for the district council to consider land issues between neighbors. This also suggests that people in urban areas turn to the formal system not because it is a particularly effective means of resolving disputes but because the social distance between neighbors is likely to be much greater than it is in rural areas.

Some cases appear more likely to be resolved quickly. For example, to resolve commercial disputes, businesses often set up effective mediating bodies, such as the tejarati councils discussed above. As a result, among thirty-six local elders in Nangarhar, only one claimed to have resolved a commercial dispute. Much of this may stem from the fact that in many commercial cases the costs for both sides increase the longer a case drags on because disputes tend to lower profits. Understandably, there is pressure to reach a resolution quickly. This is opposed to blood feuds where the victim's family and the murderer's family may not want to appear weak by attempting to settle the dispute, but they also may not have the desire to continue killing.[14] As these cases demonstrate, dispute-resolution mechanisms tend to be most effective when the majority in the community are invested in a quick resolution. Thus there is pressure to resolve family disputes and commercial disputes since discord may disrupt social and economic lives in the community.

In many cases, disputes have deep political implications, particularly given the fact that instability means that the political authority of both government officials and elders is often contested at a local level. This contestation then spills into the effectiveness of dispute resolution. The ability to resolve a dispute demonstrates political strength, whereas the inability to resolve a dispute can significantly damage a leader's reputation.

In a village in the Behsud district of Nangarhar, there was a significant dispute over local leadership, and an informal election was held to select the *malik* (an informal representative to the government) for the area.

After the selection of one man over another, a large dispute over land arose between two of the supporters of the men—with the elder, who had lost the election, clearly exacerbating the conflict. To pave the way for a resolution to the situation, a *jirga* was formed to address the issue of leadership in the village. The land being argued over was of secondary importance, and, after the leadership issue was fully addressed, the land dispute was resolved fairly easily.

Local dispute resolution in Afghanistan has become more difficult due to the instability of the past three decades and the fact that in many areas the fighting and rapidly shifting economic conditions have eroded historical checks on power. Part of what has made local dispute resolution effective outside of state regulation is that, on a local level, Afghan leaders are historically beholden to the communities they belong to because their power derived from local consent. Leadership among almost all groups in Afghanistan tends to be hereditary, but this often is the norm and not the rule. This means that local leaders, as well as religious leaders such as mullahs, are forced to respond to community pressures and demands. They lead by cajoling, not commanding, and due to the fierce individualism found among most groups in Afghanistan, leaders tend to be primus inter pares, or first among equals.[15] Relying on marriage alliances, with a relatively limited gap in wealth between leaders and followers, local communities were often able to keep leaders accountable with the constant threat of their replacement.

The entrance of sizable political and economic resources from external sources has altered this system in the past thirty years. Starting during the war against the Soviets, local leaders acquired guns and money that they could use to purchase support instead of relying on traditional patterns. The threat of violence and the limited provision of services meant that communities were unable to prevent and thus simply turned a blind eye to local commanders who grabbed land or favored one particular side in disputes. In the case of one commander involved in multiple case studies, people praised the fact that during the end of the Soviet period and in the early years of the Taliban he provided people in his community with security and basic services. Since then, however, his reputation has deteriorated, primarily as his close allies have been accused of grabbing land or committing other offenses against the community. The commander is still involved in the resolution of numerous disputes in the area, but his ability to resolve disputes now seems to stem more from his ability to threaten violence. The disputes may appear resolved, but the situation is clearly creating resentment in the community. Land disputes previously resolved now seem likely to reappear once the political balance of power shifts again.

Elsewhere, former roles have been refigured by the presence of new resources. In districts in the Shomali Plain, for example, a local elder known as the *mir aw* was responsible for organizing the distribution of water from various irrigations channels. In some of these communities where USIP had researchers, this model continued, but in another, a local commander seized the position of *mir aw* and during the civil war began to charge for the right to use the water (historically, only a small maintenance fee was expected). Following 2001, the commander pulled back from this blatant extortion but continued to distribute the water in ways perceived by many as inequitable. Eventually, one man complained and was killed by the commander.

Given the political and economic instability of the past thirty years, there is often an incentive for many to ensure that disputes remain unresolved. Thus, in the case of the murder described above, the dispute between the nephew and uncle's families remained unresolved initially because one of the men had moved to Iran as a refugee. Later, after he returned and was arrested, community members put pressure on officials to have the families resolve the dispute and release the man. In Afghanistan, there is a good deal of political uncertainty and a lack of consensus over who will be in power in the future on both the national and local levels. The resolution of disputes generates political capital, and, given the current political uncertainty and lack of security, such capital may be considered a valuable resource in other political struggles. In an example of this, when a new irrigation project increased the water flow into Qara Bagh, one local elder was widely regarded as the primary mediator in resolving how the new water would be supplied to various farmers. Even though most credited several others with actually securing the funds for the project, the elder who had resolved the water-sharing disputes handily won a seat when he ran for provincial council in 2009—despite the fact that he was not an incumbent. In more unstable conditions and in areas where there is more antigovernment activity, leaders are less inclined to demonstrate their influence publicly, and local elders actually work to mask their influence from both antigovernment forces and from the government and coalition forces, fearing reprisals from both sides.

Some of these issues are exacerbated when the international military is involved. For example, in Kunar, an elder who was a member of the DRC helped negotiate the release of several local, young men who the community claimed had been falsely detained by the international military in the area. The elder, who was respected in the area and known by some in the local U.S. military Provincial Reconstruction Team (PRT), was able to negotiate between the community and the PRT. The success of this case, however, demonstrates some of the challenges in other cases. Community members, in particular, claimed it was very difficult to access the internationals working at the PRT and felt they could only do so through the elder. Furthermore, the active Taliban presence in the area meant that everyone involved feared reprisals from antigovernment forces. The elder worked hard to ensure that few people knew about his involvement—a striking contrast with the idealized version of the informal dispute-resolution system in which the negotiator gains political capital from his fame as a conciliator.

While the reach of the coalition forces and development projects into the Afghan countryside is limited in much of the country, the resources these groups bring are still clearly important drivers of local conflict. In cases registered by the DRCs, for example, 8 percent included issues having to do with coalition forces or with the distribution of international aid. Such complaints demonstrate how excessive international funds meant to stabilize areas can create more incentives for conflict.

Conclusion: Promoting the Resolution of Local Disputes

As the examples highlighted suggest, the current issues with informal mechanisms of dispute resolution in Afghanistan have little to do with the mechanisms themselves—and a great deal to do with the current political, social, and economic contexts that are undermining them.[16] As the international community has switched its approach in the country to increasingly focus on counterinsurgency, there have been attempts by coalition forces, the U.S. and British embassies, and other international organizations to engage directly with informal systems. As this report suggests, however, the elders and councils that constitute the informal sector do not need to be strengthened (and they certainly do not need training in dispute resolution—an art they are already skilled at), as much as they need to be provided secure space in which to operate. Corrupt local officials, the continued presence of commanders and other strongmen, and insurgents all erode the traditional mechanisms that resolve local disputes and provide accountable local governance. Furthermore, in some instances, the very presence of international funds and military forces further encourage disputes, as opposed to their resolution.

International efforts should instead focus on providing security and more predictable access to political and economic resources in order to promote the historical space between local elders and government officials in which disputes can be resolved. Local disputes are not generally the cause of local insurgency, but they can create instability and violence that contribute significantly to conditions that facilitate insurgency. It is important for the international community to support the formal judiciary in setting up legitimate, transparent processes in places—cities, in particular—where there is demand for such mechanisms. It also means putting more emphasis on ensuring that local leaders are appointed based upon merit and ability, as opposed to supporting local strongmen who provide short-term stability but ultimately undermine the legitimacy of the government, the international presence, and the historical relationship between elders and communities.

Notes

1. An often-cited UNDP report claims that approximately 80 percent of all disputes in Afghanistan are resolved by the informal justice system as opposed to the state justice system. This has led to a series of aid programs aimed at working with the informal system to complement those building capacity in the formal system. See Afghanistan *Human Development Report 2007: Bridging Modernity and Tradition—The Rule of Law and the Search for Justice* (Kabul: Center for Policy and Human Development [CPHD], 2007). According to an unpublished report published by TLO, in Paktya, between 5 and 10 percent of cases are being resolved by the formal system.

2. Within USIP's work with various organizations in Afghanistan on informal dispute resolution, a template was created for gathering data on disputes. It allowed comparison of quantitative data from certain areas. Despite this, it is important to make clear that even when serious attempts were made to standardize data-collection methods there was still significant variation based upon the way the data were collected, but more importantly, the way that disputes manifested themselves in different regions across Afghanistan. To describe this diversity, researchers also conducted follow-up research on a series of case studies from each district. The downside to this case study–oriented approach is that many of the statistics in this report should be thought of as signpost indicators, rather than precise indicators, of the types of disputes in a certain area. On the other hand, the fact that disputes were deeply shaped by their political, economic, and social contexts means that studies about local context in Afghanistan do not simply describe how small-scale disputes were resolved in a certain area; they reveal much more about the individual lived experience of the political context of each area studied, particularly in relation to justice, instability, and many of the other drivers of the insurgency.

3. Deborah Smith, *Community Based Dispute Resolution Processes in Nangarhar Province* (Kabul: Afghanistan Research and Evaluation Unit [AREU], 2009); Deborah Smith and Shelly Manalan, *Community Based Dispute Resolution Processes in Bamiyan Province* (Kabul: AREU, 2009); The International Legal Foundation, "The Customary Laws of Afghanistan," 2004, www.theilf.org; Sarah Ladbury, *Helmand Justice Mapping Study, Final Report for the Department of International Development Afghanistan* (Coffey International Development Limited, July 2010); Rebecca Gang, *Community Based Dispute Resolution Processes in Balkh Province* (Kabul: AREU, 2010); Rebecca Gang, *Community Based Dispute Resolution Processes in Kabul City* (Kabul: AREU, 2011).

4. For a study on land issues, see Liz Alden Wily, *Land Rights in Crisis: Restoring Tenure Security in Afghanistan, Issue Paper* (Kabul: AREU, March 2003); for a report focusing on dispute resolution in Helmand, particularly in instances brought before Prisoner Review Shuras, see Sarah Ladbury, *Helmand Justice Mapping Study, Final Report for the Department of International Development Afghanistan* (Coffey International Development Ltd, July 2010). For specific case studies analyzing the relationship between instability and conflict, see Coburn, *Bazaar Politics: Pottery and Power in an Afghan Market Town* (Palo Alto, CA: Stanford University Press, 2011) and for a more general overview see Coburn and John Dempsey, *Informal Dispute Resolution in Afghanistan* (Washington, DC: USIP, 2010).

5. Previous work on what is sometimes referred to as informal justice systems often focuses first on the bodies that resolve disputes (often councils known as *shuras*) or more ad hoc bodies, usually referred to using the Pashtu term *jirgas*. This approach, however, tends to be overly structural and ignores the more important issues in shaping these bodies: the disputes themselves and the relationships of those involved. *Shuras*, *jirgas*, and other bodies in Afghanistan are primarily mechanisms; they exist in order to resolve disputes or address some other local concern. Furthermore, it can be argued that this focus on dispute-resolution bodies, as opposed to a focus on the disputes themselves, has led to much of the debate over terminology—which includes informal justice, traditional justice, the nonstate sector, or community-based dispute resolution. All of these terms have shortcomings (e.g.,

state actors are often involved in nonstate justice, the system itself is highly formalized in some places, and community-based dispute resolution often involves religious figures from outside the community). With these flaws in mind, this report tends to use the term informal justice with the understanding that there is no strict dichotomy between the informal and state justice sectors and that aspects the informal sector can be highly formalized.

6. While some in the development community have promoted increased work on a national land registry due to the lack of written records, it is interesting to note that in almost all areas where USIP has conducted research, even among highly illiterate communities, it is normal to find some sort of written deeds outlining ownership. The real problem concerns the standardization of these documents, something that coalition forces have complained about when multiple "owners" demanding rent have brought deeds to troops who have set up bases on private land. As a result, international groups are likely to encounter resistance to such a system by the ruling elite, many of whom have profited from the haphazard grabbing of land over the past 30 years.

7. TLO, unpublished report.

8. The definitions of these bodies vary from community to community, and other terms, such as *jalasa*, are occasionally used as well. This flexibility makes informal mechanisms more difficult to analyze but also allows them to be adapted to fit a great variety of issues.

9. TLO, unpublished report.

10. This system extends far beyond remote, Taliban-controlled areas. Rumors abound that Taliban courts are currently issuing subpoenas for land cases, and that these are being delivered in urban Kandahar city.

11. See Peyton Cooke, TLO, forthcoming.

12. For the use of informal conciliators in the Kabul court system, see Karima Tawfik and Zuhal Nesari, (Washington D.C.: USIP, Peace Brief 101).

13. See, in particular, Integrity Watch Afghanistan, *Afghan Perceptions and Experiences of Corruption: A National Survey* (2010), and Stephen Carter and Kate Clark, *'Snakes and Scorpions'; Justice and Stability in Afghanistan* (Kabul: Report prepared for the Office of the High Commissioner for Human Rights, 2010).

14. As a result of this, there are rumors of several high-ranking government officials who refuse to sit in the same room together because their families are involved in feuds. To acknowledge the other would damage their reputations, but they also clearly have little interest in actually fulfilling the blood debt.

15. For more on this, see chapter 2 in Thomas Barfield, *Afghanistan: A Cultural and Political History* (Princeton, NJ: Princeton University Press, 2010) or Noah Coburn, Bazaar Politics.

16. A similar argument can be made about the issue of women's rights in informal justice, a topic that cannot be covered here due to inadequate space. For more on how informal justice mechanisms are not the cause of discrimination against women as much as the current social context in which these mechanisms is embedded, see Coburn and Dempsey, 2010.

4

Dangerous Liaisons with the Afghan Taliban
The Feasibility and Risks of Negotiations

Matt Waldman

W aldman's 2010 analysis explores insurgents' motivations based on field interviews with current and former Taliban as well as other actors. He argues that despite the U.S. military surge in Afghanistan, security deteriorated and the number of insurgent attacks increased. This evidence made it "questionable whether it is even possible for the coalition to achieve a position of strength." Meanwhile, surge tactics were further undermining the already thin filament of trust needed to begin negotiations with the Taliban.

Waldman argues for a policy based on confidence-building measures, which could include delisting the Taliban from UN sanctions lists, partial ceasefires, or a reduction in hostilities. Policymakers and other analysts searching for possible openings to negotiations have since adopted many of these proposals. However, his analysis is unsparing regarding the obstacles facing negotiation efforts with the Taliban. Any process would require a significant amount of time to bear results. There is no shortage of spoilers on both sides, and there is a "deep-seated mistrust" between the most important actors in any potential negotiation.

Despite the obstacles, Waldman concludes that "the potential for negotiation should be explored." In retrospect, this recommendation appears to be cautious. The justification for this caution, however, can be seen in the many challenges that remain to a negotiated settlement.

Originally published as Matt Waldman, "Dangerous Liaisons with the Afghan Taliban: The Feasibility and Risks of Negotiations," Special Report 256 (Washington, DC: USIP, 2010).

Introduction

Although the number of U.S. and other foreign forces in Afghanistan has increased, from 30,000 in early 2006 to some 150,000 as of September 2010, there has been a steady resurgence of the Taliban and other insurgent groups. They have increased their attacks by more than 40 percent in each of the last four years,[1] causing an escalation in military and civilian casualties, and systematically attacked and intimidated civilians associated with the Afghan government. They now have control or influence in more than half the country, having expanded from the south and southeast to parts of the north, center, and west.[2] This expansion has led to profound concerns about the efficacy of conventional warfighting and an increased international emphasis on counterinsurgency, transition, and reconciliation.

The heavyweight counterinsurgency strategy formulated by General Stanley McChrystal has faced severe challenges and significant progress is unlikely without the two sine qua nons for counterinsurgency: a legitimate, functioning government and denial of external sanctuary for insurgents. The Kabul regime is largely corrupt and ineffective, and insurgents obtain sanctuary and support in Pakistan. Transition, meaning efforts to build Afghan forces and transfer responsibilities to them, also faces major obstacles and will take longer than anticipated.

Thus there is increasing consideration of the potential for reconciliation with insurgents. In October 2008, Taliban and Afghan government representatives met in Saudi Arabia, and Robert Gates, U.S. secretary of defense, has said he could envisage reconciliation with elements of the Taliban as part of an eventual political outcome.[3] In 2009, the former British foreign secretary and the previous UN special representative for Afghanistan each advocated efforts to achieve an inclusive political settlement.[4] Reconciliation was heralded at the January 2010 London Conference on Afghanistan, and in March, one insurgent group, Hizb-i-Islami, held talks with Afghan and foreign officials.[5] In June, a government-orchestrated peace *jirga* endorsed a plan to reintegrate insurgents, requested the removal of Taliban leaders from the UN blacklist, and called for talks with the armed opposition.[6] Also in June 2010, Pakistani intelligence and military chiefs met with Afghan and U.S. officials regarding the potential for talks with the Haqqani insurgent group.[7] These developments raise the question of whether negotiation with insurgents is feasible or desirable, which requires an understanding of why insurgents are fighting.[8]

Taliban Motivations and Objectives

This section considers the motivations and objectives of the Taliban, though it is reasonable to expect some commonality with other insurgent groups. It draws on the views of Taliban commanders, which may skew the findings, but they and other informed interviewees were also asked about the motivations of foot soldiers.[9] Motivations and objectives cannot be understood in isolation; the section therefore begins with observations derived from interviews about the general state of the movement.

State of the Taliban

Commanders acknowledged that Taliban forces were fatigued and under increased military pressure, but they were confident of the movement's prospects for eventually forcing foreign forces to withdraw. The Taliban is well-sourced in funding, munitions, and equipment, much of which commanders said is provided by or through Pakistan's Directorate for Inter-Services Intelligence (ISI) or military officials. Interviewees also reported that Pakistani territory is used for their command; for logistics, planning, training, and recruitment; and for treatment or recuperation. Many were unhappy about perceived ISI influence over the movement, especially at the leadership level.

Taliban units appear to be cohesive, and commanders regard themselves as falling within a relatively robust organizational hierarchy. However, they consider the Taliban—the largest of eight major insurgent factions—as comprising different groups with varying tactics, goals, and supporters. Many spoke of factional suspicion, mistrust, and even antipathy, especially between local and Pakistan-based groups, the latter of which they saw as more extreme.

Commanders asserted that the Taliban cause is just, but many displayed unease about certain tactics. They expressed regret for the unintended deaths of civilians, attacks on schools or non-governmental organizations (NGOs), and assassinations of tribal or community leaders. Some even said they regretted having to kill Afghan police and soldiers.

Most claimed that they were popular with locals, who provided them with essential assistance such as food and shelter. As one commander put it: "If they didn't [support and assist], the Taliban could not resist foreign forces."[10] However, some of this support may derive from insurgent coercion or intimidation, and a number of commanders from the south and southeast admitted that public support had declined because they were seen to have brought fighting to the area or caused greater hardship. As one Kandahari commander admitted, "The people in my area are kind of lost; they can't decide whether to support the government or Taliban. None of the Afghans are happy about this situation."[11] According to many local leaders or analysts in Kandahar, the insurgents are not popular but are preferred to the government. Taliban strength, they argued, was largely a function of government degeneracy and weakness.

Motivations

Insurgent motivations are variable, multiple, and difficult to ascertain. For any given insurgent there are usually several motivating factors, configured according to personal background, experience, or circumstances. Interviews suggest at least five main clusters of motivations, the first three of which insurgents often emphasized.

The first motivation is retaliation for perceived military aggression by foreign forces, especially involving civilian casualties and abusive raids or detentions. As one southern insurgent put it,

> The foreigners here do not observe the rules of their own countries; they are far wilder than the animals of the jungle. They bomb weddings, for example in Shindand, killing over two hundred innocent civilians. They shout about human rights more than most but then they kill people and call it a mistake. How can they call it a mistake after eight or nine years? If this continues, the resistance will continue.[12]

Interviews suggest that the longer the conflict has gone on, the greater the significance and prevalence of this motivation. One southern commander explained how an attack by foreign forces incited him to fight:

> I am a landowner and was working on the land. I was not a Talib. But some years ago American special forces came and entered my home without my permission at night and killed my two sons, my father, and two uncles without any reason. Another time they did the same thing in another village in my district. When I saw their acts and knew they came only to kill us, not to help, I started fighting against them. They forced me to fight them and now I will continue to fight them so long as they are in Afghanistan.[13]

Another commander argued that "if international forces keep bombing and killing civilians not only the Taliban but also all the rest of the nation will fight them."[14]

A second related but broader motivation is resistance to perceived invading infidel forces that threaten Afghan and Islamic values and culture. Taliban interviewees saw themselves as fighting a just war, a *jihad* in defense of their country and religion. Indeed, several of the commanders had attended madrassas in Pakistan where they were continually exhorted to do so. As one insurgent put it, in rejecting government plans for reintegration, "At the moment our country is invaded, there is no true *sharia*. Can we accept these [conditions] for money? How then could I call myself a Muslim and an Afghan?"[15]

Third is resistance to officials regarded as dishonest, corrupt, and unjust, who benefit from impunity. A commander from Wardak province explained: "Many, many fight because of the killing of Afghans, the invasion and order of the Holy Quran to stand up against injustice and corrupt government. The lack of *sharia* law means that if a robber or a murderer is arrested he knows he can buy his way out."[16] A senior UN official based in Kandahar argued a "sense of injustice" was driving many fighters.[17] An experienced Afghan analyst described how: "Wherever you go the government is seen as part of the trouble. Governance is not just about projects; it's about justice and impartiality in decision-making, which right now is awful."[18] As another UN official observed, foreign powers are implicated as well: "Most are fighting because of the corrupt system that we [the West] are supporting."[19]

A fourth and related motivation, not so widely acknowledged in interviews, is exclusion from power or resources. It appears that certain groups, often tribes or subclans, see allying with the Taliban as a means of challenging such exclusion or gaining leverage in local power struggles.

Fifth is social and economic security for the destitute and unemployed, which some insurgents and Afghan analysts, especially in the south, see as the main motivation for more than half of all insurgents.[20] A related factor, rarely acknowledged in interviews, is the stigma of such circumstances, and the sense of purpose, status, and solidarity associated with the insurgency. Given the danger and discomfort of fighting, as well as the potency of some of the causes mentioned above, it may be that economic and social factors do not themselves constitute a cause for fighting; rather, they may be conditions that increase the likelihood of mobilization. As a southern Talib put it, "Poverty and unemployment help a lot with recruitment."[21]

Apart from the five main motivations, there are at least two other types of motivation of varying significance. Some individuals apparently join the insurgency out of expediency: They are coerced, intimidated, or pressured into fighting, or believe it is in their personal and family interests, perhaps judging that the insurgents will ultimately prevail. There are also opportunists who exploit the insurgency for criminal purposes, such as extortion or narcotics, or to strengthen their power and influence.

Objectives

The objectives of the Taliban vary among individual commanders and groups, and are affected by a range of factors, such as local power dynamics and group leadership.[22] While the operational goals of units are local, most commanders interviewed stressed two main goals of the movement: the withdrawal of foreign forces and establishment of sharia. The interviews, however, suggest there are several separate but related goals.

First and foremost is the withdrawal of foreign troops. A small minority of insurgents appears to see the killing of foreign forces, especially Americans, as an end in itself. For the majority, however, it is justified either by their cause or retribution. Many Talibs and former Taliban officials, such as former foreign minister Mawlawi Mutawakil, saw the conflict as a "war of independence,"[23] and the struggle has been woven into the historic narrative of expelling foreign infidel invaders. A few commanders acknowledged that a rapid withdrawal of foreign forces could aggravate the conflict, as did some former Taliban officials, such as Mawlawi Mujahid. Some insurgents even claimed their aim was to curb the aggressive conduct of foreign forces: "If the Americans stop bombing, killing, and raiding then every Talib is ready to put his gun on the ground."[24] For almost all, however, the withdrawal of foreign forces was an absolute goal.

For the majority of insurgents interviewed, the concept of *sharia* as an objective was panoptic and multidimensional—not only religious and legal, but also political, moral, and cultural. Different insurgents emphasized different aspects of *sharia*, but at least four common meanings can be identified. First is the enforcement of law and order. In this sense, *sharia* means the firm, swift, and fair dispensation of justice, especially in criminal cases; there is often a concomitant assumption that *ulema* (Islamic scholars) should have a prominent juridical role. This kind of *sharia* was often defined by its corollary: an end to the bribery of judges, less crime, and greater public safety.

Second, insurgents saw sharia as the application of Islamic law but few could articulate what this meant in practice, beyond more severe punishments for criminals, including amputation and capital punishment. As one commander put it, "*sharia* is for the welfare of the communities. There will be no crimes because if robbers are caught their hands will be cut off, murderers will be killed, and good punishment given to kidnappers."[25] Another commander confided that he and some of his comrades did not support the restitution of extreme punishments as applied during the Taliban regime, but thought the majority did. Other interviewees not associated with the Taliban, including a female member of parliament, said they supported the Taliban's general position on punishments.

Most insurgents interviewed said the Afghan constitution should be changed, but were unable to say how. The commanders' support for this goal is probably attributable to their belief that the constitution was engineered by Western powers and their aversion to aspects of democracy as currently manifested in Afghanistan, rather than any profound objections to the constitutional framework. Some former Taliban leaders argued that the constitution should be changed to give *ulema* a greater role in the affairs of state, a view that the current Taliban leadership probably shares.

Third, insurgents regarded *sharia* as entailing the legitimate exercise of power. All insurgents interviewed called for an administration free from corrupt, predatory, and unjust officials, or those serving foreign interests. Some abbreviated this as a call for Islamic government.

A southern commander emphasized Taliban demands for honest government. Another explained: "The government is supposed to be reformed, but corrupt warlords are in government with loads of money and huge houses; how much money? If the international community sent money to the poor, they stole that money and put it in their pockets. If President [Hamid] Karzai took steps against these people then we would support it." He added that if foreign forces left, "they formed a proper government and stopped corruption by those in power, we are not so crazy to keep fighting."[26]

Fourth, insurgents equated *sharia* with a truly Afghan and Islamic society that resists the imposition of what are perceived as immoral Western practices, especially those associated with the liberation or sexualization of women. Insurgents argued for a strict form of *purdah*, which includes the requirement for women to use the *hijab* and conceal their form, and the separation of men and women at work and in education. They contended that such practices, which are common in southern Afghanistan, are necessary to protect women. Former Taliban figures and a number of other interviewees not associated with the insurgency echoed these views.

Some interviewees suggested that since the Taliban regime some within the movement had moderated their views on women. Whether true or not, the extreme policies of the former regime, insurgent interviews, and accounts of Taliban attacks and intimidation from the field suggest that they would seek to restrict girls' access to secondary and higher-level education; limit women's opportunities for certain types of jobs or public roles; strictly enforce social codes affecting women; curtail their access to public spaces; and require a mahram to accompany them.[27]

It is evident that Taliban commanders seek power at the local level, and the insurgency itself forms part of a national struggle for power. But it is not clear to what extent this is an end in itself or a means to the ends described above. Few of the insurgents interviewed said they wished to see the Taliban in government; most tacitly distinguished between the acquisition of power to achieve the movement's goals and the administration of government. As one southeastern commander put it, "Our target is not to capture the country, just to force the withdrawal of the infidels and bring *sharia*."[28] Some specifically rejected the idea that the insurgents would govern: "We don't want governorships or ministries. We want *sharia*—which is for the welfare of all communities." This rejection may be because field commanders are primarily concerned about their local influence, or it may be a spurious position promulgated by the leadership to conceal their real ambitions. Alternatively, Taliban leaders may believe, as a Western official remarked, "[in modern-day Afghanistan] giving people ministries is a way of removing them from power."[29] They may be seeking political rather than administrative power.

A final goal, which may seem paradoxical, is peace and security. Many commanders believed that forcing foreign troops to withdraw and imposing sharia is the only way to achieve law and order, and end the fighting. Many expressed their strong desire for peace. As one southern commander said: "I want the world to remove their young guys from Afghanistan, not to see them killed, and them not to kill our young guys; and not to cause our women and children to cry, or to make your women and your children cry. Please leave us, and our people, and our country to make our life and government by ourselves; this is our habit and history."[30]

Most commanders seemed cognizant of the dangers of ethnic and factional conflict, as well as the interference of neighboring countries. None interviewed spoke in a derogatory way about particular ethnicities or tribes, although under the former Taliban regime there was discrimination against and mistreatment of ethnic and religious minorities.

Most Taliban goals are framed within a religious narrative that binds together disparate aims and activities; it is also a source of motivation, commitment, and legitimacy. While it may have less significance in the south than in the southeast, interviews suggest that many mid- to-high-ranking Talibs have religious credentials.

The insurgents interviewed did not espouse al-Qaeda's extremist ideology, and one commander said: "We want good relations with foreign countries."[31] Interviewees regarded the Taliban as having few links with al-Qaeda, different strategic goals, and a different Islamic philosophy—a point emphasized by former Taliban deputy minister Mawlawi Arsala Rahmani. No interviewee considered al-Qaeda a significant actor in Afghanistan, which comports with recent U.S. intelligence assessments.[32]

This report does not seek to analyze the Taliban movement's copious public statements; however, many are consistent with the views of field commanders. For example, in his Eid al-Fitr message of September 2009, Mullah Omar, the movement's spiritual leader, denounced the "invading forces" for their "policy of brutality and atrocity, hoping that they will subjugate the brave people of Afghanistan by dent of military power."[33] He condemns "the rampant corruption in the surrogate Kabul administration, the existence of mafia networks, the tyranny and high-handedness of the warlords, and spread and increase of the centers of obscenity." He also echoes what commanders see as the movement's two principal aims: "Our goal is to gain independence of the country and establish a just Islamic system there."

In his 2010 Eid al-Fitr message Mullah Omar goes further than Taliban commanders in acknowledging an ambition to exercise power, and implies that Taliban leaders should hold ultimate state authority. But he is not explicit about their role in government and emphasizes the need for competency and inclusivity: "All God-fearing, experienced, and professional cadres of the Afghan society will be part and parcel of this system without any political, racial, and lingual discrimination . . . [to whom] administrative responsibilities will be devolved."[34]

His message is not consistent with al-Qaeda's transnational *jihadi* struggle and calls for a new Islamic caliphate, defining the Taliban as a "nationalist movement"[35] and stating that "we want to frame our foreign policy on the principle that we will not harm others nor allow others to harm us."[36]

Feasibility, Risks, and Implications of Negotiations

This research does not address the feasibility of local-level negotiations with insurgents. The viability of local agreements could be undermined by the insurgency's impetus and reach, or the absence of a broader supporting framework; the issue undoubtedly requires further study. In light of the above findings, this section considers whether negotiations with the Taliban, as a movement, are feasible, and if so, what the risks and implications are. (It cannot be assumed that these assessments would necessarily apply to other insurgent groups.) It considers the international and Taliban perspective on negotiations, conditions for talks, scope for confidence building, elements of a process, threats from spoilers, the role of Pakistan and regional players, and finally, the substance of an agreement.

Taliban Perspectives on Negotiations

Mullah Omar has signaled an interest in negotiations, which is ostensibly contingent on the withdrawal of foreign forces. Reaffirming the Taliban's goals of independence and an "Islamic system," he says, somewhat tautologically: "We can consider any option that could lead to the achievement of this goal. We have left open all options and ways towards this end. However, this will only be feasible when the country is free from the trampling steps of the invading forces and has gained independence."[37]

Most commanders interviewed echoed this position: "If America withdraws its troops from Afghanistan, then negotiations with the Afghan government will be possible."[38] However, this may be a tactical negotiating position, mirroring the international demands that insurgents accept the Afghan constitution and renounce violence. As Mawlawi Mutawakil points out, both demands ignore contentious issues;[39] thus, each side reinforces the obduracy of the other. As one southern Taliban commander put it, "We were, are, and will be ready for peace, but it has its conditions. Infidels cannot impose things on us—then we will not stop fighting."[40]

The Taliban leadership may have no intention to negotiate but feign an interest in doing so because Afghans widely support the idea. They may calculate that the tide of events is in their favor: They are expanding their territorial influence and inflicting more casualties on the coalition, which is increasingly looking to withdraw; the government is weak and unpopular; they have a safe haven, external support, and a steady supply of recruits. They may also believe that they can outlast international forces.

On the other hand, some interviewees, such as former Taliban deputy minister Hotak, suggested that a number of Taliban leaders support the idea of talks and, ultimately, some form of settlement.[41] They are forced to live in exile in Pakistan and endure ISI pressure; American troop presence is growing (and many are skeptical of the scheduled 2011 drawdown); large numbers of commanders are being captured or killed; fighters are fatigued; and Afghan communities are objecting to Taliban presence. Taliban leaders may also recognize the powerful yearning for peace among the population, and, as former Taliban ambassador Mullah Zaeef put it, "the responsibility for any Muslim to try to stop the bloodshed."[42]

However, interviews suggest that talks are hindered by mistrust. This is partly due to long-standing enmities, and what Taliban leaders regard as their severe and unjust treatment after the fall of their regime. Former Taliban officials say that although they publicly acknowledged the new regime in Kabul, they were harassed, imprisoned, mistreated, and forced to flee to Pakistan. They point out that they were excluded from the Bonn process and disparage past reconciliation efforts by the Strengthening Peace Commission for a lack of political will and resources. Many commanders also regard the new international emphasis on reintegrating fighters as demonstrating a disinterest in higher-level negotiations.

One senior Taliban interviewee suggested that commanders increasingly perceive power and authority in the movement as vesting with hard-line elements of the leadership. Thus, even if talks with more moderate Taliban leaders were successful, such leaders may not be able to bring the movement with them. Also, a number of Taliban foot soldiers and commanders may feel that they have little to gain from negotiations, or that it betrays their cause. Therefore, notwithstanding the movement's hierarchy, there are questions about the leadership's ability to bring field commanders with them, and of commanders to bring their fighters.

International and Afghan Perspectives on Negotiations

The Afghan government's position on negotiations is ambiguous, and there are multiple international policies on and interpretations of reconciliation. Some see it as a counter-insurgency tool to weaken and divide the enemy, involving efforts to induce individual Taliban leaders and factions to switch to the government side. Others see it as an elite pact, or series of deals, that divide power between government and insurgent leaders, allowing foreign forces to withdraw without conceding defeat. Still others see it as a process to address grievances between different groups and factions, especially those within or connected to the government and the Taliban, to resolve the core conflict, and reach a more inclusive political settlement. Finally, some emphasize the need for long-term efforts to build better relations and trust between groups in a fragmented society, thereby promoting conflict resolution at all levels.

Although the United States has given limited support to President Karzai's outreach to insurgent groups and dialogue with Pakistan, many interviewees associated the U.S. position on reconciliation with the first interpretation. This position could be considered as reintegration plus, or, as an American military manual describes it, golden surrender, which is qualitatively different from, and perhaps incompatible with, genuine negotiations.[43] One European diplomat doubted that the United States would seriously support negotiations, arguing, "They don't compromise, their model is winning ... they have a radically different perception of what a political solution means."[44] In fact, there is no clearly defined U.S. position on negotiations. This, and the mélange of international policies, appears to have convinced Taliban leaders that the West is not genuinely interested in talks, and so long as these circumstances persist, there is little prospect for serious dialogue.

Conditions for Negotiations

The prospects for negotiations are also affected by the coalition's campaign strategy and the conflict's overall dynamics. Many Western officials believe that negotiations should only be attempted once a position of strength has been achieved and that the military surge will drive insurgents to the negotiating table.

Given the constraints of counterinsurgency operations, and Taliban sanctuary and support in Pakistan, it is questionable whether it is even possible for the coalition to achieve a position of strength. An influential theory of negotiations, propounded by I. William Zartman, suggests that talks are more likely to succeed where both sides believe there is a mutually hurting stalemate.[45] Theory acknowledges that escalation can sometimes help to bring this about, but the apparent conviction of the coalition and the Taliban that each can significantly strengthen its position, or even win, is unlikely to be conducive to talks. Meanwhile, the short-term effect of the coalition's approach is to intensify the conflict and reinforce mistrust. As a southern commander asked: "Why is the West pouring millions of dollars into reconciliation and then trying to kill us with big operations like Marja?"[46] Special forces operations against insurgent commanders might also be reducing the prospects for negotiations. As an insurgent political figure observed, "Foreign forces kill commanders but they are just replaced, and the one that replaces the commander often has more confidence and more enmity. The people coming up are more aggressive, vengeful, and also become angrier."[47]

Building Confidence

Given the high levels of mistrust, substantive talks are unlikely without building confidence. One measure, called for by all the former Taliban interviewees and endorsed at the recent peace *jirga*, is to remove insurgent figures from the UN sanctions list. Some individuals have recently been delisted, although others have been added. Moreover, despite the insurgency's changing leadership, the list of 132 figures has changed little since 2002. In addition, a U.S. "joint prioritized effects list" designates a significant number of high-ranking insurgents for kill or capture. Perhaps a more pertinent and difficult question is if, when, and how that list should change.

Another confidence-building measure endorsed by the peace *jirga* is to release insurgent detainees held on the basis of "inaccurate information or unsubstantiated allegations."[48] While many prisoners have been detained arbitrarily, or are being held indefinitely without charge or trial, some observers are concerned about the potential for political interference with the judicial process, or fear that active insurgents or those guilty of serious crimes will be released.

Delisting or releasing certain insurgents may be necessary, if not sufficient, to build confidence between the warring parties. However, comparative cases suggest that unilateral gestures add little or no momentum toward talks.[49] If a dialogue were established, the Taliban could be required to reciprocate, such as agreeing in certain areas to desist from attacks on civilians and schools or allow access to NGOs or government workers. Patience and caution are required. As a senior UN official warned: "There's a strong appetite for getting out of here [among Western powers]. A concern is we'll give too much, too fast."[50] This raises the question of amnesty, which is offered to all combatants who reconcile. It is effected through Afghanistan's National Reconciliation, General Amnesty, and National Stability Law, brought into force in January 2010, and is promised in the government's Peace and Reintegration Program. However, there are questions about the eligibility for and scope of any purported amnesty, and how this can be reconciled with demands for accountability and the government's obligations under international law.

The vast majority of interviewees, including insurgents, believe that those guilty of the most serious crimes should be tried, and that this should include crimes committed since the 1978 Saur revolution. Most believe this can only happen if there is stability and a stronger, more impartial government. As one southern commander said: "If Karzai, Mullah Mohammad Omer, or others committed these crimes, we are ready to hand them over to court for trial or punishment, but not now; this can only work when there is a strong, independent government."[51]

Cease-fires or the de-escalation of hostilities could help to build confidence. A number of temporary, local cease-fires have been agreed in the current conflict, including one in 2009 in northern Kandahar, which lasted for six weeks so that a cholera outbreak could be dealt with. However, comparative cases suggest that cease-fires do little to build trust and are often exploited by one or both parties to the conflict unless they are reciprocal and part of a structured process.[52]

A more limited but still valuable confidence-building tool is regulated public statements and recognition. During 2009, in response to Taliban requests, the United Nations tacitly acknowledged the role of insurgents in allowing access for polio vaccinations. The Taliban reciprocated by removing anti-UN statements from its website. Remarks such as those by Jaap de Hoop Scheffer, Secretary General of the North Atlantic Treaty Organization (NATO), which oversimplify the conflict as a "fight against extremism and terrorism," are likely to diminish the prospects for talks.[53]

Managing the Process

If the parties do enter into talks, there are numerous questions about the form and scope of the process. Even the question of which actors are represented in talks and with what status is a minefield, given the segmentation and fragmentation within the insurgency, Afghan government, and international community. There are also questions about the involvement of political blocs outside the government, Afghan civil society—including women's organizations—and community or tribal representatives. As Afghan politicians stressed in interviews, any process not perceived as inclusive and sufficiently representative of Afghanistan's ethnically diverse population and various interest groups will be seen as illegitimate, threatening the viability of its outcome.

Given the enmity and mistrust between Taliban leaders and government figures, and misgivings about the intentions of President Karzai and his allies, the choice of mediator will be critical. Insurgents widely regard the United Nations as pursuing a U.S. agenda, and some insurgents suggested mediation could be undertaken instead by an Islamic state, such as Saudi Arabia, which hosted initial talks in 2008.[54] However, observers question Saudi Arabia's suitability given its long-standing alliance with Pakistan, and there are concerns among rights groups and organizations that represent women.[55] Other options could be mediation by Turkey, the Organization of the Islamic Conference (OIC), or the Conference on Interaction and Confidence Building Measures in Asia (CICA), perhaps in conjunction with the United Nations. Unofficial track II talks could support negotiations, as could certain influential individuals such as *ulema* in Pakistan. As one Afghan analyst remarked, "Many of them [the insurgents] don't look through the prism of political realism. The Taliban are hugely influenced by Pakistani religious leaders. Whether you like them or not, you have to bring them in; they can talk their language."[56]

The framework, scope, and guiding principles of any talks may be difficult to establish. In particular, what role should human rights considerations have, and are there Afghan and international preconditions? Without clarity, unity, and resolve on certain issues, there is a risk that too much will be conceded. But as a former senior diplomat pointed out, insisting on preconditions, or establishing ambitious red lines prematurely, might block the process altogether.[57] Also, given the diversity and complexity of actors and interests as well as widespread animosity and mistrust, any process will be lengthy. Peace processes in other countries, such as Northern Ireland, suggest that measures to improve relations between hostile groups will take years. A process without such efforts, that seeks to cut deals rather than build relations, would be acutely vulnerable to spoilers.

Spoilers

Power holders on all sides may seek to disrupt or derail a negotiations process. Whether any given actor ultimately acts as a spoiler depends on many factors, including their motivations, interests, and the structure and nature of negotiations. Some may be limited or "greedy" spoilers, whose demands can be managed; others may be total spoilers, seeking only to sabotage the process.

It is highly likely that hard-line elements of the insurgent movement would seek to scupper any negotiations. For certain ideological fighters, any dialogue with those they consider to be infidel invaders or their puppets would be anathema. Some Taliban commanders described the mentality of these insurgents, who they say are often supported by the ISI: "They will never stop fighting in the country; they want to destroy the government and bring chaos. They feel that only the Taliban are Muslims, but those who are just normal, working Afghans—who die in the suicide attacks—they think they are all infidels."[58] The al-Qaeda leadership may regard negotiations as betraying their cause and seize the opportunity to intervene; the network of militant Islamist groups known as the Pakistani Taliban, which have so far focused their attacks on the Pakistani state, may do likewise.

In addition, political figures and strongmen inside or associated with the Afghan government believe that negotiations could diminish their share of power or opportunities for graft. A number of interviewees, including a European diplomat, questioned whether senior government figures are genuinely interested in achieving peace.[59] Many individuals are accumulating vast profits from the conflict, especially through security, supply, or reconstruction contracts, and resolving the conflict would threaten their lucrative activities. Likewise, criminal groups and drug traffickers are likely to perceive negotiations as a threat to the status quo—an environment of pervasive instability, corruption, and impunity that facilitates their illicit activities.

Strategies for dealing with spoilers must be developed. It may be necessary to integrate some into the process and provide guarantees, but it will undoubtedly be necessary to seek to marginalize, exclude, or contain certain others.

Pakistan and the Region

Due to its latent conflict with India, parts of the Pakistani military and ISI have long aspired to have significant influence, or "strategic depth" in Afghanistan.[60] They are anxious about what they regard as a strong Indian presence in the country and a Kabul–New Delhi alliance. This anxiety is reinforced by concerns about the disputed Durand Line that divides Afghanistan and Pakistan, along with an enduring insurgency in Balochistan. They see the Taliban as allowing them to maintain strategic influence, and thus, according to almost all interviewees, they provide them with sanctuary and significant support. As one Western official put it, "From the point of view of Pakistan, the Taliban are an instrument of pressure against Afghanistan, the U.S. and NATO, in order to provide leverage to realize their strategic interests in Afghanistan, which primarily are the reduction or elimination of Indian presence and getting the cooperation of Afghanistan in Pakistan's internal issues, especially Pashtun and Baloch issues."[61] This puts Pakistan in the powerful position of potential facilitator or spoiler of negotiations.

In early 2010 the ISI arrested the Taliban's supreme military commander, Mullah Baradar—who was believed to have had independent contacts with the Karzai regime—as well as other members of the Taliban leadership council, known as the Quetta Shura. Virtually all interviewees, insurgents and otherwise, interpreted this as an effort to block negotiations. As one diplomat put it, "Until today [February 2010], every single person who was willing to talk about peace, they've [the Pakistani authorities] arrested."[62] The arrests were probably an attempt to demonstrate that Pakistan would obstruct talks unless it was fully involved in the process.

Taliban commanders' opinions differed on whether Pakistan should be directly involved in talks, as they did about the direct involvement of international forces. However, virtually all interviewees, both insurgent and not, believed that negotiations could not succeed without Pakistan's backing. Some interviewees thought that if Pakistan's military and ISI chiefs believe they have influence over the process they might support negotiations, which perhaps accounts for their recent overtures regarding the Haqqani network. A senior Western official argued that "Pakistan does not want an Afghanistan controlled by the Taliban."[63] A Pakistan analyst concurred, pointing to concerns within the Pakistani military that this could lead to an alliance between the Afghan and Pakistani Taliban, who could benefit from "reverse strategic depth" inside Afghanistan.[64]

However, given the persistent role of Pakistan's military and ISI in supporting insurgents, especially the ruthless Haqqani network, their inclusion in talks must be handled cautiously. It requires a difficult balance to be struck between expediency and Afghan sovereignty. If Pakistan believes its influence is insufficient, it will not support the process, yet the perception of excessive influence could provoke opposition inside Afghanistan or countermeasures by neighboring countries. Moreover, the best means to bring about Pakistan's constructive engagement is to address the underlying causes of its conduct: the perceived threat from India. Ultimately, this depends on improved relations between the two adversaries, which requires persistent encouragement, pressure, and support from the international community. It could be reinforced by more effective use of U.S. incentives and disincentives in Pakistan; modifications and perhaps a diminution in the scope of India's presence in Afghanistan; and, conceivably, Afghanistan's commitment to geopolitical nonalignment.

Any negotiations process must involve consultation and engagement with other states in the region—not least India, Iran, Russia, and China—who are maneuvering to protect their interests in anticipation of U.S. withdrawal. The shape of such a process is beyond the scope of this study, but it will require concerted efforts to identify, and as far as reasonably possible, accommodate their legitimate security concerns and strategic interests.

Substance of an Agreement

It is impossible to predict the terms or tacit understandings of any possible agreement between the Afghan government and the Taliban. However, interviewees identified key issues and questions with regard to power sharing, troop withdrawal, al-Qaeda, and human rights.

Most analysts interviewed assumed that the essence of an agreement would be power sharing, an approach espoused by theorists such as Caroline Hartzell, Matthew Hoddi, and Barbara Walter.[65] In other words, the Taliban might acquire a direct or indirect share of central power, or govern certain areas. Either way, their de facto control of large parts of the country could become de jure authority. As one Afghan analyst pointed out, power sharing "is happening right now, in Ghazni, Uruzgan, and Kandahar,"[66] arguing that there were understandings among power holders, including the Taliban, over the division of resources. Arguably, this fuels corruption, entrenches impunity, and perpetuates conflict; a number of interviewees questioned whether any arrangement could be functional or durable, and how the parties could be held to their commitments. They also raised concerns about post-agreement spoilers should certain factions believe they have been excluded, or how, in practice, state political, economic, or military power could be shared.

Interviewees did not perceive the withdrawal of international forces as problematic per se, so long as it was incremental and according to terms agreed by all sides. Questions were raised, however, about what forces would take their place; the impartiality and effectiveness of Afghan national security forces; and what measures might be required to demobilize insurgents.

The coalition will require some form of commitment regarding al-Qaeda. Some insurgent interviewees suggested that the inclinations and connections of certain Taliban leaders may make it difficult for them to renounce the group expressly. However, as noted above, interviews also suggest that links between the Taliban and al-Qaeda are minimal—though perhaps more substantial with respect to the Haqqani group—and that the Taliban might conceivably commit to seeking to prevent Afghanistan's territory being used by groups that threaten foreign states. Nevertheless, there are questions about what form of commitment, given by whom, the United States would accept, and how adherence would be monitored. Furthermore, would the United States be granted the capability to launch air strikes against extremist groups, as it does in northwest Pakistan?

As part of an agreement, it may be that certain Afghan laws are altered, or steps initiated to amend the Afghan constitution. Given Taliban commanders' demands for sharia, they could defy the leadership's accession to any agreement that did not include such measures.

Any curtailment of women's rights is likely to provoke Afghan and international resistance, but what would happen in practice? In much of Afghanistan, whether insurgent or government controlled, there are already significant restrictions on the rights, freedoms, and opportunities of women and girls. The government has done little to tackle abuses against women, and in some cases has connived in their mistreatment or marginalization. The key questions are therefore: If there were any agreement with insurgents, what changes would be instituted, or might ensue, especially in the areas of health, education, work, and family life? Would such changes be acceptable to Afghan women, and Afghan society at large?

It should not be assumed that the current Taliban movement is a replica of the former regime; new circumstances may impose new constraints. However, given the record of the former Taliban regime, serious questions must be asked about the likely implications for women and girls. There are questions, too, about the protection of civil and political rights, especially rights to equality and nondiscrimination; democratic rights and freedom of expression for individuals and the media; rights against inhuman and degrading treatment; and rights to a fair trial. These issues are germane to the evolving nature of Afghan society.

The international community must make efforts to protect fundamental rights, but perceived attempts to impose Western standards in a predominantly conservative, patriarchal society are likely to be counterproductive. If such efforts are seen as too uncompromising, they could derail negotiations altogether. The potentially unsatisfactory outcome of negotiations must therefore be weighed against the potential threat to rights by a possible expansion of the insurgency or intensification of the conflict.

Conclusions and Recommendations

Insurgent tactics have involved the massacre of civilians through indiscriminate roadside and suicide bombs, as well as the assassination of hundreds of community, tribal, and religious leaders and officials. Since the beginning of 2007 insurgents have killed more than 4,400 Afghan civilians.[67] Nevertheless, the predatory and abusive conduct of many government officials or connected power holders is also reprehensible. Moreover, the focus of Taliban attacks has been foreign and Afghan forces, and in this respect, some of the insurgents' motivations are understandable. Many are fighting what they perceive as aggressive invading forces and their proxies. Their resistance is reinforced by the egregious and widespread abuse of power; the supply of recruits is increased by conditions of severe social and economic hardship.

Thus, while Taliban tactics may be abhorrent, many of their stated goals could be considered valid. Their demands for law and order, and honest governance coincide with the aspirations of the Afghan population and the international community. It is primarily for this reason, and because some groups are more moderate or protect local interests, that in some areas they have community sympathy or support.

The potential for negotiations should be explored, given that, first, the Taliban's chief objective is a withdrawal of foreign troops, which ultimately coincides with Western and Afghan interests; second, certain Taliban goals, and the idea of talks, are broadly supported by Afghans; and third, there are severe constraints on counterinsurgency and transition strategies. This process requires controlled, incremental, and reciprocal confidence building as well as a U.S. willingness to engage, directly or indirectly, with insurgents. However, the process faces an array of challenges, especially division within the international community, Afghan government and insurgency, and deep-seated mistrust, which is compounded by the current military strategy.

A settlement could threaten the rights and opportunities of women and girls as well as ethnic or religious minorities. It threatens the civil and political rights of all Afghans. Thus, the Afghan people, through their leaders and legitimate representatives, must be involved in the process. As an Afghan female official from Kandahar put it, "The constitution is not against *sharia*. If they want to change it, this is an issue, a decision, which belongs to the Afghan ordinary people—the population."[68] Strategies are also required to deal with spoilers on all sides and involve Pakistan. Given Afghanistan's place in the Pakistan-India power struggle, concerted international efforts must be made to improve their relationship and to accommodate Pakistan's legitimate geopolitical concerns.

With the immense challenges involved in negotiations and the Afghan government's lack of credibility, the entire process requires strong, proactive international support as well as effective mediation. However, it should not lead to the neglect of efforts to improve governance, build effective security forces, or promote development. The outcome is uncertain, and a rush to negotiate might reinforce the determination of insurgents to win, or of opposing factions to disrupt the process.

Moreover, reaching a settlement is no guarantee of peace. It would be extremely difficult to implement, given the myriad of local, national, and regional conflicts and power struggles. Nearly half of all settlements of civil conflicts collapse within five years.[69] The 1988 Geneva Accords that formalized the withdrawal of Soviet forces from Afghanistan were succeeded by civil war. A negotiation process should thus prioritize long-term efforts to build relations between hostile groups and to address the fissures that divide Afghan society. Afghans must broadly regard any political settlement as both inclusive and just; an agreement that does not reflect the aspirations of Afghanistan's different social, ethnic, tribal, and other groups or factions, or one that is perceived to trade justice for expediency, is unlikely to endure. It will almost certainly require credible guarantees from foreign countries or international organizations to ensure that its principal terms are respected.

There is also the risk of a settlement with no real efforts to address the causes of the conflict. One tribal leader from Kandahar warned of a deal between discredited leaders, regarded as the proxies of foreigners, and called for political reform: "If you don't remove the killers and the corrupt from government, and stop the abuse of the people, we will not solve this conflict."[70] And in the words of an ISAF General: "We know that the Taliban will have to be accommodated on terms that the Northern Alliance will accept, and Pakistan will accept . . . but there's a danger of a 'thieves' pact' which leaves the power brokers in place, with people no better off and that's the reason why many joined the fighting in the first place."[71] The goal should not only be to end the core conflict but to address its underlying causes, which is essential for the achievement of an enduring peace.

Notes

1. See the quarterly reports of the Afghan NGO Safety Office, 2006–10, http://www.afgnso.org/index_files/Page447.htm (accessed September 2010).
2. Quarterly reports of Afghan NGO Safety Office.

3. "Gates: Afghan Militants Key to Country's Future," *The Associated Press*, July 10, 2008.

4. For example: David Miliband, Council on Foreign Relations speech, July 27, 2009, http://www.cfr.org/publication/19909/(accessed August 30, 2010).

5. Jon Boone, "Karzai Reveals Talks with Afghan Rebels," *The Guardian*, March 22, 2010.

6. See: "Resolution Adopted at the Conclusion of the National Consultative Peace Jirga," Kabul, June 2–4, 2010.

7. Karin Brulliard and Karen DeYoung, "Pakistan, Afghanistan Begin Talks about Dealing with Insurgents," *The Washington Post*, June 19, 2010.

8. This report represents an attempt to identify and understand key issues relevant to negotiation. It is not intended as a detailed anatomy of the insurgency; see Afghanistan Analysts Network, *The Other Side: Dimensions of the Afghan Insurgency* (Kabul: AAN, July 2009).

9. The author conducted semistructured, in-depth, face-to-face interviews with seventy-six individuals who were contacted and interviewed separately: ten Afghan insurgents (nine insurgent commanders, seven from the Taliban, two from the Haqqani network, and one Taliban intermediary); ten former senior Taliban officials; twenty Afghan and foreign analysts, academics, NGO workers, or journalists; twelve foreign diplomats or officials; eight Afghan politicians or officials; six UN officials; five Afghan religious, community, and tribal leaders; and five foreign soldiers. A research assistant conducted a further four interviews with Afghan insurgents (three Taliban commanders and one political figure). The author extends his thanks to Obaidullah Ali, Gran Hewad, Iris Ruttig, LPB, who wished to remain anonymous, and former Harvard students for their extensive assistance and support.

10. Interview, March 2010.

11. Interview, March 2010.

12. Interview, March 2010.

13. Interview, May 2010.

14. Interview, March 2010.

15. Interview, March 2010.

16. Interview, March 2010.

17. Interview, February 2010.

18. Interview, February 2010.

19. Interview, February 2010.

20. Interview, March 2010.

21. Interview, March 2010.

22. Generally, insurgent interviewees did not claim to know the particular objectives of the leadership.

23. Interview, February 2010.

24. Interview, May 2010.

25. Interview, March 2010.

26. Interview, May 2010.

27. *Mahram* refers to all those male relatives whom a woman cannot marry at any time in her life.

28. Interview, March 2010.

29. Interview, June 2010.

30. Interview, May 2010.

31. Interview, March 2010.

32. "Panetta: Afghan War Has 'Serious Problems,' But Progress Being Made," *CNN.com*, June 27, 2010.

33. Mullah Omar's Eid al-Fitr message, September 2009. A translation is available on the website of the Middle East Media Research Institute: http://www.memri.org/report/en/0/0/0/0/0/0/0/3646.htm (accessed September 2010).

34. Mullah Omar's Eid al-Fitr message, September 2010. A translation is available on the website of http://zakiraah.wordpress.com/ (accessed September 2010).

35. Mullah Omar's Eid al-Fitr message, September 2009.

36. Mullah Omar's Eid al-Fitr message, September 2010.

37. Mullah Omar's Eid al-Fitr message, September 2009.

38. Interview, March 2010.

39. Interview, February 2010.

40. Interview, March 2010.

41. Interview, February 2010.

42. Interview, February 2010.

43. U.S. Military Joint Chiefs of Staff, *Counterinsurgency Operations, Joint Publication 3–24* (Washington, DC: Joint Chiefs of Staff, 2009), VI-20–VI-21.

44. Interview, March 2010.

45. I. William Zartman, *Negotiation and Conflict Management: Essays on Theory and Practice* (Oxford: Routledge, 2008).

46. Interview, March 2010.

47. Interview, March 2010.

48. "Resolution Adopted at the Conclusion of the National Consultative Peace Jirga," section 8.

49. John Darby and Roger Mac Ginty, eds., *Contemporary Peacemaking: Conflict, Peace Processes, and Post-War Reconstruction*, 354–56 (London: Palgrave Macmillan, 2008).

50. Interview, February 2010.

51. Interview, May 2010.

52. Darby and Mac Ginty, *Contemporary Peacemaking*, 354.

53. Mina Al Oraibi, "Can Afghanistan be Saved?," *Christian Science Monitor*, November 3, 2009.

54. Carlotta Gall, "Afghanistan Tests Waters for Overture to Taliban," *The New York Times*, October 29, 2008.

55. Interviews, March 2010.

56. Interview, May 2010.

57. Interview, June 2010.

58. Interview, May 2010.

59. Interview, February 2010.

60. Ahmed Rashid, *Taliban: Islam, Oil and the New Great Game in Central Asia*, 186–87 (London: IB Tauris, 2002). See also Steve Coll, "Letter from Afghanistan: War by Other Means," *The New Yorker*, May 24, 2010.

61. Seminar on Afghanistan, Washington D.C., June 2010. The seminar was conducted under Chatham House rules.

62. Interview, February 2010.

63. Interview, June 2010.

64. Seminar, June 2010.

65. Caroline Hartzell and Matthew Hoddie, *Crafting Peace: Power-Sharing Institutions and the Negotiated Settlement of Civil Wars* (State College, PA: Pennsylvania State University Press, 2007); and Barbara Walter, *Committing to Peace: The Successful Settlement of Civil Wars* (Princeton, NJ: Princeton University Press, 2002).

66. Interview, February 2010.

67. Statistics compiled by analysis of the UN Annual and Mid-Year Protection of Civilians In Armed Conflict Reports, United Nations Assistance Mission in Afghanistan, http://unama.unmissions.org/Default.aspx?tabid=1816 (accessed September 2010).

68. Interview, March 2010.

69. Christine Bell, "Negotiating Human Rights," in Darby and Mac Ginty, Contemporary Peacemaking, 212.

70. Interview, March 2010.

71. Interview, March 2010.

5

Afghanistan and Its Neighbors
An Ever Dangerous Neighborhood

Marvin G. Weinbaum

By the time Weinbaum wrote the following chapter in 2006, it was becoming evident that, despite successes in the formal statebuilding processes outlined in the Bonn Agreement, the insurgency was expanding, and its viability was linked to the perceived interests of other countries in the region. With the focus on implementing the agreement, there had been a tendency to view Afghanistan's problems as self-contained, under a belief that if a strong Afghanistan was built quickly enough, the country would be able to manage its own regional relations. As Weinbaum notes, however, "Many of Afghanistan's challenges, often thought of as domestic, are also regional in character, necessarily addressed with regional strategies and cooperation."*

Waldman was among the first to begin describing the implications of the interests of Afghanistan's neighbors for the country's future stability. Weinbaum considers that countries in the region had decided that "support for a stable, independent, and economically strengthening Afghan state is preferable to any achievable alternative." He adds, however, the important caveat that "the strategic approaches to Afghanistan by its neighbors are, however, always subject to readjustment. No regional state is prepared to allow another to gain a preponderance of influence in Afghanistan. Moreover, each retains links to client networks that are capable of fractionalizing and incapacitating an emerging Afghanistan." As Rubin and Siddique do in chapter 6, Waldman makes an exception for Pakistan, noting that Islamabad, while maintaining a strategic partnership with the United States, had given up on the idea it could impose friendly rulers in Kabul. Instead it had "chosen to rely on its personal networks with Pashtun leaders built up by its Inter-Services Intelligence (ISI) directorate," and some of these leaders opposed the government.

Originally published as Marvin G. Weinbaum, "Afghanistan and Its Neighbors: An Ever Dangerous Neighborhood," Special Report 162 (Washington, DC: USIP, 2006).

Weinbaum methodically addresses the interests of all of Afghanistan's neighbors and near-neighbors, analyzing both the complex security dilemmas as well as the possible benefits from trade and economic growth if these dilemmas are resolved. He argues that the best strategy might be for the international community to create an environment conducive to the establishment of a "regional security community built on pure national interest."

Several years later international policymakers would take up Weinbaum's ideas. A number of initiatives, such as the New Silk Road, the Heart of Asia, and the Istanbul Process, would be initiated to better incorporate regional interests into a strategy for Afghan stability. However, policymakers may have warmed to Weinbaum's conclusions too late: "Along with the international community, the United States might also begin to address how it can benefit Afghanistan's quest for security and recovery through aid projects and other policies specifically intended to promote regional cooperation and integration. For this to occur, U.S. policies that are now so unidimensionally focused on counterterrorism must be better aligned with the aspirations of citizens of Afghanistan and those of its neighbors."

Introduction

Landlocked and resource poor, Afghanistan is at risk of unwelcome external influences, its sovereignty and traditions vulnerable. The competition among external powers has at times enabled the country to enjoy their beneficence. More often, it has suffered at their hands. For more than a century, Afghanistan served as the classic buffer state between the British and Czarist empires. During the Cold War it was first neutral ground and then contested terrain between Soviet and surrogate American power. Under the yoke of the Soviet Union's occupation during the 1980s, at least one-third of the population went into exile and most of the contested countryside lay in waste. The state itself suffered near disintegration in a following decade of civil war sponsored in part by regional powers. By the late 1990s, Afghanistan hosted the opening salvos in a war between radical Islamists and their designated, mostly Western enemies. A post-Taliban Afghanistan, still not free from conflict, extracts benefits for its recovery from international patrons and hopes for the forbearance of traditionally predatory regional states.

Framing the discussions in this study is the assertion that Afghanistan's future and that of the regional states are closely bound. Constructive partnerships involving Afghans and their neighbors are essential to regional stability. Just as the capacity of Afghanistan to overcome its political and economic deficits will have deep bearing on the region's security and development, the domestic stability and foreign policies of the neighboring states will affect the prospects for progress in Afghanistan. Many Afghans insist that outside forces drive the current insurgency in the country, while for the regional players Afghanistan remains a potential source of instability through the export of arms, drugs, and ideology.

The study posits that over much of the last four years Afghanistan's neighbors have assessed that support for a stable, independent, and economically strengthening Afghan state is preferable to any achievable alternatives. None have directly opposed the internationally approved Hamid Karzai as president or seriously tried to manipulate Afghan domestic politics. All have pledged, moreover, some measure of development assistance. Undoubtedly, the presence of foreign military forces and international attention has contributed to their restrained policies.

The strategic approaches to Afghanistan by its neighbors are, however, always subject to readjustment. No regional state is prepared to allow another to gain a preponderance of influence in Afghanistan. Moreover, each retains links to client networks that are capable of fractionalizing and incapacitating an emerging Afghanistan. States in the neighborhood may well sponsor destabilizing forces in the event that Kabul governments fail over time to extend their authority and tangibly improve people's lives, or should Afghanistan's international benefactors lose their patience and interest. More immediately, as described below, political currents in several regional countries may be overtaking the economic forces on which more optimistic projections for regional cooperation have been based. Poorly considered policies by international aid givers and the Kabul government have in some cases helped to increase suspicions and tensions with neighbors.

This study first examines how Afghanistan has historically engaged and been impacted by neighboring states and other foreign stakeholders. The section looks at the way the country has at different times tried both to insulate itself and attract benefactors. A second section focuses on the dynamics of contemporary political and economic relations among countries of the region. It considers how as a regional fulcrum Afghanistan is leveraged by external powers pursuing competing interests. The two sections that follow focus on Pakistan and Iran, countries providing Afghanistan's most imposing and critical regional bilateral relationships. For each country, the study describes motives and forces driving policies that have been at times obstructionist and at others constructive. A fifth section looks more briefly at the stakes and changing parameters of engagement for each of the other countries bordering Afghanistan as well as noncontiguous Russia and India. The study concludes with an examination of the broader international community's contributions to the shaping of regional security. The section looks as well at how the international community can help create the opportunities and conditions that could foster cooperation in the region and safeguard against future instability. It also assesses briefly U.S. priorities and policies in the region and their bearing on the Afghan project of state building.

The Historical Backdrop

Much of Afghanistan's modern history has been taken up with its own political consolidation. Though outside influences penetrated in important ways, affecting the outcome of domestic struggles, Afghanistan was not a visible player on either the regional or world stage until the 1950s. For centuries the country was best known for the foreign armies crossing its territory. Iran has had a long history with Afghanistan and until the mid-nineteenth century controlled large areas in the country's far west. Afghanistan's legendary status over two centuries as a pawn in the Great Game between the region's imperial giants precluded the country from having an independent foreign policy even while it was spared colonial status. Efforts to open the country to modernization through contacts with Europe were undertaken by King Amanullah in the late 1920s. But with the monarchy's overthrow in 1929 by reactionary elements, these policies abruptly ended. Within a year the royal line was restored with British assistance, as was the traditionally ascendant Pashtun ethnic group. Afghanistan resumed its relative isolation under a new, more conservative king, Nadir Shah. In the late 1930s, British efforts to thwart Nazi Germany's efforts to gain an economic and political foothold in Afghanistan drew the country into international politics. Iran's strategic location prompted the Allies to remove its distrusted king, Reza Shah, in 1941 and to occupy the country. But neutrality sufficed for Afghanistan, a backwater in the global conflict.

Adjusting to the new, postwar international order, the Afghan royal family sought to avail Afghanistan of security and development assistance. Initially, however, the country was not high on anyone's strategic agenda. Even with the Cold War under way, the Soviet Union was at first mostly occupied with institutionalizing aid relationships with other newly minted communist countries. Communist doctrine through the early 1950s generally ruled out aid to nonaligned, less developed countries like Afghanistan. Economically and socially backward, Afghanistan held even less interest for a United States engaged in trying to prevent European countries from falling within the Soviet orbit. The death of Stalin and a containment policy of regional alliances forged by John Foster Dulles brought a major reorientation. Soviet strategy now called for mobilizing nonideological support through assistance to countries, most of them less developed states, that could be weaned away from Western influences. Moscow tested its new policies on regimes in the just-emerging Third World Movement and countries like Afghanistan.

By the mid-1950s, Soviet leaders were offering substantial development and military assistance. And, as occurred in India and Egypt, the United States responded with its own aid programs designed to keep countries from tilting entirely in the Soviet direction. In the case of Afghanistan, however, Washington was willing to cede most of the development and the defense sectors to

Russia as the price for pleasing the more valued Pakistan. Pakistan had already been enlisted as an American military ally in the Baghdad Pact in 1954 and its relations with Afghanistan were poor, mostly because of the Afghan government's advocacy of a Pashtun ethnic state to be carved out of Pakistan.

Unlike neighboring states, Afghan governments remained formally non-aligned until the communist coup in 1978. Moreover, to a remarkable degree, despite the preeminence of Soviet involvement, the country's leaders showed themselves adept at playing off the Soviet Union and the United States in order to extract more aid from each. In fact, for more than twenty years Afghanistan saw a degree of accommodation between the superpowers found in no other country during the Cold War. Meanwhile, however, Kabul governments were less successful in relations with the two countries to their east and west.

Serious disputes erupted during the 1950s and 1960s between Afghanistan and Iran and Pakistan. Both states were critical to trade routes for Afghan imports and exports. Relations with Pakistan had gotten off to a bad start in 1947 as a result of a border drawn by the British more than a half century earlier to divide Afghanistan's principal ethnic group, the Pashtuns. Afghanistan was the only country to refuse to support Pakistan's UN membership. In response to Afghan governments' continuing irredentist rhetoric during the 1950s and early 1960s promoting a Pashtun state, Pakistan on several occasions closed its border, creating serious economic difficulties for Afghanistan. The country's economy was denied access to the port of Karachi, the principal entry point for Afghan imports and exports. Iran objected to any attempts by Kabul to divert the Helmand River because of the adverse effects on water reaching Iran's parched southeast. Although treaties were agreed to with both countries in the 1970s that largely normalized relations, suspicions of malicious intentions remained.

While the Soviet Union as a regional state was understood to be the senior aid partner, the Afghan leadership maintained stronger cultural ties with Europe and the United States. As increasing numbers of Afghans went to the West and India to study, they tended to avoid the Soviet Union. When King Zahir Shah decided to open the political system with a new constitution, he named Western-oriented officials to undertake the drafting. They produced a document in 1964 that aimed at establishing Western-like institutions and democratic values, defying not just local communist sympathizers but political Islamists in the country who sought a system built on principles enunciated by Egypt's Muslim Brotherhood. But if the constitution opened opportunities for popular participation in a liberal government, it also offered the country's Marxists and Maoists greater opportunities to organize and, significantly, to infiltrate the military ranks.

The failure of the constitutional experiment was marked by the fall of the monarchy in a military-led communist coup in 1973. But over the next five years, although the Soviet Union was now clearly preeminent in its influence over the country, President Mohammad Daoud gradually sought to dilute Moscow's influence. Daoud, a former prime minister and cousin of the king, reached out not to the West but to other Islamic countries. He hoped to counterbalance the Soviet Union with massive financial assistance from oil-wealthy Arab states and Iran. Before he was deposed and killed in 1978 by communists, again led by the military, Daoud had even tried to reconcile with Pakistan.

Replacing Daoud were dedicated Afghan communist party leaders who were determined to impose a Marxist-Leninist government and society. With their takeover, Afghanistan became, in effect, a willing satellite of the Soviet Union. The communist regime's attempts to impose their ideologically driven policies were crude and culturally offensive. They soon provoked an Islamic-led insurgency, whose successes over the next year and a half threatened the communists' grip on power and drew the intervention of the Red Army in December 1979.

The jihad mounted from Pakistan during the 1980s, supported by the United States and Saudi Arabia, among others, drew Pakistan into Afghan affairs as never before. By funneling assistance to the mujahideen, Pakistan enlisted in the geostrategic effort to keep Soviet forces tied down in Afghanistan. Pakistan's participation also suggested the possibility of eventually liberating Afghan territory to provide strategic depth against India. As a payback for assistance to the insurgency and its acceptance of Afghan refugees, the Pakistani military took a healthy cut of the military aid intended for the mujahideen. Islamabad expected to be further rewarded with an indebted, friendly government taking power in Kabul when Afghanistan's communist government finally fell, three years after the Soviet army's withdrawal.

But the Afghan mujahideen parties, following their return, battled one another for power and brought the country to near anarchy and commercial paralysis. Resisting subordination to Islamabad, government leaders in Kabul turned to India for a political and economic counterweight. In reaction, Pakistan's security forces in league with commercial interests took sponsorship of a group of religious students seeking to overthrow the Kabul regime. By 1996 the largely Pashtun-led Taliban had swept much of the country and captured Kabul, thanks in no small part to Pakistan's poorly disguised military assistance. With territory continuing to fall in the country's north, Afghanistan's other neighbors took alarm that the Taliban might foster insurgency in their countries. More distant countries, but especially the United States, took aim at Islamic extremism in the person of Osama bin Laden and his terrorist network in Afghanistan. Despite UN sanctions, the Taliban were probably just months away from a total victory when the events of September 11, 2001, forced Pakistan to cooperate with efforts to eliminate al Qaeda and bring regime change in Afghanistan.

Table 1. Afghanistan's Major Ethnolinguistic Groups

Ethnic Group	Population (% est.)	Primary Language	Islamic Sect
Pashtuns	40	Pashto	Sunni
Tajiks	25	Dari dialects	mostly Sunni
Hazara	20	Dari dialects	Shia
Uzbek	7	Uzbek dialects	Sunni
Turkmen	3	Turkic dialect	Sunni
Baloch	3	Balochi	Sunni

Regional Dynamics

At focus is a region reaching across Central and West Asia to the Indian subcontinent, with shared roots, and whose parts to a large extent intersect in Afghanistan. Historically it is the land bridge over which great powers have crossed in pursuit of imperial ambitions and commercial goals. It proved vital in helping to seal the fate of armies of Greeks, Arabs, Persians, Mongols, and, most recently, the Soviets. There is much today that integrates Afghanistan socially with the region. The country's diverse population of Pashtuns, Tajiks, and Uzbeks, among others, suggests the close ethnic, linguistic, sectarian, and cultural links it maintains with the states it borders. Although encompassing various nationalities and ethnicities, the countries of the region also share in many respects a common future in which a revived Afghanistan can contribute to their chances of peace and prosperity. Mohammad Iqbal, Pakistan's national poet, once called Afghanistan "the beating heart of Asia" (see table 1).

As is often stated, Afghanistan stands in a dangerous neighborhood. Responsibility for much of the political instability and misery of its people can be traced to external powers seeking to realize their own strategic, ideological, and economic interests in the country. The close and more distant neighbors of Afghanistan have regularly intervened in its politics and economy. Foreigners have sometimes acted on behalf of domestic clients and have organized and armed them to dominate large portions of the country. Although renowned for resisting foreign intruders, Afghans cannot thus be absolved of responsibility for much of the fratricide and destruction that has occurred in recent decades. Still, the aggravating role of outside states, near and far, has also made civil conflicts more sustained and lethal.

In a region that is broadly contentious, external rivalries as well as domestic unrest among neighbors can easily spill onto Afghan soil. Political instability in Uzbekistan or Tajikistan, a radicalized Pakistan, U.S. military action against Iran, and another major war between Pakistan and India could all impact strongly on Afghanistan. For some time, both Pakistani and Indian calculations have included gaining an advantage in Afghanistan. The quest for strategic depth dominated Pakistani thinking beginning in the late 1980s. Afghanistan was designated to provide safe harbor for Pakistani forces in the event of conflict with India. A cooperative, if not altogether satellite Afghan state would also provide assurance that India or any forces aligned with New Delhi would not pose a threat to Pakistan from across its northwest frontier. Supporting the cause of a pure Islamic state in Afghanistan not only promised to neutralize Pashtun irredentism but also helped to train and indoctrinate jihadis for the struggle against India in Kashmir.

Regional competition between Pakistan and Iran also carries over into Afghanistan. While the interventions of other countries have come and gone when expedient, these two neighbors have remained perennial meddlers in Afghanistan's internal affairs. While usually downplaying their differences, Iran's Islamic Republic's dissatisfaction with Pakistan is directly traceable to Islamabad's military partnerships with the United States and close economic and cultural ties to Saudi Arabia. Within Pakistan, sectarian attacks on Shia by Sunni militants have prompted Iranian clandestine operations on behalf of their coreligionists, and both countries suspect the other's involvement in insurgencies among their respective ethnic Baloch populations. The strategic rivalry between Pakistan and Iran is also fueled by their mutual nuclear programs, notwithstanding the possibly rogue role that Pakistani scientists have had in assisting Iran's nuclear development.

Many of Afghanistan's challenges, often thought of as domestic, are also regional in character, necessarily addressed with regional strategies and cooperation. Policies that have sometimes been used to insulate the country against interfering neighbors have denied Afghanistan the advantages of joining with neighbors to face common threats and realize new opportunities. Prospects for limiting the transit of arms and smuggling activities rest on regional approaches. With Afghanistan the originating point of a transnational drug trade, regional efforts are indispensable to interdicting traffickers. For all of the fears of porous borders, the free movement of labor across frontiers offers a source of needed skills for an Afghan recovery. The economic interdependencies that emerge in a regional open market system are thought likely to give its neighbors a greater stake in Afghanistan's stability and prosperity.

All of the region's economies carry on the greater portion of their trade outside the region. Every country in the region, not just landlocked Afghanistan, is anxious to create alternative routes to international markets. Road and rail transportation projects are also likely to promote intraregional economic growth. As Barnett Rubin points out, trade could be facilitated with customs procedures that expedite the movement of goods and the removal of tariffs and taxes. He also notes the values of harmonizing customs policy and procedures along with border security arrangements. Afghanistan is particularly handicapped by a badly deficient infrastructure. Its road system is limited even if rehabilitated to its preconflict status. Investment is required for building and repairing roads and for the eventual construction of an internal rail network linked to Afghanistan's neighbors.

External investment in the country hinges on addressing the requirement of expanded water supplies and hydropower as a regional project. Water issues focus on the sharing of the Amu Darya-Panj River system in the north, the Helmand River in the southwest, and the Kabul River in the east. Each of these is critical to agricultural development across borders with nearly all of Afghanistan's neighbors. Improved security and a strengthened legal system in the country could attract increased private capital from within the region and elsewhere. The case can also be made that if regional trade and other economic relations between Afghanistan and its neighbors are encouraged, more pragmatic forces will be strengthened at the expense of radical Islamic forces.

Afghanistan has enough security interests in common with its neighbors that, with international encouragement and patronage, a regional security community built on pure national interest would seem a logical step. To be effective, however, any regional arrangements for cooperation on security issues will have to take into account the limited resources that Afghanistan, the regional powers, and the international community have available or are willing to commit. A cooperative approach would of course stand the best chance of success if all the countries in the region were developing economically and progressing toward democratic, legitimate regimes.

Whether on security or economic issues, regional relations are underinstitutionalized. Region-wide organizations could facilitate cooperation that, among other objectives, would discourage interference in Afghanistan. In December 2002, regional states together with Russia and the United States that had been members of the Six-Plus-Two grouping created to contain the Taliban joined with Afghanistan in the signing of a Kabul Declaration of good-neighborly relations. The group had pledged to support the Afghan people in the political process and throughout reconstruction, and some called for extending the group to include India and Saudi Arabia. Although Afghanistan and neighboring states have since reached multilateral and bilateral agreements on controlling drug trafficking and easing border restrictions, few have been effectively implemented. Nor has the group contributed much toward solidifying trade ties.

Another grouping of countries, the Shanghai Organization for Security and Cooperation, deals with concerns that broadly affect Afghanistan, such as security and economic issues, but excludes Afghan membership. The Shanghai group, formed in 1996 by China and Russia together with the former Soviet Central Asian republics except for Turkmenistan, was primarily designed to thwart Islamic challenges in the region. Russia and China continue to endorse U.S.-led operations that are aimed at defending Afghanistan against insurgency. But a long-term U.S. military presence anywhere in the region is unacceptable to the Russians and Chinese, both of whom see the Americans as trying to cut them out of spheres of traditional influence.

Afghanistan has been admitted to several regional organizations. It belongs to the Economic Cooperation Organization (ECO), the Asian Development Bank (ADB), and the Organization of the Islamic Conference. In November 2005, with the backing of both India and Pakistan, Afghanistan became the eighth member of the South Asia Association for Regional Cooperation (SAARC). Afghanistan became the tenth member of the ECO in 1992, when the group was expanded from its original three, Turkey, Iran, and Pakistan, along with the newly born Central Asian republics. But aside from the ADB, all of these organizations have fallen well short of their original promise. The ECO has embarked on several projects in the energy, trade, transport, agriculture, and drug control sectors, but few have had impressive results. As a regional forum, SAARC aims to promote trade and cooperation on security matters, including narcotics and terrorism. Afghanistan's admission could help to draw the country economically, politically, and psychologically closer to South Asia. Most observers agree, however, that lingering political differences among members retard progress toward regional solutions. Thus it is that Pakistan still prohibits India from transporting goods across its territory to Afghanistan.

Possibly the most hopeful sign of regional cooperation was a December 2005 Regional Economic Cooperation Conference attended by nearly all of the countries across a broad region that included India, Turkey, and Russia. The Kabul conference was considered largely successful for Afghanistan's attempt to reach out to its neighbors to solve its problems and their acknowledging the country's importance to regional growth. Still, the sessions, supported by the G8 nations and World Bank, failed to produce much beyond general agreement to facilitate trade, transportation, and energy transfers, and a willingness to work together on such specific issues as fighting drugs and improving security.

A Greater Central Asia organization that formalizes cooperation for the mutual economic benefit of the region, as proposed by Frederick Starr, would be a natural extension of the Kabul conference. For the near term, Starr sees the cooperation probably occurring on an à la carte basis. However, to envision a newly viable geoeconomic entity emerging any time soon probably overstates the compatibility and common interests at present among the regional states. The idea of a greater region is complicated by their different political systems. The five former Soviet republics in Central Asia are still largely chips off the old Soviet bloc and more nationalist than regional in their attitudes. Many of the expected synergisms of the post-Soviet era have failed to materialize as the region has become an arena of competition among regional players. As a

Table 2. Regional States: Statistics

	Population (in mil.)	Population Growth Rate (%)	GDP Growth Rate (%)	GDP Per Cap (US$)	Exports to Region (mil. US$)	Below Poverty Line (%)	Literacy (%)	Political Stability Index
Afghanistan	28	2.67	8	300	1,003	53	36	3.4
Pakistan	152	2.09	7.8	632	5,149	40	49	6.3
Iran	67	1.10	4.8	2,431	10,308	32	77	19.9
Tajikistan	6	2.19	8.0	323	666	64	90	13.1
Uzbekistan	26	1.70	7.2	461	1,389	28	91	9.7
Turkmenistan	5	1.83	11.0	1,251	13,727	58	93	18.9
China	1,269	0.59	9.3	1,272	22,561	10	90	46.6
India	1,080	1.38	7.6	638	12,694	25	61	24.3
Russia	143	-0.37	5.9	4,078	15,669	18	95	21.8

result, these Central Asian republics together with their southern neighbors are likely to fail for the foreseeable future to measure up to their regional responsibilities (see table 2).

A recent World Bank study casts doubt that the region's economies form natural trade partnerships, or that Afghanistan is especially suited to serve as the hub of a regional trade zone. The study finds potentially greater compatibility in sharing energy and water resources, with the best prospects coming through bilateral rather than multilateral agreements. The Bank points out that although trade between Afghanistan and neighboring Pakistan and Iran is significant, trade activity is minimal among former Soviet republics, and between them and Afghanistan, Pakistan, and India. It suggests that even if transport and border policies currently acting as restraints were removed, regional trade would still face serious limitations. In any case, serious infrastructural and security obstacles stand in the way of Afghanistan becoming a trade crossroads for the region any time soon. Indeed, whatever the benefits of regional integration, the underdeveloped Afghan state and economy may be for the time being the weakest link.

Pakistan: The Covetous Neighbor

Afghanistan's border with Pakistan is longer than its border with any other neighbor. The Afghan economy is tightly tied to Pakistan's, and the two countries are closely linked culturally and historically. Provincial and interethnic rivalries in Pakistan and Afghanistan are well known to have fueled insurgencies across their border. The division of the region's large Pashtun population has been especially responsible for both bringing the two countries together and setting them apart. A Pashtun-dominated Afghanistan has promised its neighbor a source of security through the hoped-for strategic depth against India mentioned above and at the same time offered a potential threat to Pakistan's territorial integrity. Islamabad's policies have worked to maximize the possibilities of one and minimize those of the other by championing control over the Afghan central government by those Pashtuns espousing conservative, transnational Islamic beliefs and a religious agenda for Afghanistan.

To ensure the dependence of a Pashtun-dominated Afghan leadership on Pakistan, Islamabad is often accused of promoting adversarial relations between Pashtuns and other ethnic groups. Many Afghans are convinced that cross-border clientalism represents a deliberate effort by Pakistan to exploit Afghanistan's ethnic mosaic for its strategic interests. They cite Islamabad's favoritism toward the Pashtun mujahideen against other anticommunist parties through 1992, as well as the political and military assistance furnished to the largely Pashtun Taliban movement beginning in 1994. Whatever the regime in Kabul, Pakistan's policies have usually seemed aimed at creating accommodating, if not subservient, Afghan governments.

The degree to which Pakistan has been prepared to go toward installing cooperative regimes can be measured by the political price it was willing to pay for its backing of the Taliban. That policy poisoned Islamabad's relationship with Iran, the Central Asian republics, and Russia. It also created serious complications with other countries, including its traditional ally China. Each of these countries viewed the Taliban rule as giving sanctuary to extremist elements. Islamabad was increasingly isolated in trying to justify the Taliban to the outside world. Pakistan's Afghan policy appeared for much of the international community as one piece with its support for the Kashmir insurgency and terrorism. Even as the Taliban were falling, young Pakistani men were being openly recruited to fight in Afghanistan against the Northern Alliance and the Americans. Pakistan also paid for its jihadi policies with blowback from Afghanistan that through the 1980s and 1990s was responsible for increased domestic violence and political radicalization.

Musharraf's turnabout on the Taliban in 2001 and his regime's strategic partnership with the United States on counterterrorism would seem to be a watershed in relations with Afghanistan. Islamabad post-9/11 has had to give up the idea that it can install Afghan leaders of its choice and dictate foreign policy to Kabul. To retain influence, Pakistan has instead chosen to rely on its personal networks with Pashtun leaders built up by its Inter-Services Intelligence (ISI) directorate. It backs certain Pashtun regional political figures, some of them opposed to the central government, and has endorsed Pashtun claims of being disadvantaged in the distribution of government offices and development funds. For some time after Pakistan's reversal of policy on Afghanistan, pro-Taliban officials in the ISI, some officially retired, continued to be retained in their previous positions. It is frequently alleged that Taliban sympathizers continue to remain active within Pakistan's security apparatus.

High Afghan officials have regularly accused Pakistan of tolerating militant recruitment, training camps, and arms depots on its territory. On a February 2006 trip to Islamabad, Karzai presented the Pakistani president and his aides with a list of names, addresses, and phone numbers of ranking Taliban figures, more than implying that their presence and movements were with the knowledge and perhaps approval of Pakistan's ISI. Musharraf's reaction a week later, personally criticizing Karzai, broke sharply with what remained of attempts to keep their differences at the official level couched in diplomatic tones. Coming as it did just shortly before a state visit by President Bush, Karzai's actions were intended to maximize impact on Pakistan at a time when increasing Taliban activity in Afghanistan has drawn American concern. While Afghans are probably too quick to blame Pakistan for contributing to their security problems, there is little doubt that top Taliban commanders find sanctuary within Pakistan and opportunity to plan and launch operations. Islamabad's efforts to check extremism and prevent the infiltration of antiregime insurgents are accurately described as inconsistent, incomplete, and at times insincere.

The Islamabad government can be seen as pursuing a two-track foreign policy toward Afghanistan. At the official level, good relations with the Kabul government are sought through policies that promote Afghan stability and economic recovery. Islamabad can live with a strengthened central government in Afghanistan as long as it is reasonably friendly and, above all, sensitive to Pakistan's security needs. A regime that is pliable or openly pro-Pakistan would of course be preferred; but Islamabad has little choice at present but to respect the Afghan political process. To charges that the Pakistan government or specifically the ISI is complicit in the insurgency, Musharraf and others are quick to point out that over 70,000 troops are deployed in the border areas and that Pakistan has arrested more than 700 it labels as terrorists. Pakistan's army has lost more than 600 soldiers in these operations, though mostly in fighting with uncooperative local tribesmen. Indeed, the Islamabad government has incurred heavy domestic political costs for engaging militarily in the heretofore out-of-bounds tribal areas, and for acknowledging its coordination with the United States in intelligence gathering.

Pakistan refrained from serious interference in Afghanistan's October 2004 presidential election. Its military apparently made it more difficult for insurgents to mount cross-border attacks to disrupt the election. Karzai would probably have been denied his popular vote majority had Pakistan been determined to keep large numbers of Pashtuns from voting in refugee camps in Pakistan. Nor has Pakistan been accused of trying to influence the outcome of individual contests in the September 2005 parliamentary vote or held responsible for the militants' intimidation of Pashtun voters that held down the turnout in Pashtun-dominated provinces.

Pakistan's commercial interests in Afghanistan would prefer a stable neighbor. Indeed, a prospering Afghanistan offers opportunities for Pakistani industries and business. Some 60,000 Pakistanis are believed currently employed in Afghanistan. Private investment in Afghanistan shows signs of growing. Pakistan's wide-ranging exports to Afghanistan stand at roughly $1.2 billion per year as opposed to the $25 million in exports during the Taliban era. Pakistan imports more than $700 million worth of goods, mostly fresh and dried fruits and herbs. Offers by Pakistan to help improve airports, civil aviation, roads, and highways are all meant to create a better infrastructure for trade. A promised $200 million development aid package is also pledged for education, health care, housing, and other social sectors, in all, some twenty projects. As with other aid benefactors, many of these development projects have in fact been slow to materialize. Bitter words between Kabul and Islamabad and rising anti-Pakistan sentiment in Afghanistan could further delay delivery. The October 2005 earthquake in northern Pakistan may also affect Islamabad's ability to meet its aid commitments to Afghanistan.

Policies that contribute to Afghanistan's reconstruction and rehabilitation would seem to be in Islamabad's interest as a means of accelerating the repatriation of Afghan refugees, more than two million of whom remain in Pakistan. The country's hospitality to the refugees over the years, however admirable, has worn thin. But the preference toward stability in Afghanistan and efforts to avoid confrontation cannot be understood apart from Pakistan's partnership with the United States. With U.S. policies dedicated to defending the Kabul regime and resisting the reemergence of radical Islam in Afghanistan, a serious falling out between Islamabad and Kabul could have an adverse effect on both. The usually pragmatic-minded President Musharraf is undoubtedly unwilling to jeopardize Washington's military and economic assistance or, as some in Islamabad fear, give the Americans reason to further tilt toward India.

There exists, however, a second track in Pakistan's policies toward Afghanistan that undermines the first. The Musharraf regime's actions toward the insurgents cannot be separated from the way Pakistan has managed its domestic extremist Islamic groups. Many of those radical groups sympathetic to the Taliban and critical of Pakistan's cooperation with the United States on Afghanistan are also ones with which the Islamabad government continues to maintain close relationships. Militantly Islamic, they were either created or were otherwise indulged by Pakistan's security forces as instruments of government jihadi policies in Kashmir and earlier in Afghanistan. In recent years this jihadi network is thought to have revived and strengthened its working relations with al Qaeda and the Taliban.

While some jihadi groups have parted ways with Musharraf, even targeted him, others remain under the unofficial protection of the government. By keeping jihadi organizations mostly intact and their mission alive, the government hopes to better monitor them and channel extremist forces away from anti-regime activity. Were the jihadi movements to be entirely dismantled, it is feared that many indoctrinated and armed people would be seeded across the country, adding to the violence in urban areas. Following the London terrorist bombings in July 2005, Musharraf declared his renewed determination to end backing for radical groups that are also fueling the Afghan insurgency. His policies are constrained, however, by the large majority in the tribal belt of Pakistan that does not view the Taliban or al Qaeda as enemies. The reality is that after nearly two years of military action in tribal Waziristan, those elements financially and ideologically linked to al Qaeda rule the territory, not the Pakistani army.

For the near future, the Taliban cannot seriously threaten the Kabul government. The insurgents' strategy is long-term, to remain on the scene with their small-scale operations, with the hope that their chance will come when—as they believe—Afghanistan's international supporters will move on. The insurgency, focused mainly in the country's east and south, is designed to register doubt that international peacekeepers and the central government can protect the mostly Pashtun population. It is also intended to keep NGOs and international agencies from contributing to reconstruction and improvement in the lives of ordinary Afghans in these areas. To defeat the Taliban will require a long-term commitment of the international community to Afghanistan's security and a Pakistani government more willing and able to deny anti-Kabul forces safe haven.

Iran: A Concerned Neighbor

Iran's ambitions as a regional power have not focused on its eastern neighbor. Regimes in Tehran have for some time seen Iran's major strategic interests as lying with developments in the Persian Gulf and, above all, Iraq. The Afghan state stands today more as an opportunity for Iranian expansion economically and culturally than as a rival politically and militarily. Yet Afghanistan comes into view strategically mainly out of concern that other powers might take advantage of a weak Afghan state to menace Iran. Iran has had in recent years to compete for influence in Afghanistan with Pakistan and Saudi Arabia, and since 2001 particularly with the United States.

Iran's interests have been best served by regional stability. Tehran has shown little interest in exporting Islamic revolutionary zeal to Afghanistan's Shiite minority, roughly one-fifth of the population. As with Pakistan, attitudes toward Afghanistan have been shaped by taking in Afghan refugees for more than two decades. Both countries acted on the basis of brotherly Islamic obligations, and each became in time highly resentful of the burdens that providing refuge placed on their societies. But unlike Pakistan, Iran never served as a base for insurgency against Soviet occupiers or the Taliban. By not creating refugee camps, Iran better integrated those Afghans in exile into its society, although Pakistan provided greater educational opportunity and social acceptance. Like Pakistan, Iran could be faced with a fresh wave of refugees if Afghanistan again becomes unstable. By one estimate, there are still 1.2 million Afghan refugees in Iran, with only 275,000 having returned home since 2001. Instability in Afghanistan would also further reduce what possibility exists for Afghan authorities to gain control over poppy cultivation. The interdiction of drugs from Afghanistan's southwest provinces—transiting Iran for foreign markets or meeting Iran's strong domestic demand—have taken a heavy toll on Iran's border security forces in clashes with better-armed drug gangs.

Iran is anxious to prevent the reemergence of a radical Sunni regime in Afghanistan, whether the Taliban or a like group. During the period of Taliban rule, Tehran was convinced that the militant movement was a creation of its enemies intended as a strategic distraction. Tehran is particularly on guard that Saudi-sponsored Wahabbism does not become ascendant. Iran considers itself a patron of its coreligionists in Afghanistan and takes seriously its advocacy of good treatment for Shia, mainly ethnic Hazaras. While Tehran's relationship with Afghan Shiite political parties and militias has not always been close, it has consistently favored a multiethnic Afghan government. Iran also prefers a government in Kabul strong enough to act independently of Islamabad, Riyadh, and Washington.

More than Pakistan, Iran has seen things going its way in Afghanistan. If Pakistan is sometimes accused of sponsoring those who pursue violence in serving Islamabad's interests, Iran's involvement has seemed more benign. For the most part, Iran's foreign policy toward the Karzai government has been low-key and cooperative. Karzai was probably not Tehran's first choice for leadership, but Iran demonstrated early on its willingness to take a constructive attitude at the Bonn Conference in December 2001. The same cooperative policy has been visible through the process that saw Afghanistan pass from transitional government, to writing a constitution, to presidential and parliamentary elections. Tehran refused to encourage Ismail Khan, Herat's governor/warlord and its former patron, to resist his removal by Karzai in 2004 from his power base to a ministry in Kabul. During the October 2004 election, Iran joined with Russia and India in trying, unsuccessfully, to convince the leading Tajik political figure, Younis Qanuni, not to stand against Karzai. Despite previously having backed the Tajiks and the Northern Alliance, the three countries saw more to gain for Qanuni in striking a deal with

Karzai before the election. After the election, Iran weighed in with the Hazara Shiite candidate to accept the results of the election and also convinced Qanuni to do the same.

Iran has every intention of creating an economic sphere of influence in Afghanistan. Its consumer goods already compete favorably with those from Pakistan. Between 400 and 500 trucks cross the border with Afghanistan daily. Iran's nonoil commodities exports to Afghanistan have expanded to roughly $500 million per year. An Iranian bank to facilitate trade opened in Kabul in late 2004. To further strengthen the Afghan market, Tehran has given generous support for reconstruction of the Afghan infrastructure. Pledges of $560 million in reconstruction assistance over five years have included extending its electric grid inside Afghanistan. A 132-kilowatt power transmission line to Herat was inaugurated in January 2005, with promises for a later tenfold increase in power exports to other cities. Iran has opened a 122-kilometer-long highway that connects Herat with northeast Iran at an estimated cost of $68 million. Other reconstruction projects are planned, including the extension of the Iranian rail system into western Afghanistan to link it with the Iranian port of Chabahar, making Chabahar an attractive alternative to Pakistan's new port at Gwadar for both Afghanistan and Central Asia. But continuing U.S. objections to projects economically and politically beneficial to Iran may limit its future role in regional development.

Afghan-Iranian relations are, then, increasingly dictated by Kabul's relationship with the United States. Tehran has always felt uneasy about the Afghan government's strong reliance on the United States but felt unable to do much about it. Support for a stable Afghanistan and a politically secure Karzai was expected to enable Afghanistan to lean less on the United States.

Ironically, since the fall of the Taliban, U.S. and Iranian foreign policies have found considerable convergence on Afghanistan. Iran is believed to have offered search and rescue assistance as the United States readied its attack on the Taliban regime. In February 2002, Iran expelled the anti-American mujahideen leader Gulbuddin Hekmatyar, who had been living for five years in Iran. Tehran has Washington to thank for removing both the Taliban and Saddam Hussein, thereby opening the region to a more muscular Iran and the possibility of regional leadership. For nearly four years, U.S. and Iranian mutual support for the Karzai government had offered what few opportunities there were for the two countries to communicate their views more or less directly.

Two events in 2005 accelerated the rupture of Iranian and American cooperation on Afghanistan. One, a "Memorandum of Understanding" between Washington and Kabul in mid-2005, created a "strategic partnership" that could lead to permanent U.S. military bases close to the Iranian frontier. The possibility of the long-term presence of U.S. military forces in western Afghanistan naturally makes Iran nervous since it would position them within easy striking distance of strategic targets inside Iran. Even now, intelligence units and U.S. Special Forces are believed to be operating along Afghanistan's western border with Iran. Also, in Karzai's desire to please Washington, further differences with Iran could emerge over the possibility of Kabul's recognition of Israel. While the Tehran government challenges the very existence of the Jewish state, the Afghan president has gone on record as being prepared to recognize Israel upon the creation of a Palestinian state. Moreover, he has not ruled out meeting with Israeli leaders.

The second event was the election in June 2005 of Mahmud Ahmadinejad, Iran's new hard-line president. The carefully modulated policies long associated with Iran's Foreign Ministry soon came under attack with the removal of large numbers of officials in the Iranian Foreign Service and elsewhere in the bureaucracy. A more ideological, aggressive foreign policy has apparently replaced Iran's heretofore essentially defensive strategy in Afghanistan. Of late, there are reports of attempts to recruit Afghan journalists to disparage the American presence in the country, and a stronger line against the U.S. role in Afghanistan has been observed on Iranian television broadcasts, which can be seen in Afghanistan's western provinces. Iran's interests are enduring. Iran's Revolutionary Guards are accused of having set up new security posts along the border and of making incursions into Afghanistan to incite unrest among Afghan factions. Mischievous Iranian policies in Afghanistan may increase if tension between Washington and Tehran rises, especially if the United States and its allies press for UN-approved economic sanctions on Iran for its nuclear weapons program.

The sharp rise of oil prices and Iran's cash surpluses offer additional ways for Tehran to exercise its influence regionally. Iran has recently increased its funding for favored groups and individuals in Afghanistan and reportedly funneled money to candidates, including several non-Shiites, in the September 2005 parliamentary elections. Iran's business practices in Afghanistan are reportedly becoming more assertive, even cutthroat. If Iran succeeds in further extending its influence in Afghanistan, it will most likely be through the agency of Iranian commercial interests and their expanding markets in Afghanistan.

Post-Soviet Central Asian States and Other Powers

The increasing differences among post-Soviet Central Asian republics rule out a single approach to engaging them as regional players. In the recent past, these states shared a continuing dependency on Russia and a perceived threat to their sovereignty from Moscow's exploitation. Over time, their relationships with Russia have become more complex, and their politics and economic destinies have diverged with differences in natural resources, demographic mix, cultural imperatives, and leadership styles. Unchanged, however, are their need for external sources of development assistance and the gains possible with mutual approaches to common problems. Also remaining, despite the region's remarkable regime stability, are their common fears of insurgency, mainly from Islamic extremists.

So motivated, most of these Central Asian states welcomed the generous U.S. military and nonmilitary assistance that since 2001 has insured logistical support for operations in Afghanistan. But more recently, these former Soviet republics have "hedged their bets" mostly by raising their price of cooperation with the United States and its allies. Even then, their suspicions about U.S. strategic designs fed by the Russian and Chinese governments are no deeper than what they feel toward one another. Among the three states that form Afghanistan's northern border, nationalist rivalries between Uzbekistan and Tajikistan have become a major impediment to trade, and an erratic, egocentric leadership in Turkmenistan makes it an unreliable partner for its neighbors.

Uzbekistan had special concerns during the 1990s about the radical Islamic Movement of Uzbekistan (IMU). Its leader, Juma Namangani, and many of his followers were known to be located in Taliban-controlled parts of Afghanistan, where they attended training camps and joined the fight against the opposition Northern Alliance. Namangani was killed when Mazar-e-Sharif fell during the U.S. military campaign that began in October 2001. Despite Karzai's assurances that Afghan soil will not be used for carrying out cross-border terrorism, Uzbekistan and the other northern neighbors fear an unstable Afghanistan that will again become a base for subversive activities. Truth be told, the leadership of these states also exaggerates the threat of Islamic militancy as a means of retaining power and discrediting and oppressing opposition elements.

The bitter falling out between the United States and the Karimov regime in Uzbekistan that led to the closing of Uzbekistan's K2 air force base in mid-2005—following Washington's strong condemnation of the brutal suppression of anti-regime demonstrations—carries implications broader than the loss of an air base for U.S. forces operating in Afghanistan. The rupture may have put in jeopardy international financing for a project designed to relieve by 2007 Afghanistan's serious electricity deficit with transmission lines from Uzbekistan. Karimov's stridently anti-Western rhetoric could also affect plans to extend, with the help of Japanese financing, a rail line to the Afghan border along with other sorely needed projects intended to help Uzbekistan develop its regional trade links.

Although a modus vivendi appears in place with Tajikistan's Islamists, the Rakhmanov regime continues to worry about a resurgence of Muslim radicals like those who fought during the 1994–97 civil war. Until 2001, the Dushanbe government, anticipating that the Taliban were likely to extend their control over all of northern Afghanistan, feared the export of instability from Afghanistan. Like Uzbekistan and Kyrgyzstan, Tajikistan facilitated military operations against al Qaeda and the Taliban in November 2001. A NATO base, under French command, has taken on increased importance with Uzbekistan's decidedly anti-American policies. Russia has continuously maintained an air base within Tajikistan, a facility that the Indian air force has been invited to share. Until they were withdrawn in 2005, Russia deployed 25,000 troops along the border ostensibly to block drugs entering from Afghanistan. Although Moscow maintains a military presence in the country, efforts to stanch the flow of the more than 100 tons of heroin that cross the frontier annually have been left to an underfunded, poorly trained, easily corrupted Tajik security force.

Tajikistan has stronger ethnic and cultural ties with Afghanistan than any of its other northern neighbors. Although human traffic across their border is substantial, their commercial trade, mostly in raisins and nuts, is modest. But as noted by Ahmed Rashid, a new road from western China and the completion of an American-built bridge across the Amu Darya could open up Tajikistan as a new transit route for Chinese goods and those from elsewhere in Central Asia. For this to occur, however, much remains to be done in reducing trade barriers and protectionism. Tajikistan's participation in a regional energy plan is closer to realization. Iran has offered to fund a $200 million hydroelectric power project that provides for high-voltage transmission lines to Afghanistan and Iran. Together with a companion Russian-built plant, Tajikistan's energy production should more than double, meeting even broader regional demands for energy.

Turkmenistan alone among the former Central Asian republics had cordial relations with the Taliban. Although Afghanistan's current ties with Turkmenistan are positive, the poor record of participation by Turkmenistan in regional forums leaves its future contribution to regional projects uncertain. A proposed 1,000-mile gas pipeline to Pakistan through Afghanistan attracted considerable interest among Western investors during the mid-1990s. The project, however, became a victim of international condemnation of the Taliban regime. Skeptics also questioned the size of Turkmenistan's gas production capacity. Talk of a pipeline resumed with the post-Taliban Afghan government. Influenced by a favorable Asian Development Bank study, the affected countries formally endorsed the project in early 2006. Revenues from transit fees could bring as much as $450 million to Afghanistan annually. But completion of a gas pipeline remains unlikely. None of the countries that would benefit have the funds or engineering expertise to build the pipeline. Construction costs of at least $3.5 billion and the difficult and dangerous land route through Afghanistan and Pakistan make financing from abroad doubtful.

Russia was together with Iran a main backer of the Northern Alliance. Moscow had acted in concert with other states to try to contain Islamic radicalism, particularly because of the known presence of Chechen rebels under Taliban protection. Afghanistan was the only country to recognize Chechen independence. Moscow went along with Washington in promoting UN resolutions imposing sanctions against the Taliban and welcomed their rout by American-led forces. Since the removal of the Taliban government, many Afghans who had collaborated with the Soviet Union's occupation have been socially and politically rehabilitated. At the same time, relations between Moscow and Kabul have never recovered, and most Afghans continue to view Russia with bitterness and distrust. Russia has figured only minimally in Afghanistan's reconstruction. Late in 2005, Moscow renewed its demand for repayment of some $10 billion in loans that were extended to Afghanistan over several decades, mostly for heavy weapons and the service of Russian military experts. However, in February 2006 the Russian government went along with a Paris Club of creditor countries agreement aimed at heavily indebted poor countries that wrote off the Afghan debt.

For some time the Russians have been uncomfortable with the U.S. role in Central Asia, an area where Moscow's preeminence had been long established. Moscow sees the promotion of democracy by the United States and NATO as a pretext for continued, even accelerated, interference in its former republics. The Karzai government's strategic partnership with Washington, which could allow a long-term U.S. military presence in Afghanistan, seems to confirm these fears. President Karzai vigorously denies that his strategic partnership with the United States is aimed at any country in the region and accuses the Russians of spreading "suspicion and untrue beliefs." Especially troublesome are reports of Russian arms and funds reaching previously favored militia commanders in the north.

China shares only a small mountainous border with Afghanistan that is virtually impassable and barely inhabited. Beijing's involvement with Afghanistan increased during the Taliban rule, after Chinese Uighurs trying to stoke an insurgency among southwest China's Muslim population took sanctuary and training among the Afghans. Some Uighurs also fought together with the Taliban and al Qaeda. Lest it again become a safe haven for foreign militants under the protection of radical Islamists, China's present interests lie with an Afghanistan that is politically stable and enjoying reconstruction. Yet Beijing's contribution to date has been relatively modest, a mere $150 million pledged by late 2005 compared with $900 million from Japan. Of late, China seems mostly engaged in using diplomatic means to thwart an open-ended U.S. military presence in Afghanistan and the region.

India has maintained historically strong business and cultural links to Afghanistan, bolstered by a sizeable Indian resident community. Afghanistan has also served as a theater for Indo-Pakistani enmity. New Delhi fears most the Islamic radicalization of Afghanistan, especially where seen as Pakistan-sponsored. Important jihadi organizations in Pakistan have always viewed their offensive operations in Afghanistan and Kashmir as part of the same religious calling. Because of India's thinly disguised endorsement of pro-Soviet regimes in Kabul during the 1980s, Pakistan was concerned by the possibility of being outflanked by its traditional adversary. This concern should have ended with the ascent to power of a mujahideen government in Kabul in 1992. But Afghanistan's new rulers, anxious to free the country of Pakistan's influence, soon sought out India as a counterweight to their former patron. This rapprochement promptly ended with the fall of Kabul in 1996 to the Pakistan-backed Taliban insurgency.

India has worked hard to win the confidence of the post-Taliban government in Kabul. New Delhi has contributed $565 million toward Afghan reconstruction—the sixth largest contributor—divided among infrastructure repair, humanitarian assistance, and institutional and human resource development. A wide spectrum of programs includes highway repair, communications, energy, health care, and capacity building in contributions to secondary education and the training of diplomats and bureaucrats. India will finance the construction of a new parliament building at a cost of $50 million. Indian-donated Tata buses are a key part of Kabul's public transportation. Assistance to Afghanistan's reconstruction advertises India's claims to be a regional economic power, ready to assume regional responsibilities.

Indian activities in Afghanistan regularly draw complaints from Pakistan. Few actions rankled the Pakistanis more than the opening of Indian consulates in several Afghan cities, where they seem designed mostly as listening posts to monitor Pakistani influences and activities. But Pakistan sees more sinister motives than simple intelligence gathering, accusing the Indians through its consulates in Kandahar and Jalalabad of fostering an insurgency inside Pakistan's Balochistan. Pakistan takes this especially seriously because the Chinese-built port at Gwadar stands at the southern boundary of the province. The port is central to Pakistan's plans to create a new international route for sea traffic that could serve China, but also Afghanistan and Central Asia. Meanwhile, India is building an $80 million road linking Afghanistan's Kandahar Province with the Iranian port at Chabahar, and providing a 300-man paramilitary force to ensure the security of Indian workers. Until recently, a projected gas pipeline to carry Iranian gas through Pakistan to India stood a better chance of completion than the more problematic American-backed route from Turkmenistan through Afghanistan and Pakistan. But New Delhi's ardor for Iranian gas began to cool following a March 2006 agreement with Washington on cooperation in India's civilian nuclear power program. Although this may boost interest in the Afghan route, India cannot ignore gas-rich Iran as the prime long-term energy resource supplier for South Asia.

Afghanistan's Future and the International Implications

Following the events of 2001, the region's states seemed poised to accelerate their movement away from traditional rivalries toward greater cooperation. A rising tide of regional economic cooperation, it was hoped, would complement international assistance programs in carrying Afghanistan through the post-conflict years. But as this study has shown, the region contains as many problems as it does solutions. Particularly disconcerting are the indications that several states in Afghanistan's neighborhood are becoming more assertive, possibly reviving older geostrategic aims. While none of its neighbors and other interested powers have yet pursued a course to destabilize the Afghan state or threaten its recovery, some seem prepared to extend their influence in Kabul through their traditional, divisive Afghan clients. Only with a renewed commitment of the international community to Afghanistan will it be possible to succeed in holding back these potentially disruptive political currents.

Securing and rebuilding post-Taliban Afghanistan has been from the outset an international effort. At Bonn, the responsibilities were divided among several countries designated to lead in the areas of training a national army and police forces; constructing a legal system; eradicating poppy cultivation; and disarming, demobilizing, and reintegrating into society (DDR) hundreds of private militias. Similarly, the financing of Afghanistan's humanitarian and developmental recovery began as a shared international project. Arguably, the failure of Bonn to assign the regional powers defined roles in the recovery missed an opportunity for them to become more responsible players and long-term partners with Afghanistan. But leaving them with less specified political and financial responsibilities probably prevented any of these countries from using means at their disposal to monopolize sectors of the recovery. It may also have been to Afghanistan's advantage to have regional states compete constructively in providing development assistance.

While most regional states have permanent interests in Afghanistan, international players have repeatedly demonstrated short attention spans. Bitter memories exist over how, soon after the Soviet withdrawal in 1989, Afghanistan's prospective international benefactors backed away from their commitments, and then almost entirely washed their hands of Afghanistan during its more-than-decade-long civil war. Only the rise of international terrorism and the more repugnant actions of the Taliban brought Afghanistan back onto the international agenda. Many Afghans, like the Pakistanis, are convinced that Washington will quickly lose interest with the capture of the al Qaeda leadership, and that without the Americans most donor countries and international agencies will soon drift away. The expansion of NATO peacekeeping forces and redeployment to several southern provinces, replacing U.S. combat troops scheduled for a 12 percent drawdown in the country, have fanned speculation that the United States is reassessing its commitment.

Predictably, the levels of financial assistance and the presence of foreign military and aid personnel will decline over time. But deserting Afghanistan may not be a prudent option for the United States and others. To deprive Afghanistan of humanitarian and development aid would be cruel in light of how the country has suffered and sacrificed. Realpolitik would also dictate that this resource-poor country should not be left vulnerable. Without a visible international involvement, there exists a strong possibility of domestic political turmoil and economic failure that could condemn Afghanistan to become a narco-state, and leave it prey to rapacious neighbors. Once again, Afghanistan could easily become a breeding ground for an Islamic militancy that is regionally and globally contagious. A nuclear-armed Pakistan and the dangers of its becoming a jihadi state also raise the regional stakes for the international community, and especially the United States.

The investment of the international community in keeping Afghanistan from becoming a narco-state has more immediacy than any of the other threats facing Afghanistan. As a direct consequence of a broken economy and a weak state system, opium poppy cultivation has spread across the entire country and criminalized much of its economy and governance. It has created a community of interests among dealers, local militias, government officials, and antiregime militants that defies the enforcement efforts of the Kabul government and those assisting it. The country's weak judicial institutions also stand as a major impediment. With Afghanistan accounting for almost 90 percent of the world's heroin output, it is not surprising that the United States and others continue to call for a more robust counternarcotics strategy. Attempts at wholesale eradication could, however, be politically destabilizing owing to the dependence of more than 2 million farm families on their poppy crops for their livelihood. The longer-term introduction of alternative crops within a comprehensive rural development program strikes most experts as a more feasible and sustainable strategy. But these and other supply side measures conveniently ignore that the explosion of drug production in post-conflict Afghanistan is only in response to the high demand for drugs in neighboring states and more distant international markets.

The more impressive political gains and the passing of the milestones laid out in Bonn have occasioned the recommitment of the international community. The January 2006 London conference, attended by more than sixty countries and international agencies, pledged $10.5 billion in development assistance over five years. The focal point of the conference was an Afghanistan Compact, drafted by the Karzai government, predicated on international engagement for progress in governance, the rule of law, human rights, and economic and social development. The conference participants were sympathetic to the requests by the Karzai government that it be handed primary control over aid resources. But strong doubts remain about the central authority's capacity to receive and spend the aid effectively. Agreement was reached, however, to create a trust that could release more funds to Kabul with evidence of greater transparency and accountability. Regarding concerns about Afghanistan's continuing security challenges, Pakistan was not named in connection with the growing insurgency. Instead, the Compact calls for "full respect of Afghanistan's sovereignty, and strengthening dialogue and cooperation between Afghanistan and its neighbors."

Washington to date has been equivocal regarding Pakistan's Afghan policies. U.S. officials periodically press Musharraf to do more to rein in the Taliban and others engaged in anti-Kabul activities, and publicly praise the Islamabad government for its cooperation in apprehending Islamic terrorists. Actually, for most of the last four years Pakistan's leaders have had reason to conclude that curtailing the activities of the Taliban and their allies was of lesser importance to Washington than capturing those who could be linked directly to al Qaeda. Meanwhile, the United States has given Musharraf considerable slack in meeting his commitments to deal with domestic extremism or his promises to restore authentic democracy. The U.S. partnership with Pakistan would probably be on firmer footing through conditioned programs more dedicated to building the country's political and social institutions than rewarding its leadership.

Like Musharraf, Karzai is one of the pillars supporting U.S. policy objectives in the region. However, a military-focused partnership with Afghanistan may be the wrong way for the United States to demonstrate its commitment to Karzai and Afghanistan. It slights the contribution of reconstruction and improvement in the lives of most Afghans in making the country secure from its enemies. Many Afghans view a concession to Washington on long-term military basing as akin to those demands associated with an occupying power, having little relation to Afghanistan's own needs. A strategic partnership could also undermine what has been the Afghan president's largely successful personal rapport with most of the region's leaders. As this study has shown, Afghanistan is unlikely to succeed without coming to terms with its difficult neighborhood.

The United States is frequently accused of lacking a holistic approach to this turbulent region. Its regional policies on security, democracy, and development are said to be often inconsistent if not contradictory. The decision by the U.S. State Department to incorporate Central Asia's Islamic states into the same bureau as Afghanistan can contribute to a strengthened region-wide perspective. Along with the international community, the United States might also begin to address how it can benefit Afghanistan's quest for security and recovery through aid projects and other policies specifically intended to promote regional cooperation and integration. For this to occur, U.S. priorities that are now so unidimensionally focused on counterterrorism must be better aligned with the aspirations of citizens of Afghanistan and those of its neighbors.

6

Resolving the Pakistan-Afghanistan Stalemate

Barnett R. Rubin and Abubakar Siddique

Rubin and Siddique describe the complexities of the border area between Afghanistan and Pakistan, the dynamics of which involve more than state-to-state relations. Originally published in 2006, as the insurgency was heating up, this chapter notes that more members of Afghan and international forces were killed by the insurgency in 2005 than between 2001 and 2004 combined. Islamist militia–inspired violence also increased in the tribal districts on the Pakistani side of the border, while anti-Islamabad insurgent activity continued in the Pakistani province of Baluchistan, where there is a long-standing separatist movement.

The authors link the conflicts to the unsettled border between Afghanistan and Pakistan—the so-called Durand Line—which has been delineated on maps but never demarcated on the ground, and which Pakistan recognizes but Afghanistan contests. The long and porous border is seen as a major enabler of the insurgency in Afghanistan, and its mountainous and remote geography permits the sanctuary of groups such as al-Qaeda. Today, despite international efforts to mediate border disputes, Afghanistan and Pakistan each trade accusations over the operations of militant groups operating from the other's territory and their respective military responses to those threats.

Rubin and Siddique provide a succinct history of the Durand Line, connecting it to the Great Game rivalry between the British raj and imperial Russia, the uneasy efforts of the raj in dealing with the unruly Afghan tribes that lived in the mountains along the western fringes of the settled and fertile Punjab, and the conscious choice of British Delhi to establish a "frontier of separation" rather than a "frontier of contact." Tribal areas on the Pakistan side of the border were controlled by the military, while tribes on the Afghan side were "managed" by a combination of influences that, with few exceptions, stopped short of attempts at total control.

Originally published as Barnett R. Rubin and Abubakar Siddique, "Resolving the Pakistan-Afghanistan Stalemate," Special Report 176 (Washington, DC: USIP, 2006).

The peculiar legacy of the borderlands affected relations between the two countries and the larger region. The authors describe the Taliban as "a phenomenon of the borderland, a joint Afghan-Pakistan network and regime." Pakistan's use of the Taliban in the 1990s to stabilize Afghanistan—and after 2001 to destabilize it—are "a reprise with variations on the theme of a forward policy composed by the British empire." The authors make a point, too often overlooked by over-optimistic policymakers, that "Pakistan and other neighbors of Afghanistan see the consolidation [in Afghanistan] of a state dependent on the United States as a long-term threat." Pakistan's policy of undermining "the status of the Durand Line as an international border" has, the authors argue, "neutralized Afghan nationalism," making the statebuilding process far more difficult.

If the anomalous isolation of the tribal areas has allowed the fractious border area to become a base for ideological extremists and a shelter for armed groups who feel no part of any state, the authors argue that the only solution is to begin breaking down that isolation, and they describe how this might be done.

Introduction

On January 13, 2006, the sleepy village of Damadola in the Bajaur tribal district of Pakistan on the Afghan frontier became the focus of global attention. With the American news networks in the lead, global media broadcast coverage of the Central Intelligence Agency's attempt to kill al Qaeda's number two, Ayman al-Zawahiri, who had reportedly attended a dinner in the village to commemorate the Muslim holiday `Id-ul-Adha. Pictures of tribal members digging dead bodies from the debris of their bombed-out mud houses were beamed around the globe. Pakistan's Islamist political parties called for severing all ties with the United States for this attack on the country's sovereignty.[1] President Pervez Musharraf, who initially minimized the attack 's importance, later announced that at least five top al Qaeda figures had been killed, although al-Zawahiri himself had escaped.[2]

Three days later, in what appeared to be a reprisal, a suicide bomber riding a motorcycle blew himself up among spectators of a wrestling match in the southern Afghan town of Spin Boldak, across from the Pakistani border town of Chaman. It was Afghanistan's worst suicide attack, killing twenty-two civilians and leaving dozens more injured.[3]

This was the largest in a rash of suicide attacks in Afghanistan, some of which have taken place even in the relatively secure northern and western provinces.[4] With 1,500 violent deaths, more members of the Afghan security forces and the U.S.-led international coalition were killed in combat in 2005 than in any year since the overthrow of the Taliban regime in late 2001. In the first six months of 2006, Afghanistan faced thirty-two suicide attacks, unprecedented in the country's three decades of violence.[5] Since May 2006 violence has reached new levels. Some 800 insurgents, civilians, and soldiers died in the four southwestern provinces. The reorganized Taliban, operating in Afghanistan from bases in Pakistan, form the bulk of the insurgency, which also includes elements led by Afghan Islamist Gulbuddin Hikmatyar's *Hizb-i-Islami* and foreign jihadi forces, including the leadership of al Qaeda.

The violence, which has spread to both sides of the frontier, escalated in the run-up to President Bush's mid-March 2006 visit to South Asia—especially in Waziristan, a craggy region of 5,000 square miles divided into the South and North Agencies, or tribal districts. Some 300 Islamist militants, civilians, and Pakistani soldiers died in the fighting, which forced tens of thousands of people to flee the Pakistani town of Miran Shah, administrative headquarters of the North Waziristan tribal district. In neighboring South Waziristan, skirmishes, rocketing, assassinations, and land-mine blasts continue.[6] Since al Qaeda's retreat from Afghanistan in winter 2001, some tribal areas have become a small-scale copy of Taliban-controlled Afghanistan, where Islamist militants can recover and plan fresh operations while gradually imposing their will on the secluded region. Violence also has spread into the adjacent districts of the Northwest Frontier Province.[7]

Hot Wars on the Borders

Despite the presence of some 80,000 Pakistani soldiers, Islamist militias have grown along the border. Before the fighting in Miran Shah in spring 2006, the violence in Waziristan had claimed the lives of some 250 members of the security forces and 300 civilians. Unofficial casualty counts place the figure much higher.

The Pakistan military also claimed to have killed 194 foreign militants and 552 of their local supporters in periodic operations since mid-2002. The majority of these fighters were Uzbeks, Chechens, and Arabs led by Qari Tahir Yuldashev, erstwhile leader of the Islamic Movement of Uzbekistan, who survived American bombing in the northern Afghan town of Kunduz in 2001. Two senior al Qaeda figures, Haitham al-Yamani and Abu Hamza Rabia, were killed in North Waziristan in 2005. International media attributed their deaths to Hellfire missiles fired from CIA drones.[8] In April 2006 Pakistani forces killed Muhsin Matwalli Atwah, an Egyptian known as Abdul Rahman, in an air raid north of Miran Shah. Charged with being a bomb maker who had participated in the 1998 bombing of the U.S. embassies in Kenya and Tanzania, Rahman had a $5 million price on his head.[9] A week later a Saudi national, Abu Marwan al-Suri, was killed at a checkpoint in Khar, the administrative headquarters of the Bajaur tribal district. Known for his expertise with explosives, he had been one of the targets of the January 13 strike in Damadola.[10]

Another insurgency along the border, in resource-rich southwestern Baluchistan province, also remains a major headache for Islamabad. Desolate but rich in mineral resources and hydrocarbons, Baluchistan is important to Pakistan's future development. This province provides Pakistan with most of its gas. With $150 million in Chinese assistance, Pakistan is building a major deepwater seaport in the small fishing town of Gwadar. Elsewhere it wants to dig oil and gas wells and excavate gold and other minerals. Today's Baluch nationalist rebels view these projects as exploitation of their province's wealth for the exclusive benefit of the Pakistani state, dominated by military officers and bureaucrats from Punjab and Urdu-speaking migrants from India who often call themselves *mohajir* (immigrants). The Baluch nationalists call for maximum provincial autonomy and control over their resources before they will agree to mega-development projects such as the Gwadar port.

Since the 1947 creation of Pakistan, autonomy-minded Baluch nationalists have carried out five insurgencies, in 1948, 1958–59, 1962–63, 1973–77, and 2004–06. The military suppressed all of these revolts. During the 1970s insurgency 6,000 Baluch tribesmen and 3,000 Pakistani soldiers died. Some 30,000 Baluch tribesmen went into exile in southern Afghanistan for more than a decade.[11]

A dormant insurgency in the region escalated in December 2005, when Baluch nationalist guerillas fired rockets at a gathering presided over by Pakistani President Gen. Pervez Musharraf while he was visiting Baluchistan. By June 2006, hundreds of Baluch militants, civilians, paramilitary fighters, and soldiers had died in the skirmishes and as a result of insurgent sabotage. The killing of Nawab Akbar Bugti, a respected politician and former governor of Baluchistan, made the insurgency both a major national crisis and a critical factor in Pakistan's relations with Afghanistan and India, where governments, parliamentarians, and the press condemned the killing.

The Islamist militancy and ethnic revolt on both sides of the Durand Line, the 2,400-kilometer frontier between Afghanistan and Pakistan, are linked to many complex global and regional problems. Policymakers and journalists say Osama bin Laden and his deputy Zawahiri are hiding somewhere in the northeastern part of this rugged region. In December 2001, under intense U.S. pressure, Pakistan deployed regular military units in the Kurram and Khyber agencies to block al Qaeda's exodus from Tora Bora, but a delay in their arrival and the U.S. decision not to deploy available U.S. Marines to the area allowed bin Laden and his followers to escape. The number of Pakistani troops steadily grew to 80,000 and drastically changed the region, which had been under "indirect rule" for more than a century.

Afghanistan never has recognized the Durand Line as an international border. The administration of President Hamid Karzai, charging Pakistan with supporting the Taliban, has leaned toward India. Further antagonized, Pakistan blames rising Indian influence in Afghanistan for the violent nationalist insurgency in Baluchistan. This dispute presents a problem for the United States, which has been trying to dislodge al Qaeda and the Taliban from the region since early 2002. U.S. policies, however, have not addressed the long-standing conflicts over the frontier region.

Pakistan and Afghanistan inherited their multilayered border and its complex governance mechanisms from the British Empire. In the late nineteenth century the British tried to make Afghanistan an isolated buffer state between their empire and Russia, but nineteenth-century border arrangements on the margins of an empire do not work in an area at the heart of twenty-first-century global strategy.

The neighbors now need to resolve the myriad problems of the border region. They have to overcome past differences and circumvent the violence unleashed by nonstate actors, sometimes with official support, to reach a comprehensive settlement. The international community in general and the United States in particular have to facilitate such a process through diplomacy and help pay for the long overdue reforms and economic development on the rugged frontier. They also may have to press reluctant actors to explore alternatives to deeply entrenched policies. Kabul and Islamabad must formulate policies to promote a peaceful and prosperous future rather than remaining hostages to the bitter disputes of the past.

Old Conflict and New Bitterness

The Durand Line is named after the British foreign secretary, Sir Henry Mortimer Durand, who demarcated the boundary with agents of the Afghan Amir Abdul Rahman Khan in 1893. The Pakistan side of the border area includes the provinces of Baluchistan, the North West Frontier Province (NWFP), and the adjacent FATA. On the Afghan side the frontier stretches from Nuristan province in the northeast to Nimruz in the southwest. The border region is predominantly inhabited by ethnic Pashtuns, who were divided by the Durand Line. The 30 million to 35 million Pashtuns in Pakistan represent 15 to 20 percent of the country's population. In Afghanistan they are the largest ethnic group, comprising about half its estimated 30 million people. The Baluch also live on both sides of the Durand Line in the southwest border region, as well as in neighboring Iran.

This region's passes and trading routes have connected South Asia to Central and West Asia for millennia. The political and legal structure of the region is a product of centuries of empire building and resistance, but it started to assume its contemporary form in the early nineteenth century, when the British East India Company was expanding toward northwest India. About 25 years after taking Delhi in 1804, the British became concerned about czarist expansion toward Central Asia. During the first Anglo-Afghan war (1840–42), the British invaded Afghanistan but were defeated by an uprising in Kabul that turned into a rout.

By 1876 Russian advances in Central Asia reached the Amu Darya, the river that now constitutes Afghanistan's northern border. The Afghan amir's efforts to establish friendly relations with his northern neighbor led the British to launch the second Anglo-Afghan war in 1879, deposing the amir and occupying Kabul. This was the peak of the "Great Game," when the European powers vied for control of Central Asia, with Afghanistan as the central arena.

The British forced Amir Yaqub Khan to sign the Treaty of Gandamak in 1879, while their army was occupying Kabul. Successive Afghan governments have repudiated this treaty, claiming it was signed under duress. Afghanistan agreed to let the British open an embassy and gave up control of several frontier districts, including most of today's FATA and parts of Baluchistan. The treaty guaranteed British support to Kabul against external aggression and provided an annual subsidy of money and arms with which the Afghan ruler was to subdue his own territory. Anglo-Russian commissions demarcated Afghanistan's northern and western borders with Central Asia, Iran, and China between 1870 and 1896.

Following the second Anglo-Afghan war, the British set about developing what they hoped would be a durable border regime, involving separate statuses and mechanisms for Afghanistan, the border tribes, and the Pashtun and Baluch territories under the administration of British India. They invited Abdul Rahman Khan, a nephew of Amir Sher Ali Khan living in exile in Russian Turkistan, to assume the throne in 1880. During a brutal twenty-year reign, the "Iron Amir" laid the foundation of modern Afghanistan. He gave the country its administrative institutions and agreed to the formal demarcation of its borders, including the Durand Line. The amir always contended that excluding the tribal territories from Afghanistan was a mistake, as he could control the tribes better than the British could.

The demarcation of the Durand Line required the British to establish a regime to deal with the tribal borderlands. Five tribal regions were placed under the direct control of the central government in Delhi. After the creation of Pakistan in 1947, three new agencies were carved out of other tribal districts. The British devised a special legal structure called the Frontier Crimes Regulations (FCR). Evolving through the late nineteenth century, the regulations were finally promulgated as statutory law under Viceroy Lord Curzon in 1901 and are still the legal regime in FATA.

After the failure of the British "forward policy" in the first Anglo-Afghan war, Delhi settled on a "close border" policy to make the frontier into a buffer. To British administrators, frontier meant a "wide tract of border country, hinterland or a buffer state." The most important feature of this arrangement was its transformation into a "frontier of separation," in contrast to a "frontier of contact." The result was the "threefold frontier." The first frontier was the outer edge of the directly administered territory (the river Indus in the nineteenth century and the settled districts of NWFP in the mid-twentieth century); the second was the Pashtun tribal area between Afghanistan and the settled districts of NWFP, which was placed under indirect rule; and the third comprised the protectorates of Nepal and Afghanistan on the outer edge of the sphere of influence.

In recent times Pakistan has used its support for the anti-Soviet *mujahidin* and then the Taliban to ensure that in the event of conflict with India, Afghanistan would provide Pakistan with support and use of its land and air space if needed. Pakistani military planners referred to this as the quest for "strategic depth." The similarity of the threefold frontier to this quest in Afghanistan illustrates the continuity of strategic policy in this region.

The 1907 Anglo-Russian convention formally ended the Great Game. It divided Persia into zones of influence of the two great powers, protecting Afghanistan's western borders from Russian penetration. Both powers agreed to recognize Chinese control over Tibet. Russia conceded Afghanistan to the British sphere of influence, but Britain was not to occupy or annex any part of the country or interfere in its internal affairs. Amir Habibullah of Afghanistan declared the convention illegal because Afghanistan was not a party to the agreement, but his protest went unheeded.

Popular resistance movements throughout the century of British rule also shaped the border region. At times these were local affairs, as when a clan or a tribe resisted the British; but on other occasions the tribes launched wider movements, sometimes coordinating with the larger Afghan and Indian struggles against European colonialism. Charismatic tribal leaders or clerics led many such rebellions. These leaders fought small-scale battles and larger wars, such as the one in Waziristan, where the British kept 50,000 soldiers, more troops than on the rest of the subcontinent, as late as the 1930s. On other occasions the British used more indirect counterinsurgency methods. Seventy thousand tribal members serving as scouts under British officers suppressed the Great Tribal Uprising of 1897, in which most Pashtun tribes east of the Durand Line joined in an uncoordinated war against the British.

As Afghanistan lacked a modern army, the rulers of Kabul often mobilized the tribes to fight in the early twentieth century. The modernist and nationalist King Amanullah declared jihad for full independence from the British in 1919. Pashtun tribal *lashkars,* or posses, from both sides of the Durand Line fought the month-long war. Afghanistan subsequently obtained full sovereignty from a weakened British Empire in the 1919 Treaty of Rawalpindi.

In 1929, King Amanullah lost his throne in a revolt led by a Tajik guerrilla leader, Habibullah Kalakani, who was supported by conservative clergy. A tribal posse headed by the king's distant cousin, Nadir Khan, and composed of Pashtuns from both sides of the Durand Line, put an end to the rule of Amir Habibullah II, commonly known as *Bacha-yi Saqao* (son of the water carrier) in admiration or mockery of his humble origins.

In return for their military services, Nadir Shah gave the tribes of the *Loya,* or Greater Paktia region of southeastern Afghanistan, maximum tribal autonomy. He exempted them from taxation and conscription on the assumption that they could mobilize lashkars if needed. Throughout the twentieth century Afghanistan also maintained a sizable number of tribal sympathizers east of the Durand Line through honorary and material rewards, including recruitment into the officer corps.[12] Members of the tribes that had fought for Nadir Shah from both sides of the Durand Line predominated among the military officers trained in the Soviet Union, who joined or sympathized with the Afghan communist groups.

Modern Pashtun nationalism emerged in NWFP in 1930, when British troops killed unarmed protestors in Peshawar. Khan Abdul Ghaffar Khan headed the Afghan *jirga*, which was later called the *Khudai Khidmatgars* (servants of God). Ghaffar Khan allied with the Indian National Congress to win the 1937 and 1946 elections in NWFP, after which his movement formed the provincial governments. The Khudai Khidmatgars parted ways with Congress in 1946, when the latter accepted the British partition plan providing for a plebiscite in the province on joining India or the new state of Pakistan. This movement demanded inclusion of an option to establish an independent state of Pashtunistan.

In August 1947 two states, India and Pakistan, emerged from the British Indian empire. The Afghan government voted against Pakistan's admission to the United Nations in 1947, arguing that Pakistan should not be recognized as long as the "Pashtunistan" problem remained unresolved. Afghanistan withdrew this objection after only a month, however, and in February 1948 it became one of the first nations to establish diplomatic relations with Pakistan. The Pashtun nationalist Khudai Khidmatgars moderated their stand soon after partition and declared their loyalty to the new country. Some tribal leaders in FATA maintained militias in the name of Pashtunistan. Successive governments in Pakistan tried to handle the Pashtun nationalist claims by suppressing their advocates.

Pakistan then ended the British policy of military control of tribal areas by withdrawing army units from the agencies. Soon Pakistan was able to mobilize a sizable Pashtun tribal posse from both sides of the Durand Line to fight for control of Kashmir, a Muslim majority state, when its maharaja declared accession to India in 1947. Although the tribal members made a spectacular march, they failed to capture Srinagar, the capital of Kashmir. Since 1947 Pakistan and India each have occupied parts of Kashmir, divided by the line of control.

Today Kashmir remains divided between India and Pakistan. India claims that the state of Jammu and Kashmir is now an integral part of the Republic of India, while Pakistan still demands implementation of UN Security Council resolutions calling for a plebiscite on whether Kashmir should join India or Pakistan. Some Kashmiri movements have demanded independence.

The Durand Line border dispute soon brought the Cold War to the Khyber Pass. In July 1949, after a Pakistani bombing raid on an Afghan border village, the Afghan government convened a *loya jirga*, or grand tribal assembly, in Kabul. This supreme national decision-making body declared support for the Pashtunistan demand. The jirga affirmed the Afghan government's position that Pakistan was a new state rather than a successor state to British India, and all past treaties with the British pertaining to the status of the border were therefore null and void. Such agreements included the 1893 Durand Agreement, the Anglo-Afghan Pact of 1905, the Treaty of Rawalpindi of 1919, and the Anglo-Afghan Treaty of 1921. It reaffirmed Afghanistan's rejection of the 1879 Treaty of Gandamak. Afghanistan eventually turned to the Soviet Union for military aid, because its position on Pashtunistan made it impossible to receive aid from the United States, which was allied with Pakistan.

For Pashtun nationalists in Pakistan and Afghanistan, Pashtunistan meant different things, ranging from an independent country to an autonomous province of Pakistan to an integral part of Afghanistan. The Soviet Union and India paid lip service to Pashtunistan for decades. The Soviets wanted to prevent Afghanistan from joining any Western military alliance and to pressure Pakistan; India wanted to divert Pakistan's military resources by cultivating the fear of an unstable western border.

The Pashtunistan demand served domestic Afghan political purposes as well. In the twentieth century successive Afghan rulers used the issue to strengthen Pashtun ethnic support for the state. By harnessing the state to the Pashtun ethnic cause, however, the government intensified ethno-linguistic rivalry between Pashtuns and non-Pashtuns.

In 1961 relations between the neighbors hit rock bottom when Pakistan closed the border and the countries broke off diplomatic relations. With Afghanistan's principal trade route cut off, the Afghan economy was pressed to the breaking point. Differences within the royal family led to the resignation of Prime Minister Daud Khan in 1963. After ten years of constitutional monarchy with a contentious but ineffective parliament that dissolved the government three times, Daud launched a bloodless coup against his cousin, Zahir Shah. He justified it in part by claiming that Zahir's government had neglected Pashtunistan to improve relations with the United States and Pakistan.

Zahir's government was accused of not responding forcefully to the firing of the National Awami Party provincial governments in NWFP and Baluchistan by Pakistani Premier Zulfiqar Ali Bhutto in 1973. These governments were composed mainly of Pashtun and Baluch nationalists. After the dismissals, Nawab Bugti was appointed governor of Baluchistan. Eventually he became the political leader of the 2005–06 Baluch insurgency and was killed by the Pakistan military on August 26, 2006.

After the creation of Bangladesh in 1971, the Pashtun and Baluch nationalist movements along the western borders posed the most active secessionist threats to the remainder of Pakistan. Thus the 1972–77 government of Zulfiqar Ali Bhutto both cracked down on nationalists and sought to extend Pakistani state authority by bringing economic development to the border region and FATA. It built some roads and hospitals and a few factories.

This meager development effort, however, was not matched by any political reforms. On the contrary, Bhutto's administration strengthened the colonial system by incorporating the border regime into the 1973 constitution. Pakistan also started supporting Afghan Islamists who opposed Daud's secular ethnonationalism. The Islamists had publicly opposed the partition of Pakistan to create Bangladesh in 1971 and protested against foreign influence in Afghanistan by both the Soviet Union and the West.

The long history of each state offering sanctuary to the other's opponents has built bitterness and mistrust between the two neighbors. This intensified in the 1970s, when Kabul extended shelter to some 30,000 Marri Baluch tribesmen who had escaped a Pakistani military crackdown after the nationalist insurgency in Baluchistan. Islamabad then extended refuge and military training to Afghan Islamists such as Ahmed Shah Massoud and Gulbuddin Hikmatyar, who staged an abortive uprising with Pakistani support in 1975. Pakistan hosted the Afghan mujahidin in the 1980s, while Afghanistan's pro-Soviet regime provided safe haven to *al-Zulfiqar*, a militant offshoot of the Pakistan Peoples Party. Headed by Murtaza Bhutto, the group intended to destabilize Gen. Muhammad Zia-ul-Haq's military regime, which had overthrown and hanged Murtaza's father, Zulfiqar Ali Bhutto. The current claims and counterclaims of sheltering each other's opponents indicate that the same strategies may be continuing.

Globalization of the Conflict around the Borderlands

The final collapse of the Afghan Durrani ruling dynasty with the overthrow of President Daud by communist factions in April 1978 shattered cooperative relations in the borderlands, precipitating the rounds of war that continue. The Christmas Eve 1979 Soviet invasion was the first major step toward globalizing the conflict in the border region.

The Soviet invasion made Pakistan a frontline ally of the United States. The country's ruling military virtually had a free hand to shape the Afghan resistance based in the refugee camps along the Durand Line. Pakistan wanted to prevent the establishment of Afghan nationalist guerillas on its soil and thus refused to recognize parties and exiles associated with the old regime. It guided the supplies from the United States, Saudi Arabia, Western Europe, and China toward the Islamists, who were also generously funded by wealthy private donors in the Gulf. The regime of Gen. Muhammad Zia-ul-Haq promoted the jihad in neighboring Afghanistan as part of its overriding priority: using the "Islamization" of Pakistan to legitimize military rule. In the process it militarized and radicalized the border region.

From the funding of thousands of Islamic *madrassahs,* or seminaries, to the arming of domestic Islamist organizations, Pakistan experienced a major transformation. Pakistan engaged in the successive wars in and around Afghanistan—the Cold War struggle, the post–Cold War civil conflict, and the war on terror—as a way of dealing with its basic national security threat: India, a country with more than eight times its population and economic resources. India's elites, at least in Pakistani perceptions, do not fully accept the legitimacy of Pakistan's existence. Pakistan's support for Islamist parties (especially for the Islamic Party of Gulbuddin Hikmatyar) and then for the Taliban constituted attempts to impose on Afghanistan a government that would never allow an Indian presence on its territory, giving the Pakistani military a secure border and strategic depth. In other words, Pakistan sought to support a client regime in Afghanistan that was supposed to provide a space for the retreat and recuperation of the Pakistani military in case of a confrontation with India. This policy was a continuation under different conditions of the British policy of treating Afghanistan as part of the security buffer zone of South Asia.

After the Soviet withdrawal under the Geneva Accords of April 14, 1988, completed in February 1989, a U.S.-Soviet dialogue tried to prepare the ground for a transitional government to preside over elections. Had they been implemented, the Geneva Accords would have resulted in a weak Afghan government, still close to the Soviet Union but without a Soviet troop deployment. In effect, Afghanistan would have become a de facto buffer within the Soviet sphere of influence. The war continued, however, in the absence of great-power agreement over the political settlement in the borderlands, eventually resulting in state collapse in Afghanistan. The United States and Pakistan pursued an anti-Soviet "rollback" policy (equivalent to the British "forward policy") to wipe out Soviet influence in Afghanistan by continuing to aid and arm the anti-Soviet Afghan guerrillas, the mujahidin. During this period, when many Afghans considered the jihad ended with the departure of Soviet troops, the rollback policy increasingly relied on Salafi Arab fighters who joined the jihad for very different reasons than Afghans had.

Representative rule in Pakistan was restored following Zia-ul-Haq's death in an air crash in August 1988. The Pashtun nationalist political parties with seats in the Pakistani national and provincial legislatures moderated their demands, replacing the name Pashtunistan with "Pashtunkhwa," denoting a province for all Pashtuns living east of the Durand Line. Such a province would include NWFP, some districts of Baluchistan, and the tribal agencies. The change to superficially civilian government between 1988 and 1999 hardly affected Pakistan's Afghan policy, which remained in the hands of the military.

In October 1994, the Taliban, a previously unknown group of clerics from the puritanical Sunni Deobandi sect, initiated a military movement to overpower the mujahidin factions. The Taliban originated in Kandahar province of Afghanistan and the neighboring Baluchistan province of Pakistan. They showed to what extent the mass violence, migrations, and ideological mobilization of the past three decades had transformed the border region. They are a phenomenon of the borderland, a joint Afghan-Pakistan network and organization. Afghan refugees, their children, and their grandchildren have coped with and interpreted their experiences in the refugee camps, tribal territories, and urban slums of Pakistan through the lens of the Islamist education that Pakistan's military regime and its Saudi and U.S. patrons offered them alongside their classmates from Pakistan, including FATA.

The unmonitored border and the ungoverned frontier between the two countries provided the space in which Pakistan could use the resulting social networks for asymmetrical warfare that served its strategic purpose on the Afghan and Kashmiri fronts, while sheltering itself through nuclear deterrence from conventional reprisal. The instability of this arrangement twice has precipitated the threat of nuclear escalation, once over the 1999 Pakistani intrusion in Kargil, in Indian-occupied Kashmir, and then over the 2002 attack on the Indian parliament by a Pakistan-based terrorist group.[13]

Pakistan's attempt to stabilize Afghanistan and gain strategic depth through control by the Taliban constituted a reprise with variations on the theme of a forward policy composed by the British Empire. This policy was to place Afghanistan under a nonhostile regime, harsh enough to control opposition with some military and financial assistance, and guarantee that hostile forces (mainly India, but also Russia and Iran) would not gain a foothold in the adjacent territory. Under the British, however, the Afghan ruler was an autocrat who used Islam to strengthen the central state while bringing the clergy under control. Founded as a state for Indian Muslims and basing its power on an alliance of the military and the mosque, Pakistan used Afghan clerics. Their Islamic allegiances would ensure their cooperation against secular Hindu India, Pashtun nationalists, and tribal leaders on both sides of the Durand Line.

The Taliban captured Kabul in September 1996. They moved north of the capital in a failed offensive in May–June 1997 but captured most of the north and center of Afghanistan by August 1998, only a few days after the bombing of U.S. embassies in Kenya and Tanzania. These bombings revealed to high-level policymakers and the general public a new dimension of globalization of the Afghan conflict—the consolidation of Osama bin Laden's international network of anti-Western Islamist militants now known as al Qaeda.

In the 1980s thousands of Islamist radicals from the Arab world and a lesser number from Southeast Asia flocked to Pakistan to fight and assist the anti-Soviet jihad in Afghanistan. They established support networks in NWFP and bases along the Afghan side of the Durand Line in areas such as the Jaji district of Khost (the al-Masada or "lion's den" camp) and Khugiani district of Nangarhar (Tora Bora). The concept of al Qaeda formed in Peshawar, Pakistan, in the late 1980s. A decade later it had a somewhat formal organizational structure whose aims and objectives bin Laden and Zawahiri announced to the world from Khost, Afghanistan, in 1998.

Al Qaeda was founded in the borderlands, but none of its leaders was Pakistani or Afghan. The war in the borderlands produced the leaders and ideologues of modern global jihad such as bin Laden, Zawahiri, and the Palestinian scholar Abdullah Azzam, who was killed in Peshawar in November 1989. After the Soviet withdrawal in 1989, many Arabs remained, and a second wave of jihadis gathered in the borderlands. During the 1990s additional waves of Islamists from Chechnya, Central Asia, Chinese Turkistan, Southeast Asia, and Europe joined the Arabs to form a truly global conglomerate.

This globalization of the Afghan conflict also introduced structural changes to Pashtun society and politics on both sides of the Durand Line. The fragmented tribal nature of this polity provided fertile ground for ideological penetration. Pashtun nationalism was modernist and secular, associated with the royalist elite, tribal leaders, and intellectuals. The Islamic conservatives joined the nationalists to oppose foreign domination during British colonialism, but they opposed the adoption of Western or liberal social or political institutions or values. The radical Islamists who began to organize in the 1960s opposed liberal institutions with at least equal fervor, but they tried to Islamize rather than reject institutions or concepts such as the nation-state, political ideology, political party, revolution, and development.

Pashtuns are no more or less prone to extremism than members of any other ethnic group in the region, but intelligence agencies and radical movements have used their cross-border ties and strategic location to spread extremism. The war in Afghanistan provided Pakistan with a golden opportunity to act on its long-standing desire to weaken Pashtun nationalism. It actively supported pan-Islamism among the Afghan refugees while bankrolling Pakistani Islamist parties in the border region. This resulted in a newer brand of Pashtun Islamism, some of whose characteristics were manifested and reinforced during the Taliban's ascent to power in Afghanistan, where pan-Islamist solidarity surpassed tribalism and ethnic cohesion.

While decades of Pakistani investment in Pashtun Islamism turned it into a formidable political force and reduced the nationalist threat, it also created its own transborder ethnic realities, which are backfiring against its original sponsors, whose primary allegiance is to the state of Pakistan. The operational and strategic vision of a Pakistani nation-state directly clashes with the pan-Islamism of Talibanization, which demands a complete overhaul of the state and society in Pakistan, Afghanistan, and beyond. This new reality, however, corresponds to the goals of some in Pakistan who envisage a broader Islamist union of Pakistan, Afghanistan, and Central Asia.

During the early 1990s, Afghanistan became an international pariah as the United States walked away from the Cold War's last battleground. Successive U.S. administrations did not consider the collapse of Afghanistan as a threat to the United States or a global strategic issue. Not until the attacks of September 11, 2001, did they heed warnings that in the absence of legitimate order in the borderlands, a global terrorist opposition was consolidating its links and building its skills, using the human and physical capital they had supplied to these networks through Pakistan in pursuit of the Cold War strategic agenda.

The hurried negotiations between the United States and Pakistan immediately after 9/11 changed Pakistan's behavior, but not its interests. Pakistan first asked for a pause to allow it to install a "moderate Taliban" government in Afghanistan that would break with al Qaeda. When that failed, Pakistan demanded that the Northern Alliance, backed by Russia, Iran, and, most importantly, India, not be allowed to enter Kabul or form the government. The U.S. agreement to support UN efforts to dilute Northern Alliance control with remnants of Afghanistan's royal regime and some technocrats did little to mollify the generals in Islamabad. Nonetheless, to save its nuclear deterrent and military supply relationship with the United States, Islamabad acquiesced in reining in its use of asymmetrical warfare, while keeping the capacity in reserve.

The presence of the United States, the UN, and the International Security Assistance Force (ISAF, the UN-mandated, multinational force in Afghanistan, under NATO command since August 2003) initially acted as a deterrent to both overt external subversion and open warfare among the power-holders the United States had re-armed in the war to oust the Taliban. This deterrent created an opportunity to build an Afghan state that could be reintegrated into the regions it borders. Given the cross-border movements of capital, trade, population, arms, ideologies, and identities, however, it was no longer possible for Afghanistan to play the role of a buffer or insulator state separating South Asia, Central Asia, and the Gulf. Instead, Afghanistan would have to become what its government calls a "land bridge" linking these areas.

The prerequisite for the stabilization of Afghanistan under these conditions has been the formation of an Afghan state with sufficient resources and legitimacy to control and develop its territory while posing no threat to any of its neighbors, especially Pakistan. Its deep interpenetration of Afghan society and politics enables Pakistan to play the role of spoiler whenever it chooses. For the United States, such a project would have required additional troops, whether from the coalition or ISAF, especially in border provinces; rapid investment in the infrastructure and development of the country; and an active program of diplomacy and regional cooperation. The Bush administration's opposition to U.S. investment in "nation-building," which it did not relax until 2003, led to delays in all such projects. Nor did the United States or others address the long-standing conflicts over the frontier.

In this context, especially given the new U.S. doctrine of preventive war, Pakistan and other neighbors of Afghanistan see the consolidation of a state dependent on the United States as a long-term threat. Pakistan sees the United States increasingly favoring India, particularly in the area of nuclear cooperation, and faces an Afghan government whose rhetoric has become more confrontational. As a result, Pakistan sees no strategic advantage in eliminating the Taliban, who have established themselves in parts of southwestern and southeastern Afghanistan, control parts of FATA, and have their main headquarters and support networks in Baluchistan. The ability of this Pakistan-based group to destabilize Afghanistan sends a message that Islamabad, not Delhi or Kabul, is the key to stability in the region.

These transborder political and military networks are reinforced by the economic components of "network war," which relies on transnational links of communications, funding, recruitment, and armament, rather than a territorial base. Trafficking in drugs, arms, and other items, including people, is an important element of network war, and smuggling is the classic livelihood of the borderlands; both of the major frontier ethnic groups —Pashtuns and Baluch—gain much of their income from it. The borderlands already have become a land bridge for the criminal (drugs) and criminalized (transit trade) economies of the region. The transnational economic actors exploit the weakness and illegitimacy of statehood in the region to pursue profit, part of which pays for protection provided by transnational and parallel military and political forces. The fight to protect these transnational economic activities is increasingly inseparable from the armed conflicts around the borderlands.

The Anomaly of FATA

With an area of 27,000 square kilometers, slightly larger than Luxembourg, and a 600-kilometer border with Afghanistan, FATA is the real administrative, political, and economic anomaly in the border region. FATA is divided into seven agencies, or administrative units, which from north to south are Bajaur, Momand, Khyber, Orakzai, Kurram, and North and South Waziristan. A few more frontier regions adjacent to the settled districts of Peshawar, Kohat, Dera Ismail Khan, Bannu, and Tank are also part of FATA. The area had a population of some 3.1 million people at the time of the 1998 census, and current unofficial estimates range up to 7 million, mostly ethnic Pashtuns whose tribes straddle the Durand Line.[14]

Pakistan's 1973 constitution gives the president executive authority over the region. But he does not exercise this authority in Islamabad, where the people of FATA have representatives in the national assembly. The area is largely ruled from Peshawar, where the governor of NWFP, a presidential appointee, exercises enormous authority with no legislative check. The provincial government controls all the agencies that deliver services such as health care, education, support for agriculture, and communications in the tribal areas, but the people of FATA have no representation in the NWFP provincial assembly to which the government is accountable.

The real authority in a tribal agency is the political agent. He combines legislative, law enforcement, and economic management functions. Apart from being the top civilian official in the territory, the political agent is the judge, jury, police chief, jail warden, district magistrate, and public prosecutor. He collects and disburses revenue with virtually no accountability. He also oversees all development schemes and public service departments.

The political agent governs through the Frontier Crimes Regulations (FCR). For more than a century these regulations have been used as a whip to control the border tribes. Under them a political agent may impose an economic blockade or siege of "hostile" or "unfriendly " tribes or inflict fines on whole communities where certain "crimes" have been committed. He can prohibit the construction of houses and raze houses of tribal members as punishment for not meeting the agent's demands. Some of the harshest clauses establish collective responsibility, under which an entire tribe can be held responsible for crimes committed by a single member or occurring anywhere within that tribe's territory. The law empowers the political agent to deliver multiyear jail sentences without due process or right of appeal to any superior court. The political agent also can appoint and refer civil and criminal cases to a hand-picked jirga, or tribal council. During the 2003–06 crises in Waziristan, political agents invoked all of these clauses.

The administration also manipulates local politics through its exploitation of the *lungi* or *malaki* system of appointed tribal leadership. Hand-picked tribal leaders are showered with government allowances and other economic incentives in return for loyalty. Every tribal administrator controls millions of dollars in secret funds to buy loyalty, leading to widespread corruption in the administration.

The British and their Pakistani successors have claimed that the FCR are rooted in tribal customs and traditions, but they contradict the egalitarian Pashtun ethos. The regulations also contradict the Pakistani constitution, which guarantees fundamental rights for all its citizens, and respect for international human rights conventions. The administrative arrangements of FATA deprive tribal members of political participation and economic development. All political parties, aid agencies, and civil society organizations are banned from working in the tribal areas, although radical extremist clerics are free to preach and campaign. Such clerics consequently won most of the elections held on a nonparty basis after adult franchise was introduced in 1996.[15]

The economic situation in the borderlands is equally dire. The wars in and over Afghanistan during the past three decades have transformed the economy of these tribal territories from one based on subsistence agriculture and nomadic pastoralism to dependence on the unregulated, cross-border trade of goods, including contraband such as drugs and arms. The area depends on smuggling routes that exploit the Afghan Transit Trade Agreement, under which goods may be imported duty-free into Pakistan for re-export to Afghanistan; many are illegally re-exported to or simply sold in Pakistan. In 2001 the World Bank estimated the value of such trade, as well as other transit trade through Afghanistan, at nearly $1 billion per year.[16]

The deployment of military forces along Pakistan's western border, however, has threatened this cross-border trade. Pakistan and Afghanistan have set some of their respective tariff levels at par, eliminating most of the profit for smugglers. As both countries approach admission to the World Trade Organization, the cross-border trade may dry up. The unavailability of alternative livelihoods for FATA is likely to add a new dimension of economic resistance to the struggles in the region, as does the lack of alternative livelihoods for opium poppy farmers and opiate traders in Afghanistan.

Human development indicators in FATA are no better than in neighboring Afghanistan. Poverty levels are as high as 60 percent, twice those in the rest of Pakistan.[17] Official statistics estimate the literacy rate in the tribal territories at 17.4 percent: 29.5 percent for men and less than 3 percent for women. The primary school enrollment rate is 68 percent for boys and 19 percent for girls. Only 102 colleges (equivalent to Western high schools) exist in the tribal areas, and only two or three of them are for women. On the other hand, madrassahs have mushroomed, and today up to 300 operate in the region. Only 524 medical doctors practice in FATA, one for every 6,307 people, and there is no healthcare infrastructure in some remote regions. Only two or three hospitals in all of FATA have rudimentary facilities for complex surgical procedures.[18]

With 2.4 percent of the national population, FATA receives only about 1 percent of the national budget. The per capita development allocation is one-third of the national average. No aid agencies or NGOs can work in the tribal belt, while in the other regions of the country they run substantial development projects. The per capita income in FATA is half that of Pakistan's national average. The region had the country's highest emigration ratio even before the advent of Islamist militancy, which, along with army offensives, has further displaced tens of thousands of people. The unemployment rate is 60 to 80 percent, or even close to 100 percent seasonally, if remittances and migrant labor are not counted.[19]

Toward a Border Settlement

Pakistan enunciated its position on the border in 1947:

> [The] Durand Line delineated in the 1893 treaty is a valid international boundary subsequently recognized and confirmed by Afghanistan on several occasions. The drawing of this international border terminated any Afghan sovereignty over the territory or influence over the people east of [the] Durand Line. Pakistan as a successor state to British India derived full sovereignty over this region and its people and has all the rights and obligation of a successor state. In addition, the question of self-determination for Pashtuns was foreclosed by the British supervised plebiscite held in 1947 in NWFP in which 99 percent of votes cast were in favor of joining Pakistan.The Tribal Areas too expressed their assent through special Jirgas.[20]

No Afghan government has accepted these claims. Despite Afghanistan's formal position, however, no government has made any serious effort to advance territorial claims either bilaterally or in international forums. Instead, its governments have used these claims as bargaining chips or to address domestic political concerns.[21]

In practice, Pakistan has done more than Afghanistan to undermine the status of the Durand Line as an international border. Successive governments in Islamabad have exploited the porosity of the threefold frontier to use covert asymmetrical warfare as a tool of national security policy. While the Pakistani military's deliberate fashioning of the Afghan resistance on an Islamist model gave Pakistan strategic depth and neutralized Afghan nationalism, it also relied on transnational networks that ignored the Durand Line as consistently as any border tribe. Pakistan is now paying the price for this policy by losing control of much of the frontier area to groups it has supported, groups that exploit their ties in Afghanistan just as the Taliban exploit their ties in Pakistan.

The Pakistan military's relationship with cross-border Islamist groups also affected the domestic situation in Pakistan. It strengthened and spread beyond an alliance vis-à-vis Afghanistan and Kashmir to cooperation in domestic politics, including elections. In the words of Husain Haqqani, Pakistani author and former adviser to the country 's government, "[The] Islamists staunchly adopted the Pakistani state's national security agenda and, in return, increasing number of officers accepted the Islamist view of a more religious state".[22] Increasingly, however, Islamist transnational goals have triumphed over the state's strategic objectives, as the Islamists have established a strategic presence in Pakistani state institutions, military, civil society, and campuses.

Since 9/11, a clear tension has developed between these visions. Pakistan's stated position as a frontline ally in the "war on terrorism" has led to tensions within the Islamist-military alliance over arresting al Qaeda leaders, cooperating with the United States, and cracking down on the Taliban and local militants. Islamist militancy, however, remains Pakistan's most successful strategic weapon against Indian regional hegemony, including its penetration into Afghanistan. However, by providing $650 million in economic and military assistance to the Karzai government, India is consolidating its position in Afghanistan. The semi-military Indian Border Roads Organization is building a major highway on the Pakistan border in the southwestern province of Nimruz, bordering on Baluchistan.

Pakistan is increasingly wary of this growing Indian influence and also accuses Indian consulates in the border cities of Jalalabad and Kandahar of fueling the Baluch nationalist insurgency. Pakistan sees the Indian presence as a major strategic defeat and a loss of years of investments that established an Islamist regime that kept all things Indian away from Pakistan's western borders.

Pakistani Pashtun nationalists, now organized in two major political parties, the Awami National Party and the Pashtunkhwa Milli Awami Party, view their relations with the Pakistani state and Afghanistan differently than do Pakistan's civil and military establishment and the Islamist political parties. Since 1947, the Pashtuns have been integrated to varying degrees into Pakistan's economy and state institutions such as the army and bureaucracy, weakening separatist sentiments. They have relied mostly on parliamentary politics to demand democratization, provincial autonomy, and friendly relations with Afghanistan.

Although it still lacks internal communications, the remote border region has been linked more closely to the rest of Pakistan through the extension of roads and communication networks. The lack of economic development in the borderlands has motivated Pashtuns to use this transport infrastructure to migrate for employment to Punjab and Sindh, particularly the southern seaport city of Karachi, which after Peshawar contains the largest urban concentration of Pashtuns—some 12 percent of its estimated population of 12 million.

Pashtun nationalists now propose restructuring the Pakistani state to unite all Pashtun regions in FATA, NWFP, and northern Baluchistan into a new province of Pashtunkhwa. This new province would form part of a revitalized federal structure in which provinces would enjoy enhanced powers within a genuinely democratic Pakistan. Once such restructuring occurred, the Awami National Party would support the recognition of the Durand Line as an international border between Pakistan and Afghanistan and encourage Afghanistan to move in that direction. As long as Pashtun nationalists conclude that Pakistan is still essentially a centralized military dictatorship, however, they say they will maintain their present position.

In the interim, Pashtun nationalists are calling for fast-paced economic development and reforms in FATA. They maintain that the border between Pakistan and Afghanistan can be pacified only if Pashtuns in both countries have unhindered, cross-border movement through formal recognition of open borders. As Pashtuns dominate regional trade and transport, regional peace and open borders will bring major improvements to the economy of the borderlands.[23]

Unlike the Pashtuns, the Baluch are divided among three states: Pakistan, Afghanistan, and Iran. The Baluch nationalists hold that the colonial boundaries weakened them economically and culturally, resulting in their impoverished life as minorities in all three states. They have viewed Afghanistan in a relatively favorable light, however, because Afghanistan's demand for Pashtunistan led Kabul to extend moral and material support to the Baluch nationalists as well.

As the fifth Baluch nationalist insurgency rages and expands into a nationwide political crisis with the killing of Bugti, many members of the ethnic group feel marginalized in the Pakistani state. With a population of nearly 5 million, Baluch nationalists feel extremely vulnerable to demographic extinction if mega-development projects such as Gwadar port are implemented in their province without guarantees of provincial autonomy within a federal Pakistan. Thus the Durand Line is not the foremost concern of the Baluch. But like Pashtun nationalists, they demand federal arrangements in Pakistan with enhanced provincial autonomy as a precursor to the settlement of the border and abandonment of secessionism. In contrast to Pashtun nationalists, the Baluch have used military means to protest and bargain politically with Islamabad.[24]

Afghanistan's current government has not issued a formal policy on the Durand Line. In April 2006, however, Afghanistan's minister for border and tribal affairs, Abdul Karim Brahui, told the lower house of the Afghan parliament that Afghanistan does not recognize the Durand Line as an international border. Brahui, a member of a small ethnic group closely linked to the Baluch, stated that his government does not have the mandate to negotiate this old dispute. Only a loya jirga could settle the issue permanently, he claimed, just as a loya jirga first ratified Afghanistan's policies on the post-partition frontier.

Since 2002, Kabul has feared a regrouping of the Taliban and al Qaeda in the border region. Although the Pakistani military buildup in the tribal areas is ostensibly to support the U.S.-led coalition's effort to eliminate the Taliban and al Qaeda, Kabul has charged that these forces have occupied territory on the

Afghan side of the Durand Line. It suspects that the deployment might provide a platform for further interference. Such fears, coupled with uncertainty over western commitment, have pushed Karzai to align with India, seen as a more dependable, long-term, regional ally.

As post-Taliban Afghanistan has grappled with a plethora of domestic issues, Pashtunistan and the border region have not figured prominently in the national political discourse. Although some Pashtun publications play up the issue from time to time, the Afghan Mellat political party and other Pashtun nationalists are concentrating on domestic issues. Some non-Pashtun intellectuals and political activists, on the other hand, advocate agreement on a final border settlement in return for access to the sea and assurances of noninterference from Pakistan. Some argued for the inclusion of such an agreement in the 2004 constitution.[25]

Afghan politicians of all ethnic groups, including nationalists, Islamists, and former communists, oppose reviving the conflict and heightening tensions with Pakistan. This is an issue of such political sensitivity that every Afghan leader we interviewed on the subject reemphasized that all comments were off the record before proceeding. Many call for confidence-building measures, such as open borders, enhanced bilateral trade, and more people-to-people contact, including direct interaction between the two countries ' parliaments. Some argue that the time is ripe to seek a settlement. "If we cannot solve this now, with the support of the entire international community, we will never resolve it," said a leader of the parliamentary opposition.

Paktia Governor Hakim Taniwal, assassinated September 10 by a suicide bomber, noted how much this dispute had cost Afghanistan: "The reason that Afghanistan adopted friendship with the Soviets was for Pashtunistan . . . and the result was, we did not gain Pashtunistan, but we almost lost Afghanistan. It would be good if we recognized the Durand Line—good for FATA, NWFP, Pakistan-Afghanistan relations. But we have to get something in return, such as a corridor to Karachi or Gwadar."

Others echo the traditional view that Pakistan, an "artificial state," is destined to dissolve, and that Afghanistan should not make any concessions while it is weak. Local leaders are discussing the issue as well. At a meeting of elders from eastern Afghanistan, one volunteered that this unresolved issue gave the neighbors an opportunity to meddle in internal Afghan affairs. Just as Afghanistan no longer claimed territory it once ruled in today's Iran or Uzbekistan, "we should accept this border as a border." This proposal, however, prompted loud protests from others, who insisted that the Durand Line Treaty under which Afghanistan ceded control of the areas across the Durand Line, expired after 100 years (in 1993), and Pakistan was obligated to return the territory. Among the leaders we interviewed, the myth of the expiration of the Durand Line Treaty was almost universally accepted.[26]

Given the political sensitivity of the issue and opposition to Pakistan's Afghan policy, which people across all factions and ethnic groups see as a major threat to Afghanistan, no major leader has publicly supported rapid settlement of the border issue. Although the Karzai government has not aggressively raised the Pashtunistan issue, it has begun to follow the path of previous Afghan governments in using border issues and Pashtun cross-border ethnic solidarity as political tools. It has revived relations with Pashtun nationalists in Pakistan and fallen back on Afghan nationalism to wage a war of words with the neighbor.

Recommendations and Conclusion

Afghanistan, Pakistan, and the neighboring regions would all benefit from a recognized open border between the two countries. Such a border would clarify that all Pashtuns have rights as citizens of one or another state and would enable them to communicate, trade, and develop both their economy and their culture in cooperation with one another. Such a settlement would strengthen democracy in both states and facilitate both Pakistan's access to Central Asia and Afghanistan's access to the sea. It would lessen domestic ethnic tensions and strengthen national unity in both states. It would, however, require difficult internal changes in both countries, a reversal of the hostility that has predominated in relations between the two governments for sixty years, and credible international guarantees.

A major challenge to such objectives is the Islamist insurgency on both sides of the border. In 2005 Musharraf responded to charges that the Taliban were engaging in cross-border activity by proposing to fence and mine the Durand Line, a solution reminiscent of the policies of Israel and Uzbekistan. As in Central Asia and the Middle East, such a solution will not work for many reasons. International political and military officials in Afghanistan, as well as counterinsurgency experts, agree that the key to strategic success is disrupting the Taliban's command and control, mainly in Quetta and Waziristan, not wasting resources on the impossible task of blocking infiltration by easily replaceable foot soldiers across snow-capped mountains and trackless deserts.[27] Fencing would further isolate the border region and create an additional obstacle to its economic development.

Crafting a twenty-first-century border settlement will require ending the nineteenth-century regime in FATA. Since 9/11, Pakistan has ended FATA's autonomy by deploying 80,000 troops in the mountainous region, but these operations have not been matched by political and economic reforms. Stabilizing the border region must include the political integration of FATA into Pakistan. Almost all Pakistani political parties have urged reform packages. The extension to FATA of the Political Parties Act of 2002 would allow mainstream political parties to organize there and counter extremist propaganda. These parties would provide an opportunity for tribal members to campaign for their rights in national institutions.

The Awami National Party, one of the most vocal proponents of reforms in FATA, wants to overhaul the administrative and judicial system. It supports tribal representation in the legislature of an NWFP that would include FATA. The Awami National Party emphasizes the fact that in the 1960s and early 1970s FATA was represented in the provincial assembly of a united West Pakistan. Over the past decades, many tribal members have acquired farmland and businesses in the settled areas. They also obtain health care and education in NWFP's urban centers.[28]

The Frontier Crimes Regulations have remained virtually unchanged since Lord Curzon promulgated their final version in 1901. Today human rights advocates and tribal intellectuals call for an overhaul of the law. They demand

- Conformity of the law to contemporary human rights standards;
- Transfer to parliament of all legislative and administrative powers over FATA now resting with the president;
- Extension of the jurisdiction of higher Pakistani courts to FATA and separation of the region's judiciary from the executive;
- Abolition of collective punishment and territorial responsibility;
- Extension of political and civic freedoms to FATA; and
- Implementation of a comprehensive disarmament and demobilization program in the region.[29]

No reform program would be successful without a complementary strategy for economic development. It is crucial to reinforce reconstruction in Afghanistan with a compatible model across the border in FATA. The Awami National Party has asked for a detailed baseline survey by the World Bank or another international agency to assess the economic situation and help Pakistan and the people of FATA devise a comprehensive strategy. Linking FATA to Afghan reconstruction and creating special opportunity zones along the Durand Line will be first steps in this direction. Work is under way to establish such zones on the Afghan side. In May 2006 Musharraf hinted at establishing them with the help of the U.S. government. Such development would also open U.S. markets to products produced in FATA.[30]

FATA's isolation can be broken only by improving its infrastructure. A major highway spanning FATA, from Bajaur in the north to Waziristan and Zhob in the south, is needed to encourage contact. Pakistan's bilateral trade with Afghanistan now surpasses $2 billion a year (with Pakistani exports to Afghanistan totaling $1.2 billion, and Afghanistan's exports to Pakistan totaling $700 million).[31] But so far there are only two official border crossings, Torkham in the north and Chaman in the south. At least a dozen more border crossings could be opened to facilitate trade.

More than seventy FM radio stations broadcast illegally in FATA, often inciting sectarian violence and hatred, but the region has not joined the telecommunication revolution in the rest of Pakistan. The area needs mobile telephony and Internet access. Trade and commerce also should be modernized by establishing tribal chambers of commerce and accounting and financial information systems. Since most of the land in the region is communal, there is a need for a baseline study of land rights and a strategy for reform. To accomplish this, the government should extend the municipal laws of land settlement to FATA. Proper utilization of several known mineral deposits in FATA will result in the growth of labor-intensive mining and manufacturing industries in marble and precious stones. Agriculture in general, and fruit in particular, can be made profitable by introducing new techniques to tribal farmers and helping them gain access to markets.[32]

Such a transformation requires complementary measures by Afghanistan, the United States, the UN, and NATO. The persistence of a safe haven for the Taliban insurgency in Pakistan threatens the objectives of the international community in Afghanistan. Success in Afghanistan is fundamental to the U.S. "war on terror," the UN's credibility, and NATO's viability. Forces whose command and control and networks of recruitment, funding, training, and equipment are located in Pakistan are killing Afghan, American, British, and Canadian troops and civilians. The United States, the UN, and NATO must agree quickly to send a message to Islamabad that the persistence of Taliban havens in Pakistan is, in the words of the UN Charter, a threat to international peace and security that Pakistan must address immediately.

The United States, UN, and NATO also must agree on sending a message to Afghanistan and India that they must do all in their power to encourage Pakistan to make such difficult decisions by addressing sources of Pakistani insecurity, including issues related to the border region and Kashmir. The international community must offer generous aid and support to Pakistan if it undertakes needed reforms in the governance of FATA and creates a development area along the border in coordination with the reconstruction effort in Afghanistan.

The United States should use its influence to impress on Pakistan the gravity of the risks it is taking by not disrupting the Taliban command and to persuade all governments in the region to lower the tone of confrontation. Only the United States is likely to be able to persuade Pakistan and Afghanistan to keep India out of their bilateral relationship by agreeing to a set of ground rules and to press India to abide by them. India's contribution to Afghanistan is welcome and mostly constructive, but it should reduce its staff and activities in the border regions for the sake of regional stability. The size of the Indian consulates should be limited and their roles strictly defined.

U.S. diplomacy prevented nuclear confrontations between India and Pakistan in 1999 and 2002 and helped these arch-rivals begin talking. It also should facilitate a political process between Pakistan and Afghanistan. The United States helped set up the tripartite commission composed of senior Afghan, Pakistani, and U.S. military officials in 2003; it now includes NATO but still deals only with military coordination. Until now, Pakistan has delayed responding to a proposal to expand the consultations to the political level. As part of their joint initiative, the United States and NATO need to press Pakistan for a positive response.

Afghanistan has more international backing and support than ever. A growing segment of opinion privately holds that now is the time to address these issues; but only leadership can encourage those harboring such ideas to propose them in public. The Karzai administration should take advantage of this situation to begin a national dialogue to develop a consensus on resolving the conflicts with Pakistan that have caused so much damage to both countries. Afghanistan needs to show good will to Pakistan regarding the border issue and make a historic compromise.

Both countries should facilitate and encourage people-to-people contact as well as contact between officials at all levels across the border. If the wars in Afghanistan had any positive impact it was to expose Afghans to the outside world. Nearly half of today's Afghan population has visited Pakistan at some point, making it the country that Afghans are most familiar with outside their homeland. About 60,000 Pakistanis currently work in Afghanistan, and 10,000 of them cross the border daily. Pakistan's exports to Afghanistan grew from $221 million in 2001 to $1.2 billion in 2006, but the economy in the border region faces a sharp decline. Despite the intimate contact of the two peoples, however, the governments remain isolated from each other. The governors and chief ministers of NWFP and Baluchistan should meet with counterparts in the Afghan border provinces regularly, as should police chiefs, customs officers, and other officials.

In 2006, no secessionist nationalist movement operates among the Pashtuns in Pakistan, and Afghanistan has not revived its irredentist claims. Tribes on both sides of the border are clamoring for development. Economic pressures have forced Pashtuns to migrate to Karachi and the Gulf region in huge numbers. Only policy changes in both Kabul and Islamabad can involve their Pashtun populations in mutual confidence building, which could lead to an amicable resolution of the border issue.

Three contending visions of relations between Pakistan and Afghanistan emerged in spring 2006. One was the launch of the friendship bus service between the eastern Afghan city of Jalalabad and the western Pakistani city of Peshawar. People in both countries celebrated the occasion and greeted the arriving delegations by showering them with rose petals, playing music, and dancing in joy.[33] Another vision of cross-border relations was expressed in the rather implausible proposal of fencing the Durand Line.[34] A third and worrying trend is Talibanization and escalating violence in the areas around the Durand Line. People in both countries have chosen the peaceful alternative; now their governments and leaders should follow suit.

Sources

Bangash, Mumtaz A. *Political and Administrative Development of Tribal Areas, A Focus on Khyber and Kurram,* unpublished Ph.D dissertation, University of Peshawar, 1996.

Benjamin, Daniel, and Steven Simon. *The Age of Sacred Terror.* New York: Random House, 2003.

Dupree, Louis. *Afghanistan.* Princeton: Princeton University Press 1980.

Kakar, Hassan. "Afghanistan; a Political and Diplomatic History, 1863–1901," unpublished manuscript.

Magnus, Ralph, and Eden Naby. *Afghanistan Mullah, Marx and Mujahid.* Boulder: Westview Press, 1998.

Roy, Olivier. *Islam and Resistance in Afghanistan.* Cambridge: Cambridge University Press, 1986.

Rubin, Barnett R. *The Fragmentation of Afghanistan: State Formation and Collapse in the International System.* New Haven: Yale University Press, 2002.

Notes

1. Reuters. "Pakistan opposition barred from US air-strike village," January 23, 2006.

2. Khan, Gulzar Ahmed. "Bajaur raid killed five foreigners: Musharraf," *Dawn*, February 12, 2006.

3. Synovitz, Ron. "Afghanistan: Are militants copying Iraqi insurgents' suicide tactics?" Radio Free Europe/Radio Liberty. www.rferl.org/featuresarticle/2006/01/71de933c-eb38-4c16-a7aa-a42f46a74250.html.

4. Qureshi, Ahmad, and Ihsan Sarwaryar. "Suicide attack at Herat PRT kills two, injures nine," Pajhwok Afghan News, April 8, 2006. www.pajhwak.com/viewstory.asp?lng=eng&id=16242.

5. Karzai, Hekmat, and Seth Jones. "How to curb suicide terrorism in Afghanistan," *Christian Science Monitor*, July 18, 2006.

6. *Economist.* "The other Taliban," March 16, 2006.

7. Hussain, Zahid. "Terror in Miran Shah," *Newsline Magazine*, April 2006.

8. ABC News. "Senior al-Qaida Operative Struck by Predator Missile," May 13, 2005; Peters, Gretchen. "Violence grows in Pakistan's tribal zone, despite Army presence," *Christian Science Monitor*, December 12, 2005.

9. Gall, Carlotta, and Muhammad Khan. "Qaida bomber is reported killed," *New York Times*, April 13, 2006.

10. *Dawn*. "Wanted Al-Qaida militant killed," April 21, 2006.

11. Hussain, Zahid. "Musharraf's Other War," *Newsline Magazine* (Karachi), January 2006.

12. Trives, Sebastien. "Afghanistan: Tackling the insurgency, the case of the Southeast," *Politique étrangère*, January 2006.

13. Coll, Steve. "The stand-off," *The New Yorker*, February 13, 2006.

14. Siddique, Abubakar, and Iqbal Khattak. "War on terror highlights development needs in FATA," *The Friday Times* (Lahore), January 23, 2004.

15. Human Rights Commission of Pakistan. "FCR—a bad law nobody can defend," 2005.

16. World Bank. "Afghanistan's international trade relations with neighboring countries." http://lnweb18.worldbank.org/SAR/sa.nsf/Attachments/8/$File/intltrade.pdf.

17. *Dawn*. "Development backlog in FATA," November 22, 2005.

18. Siddque and Khattak, 2004.

19. Awami National Party. "Federally Administered Tribal Area, A Development Framework," unpublished paper, April 2006.

20. Embree, Ainslie, ed. *Pakistan's Western Borderlands, the Transformation of a Political Order.* Karachi: Royal Book Company, 1979.

21. Interviews with experts and politicians in Islamabad in March–April 2004 and an undated, internal Pakistan Foreign Office document shared by a Foreign Office spokesperson.

22. Haqqani, Husain. *Pakistan between Mosque and Military.* Washington, D.C.: Carnegie Endowment for International Peace, 2005, page 197.

23. Interviews with Pashtun politicians in Islamabad and Peshawar, March–April 2004 and July–August 2006.

24. Interviews with Baluch nationalist parliamentarians in Islamabad, March 2004.

25. Abdul Hafiz Mansur, "*Nazari piramun-i Qanun-i Asasi*" (a look at the constitution), Kabul, December 2003, lists as its first point that "the lack of defined borders on the south and southeast frontiers of Afghanistan has created all kinds of security and other problems, and the constitution should recognize these borders."

26. Interviews in Kabul, Gardez, and Peshawar, March–April 2004 and August 2006.

27. Interviews in Kabul, July–August 2006.

28. Awami National Party, 2006.

29. Human Rights Commission of Pakistan, 2005.

30. Raza, Shahzad. "Civil, military man to be political agents," *Daily Times* (Lahore), May 10, 2006.

31. These figures do not include the Afghan transit trade.

32. Awami National Party, 2006.

33. Agence France-Presse. "First Pakistan-Afghanistan bus service runs," March 15, 2006.

34. Pajhwok Afghan News. "Islamabad's border-fencing idea irks Pashtun leaders," March 8, 2006.

7

Pakistan, the United States, and the Endgame in Afghanistan
Perceptions of Pakistan's Foreign Policy Elite

Moeed Yusuf, Huma Yusuf, and Salman Zaidi

I*n a report produced by the Jinnah Institute and USIP, Yusuf, Yusuf, and Zaidi, writing in 2011, look at the views of Pakistan's foreign policy elite regarding the Pakistani state's outlook toward an Afghanistan in transition from U.S. dependence, under the premise that Pakistan's role is "central" to stability in Afghanistan. To explore that role, the Jinnah Institute and USIP convened several roundtable discussions in Pakistan of retired civilian and military officials, analysts, journalists, and civil society activists to express their views of the complicated relationships among Afghanistan, Pakistan, and the United States. The discussions revealed that much of the "mistrust" found in the research on peace through reconciliation with nonstate actors exists at the state level as well.*

Pakistani elites generally had "very little faith in U.S. intentions" and expressed worry about a long-term U.S. antiterrorism presence on Pakistan's border. They criticized the U.S. counterinsurgency strategy as ineffective and worried that the United States would push the Pakistani military to "do more" against Afghan Taliban who had found safe haven in the Pakistani tribal areas, as well as other anti-Pakistan militant groups. The elites opined that the Pakistani state favored a clear process of reconciliation, arguing that the longer the United States pursued its counterinsurgency operations without a clear path toward a political process, the more difficult it would be for Pakistan to maintain its own internal security balance. Regarding stability in Kabul, the Afghan Taliban would most likely secure Pakistani interests in Afghanistan (which included limiting India's presence to development activities), and this regrettable state of affairs was the result of decades of myopic Pakistani policies.

Originally published as Moeed Yusuf, Huma Yusuf, and Salman Zaidi, "Pakistan, the United States, and the End Game in Afghanistan: Perceptions of Pakistan's Foreign Policy Elite," (Islamabad, Pakistan: Jinnah Institute, 2011).

In what the authors describe as a "dilemma," elites also recognized that, for all their criticism of U.S. dealings with Pakistan, a premature withdrawal would increase instability in Pakistan. Permeating the analysis is a sense of miscommunication between the United States and Pakistan despite "otherwise considerable overlap on the issue of reconciliation between the American and Pakistani positions." The American raid against Osama bin Laden occurred after the roundtables but before the report was published, and the roundtable participants' views were sought on the effects of the raid, which was generally seen to have increased doubts about the two countries' ability to collaborate in Afghanistan. The sense of distrust, if not outright hostility, worsened after the incident, which led to a wounding standoff over supplies to U.S. forces in Afghanistan and a nearly year-long stall in relations that has only recently begun to shift back toward cooperation and convergence. Despite decades of strategic partnership in the past and allegedly common interests in the present, the U.S.-Pakistan relationship remains highly sensitive to disruption. To the extent that much of this vulnerability is based on each side misreading the other's intentions, this chapter sheds light on Pakistan's views of its own interests.

Introduction

On June 22, 2011, U.S. President Barack Obama announced a withdrawal plan for U.S. troops deployed in Afghanistan. The plan marks a major step in the drawdown of the international security presence from Afghanistan, leading to the transfer of primary security responsibilities to the Afghan National Security Forces (ANSF). The December 2014 deadline for this transition, now accepted by the troop-contributing countries, increases the pressure on the international coalition and the Afghan government to find an amicable solution in Afghanistan in the interim.

While an internal consensus among Afghans is undoubtedly the most crucial element of any settlement, regional players also have an important role to play in facilitating progress towards durable peace in the so-called "endgame" in Afghanistan. Among the regional players, Pakistan's role stands out. It is often described as the most influential actor whose support will be pivotal in ensuring a peaceful Afghanistan. Despite its importance however, the evolving direction of Pakistan's Afghanistan policy is often not well understood in many of the world's important capitals. While there is somewhat greater clarity on past actions, Islamabad's outlook towards the Afghanistan endgame and policy preferences to that end remain a matter of intense debate. Too often, the Pakistani view on Afghanistan is taken as a monolith, with little attention being paid to the many competing narratives that affect official decisions directly or indirectly. Interestingly, even Pakistani foreign policy elite and policymakers do not always fully comprehend the multiplicity and range of opinion on key foreign policy issues within the country.

Given Pakistan's centrality to the Afghanistan equation and the need to ensure that Islamabad's policy complements that of other actors seeking viable peace in Afghanistan, a better understanding of how Pakistani foreign policy elite perceive the situation in Afghanistan is needed. For all those seeking to promote a durable peace settlement in Afghanistan, it is crucial to understand also how Pakistan's policy elite view Pakistan's interests and concerns during the endgame, what they consider realistic options in pursuit of these interests, and what areas of overlapping versus competing interests exist between Pakistan, the United States, Afghanistan, and other actors.

This report captures the findings of a project, convened by the United States Institute of Peace and the Jinnah Institute, Pakistan, aimed at better comprehending Pakistan's outlook (as perceived by the country's foreign policy community) towards the evolving situation in Afghanistan. The interplay of the Pakistan-U.S. relationship and the respective interests of the two countries in Afghanistan was also a key area of focus of the project.

Specifically, the project focused on four key themes:

(i) America's evolving strategy in Afghanistan;
(ii) Pakistan's short-term and long-term interests in Afghanistan, and how Pakistan *is* pursuing these interests;
(iii) In light of America's strategy and its implications for Afghanistan and the region, how *can* Pakistan best pursue its interests going forward; and
(iv) Policies that the United States, Afghanistan, India (and other regional actors) would have to pursue/accept for Pakistani objectives to be met.

To examine these themes, the project drew on the expertise of a wide spectrum of Pakistan's foreign policy elite—retired civilian and military officials, analysts, journalists, and civil society practitioners—with established expertise on Afghanistan and/or with knowledge of the modalities of policy making in the United States. These opinion makers attended roundtable discussions aimed at exploring the themes; a few were interviewed directly. Senior politicians representing the major political parties in the country were also interviewed during the project.

The project was conducted in the spring of 2011 and updated after Osama Bin Laden's killing on May 2. In total, 53 opinion makers and politicians participated in the project. They were selected in order to capture opinions from across the spectrum and to be able to present conclusions that were representative of the views prevalent among opinion makers in the country. Only participants with direct expertise—practical policymaking involvement, on-ground experience in Afghanistan, or an academic understanding of the issue at hand—were invited. While inevitably, a few influential opinion makers were unable to participate—we originally invited 70 individuals—the project team

Box 1. Methodology

The project proceeded in two phases. Pakistani foreign policy elite were brought together in off-the-record roundtable discussions in March 2011. Six roundtables, involving 39 individuals, were held; four were held in Islamabad, and one each in Lahore and Peshawar. Each roundtable was restricted to 6–10 individuals to keep the discussions interactive and manageable. The mix of experts for each roundtable was carefully selected to ensure some level of diversity (as we anticipated) of views. We directly interviewed four opinion makers who were invited but could not attend any of the roundtable discussions.

The second phase of the project entailed off-the-record, one-on-one interviews with seven politicians representing major political parties of Pakistan.[1] The interviews were meant to solicit perspectives of the political parties on the subject at hand. These were conducted between March and July 2011.

The project directors added an additional component to the project after Osama bin Laden's killing on May 2, 2011. Since all the roundtables and most of the interviews were conducted prior to the incident, we felt a need to solicit views of participants on the impact of this development on the Afghanistan calculus. We reached out to all roundtable participants via e-mail and requested answers to two questions:

(i) How do you think bin Laden's death will change the U.S. endgame in Afghanistan?
(ii) Will bin Laden's killing change Pakistan's strategy vis-à-vis Afghanistan?

We received responses from 17 of the 39 roundtable participants. Their views are reflected in the post-script to this report.

Methodological robustness was ensured through an innovative project design. All roundtables were conducted in quick succession to ensure that the policy environment and realities surrounding the issue remained constant.[2] Also, in order to confirm that the authors were able to capture the key themes discussed during the project and that the report was representative of the roundtable discussions, the project team requested four participants, chosen carefully to ensure a diversity of views among them to attend multiple sessions and subsequently review the report for errors. Between them, they attended all six roundtables.[3]

is not aware of previous undertakings on the subject which managed to summarize the views of such a diverse group of Pakistani foreign policy elite in a systematic manner.

The body of this report captures the essence of the viewpoints expressed and conclusions drawn during the roundtable discussions and interviews with the foreign policy elite. The findings from the interviews with representatives of the political parties are encapsulated separately in box 3 in the report. Responses to questions on the impact of Osama bin Laden's killing on the Afghanistan calculus are reported in the post-script to the report.

The authors of this report have refrained from conducting any independent analysis or additional research. The report is merely a reproduction of the key themes and findings that emerged from the discussions. As such, the report can be considered an objective rendering of a wide spectrum of informed Pakistani views on the conflict and possible endgame in Afghanistan.

To be sure, the authors make no claim that the elite perceptions reflected in the report are always factually accurate or objective; nor have the authors injected their own views on what this elite outlook means for the evolving situation in Afghanistan. The report simply lays out these perceptions as views that must be known and understood before informed, contextually grounded policies can be devised by stakeholders seeking Pakistan's cooperation in the Afghanistan endgame. The report is not a consensus document and does not represent the entire range of views on every issue. In fact, while every effort has been made to faithfully represent the content of the discussions, owing to the diversity of opinions expressed, the report cannot claim to have effectively articulated the opinions of all participants.

Section II of the report discusses elite perceptions of Pakistan's objectives in Afghanistan. Section III reflects participants' views on U.S. strategy in Afghanistan. This is followed by a discussion of how Pakistani opinion makers view their own country's policy towards Afghanistan. In section V, we outline participants' views on a regional framework for an Afghan settlement. Section VI lists what the policy elite highlighted as some of the key impediments to successful endgame negotiations. In section VII, we outline the main steps project participants believed the United States, Pakistan, Afghanistan, and other regional actors could take to contribute to peace in Afghanistan. This is followed by a post-script which focuses on elite perceptions of the impact of Osama Bin Laden's death on the Afghanistan equation.

Pakistan's Objectives in Afghanistan: The Ideal versus the Achievable

The Ideal

A distinction ought to be drawn between what Pakistan's foreign policy elite see as their country's long-term vision for relations with Afghanistan and what the Pakistani state will seek to achieve in the impending endgame.

Pakistani foreign policy elite are generally critical of their country's traditional, security-centric approach to Afghanistan. The security establishment, which has dominated the country's policy throughout, is seen as being overly concerned about an antagonistic Afghanistan. This fear has led it to interfere in sovereign Afghan affairs over the years. Especially since the Afghan resistance against Soviet occupation in the 1980s, there has been an urge to micromanage developments within Afghanistan in a bid to prop up pro-Pakistan governments in Kabul. The Pakistani military has persistently sought a friendly Afghanistan to avoid a 'two-front' situation which would entail a hostile India to the east and an antagonistic Afghanistan to the west.

Project participants contended that even as the Pakistani state reached out to seek amenable partners, it approached Afghanistan largely from an ethnic rather than a political or economic lens. Its policy has therefore focused virtually entirely on the Pashtun political factions in Afghanistan. For the longest period, the Pakistani state has believed in a strong feedback loop between Pakistani and Afghan Pashtuns; the state has been fearful of an ethno-nationalist Pashtun movement triggered by developments in Afghanistan that are unfavorable to the Pashtuns in Pakistan. The country's official policy towards Afghanistan has been influenced, in no small part, by this fear.

Pakistan's security-centric approach has caused the state to lose goodwill among Afghans even though the ethnic Pashtun ties at the people-to-people level have remained strong. Pakistani experts and political leaders we talked to were acutely aware of the fact that their country is widely reviled and mistrusted in Kabul while countries like India are viewed positively. Some policy elite however argued that the anti-Pakistan sentiment is confined to the northern, non-Pashtun parts of Afghanistan and that the international media has been unnecessarily hyper-sensitive to this concern.

Nevertheless, most project participants agreed that Pakistan's interference in Afghanistan's affairs over the past two decades has left many Afghans alienated and resentful of what they view as Islamabad's hegemonic tendencies. This troubles many, especially those who argue that Pakistan's geographical, ethnic, historical, and cultural links with Afghanistan gives it an inherent advantage in terms of ensuring interdependence between the two countries. A less overbearing approach, project participants felt, would have highlighted Pakistan's indispensability while retaining strong goodwill among Afghan citizens, both Pashtun and non-Pashtun. Support to Islamist forces in Afghanistan is especially criticized and is blamed for having accentuated Pakistan's problems of radicalization within its own society.

Most members of the policy elite included in our discussions held the view that Pakistan's long-term interests are best served by expanding the framework of the bilateral relationship with Afghanistan beyond security to include trade, energy, and reconstruction projects. Rather than seeking influence in Kabul through groups such as the Taliban alone, Pakistan ought to have pursued enhanced trade ties and joint investments for leverage. Indeed, the scope and strength of Pakistan's current economic and educational ties with Afghanistan is substantial and often underestimated. The Pakistan-Afghanistan bilateral trade increased from $169.9 million in 2000–01 to $1.24 billion in 2007–08 and further to approximately $1.75 billion at present.[4] However, much of these ties have developed without any holistic, visionary state policy to optimize benefits on Islamabad's part. Greater attention towards this aspect is seen as critical by

Pakistani policy elite; presently, the informal and societal links dwarf progress at the interstate level.

A reality check

Notwithstanding what the Pakistani foreign policy elite would have liked their state to achieve, or what they see as the preferred long-term vision, there is a fair bit of realism that the endgame in Afghanistan does not allow the luxury to chart an ideal course. It was largely agreed among project participants that achieving the above-recommended course would require no less than a wholesale transformation of Pakistan's traditional thinking vis-à-vis Afghanistan.

Between now and 2014, Islamabad's positioning in the Afghan reconciliation efforts will be dictated by the country's security establishment. And despite the criticism of a security-centric approach, there is a firm belief among the policy elite that Pakistan has strong interests and concerns in Afghanistan which the international community—read the United States—has often ignored over the past decade.

Pakistani policy elite believe that there has been a gradual evolution in the security establishment's thinking, hastened in recent years by the fast pace of change in the situation in Afghanistan. In terms of the endgame, Pakistani elite see their state as having defined two overriding objectives:

- The 'settlement' in Afghanistan should not lead to a negative spillover such that it contributes to further instability in Pakistan or causes resentment among Pakistani Pashtuns; and
- The government in Kabul should not be antagonistic to Pakistan and should not allow its territory to be used against Pakistani state interests.

Participants believed that translated into actionable policy, these umbrella objectives lead Pakistan to pursue the following outcomes in the endgame in Afghanistan:

(i) A degree of stability

There is broad recognition among the policy elite of the intrinsic link between stability (or lack thereof) in Afghanistan and Pakistan. A failure to evolve an amicable solution to the Afghan conundrum, and the resultant persistence of high levels of instability, will have numerous and predictable consequences for Pakistan: continuing unrest in the Federally Administered Tribal Areas (FATA); a surge in illegal border crossings leading to another Afghan refugee crisis; a surge in drug trafficking and weapons smuggling; an upswing in Pashtun nationalism seeking to support their Afghan brethren in a tussle against non-Pashtuns in Afghanistan; a reversal of the direction of the insurgency, whereby anti-Pakistan militants seek sanctuary in the large swaths of misgoverned spaces in Afghanistan; further strains in the India-Pakistan relationship as both continue to compete for presence in Afghanistan; and courtesy of this, continued dominance of Pakistan's security-centric approach towards Afghanistan. Pakistan's interests, project participants felt, are thus best served by a relatively stable government in Kabul that is not hostile towards Pakistan.

(ii) An inclusive government in Kabul
Pakistani foreign policy elite believe that only a truly inclusive government in Kabul can usher in an era of relatively efficient and stable governance in Afghanistan. Most participants defined this as a politically negotiated configuration with adequate Pashtun representation that is recognized by all ethnic and political stakeholders in Afghanistan. While far from a consensus, some opinion makers insisted that given the current situation, a sustainable arrangement would necessarily require the main Taliban factions—particularly Mullah Omar's "Quetta Shura"[5] Taliban and the Haqqani network—to be part of the new political arrangement. Specifically, a decentralized system of governance is more likely to be sustainable than an overly centralized one. Such an inclusive dispensation, it is believed, will view the relationship with Islamabad favorably and be sensitive to Pakistani concerns.

The desire to see an inclusive government in Afghanistan also signals Pakistani opposition to a return to Taliban rule in the country akin to the 1990s. Most participants agreed that the Pakistani security establishment and civilian leadership is no longer seeking to support a return to Taliban rule. The policy pursued in the second half of the 1990s which saw the Taliban as instruments of Pakistan's regional agenda received scathing criticism from policy elite across the opinion spectrum. Moreover, there is a realization that an Afghan Taliban[6] government would not be acceptable to the Afghan population or to the international community.

(iii) Limiting Indian presence to development activities
The implications of Indian activities in Afghanistan is a hotly debated issue and while a consensus was far from forthcoming, there was concern about Indian activities which could undermine Pakistan's security and stability. Most participants agreed that India, as the largest economy in the region, has a role to play in Afghanistan's economic progress and prosperity. There is also a fairly candid admission that the Pakistani security establishment exhibits paranoia when it comes to Indian activities in Afghanistan. However, many believe that the present Indian engagement goes beyond strictly development, and thus raises legitimate concerns in Pakistan. From Pakistan's perspective, this needs to be addressed as part of the endgame settlement in Afghanistan. As the Pakistani security establishment sees the dynamic, reluctance on the part of the Afghan government or the United States to address Pakistani mis-

givings increases the likelihood of a growing Indian footprint, and in turn, New Delhi's greater ability to manipulate the endgame negotiations and the post-settlement dispensation in Kabul.

Views on U.S. Strategy in Afghanistan

Perhaps the greatest convergence in Pakistani views is on the impression of U.S. policy towards Afghanistan. The policy to date is largely seen as unclear, inconsistent, and confused. It is also perceived to be counterproductive not only for Pakistan's interests, but also for durable peace in Afghanistan. The strongest criticism is targeted at the political component of U.S. policy, which is largely seen as subservient to the military surge. Hardly anyone accepted Washington's official position that the two aspects are working in tandem. The Obama administration is aware, Pakistani elite believe, that an outright military victory in Afghanistan is not possible, but it is politically compelled to find a face-saver to justify the decade-long conflict to American taxpayers and the international community. This compulsion is playing to the advantage of those who remain opposed to reconciliation talks.

Participants identified several aspects of the U.S.'s Afghanistan policy as problematic from a Pakistani perspective. Each of these directly or indirectly stems from what they saw as lack of clarity of U.S. designs in Afghanistan.

Civil-military disconnect

A disconnect between the Obama administration and the U.S. military's approach to Afghanistan is blamed for what are seen as contradictory or, as one participant called it, "perpetually evolving" preferences. Broadly, the civilian administration is perceived to favor political reconciliation while the Pentagon, seen as having excessive influence over the Afghanistan-Pakistan security policy,[7] still prioritizes the need to make greater military gains. Some argued that this divisive thinking prevented the Obama administration's December 2010 Afghanistan policy review from being an honest evaluation or re-think of U.S. strategy. This was otherwise a good opportunity to recalibrate the aims towards more modest ends.

Pakistani policy elite view initiation of a serious, inclusive political reconciliation process as the most viable means of achieving a sustainable solution in Afghanistan. During our conversations, many participants appreciated U.S. Secretary of State Hillary Clinton's February 18, 2011, speech at the Asia Society in which she stated that the United States was open to political reconciliation with the Taliban in pursuit of an integrated military-civilian diplomatic strategy.[8] Most, however, were not convinced that there is enough support in Washington for serious reconciliation efforts to take off just yet. Pakistani opinion makers feel that electoral pressure in the run-up to the

2012 U.S. presidential elections will lead President Obama to gradually begin imposing his vision on the military. However, since he is also in search of a 'narrative of victory', he will not undercut the military surge prematurely.[9] This inevitable delay in outlining a clear policy dominated by inclusive political negotiations among Afghans is seen as counterproductive to Pakistani interests, and to the prospects of peace in Afghanistan.

Finally, there was general skepticism among the participants in terms of U.S. patience and the domestic public support to pursue a long, drawn-out Afghan reconciliation process once it commences. It was often pointed out that the United States may be approaching negotiations with a view to meet the drawdown target of 2014. However, the internal reconciliation will have to continue much beyond this deadline before political stability can be expected in Afghanistan. The U.S.'s post-2014 commitment to the process remained unclear to project participants.

Failure to clearly identify the target of the military campaign

Pakistani policy elite feel that the United States is failing to define clearly the principal target of the military surge in Afghanistan. The goal posts have changed frequently as has the narrative around what the United States is ultimately after. Is Al Qaida what Washington ultimately wishes to eliminate, participants wondered? If so, just how many Al Qaida members are left in Afghanistan? Is the United States pursuing a moving target which is not easily identifiable and whose total annihilation is likely impossible? Or does the United States still consider the leadership of the main Taliban factions and other Al Qaida-affiliated groups to be primary targets as well? Until there is clarity on these questions, the United States will be unable to determine when it can consider the mission accomplished.[10]

Despite President Obama's pronouncements reflecting a desire to limit the objectives to Al Qaida, Pakistani policy elite are not convinced that U.S. policy adequately distinguishes between Al Qaida and Afghan Taliban factions like the Haqqani network and Mullah Omar's "Quetta Shura."[11] A sizable number of the participants believed that the U.S.'s strategy was still conflating the two groups, and warned against making this mistake. Participants suggested that the Pakistani state considers the Afghan Taliban political actors and part of a major ethnic group; silencing the Taliban-led insurgency through military force was considered to be impossible. In fact, many participants saw excessive use of force as generating greater sympathy for the Taliban.

Bleak prognosis of the military surge

The question of the efficacy of the military aspect of President Obama's "surge" elicited skeptical responses. The understanding of the on-ground situation in Afghanistan is that the Taliban's capacity has been degraded in the southern part of the country where the U.S. military has concentrated over the past year. However, virtually no one was convinced that this can put an end to the insurgency or that it can force the main Taliban factions to negotiate on America's terms. To substantiate this claim, experts cited the lack of precedence of such a development in Afghanistan and a belief that the United States is committing many of the same mistakes the Soviet Union made during the 1980s (and those who tried to occupy Afghanistan before it) by depending on military force and powerful, but highly tainted and corrupt strong-men and militias as partners in Afghanistan.

A sizable proportion of the policy elite present in the discussions took issue with what is perceived to be a shift towards a more heavy handed U.S. military strategy in Afghanistan under General David Petraeus, commander of U.S. forces in Afghanistan at the time of the roundtable discussions.[12] The aim of killing as many insurgent fighters as possible and tactics like aerial attacks and night raids are believed to be counterproductive. The opinion makers argued that the surge has resulted in the widespread destruction of villages, and has therefore spurred fresh Taliban recruitment and brought turmoil even to previously peaceful areas. Others pointed out that the U.S. military is focusing on stabilizing and fortifying urban areas while neglecting the Afghan countryside. This strategy is considered unsustainable given the traditional importance of the Afghan countryside in politics and will likely result in increased insecurity in the wake of U.S. troop withdrawal.

The debate about America's post-2014 footprint

There was a sense among the participants that the United States would want to retain some long-term security presence in Afghanistan. Opinions varied on the U.S. objectives behind this desire. While some were convinced that the United States views this presence in strategic terms and wants to establish a physical foothold in the South Asian region,[13] others argued that the mandate in Afghanistan is likely to be limited to ensuring that Afghan territory is not used for attacks against the United States in the future. For those who agreed with the latter, the United States would retain its military bases and use these as launching pads for a counterterrorism-dominated strategy after the 2014 transition. The aim would principally be to hunt down Al Qaida leaders and other high-value targets in Afghanistan and Pakistan. However, skeptics considered even this limited agenda to be problematic from a Pakistani perspective. As they saw it, it would amount to U.S. presence in a relatively peaceful northern Afghanistan, leaving Pakistan to deal with the fallout from the country's turbulent eastern and southern provinces.[14]

There are also divergent views among Pakistani foreign policy elite on how public knowledge of America's desire for a long-term presence in

Afghanistan may impact the political reconciliation process. At the very least, it is viewed as an additional challenge and is likely to make not only the Afghan Taliban, but also regional countries like Pakistan, Iran, China, and Russia uneasy.

The Afghan Taliban's position on foreign troop presence is somewhat contested. Some participants tended to take the Taliban's stated position of "no foreign troops" at face value. They saw no possibility that the major Taliban factions would accept foreign troop presence as part of the endgame settlement. Therefore, if the United States is unwilling to commit to total withdrawal, the reconciliation process could be stillborn. Those who held this view also tended to believe that the opposition to long-term U.S. military presence goes beyond the Taliban and extends to a number of moderate Afghan groups, both Pashtun and non-Pashtun. Others disagreed however, and argued that the Taliban's demand for complete troop withdrawal is a starting position which is aimed more for the consumption of their own rank and file than as a non-negotiable condition in talks with the United States. Ultimately, they may accept a plan for phased withdrawal as long as there is firm commitment that all foreign troops would pull out at a specified time in the not-so-distant future.

U.S. view of Pakistan's role in the reconciliation phase

Uncertainty and skepticism about U.S. policy leads to a sense of nervousness in Pakistan. The growing mistrust between the United States and Pakistan in the context of the Afghanistan strategy is front and center of Pakistani thinking. Hardly anyone among the project participants believed that the United States would willingly adjust its Afghanistan strategy to incorporate Pakistani concerns. In fact, many argued that Washington views Pakistan as a nuisance that cannot be relied upon in the negotiations phase in Afghanistan.

Pakistani policy elite believe that Washington would continue to push the Pakistan Army to "do more" to stamp out militant sanctuaries in Pakistan while it tries to open up direct channels for talks with the Taliban—thereby minimizing Pakistan's role in the negotiations, or, at the very least, signaling a willingness to explore avenues that lessen dependence on Pakistan's security establishment for reconciliation talks.[15] Not many participants were convinced that this is a viable strategy; most believed that it would undermine the prospects for successful reconciliation.

Pakistan's Afghanistan Policy: Reacting to the United States

Lack of clarity in Pakistan's policy

Pakistani opinion makers involved in the project discussions saw their country's strategy towards Afghanistan as largely reactionary; it is seen as having responded to U.S. actions in a manner that ensures continuation of the Pakistan-U.S. partnership while securing Pakistani national security interests, as defined by the security establishment. Reservations about the U.S. strategy in Afghanistan have prevented the Pakistani state from complementing America's actions outright. While the experts accepted that this amounts to divergent policies—"double game" as it is known in Washington—they also highlighted that Pakistan has to look after its own interests first and foremost. Nonetheless, there is recognition that Pakistan's outlook on Afghanistan has been unclear and ambiguous. While Islamabad has been critical of the lack of clarity in U.S. policy, it has itself failed to articulate a coherent plan towards Afghanistan that allows for long-term engagement on multiple levels—political, economic, and security-related.

A dual approach towards the United States

Project participants suggested that Pakistani policy faces a dilemma vis-à-vis the United States. On the one hand, U.S. military operations in Afghanistan are believed to be causing a backlash in terms of militancy and deepening the state-society rift within Pakistan. Militant groups such as the Tehreek-e-Taliban Pakistan (TTP) are using the U.S. presence in Afghanistan, and Pakistan's support in the fight against terrorism, as justification for attacking Pakistani state interests. On the other hand, Pakistani foreign policy elite appreciate that a premature U.S. troop withdrawal would lead to added instability in Afghanistan.

Pakistan has tried to balance these two competing aspects in its policy. It has continued to provide counterterrorism and strategic (principally, the supply routes and military bases) support to the United States to ensure that Washington continues to engage Pakistan as a partner. Moreover, Pakistan's support keeps U.S. costs in Afghanistan from becoming prohibitively high, which could potentially increase political pressure in Washington for an abrupt troop withdrawal, or short of that, force the U.S. military to prematurely retreat to its bases in Afghanistan and pursue the counterterrorism-heavy approach amidst deteriorating security in the country. As explained earlier, neither is seen to be in Pakistan's interest.

Simultaneously, Pakistan has refused to succumb to U.S. pressure to aggressively target the Afghan Taliban and other Pakistan-based groups operating against U.S. interests from Pakistani territory. Indeed, Pakistani policy elite are fairly candid in acknowledging the presence of Haqqani network fighters in North Waziristan and of the "Quetta Shura" Taliban, although the influence and reach of the latter is believed to be exaggerated by western accounts. That said, Pakistani policy elite agree that Mullah Omar's cadres do not, for the most part, conduct violent operations inside Pakistan and are therefore not targeted by the Pakistan military.

Box 2. Why is Pakistan holding out on the sanctuaries?

Several reasons were discussed for Pakistan's refusal to target militant sanctuaries being used to attack the International Security Assistance Force (ISAF) presence and the Afghan troops. The debate can be summed up as one between lack of 'capacity' and lack of 'will'. While there was agreement that both feature in the Pakistan military's decision, views differed on which of these is the primary factor.

Those who see the reluctance to target sanctuaries as primarily a "will" issue argue that the decision stems largely from Pakistan's concern about being sidelined in the reconciliation phase in Afghanistan, which could result in a manipulated process that works to the advantage of elements hostile towards Islamabad. For instance, the main Taliban factions may be left out, or certain individuals within them may be bought out to accept an outcome unfavorable to the Pashtuns.

Pakistani intelligence links with the Afghan Taliban and the presence of these groups on Pakistani soil are seen as leverage points which more or less guarantee Islamabad's involvement in the endgame. Presence of these groups in the post-transition power-sharing arrangement in Kabul also provides Pakistan some sense of security in that they will not allow Kabul to adopt an overtly anti-Pakistan policy.

A number of strong voices disagreed with this outlook. They argued that the "will" narrative reflects the traditional thinking of the Pakistani security establishment, which is no longer valid. They emphasized the need to acknowledge an evolution, however slow, in the security establishment's thinking. Those who support this narrative cite the less-than-harmonious relationship, induced as it was by Pakistan's post-9/11 offer of support to the U.S. mission in Afghanistan, between the main Taliban factions, including their leadership, and the Pakistani intelligence outfit, the Inter Services Intelligence (ISI). No longer does the ISI hold the kind of sway over the Taliban groups as it once did. Some take it

(Box continued on next page)

Support for political reconciliation in Afghanistan: Here and now

Pakistani foreign policy elite deem the strategy to support the U.S. presence in Afghanistan on the one hand, and resist pressure to target militant sanctuaries on the other, as costly in terms of the backlash Pakistan is facing from within. Project participants believed that from Islamabad's perspective, the longer U.S. military operations continue without a clear path for political negotiations, the tougher it will get for Pakistan to manage its internal security balancing act. Pakistan therefore favors an immediate, yet patient effort at inclusive reconciliation in Afghanistan. Pakistani policy elite admitted that little progress will be made until a fundamental disconnect between Pakistani and American perceptions is addressed: most Pakistani decision makers believe that large-scale military operations against militant sanctuaries in FATA are not in their national security interest. As long as the military views the

Box 2. Why is Pakistan holding out on the sanctuaries?   Continued

one step further by contending that there is a significant amount of distrust between the Afghan Taliban and the ISI which will manifest itself once the Taliban's compulsion to use Pakistani territory disappears. Therefore, while the Taliban may still be the friendliest option for Pakistan, there is little to say that they would be willing to do Pakistan's bidding. We were also reminded that even in the 1990s, the Pakistani state's relations with the Mullah Omar-led Afghanistan were seldom without problems.

This narrative views the reluctance of the Pakistani military to target the sanctuaries as principally a capacity issue. The Pakistan Army does not have the capacity to open up new battlefronts given that it remains overstretched with its commitments against anti-Pakistan militant outfits. An incomplete or ineffective military campaign against the sanctuaries could lead Afghan insurgent groups, especially the Haqqani network, to back groups like the TTP against the Pakistani state. Those wedded to this argument doubt the Pakistan military's ability to manage such an onslaught. They believe a massive backlash in Pakistan's heartland to be inevitable. The possibility of fresh Pashtun resentment in FATA and adjacent areas in Khyber Pakhtunkhwa (KPK) province is also not lost on these strategic thinkers.

Those favoring the "capacity" narrative also seek to correct the misperception that the Pakistani security establishment is unaware of the growing linkages between the Afghan Taliban and Pakistani militant groups. However, they argue that while the current links remain limited, it is precisely the fear of these growing into fullblown operational cooperation and coordination that prevents the Pakistani state from targeting Afghan insurgent groups on its soil. Moreover, the security establishment is able to take advantage of the present linkages between these groups from time to time by persuading the Afghan Taliban to pressure the TTP and other North Waziristan-based militants to curtail their activities

situation as a stark choice between ensuring security within Pakistan and taking actions to aid the U.S. mission in Afghanistan, a divergence of policy, and indeed a high level of mistrust will remain. Project participants were also of the view that Pakistan will not cease a certain level of interference in Afghanistan until a credible reconciliation process takes off. There was a virtual consensus though that this challenge can only be addressed within the framework of well-articulated, long-term Afghan policies by Washington and Islamabad.

Indeed, the need for U.S. and Pakistani positions to converge on the endgame in Afghanistan is well understood. There was a belief among the participants that what Pakistan is seeking in Afghanistan is not necessarily opposed to U.S. interests; there is considerable overlap which ought to be explored rather than allowing bilateral mistrust to overshadow the opportunity. Pakistan hopes that the United States would pursue reconciliation talks more proactively and sincerely in the coming months, but do so through an Afghan-led process that also takes regional actors into confidence. An inclusive government in Kabul, participants agreed, would inevitably emerge from an Afghan-led reconciliation effort which was genuinely representative and not manipulated by any external actor.

Pakistani foreign policy elite however tend to draw a distinction between manipulation of an intra-Afghan process and facilitation by external parties. They see their country as an important and potentially effective facilitator which could nudge the main Taliban insurgent groups to join and approach the negotiations process sincerely. That said, there was a fair bit of skepticism regarding the ability of outside parties—Pakistan and the United States included—to resist the temptation of meddling in the negotiations process rather than simply facilitating the presence of all major Afghan factions on the table. The concern about the others' meddling, most participants feared, would in turn incentivize each external actor to interfere itself, thereby undermining the potential for an intra-Afghan settlement.

To be sure, the discussions about the 'inclusiveness' of the reconciliation process and the post-2014 transition government in Kabul took the presence of the main Taliban factions in the framework for granted. Rather interestingly, while there was frank admission that the Pakistani security establishment sees the Taliban's involvement in reconciliation in Pakistan's interest, and thus will insist on it, project participants sought to clarify that this should not be seen as Pakistan's ploy to artificially impose its preferred outcome. Instead, they argued that Islamabad believes that a genuinely intra-Afghan dialogue will naturally produce an outcome which would provide the Taliban some role in the power-sharing arrangement. Based on their perceptions about the current realities on the ground in Afghanistan, members of the Pakistani elite tied to this narrative saw any attempts to alienate Pashtuns in general, and the Taliban in particular as shortsighted and impractical.

Project participants believed that the Afghan Taliban's presence in the reconciliation phase and their acceptance of the dialogue process would satisfy a number of Pakistani interests. For one, the on-ground realities and the Taliban's strength as an insurgent group imply that any attempt to isolate them would prolong the insurgency, and instability in Afghanistan. In this regard, Pakistan's support for their role in Afghanistan's future political set-up is believed to make it a force for stability.

Moreover, even if the main Taliban factions do not completely trust the Pakistani security establishment, they are not seen as groups who would actively undermine the Pakistani state's interests either. Their ethnic ties to Pakistan and long-standing relationships with Pashtun-centric right-wing Pakistani political parties will militate against this outcome. They may however, seek to chart a course that is less dependent on Pakistan than during the 1990s, which according to some participants, ought to be considered a blessing in disguise for Pakistan.[16] Next, the Taliban's acceptance of a negotiated settlement, or at the very minimum, sufficient progress in talks for them to be comfortable with ceasing violence, would lead to voluntary relocation from sanctuaries in Pakistan. Finally, a truly inclusive political dispensation, most among the project participants believed, will eliminate the possibility of an overtly pro-India dispensation or one that is outright insensitive to Pakistani concerns.

A reconciliation process that leaves out the Taliban, on the other hand, may confirm the Pakistani security establishment's worst fears. It would be seen as an effort to sideline Pakistan's importance and some in the establishment may even view it as an effort to install an anti-Pakistan—read pro-India—political dispensation in Afghanistan. The Taliban leadership may see no reason to re-locate to Afghanistan and will continue to keep the pot boiling; Pakistan will remain under pressure to "do more" and will be portrayed negatively in the international media if it resists. Pakistani Pashtuns would also be resentful of the outcome and the TTP may use this sentiment to increase recruitment and justify continued attacks against the Pakistani state.

It is important to note that even as project participants acknowledged that at present, the Taliban may be the friendliest option for Pakistan, a number of them were quick to underscore that this is a result of the state's myopic approach towards Afghanistan over the years. It is Islamabad's failure to broaden its contacts with other moderate Pashtun, and even more so the non-Pashtun groups, that has forced Pakistan to tolerate the Taliban. The policy has come at significant cost in terms of international condemnation and mistrust with much of the western world. It has also led to greater ex-posure of the Pakistani society to the Taliban's radical ideological outlook than would have been possible otherwise. There is a strong feeling of being 'stuck' with the Taliban; the state is 'forced' to fall back on the Taliban groups as its principal leverage.

The flip side: Avoiding a return to the 1990s

While some opinion makers remained unconvinced, for most, the Taliban's perceived utility for Pakistan does not translate into a desire for a return to Taliban rule in Afghanistan. The Pakistani policy of the 1990s is believed to have lost support even in the strategic establishment, not least because of the realization that Afghan citizens and the international community would not accept any such effort. Moreover, a bid to regain lost glory by Mullah Omar's Taliban would end up creating conditions in Afghanistan which run counter to Pakistani objectives, most notably stability.

Pakistani policy elite recognize that no elements within the current political setup in Afghanistan will willingly cede power to the Afghan Taliban. Large pockets of Afghan society, especially in the north, have seen the benefits of international presence over the past decade and will not accept wholesale regression to the 1990s. Pakistani foreign policy elite are cognizant that the Taliban's obscurantist, extremist views have made them extremely unpopular in Afghanistan. They are aware that what seems to be support for the Taliban in Afghanistan at present stems from the frustration and resentment towards the failure of effective governance by the Karzai regime. While this frustration may generate support for the insurgency as the only means to push back against the status quo, participants felt that it would be a mistake for the Pakistani state to see it as a desire among the Afghans to return to Taliban rule.

Experts involved in the discussions argued that any attempt by the Afghan Taliban to impose their rule will be met with fierce resistance from non-Pashtun and moderate Pashtun groups. The non-Pashtuns will now be able to draw on their improved organization, bolstered capacity, and access to sophisticated weaponry through the ANSF[17] to prevent such a development. Afghan Taliban, on their part, do not have the military capacity to take on this opposition on their own. In fact, it was often pointed out that the Taliban are no longer a monolithic entity and the various factions may well have clashing preferences in terms of the endgame and beyond. In essence, a serious attempt to return the Taliban to rule Kabul on their own could spark widespread insecurity, or even outright civil war, in Afghanistan.

Participants referred to Pakistan's attempts in recent years to reach out to more moderate Pashtun factions in Afghanistan and to forge better links with the Karzai government as evidence of the desire to broaden the scope of Pakistani contacts across the Durand Line. Islamabad's preliminary efforts to quietly reach out to former members of the Northern Alliance, some of them highly critical of Pakistan, were also seen favorably by most participants.

The Pakistani state's sympathetic view towards the Afghan Taliban and yet its averseness to a return to the 1990s raises an interesting question about just how much support the state apparatus is extending to the main Taliban factions. There was a lively and inconclusive debate on this issue among the policy elite. Some argued that the military's policy is to 'tolerate' Taliban presence and that the ISI does not actively train or materially support the Afghan Taliban factions present on Pakistani soil. Others however held the view that while this may generally be true, from time to time the ISI extends material support or directs certain actions. Yet others—this was the least common view—went a step further to state that they did not rule out the possibility that the ISI has continued to equip and actively fund some of the Afghan insurgent factions over the past decade.

Regional diplomacy

Project participants believed that skepticism about U.S. policy has also led the Pakistani official enclave to 'hedge' at a different level. Much like the rest of

Box 3. The Afghan conundrum from the perspective of Pakistan's political parties*

Representatives of the major political parties in Pakistan echoed much of the concerns and opportunities highlighted by the country's foreign policy elite. While there are a number of consensus points on which parties from across the political spectrum broadly agree, there is also a discernible difference in outlook between right and left wing parties on some issues.

Views on Pakistan's objectives in Afghanistan underscore the criticality of ensuring positive ties with Afghanistan. The fact that the stability of both countries is interdependent is recognized, as is the fact that the present situation in Afghanistan bodes ill for Pakistan. There is a general sense that Pakistan should approach the relationship with Afghanistan more holistically. A more multi-layered engagement, built around common and stable economic goals and capacity building of Afghanistan's governance and security sectors should be pursued. The military's predominance over the Afghan policy elicits significant criticism and most parties, especially those left-of-center, desire a re-balancing of geo-strategic interests towards goals that privilege gains from economic interdependence.

In terms of the evolving end game in Afghanistan, Washington is seen as part of the problem to a large extent. America's over-reliance on military force in Afghanistan is considered to be a major flaw, one that is undermining the prospects of successful reconciliation. A more aggressive political approach is believed to be essential for durable peace in the country. There is a sense that the military surge has weakened the Taliban but that rather than pushing further in pursuit of the elusive goal of 'victory', the present U.S. advantage should be used to initiate serious dialogue with all Afghan factions.

The impact of Washington's troop presence in Afghanistan is a matter of some debate. Most see military presence leading up to a political transition as essential to avoid a further deterioration of Afghanistan's security. However, a long-term international security presence is not seen nearly as favorably. The right-of-center parties remain wary of America's long-term interests and intentions for the region and remain opposed to permanent military bases or a sizable force post-2014.

Political parties profess strong support for a regional framework to ensure sustainable peace in Afghanistan. Views on how a regional framework would be developed and which countries would play the central role are not always fully thought out. While most parties would like to see an approach led by the regional states with involvement from the United States, others argue that the United States would inevitably want to dictate the process. In general however, the idea—the practicality is debatable—of Pakistan playing a pivotal role in bringing together countries like Iran, Turkey, and China to consolidate their efforts to push for reconciliation attracts Pakistani political leaders. Most still acknowledge though that India will have to be included as a legitimate stakeholder, not least because U.S. and Indian interests align closely in Afghanistan; Washington would want to see India's interests protected to some extent. Pakistan's moves to reach out directly to Kabul and to other regional actors are seen positively; this could tilt the equation back in Pakistan's favor to some extent.

On India's role in Afghanistan, there is sharp divergence of opinion. The left-of-center parties are of the view that Pakistan's Afghanistan calculus should not be dictated by a phobia of malign Indian designs. While there is little

(Box continued on next page)

Box 3. The Afghan conundrum from the perspective of Pakistan's political parties* Continued

agreement even among these parties on how to incorporate Indian presence in Pakistan's calculus, they do not see India's role as a major impediment in ensuring peace in Afghanistan on terms that safeguard Pakistan's interests. The traditionally right-of-center parties however, do view an Indian presence in Afghanistan as worrisome. India is seen as using Afghanistan to further its strategic goals in South Asia, which are perceived to be contrary to Pakistan's. According to this narrative, Indian clout in Kabul is inversely proportional to Pakistan's ability to ensure a friendly neighbor. Therefore, limiting India's presence to purely development objectives is seen as a priority.

* Based on interviews with members of seven major political parties: Khurshid Ahmad (Jama'at-e-Islami); Ahsan Iqbal (Pakistan Muslim League-N); Malik Amad Khan (Pakistan Peoples Party); Afrasiab Khattak (Awami National Party); Maulana Atta-ur-Rehman (Jamiat-e-Ulema Islam-F), Waseem Sajjad (Pakistan Muslim League -Q); Farooq Sattar (Muttahida Qaumi Movement).

the region, Pakistan is also exploring "what if" scenarios: what if the United States continues to remain incoherent in its outlook?

A parallel track aimed at energizing regional diplomacy even as the United States struggles to better define its future approach has been initiated. The aim: to forge an understanding on how reconciliation could best be entertained by regional countries. The strategy is seen not as much a means to sideline the United States—hardly anyone saw this as wise or even possible—but to signal that regional actors need to (and can) generate a momentum of their own to a certain extent. Pakistan's efforts to reach out to Afghan President Hamid Karzai and recent conciliatory overtures between the two sides were seen as positive developments that need to be continued. In the same vein, high-level Pakistani visits to Central Asian republics[18] and visits to China and Russia[19] (upcoming at the time of the roundtables) were welcomed as means to better understand how regional parties are approaching the issue and what overlaps and differences exist in their respective positions. A greater Chinese role had special resonance among most observers, although there was recognition of the tensions overtures towards China create vis-à-vis the United States. An overly aggressive approach towards Beijing was opposed for the fear of worrying Washington and prompting it to actively seek to limit Islamabad's access to Kabul in response.

A Regional Framework: Views on Neutrality and Non-interference in Afghanistan as a Viable Option

A regional framework which seeks neutrality and non-interference from countries in the neighborhood was often underscored during our conversations as a key ingredient of any plan aimed at achieving future Afghan stability. There was support for the idea in principle; normatively, the need both to pledge non-interference in Afghanistan's affairs and a region-wide agreement on the same was recognized. Some members of the roundtable discussion groups went further to state that an absence of a regional understanding would inevitably prompt neighbors, including Pakistan, to carve out their own spheres of influence in Afghanistan. This could quickly revert to a proxy war situation whereby Pakistan, Iran, India and other regional players compete with each other, to Afghanistan's detriment.

That said, there was also a sense that any understanding of "neutrality" in the Afghan context cannot ignore the varying interests and linkages different regional actors have with the country. Pakistan stands to gain or lose most from developments in Afghanistan by virtue of its geographical location and societal linkages. Pakistan's concerns can therefore not be weighted equally to those of other, one-step-removed parties. By the same token, participants believed that Pakistan's proximity and ethnic ties will naturally allow it greater interaction and influence over Afghanistan, but this ought not to be conflated with active efforts at interference, which Pakistan has admittedly been guilty of in the past.

If done right, Pakistani policy elite believe that the approach can produce substantial peace and development dividends for the region. In terms of foreign policies, a successful political reconciliation process in Afghanistan couched within a regional framework could potentially offer Pakistan significant breakthroughs. Pakistan and India could cooperate economically and politically in Afghanistan, thereby helping to normalize one aspect of their relationship. Conversely, a breakdown of a regional bid could quickly lead to a proxy situation between the two sides. There will be potential gains in the Pakistan-Iran relationship as well. Project participants believed that Iran and Pakistan are presently competing for political influence in Afghanistan. Iranian support for Hazaras and Tajiks is limiting Pakistan's ability to reach out to non-Pashtun groups. Moreover, some participants feared that Iran's involvement in Afghanistan could stoke sectarian tensions within Pakistan, as Islamabad, unlike Tehran, is not engaging Shi'a groups in Afghanistan successfully. A regionally-backed resolution to the Afghan conflict, the policy elite felt, could eliminate this competition to a great extent.

In terms of development benefits, Afghanistan's emerging markets and energy resources and the transit corridor through Afghanistan were repeatedly highlighted as high potential avenues, but ones that can only materialize if a successful endgame settlement brings stability to Afghanistan. Countries may still compete but in such a transformed scenario the competition would be commercial rather than security-dominated. For instance, the need for Pakistan to take advantage of its location to become a transit hub for energy inflows from Central Asia was noted. Also, China's growing economic interests in

Box 4. The power to spoil: Pakistan's concerns about Indian presence in Afghanistan

Indian presence in Afghanistan was presented as Pakistan's single biggest concern when it comes to accepting a regional framework of noninterference. Project participants explained the Pakistani state's fears that expanding Indian influence over a primarily non-Pashtun government in Kabul could lead the latter to be increasingly hostile towards Islamabad.

Pakistani foreign policy elite are cognizant that their state must reconcile with the prospect of a long-term Indian development presence in Afghanistan. However, in return, Pakistan seeks assurances from New Delhi, Kabul, Washington, and the international community that India's interests in Afghanistan are of an economic, rather than strategic or political nature. The potential repercussions of leaving Pakistan's concerns vis-à-vis India unaddressed is not lost on the policy elite: they believe that Pakistan's strategic establishment is fully aware that their country's geographical location gives them an unmatched advantage in the eventuality that they need to compete with Indian strategic presence in a subversive manner.

Current Indian activity patterns worry Pakistani policy elite. The Indian desire to train parts of the ANSF, the presence of the Border Roads Organization, which is partly staffed by Indian Army officers, as a road construction contractor in Afghanistan, and the location of a number of major Indian development projects in relatively close proximity to the Pakistani border raises Pakistani sensitivities. The international community's reluctance to nudge India to be more forthcoming on the issue was also raised frequently during the discussions; it is seen as being consistent with the overall discriminatory treatment towards Pakistan. Indeed, the India question continues to be seen in the context of Indian encirclement by Pakistani opinion makers. Washington's decision to isolate the India-Pakistan equation from U.S.-"Af-Pak" ties is seen as evidence of America's decisive tilt toward India. Some from among the policy elite take seriously the notion that India's Afghanistan presence is part of a regional strategy to counter China, and in that sense, it complements long-term U.S. interests in the region. For this cohort, Indian presence in Afghanistan will remain a major sticking point in the Pakistan-U.S. bilateral relationship even after 2014.

Afghanistan are seen positively in Pakistan. Project participants tended to see the warmth of the Sino-Pakistan relationship as an advantage in seeking joint investments and placement for Pakistani labor.

The normative appeal and understanding of potential gains aside, when asked whether the regional approach is likely to work out in reality, Pakistani policy elite came across as broadly skeptical. For one, there were few, if any, who believed that countries like the United States would be truly neutral in creating a regional framework. The U.S.'s long-term interests and tensions with countries like Iran would force it to seek considerable influence over Afghanistan's behavior. Moreover, a sense of discrimination prevails in Pakistan when it comes to the India-Pakistan equation vis-à-vis the United States. In the view of most of our project participants, Washington is more likely to favor India in the Afghan context, not least because the interests of the two countries align more neatly.

Second, and more discernible, participants were unsure on how a regional agreement would be enforced. Can any government or international body be tasked and trusted to guarantee non-interference? What mechanism would determine whether or if regional actors transgress, or who does so first? The Afghan state itself is seen as too weak and divided to be able to deter undesired interference. The long history of outside interference in Afghan affairs also does not generate confidence in the viability of such a regional understanding. Some participants worried that just the entrenched expectation of interference by others—as opposed to actual violation of the understanding by any party—will lead countries not to honor the arrangement in the first place. Each will seek a 'first-mover's advantage' in establishing its influence in Afghanistan. This is especially true given that regional conflicts remain active and that the foreign policies of key actors like Pakistan, India, and Iran remain competitive to varying degrees.

Other Impediments to Successful Endgame Negotiations

U.S. policy towards Afghanistan and Pakistani skepticism about the viability of a broad regional framework have already been highlighted as major impediments to successful reconciliation in Afghanistan. Project participants also pointed to other hurdles in ensuring successful negotiations and the transition to a durable settlement in Afghanistan. These cast further doubt in the Pakistani mind over prospects of the success of the U.S. mission in the country, and in turn, make the Pakistani state even less keen to conform to Washington's desires.

Political situation in Afghanistan

President Karzai, while recognized as a legitimate ruler, is increasingly seen as corrupt and ineffective. Some among the project participants even saw him as a liability for America's Afghanistan strategy, arguing that his loss of credibility is generating additional support for the insurgency and forcing Afghan groups opposed to his government to delay meaningful talks. Some participants also saw the present political government in Kabul as being compromised due to its close contacts with lobbies of status quo beneficiaries—those who have gained most from foreign assistance, reconstruction contracts, and lawlessness. These are the people who cashed in on the perverse incentives set up by the flow of international assistance and flawed aid utilization policies of international actors; they are the very vested interests that the international community sought to hold accountable but ended up empowering beyond control.

According to the Pakistani policy elite, a major challenge in this political environment lies in identifying representatives who could mediate and speak on behalf of different Afghan stakeholders. The Karzai regime will want to be seen as representing all Afghan factions in talks with the Taliban. This however, is unlikely to be acceptable to a number of political groupings. Even the High Peace Council was described by many participants as ineffective and lacking credibility and inclusiveness. While its members include former Taliban or those sympathetic to them, these individuals are no longer believed to be acceptable the Afghan Taliban leadership as interlocutors.

Looking ahead, participants suggested that the U.S. role will be important in nudging the Karzai regime to enhance its legitimacy by becoming more transparent, accountable, and effective in governance. By the same token, the United States will have to ensure that status quo beneficiaries are not allowed to hijack the reconciliation process. Under the present circumstances, Pakistani policy elite contend that the Karzai government cannot be expected to establish truly inclusive parameters for reconciliation in Afghanistan.

Taliban's willingness to negotiate

Setting the parameters for reconciliation talks and ensuring sincere participation from all Afghan groups is not a problem limited to the mainstream outfits. The Afghan Taliban's negotiating behavior and their desired role in the post-transition Afghanistan remains an even bigger question mark.

Pakistani policy elite dismiss the idea that the Pakistani security establishment can force the Taliban's hand into accepting specific U.S. demands. At best, it can get the major Taliban factions to the negotiating table. Even there, Pakistani opinion makers claim lack of clarity about the Afghan Taliban's willingness to participate in a political reconciliation process, or even to communicate directly with the United States beyond a point. This confusion is attributed to the group's evolving composition and ideological and political outlook. However, there was considerable agreement among participants that the Taliban are no longer a monolithic entity and that one should expect different, even divergent, approaches to the reconciliation process from within Taliban ranks. Different Taliban factions could lay down their own sets of conditions in the reconciliation process.

There are a number of specific aspects which lack clarity: what is the precise nature of the links of the various Afghan Taliban factions with Al Qaida? What will it take for them to divorce all links? What are Afghan Taliban's current ideological ambitions: is the group looking to impose its hard-line views on the Afghan public; or has it revised its opinion on various socio-political matters such as girls' schooling? Just how sincere will Taliban factions be during talks is not entirely clear either: will they use the talks to secure the exit of foreign troops and then seek to re-launch a violent campaign to neutralize opposing

Afghans; or will they settle for a power-sharing arrangement? Pakistani policy elite opinion is divided, although there was broad agreement that definitive answers will not be forthcoming until serious talks actually commence with the Taliban.

Regardless, participants warned against envisioning reconciliation talks with the Taliban as smooth and swift. They see reconciliation as necessarily being a long, drawn-out process with many twists and turns, and with no guarantee of success. However, it is a commonly held view that negotiations will only succeed if Afghan stakeholders, the United States, and the Taliban remain open to engagement, do not impose rigid preconditions unacceptable to the adversary, and refrain from manipulating the process to mould outcomes. Notwithstanding, in line with the desire to see a reconciliation process commence urgently, Pakistani policy elite feel that the longer inclusive talks are delayed, the more challenging it will become to bring the Taliban to the negotiating table (implicit here is the pervasive belief that the military surge will not be able to tilt the balance decisively towards the United States).

Afghanistan's fragile economy

Afghanistan's post-endgame stability is intrinsically linked to the country's economy and its ability to generate revenues. Pakistani elite see the bulk of the current economic infrastructure as a consequence of an inflated war economy and international support. In 2009–10, more than 70 percent of the Afghan budget came from foreign sources. And while Afghanistan had an $11.4 billion economy in 2010, a $4.4 billion segment was attributed to services dominated by trade, transport, and government support—agriculture amounted to $3.3 billion, and mining only to $52 million, or one percent of the overall size of the economy.[20]

As such, while the improvements in the Afghan economy and infrastructure as a result of the U.S.-led reconstruction efforts post-9/11 are recognized by Pakistani foreign policy elite, the real gains are not seen to be commensurate with the claims the international community has made during its decade-long presence in Afghanistan. The most skeptical among our participants pointed to deeprooted structural anomalies in the Afghan economy, some of which have, according to them, been exacerbated in the past decade even as the macroeconomy has continued to improve. Moreover, the Afghan government's revenue collection capacity is seen as modest, corruption levels high, job creation remaining dependent on external financing, and public infrastructure projects much too slow to take off. President Hamid Karzai's lack of credibility is seen as an additional impediment in ensuring good governance.

The international community would have to continue substantial monetary support for years after the 2014 transition to avoid an economic collapse in Afghanistan. While most participants expected such support to continue, some remained skeptical given the economic conditions in many of the donor countries and the increasing number of western voices calling for a cutback on the commitment in Afghanistan. Regardless, the perfect storm from Pakistan's vantage is a collapse of the Afghan economy once the international troops have pulled out. Not only would Pakistan's own economic investments in the country be jeopardized, but the country would be faced with a fresh influx of Afghans escaping renewed violence and seeking livelihood opportunities.

Such a possibility brings back the bitter memory of the 1980s for Pakistanis when their country had to housed over three million Afghan refugees, with attendant affects on Pakistan's economy, society, and law and order. This time round, Pakistan's own internal turbulence and weak economy leaves it ill-prepared to absorb a new refugee spillover and the possibility of increased drug trafficking and weapons inflow. Some participants pointed to already increasing tensions between Pakistanis and Afghan nationals present on Pakistani soil. Afghans have begun to face discrimination in recent years, partly as a reaction to the anti-Pakistan sentiment in Afghanistan. Moreover, there are repeated allegations of involvement of Afghans in criminal and smuggling gangs, which further stereotypes their presence in Pakistan.

The future of the Afghan National Security Forces

Pakistani foreign policy elite remain wary of the future role of the ANSF. Few participants expected the ANSF to be ready to become the principal custodians of Afghanistan's security by the 2014 transition. The improvement in their performance was acknowledged but it is considered insufficient to prevent Afghanistan from regressing into an anarchic state, should political reconciliation fail, or unravel. Former Pakistani military officials included in our discussions were particularly skeptical. They pointed to the absence of senior officers with any noteworthy track records in the ANSF, unstable ranks of the forces, and the disadvantages of operating without an air force for the Afghan National Army (ANA) as structural problems that are unlikely to be addressed satisfactorily in the medium term. Moreover, Pakistani policy elite perceive ANSF's bloated size to be both, unsustainable given Afghanistan's meager resources and a threat to Pakistani interests. Participants feared that absent organized demobilization, any efforts to prune the forces may lead to resentment among the ranks.

The ethnic composition of the ANSF was also brought up frequently. The claim that the forces are ethnically balanced was rejected for the most part and the presence of non-Pashtun officers in key positions was highlighted to suggest that the makeup is more likely to fuel ethnic hostility than to maintain peace in the country. The Pashtuns in Pakistan, and some argued even Afghanistan, have begun to see the ANA as an anti-Pashtun force. While there are varying opinions on the future trajectory of the ANSF, a sizable proportion of the participants believed that the forces may split up along ethnic lines and their rank and file could feature on opposite sides of a fresh civil war, this time with an abundant supply of highly sophisticated weapons. The spillover into Pakistan, and indeed, involvement of elements from Pakistan's Pashtun belt in the Afghan turmoil would then destabilize Pakistan further.

Moving Ahead: Key Countries and their Role in Promoting Peace in Afghanistan

While participants were not asked for specific recommendations on the way forward per se, they did spend some time examining steps (from a Pakistani perspective) that the principal regional actors would have to take to stabilize Afghanistan. The main observations made by participants (by country), not all encompassing by any means, included:

Afghanistan

(i)   While President Karzai is still seen as the best available choice to work with in Afghanistan, his regime's dwindling credibility in the eyes of Afghan citizens is considered to be a major problem and one that he and his team must work to rectify. Only then will they be able to win the trust of Afghan factions that have to be brought on board for a successful political reconciliation process.

(ii)   The Afghan government needs to identify representatives who can mediate on behalf of and across all ethnic and political groups in Afghanistan. President Karzai will have to appoint credible representatives beyond the High Peace Council to work with the Afghan Taliban as well as members of the Afghan civil society. Various Afghan political groups also need to articulate their preferred framework for an Afghan-led reconciliation process.

(iii)   The Afghan Constitution should be used as a basis to develop a framework for political reconciliation. However, an unconditional acceptance of the current text should not be held out as a precondition for a negotiated settlement with the Taliban. Clauses within the constitution should remain negotiable through an internal process that seeks the consent of all Afghan stakeholders.

(iv)   Afghanistan must focus on developing the capacity and ethnic diversity of the ANSF. The officer cadre of the ANA that wields much of the power must be more representative, with larger Pashtun presence. Moreover, the numerical strength of the ANA should be rationalized at levels that will be sustainable after the 2014 transition.

(v)   The Afghan government and business elite have to seek ways to make the Afghan economy sustainable without the present levels of foreign monetary inflows. Notwithstanding, the international community, on its part, should continue supporting the economy well beyond 2014.

United States

(i)   From Pakistan's perspective, participants felt that the United States has to articulate a coherent Afghan strategy, particularly with regard to the impending political reconciliation process. Greater clarity on the political aspect of the strategy could help avoid failure in Afghanistan, convince the Taliban of the validity of a power-sharing agreement, and urge Pakistan and other regional actors to stop hedging and play a more constructive role.

(ii)   Washington's policy is viewed as opaque; more transparency is deemed beneficial in generating trust among regional partners. Pakistan would like Washington to be forthcoming on the role it envisions for Islamabad and guarantee that attempts will not be made to sideline it.

(iii) There is a need to remain open to negotiating with all relevant actors. Rejecting talks with specific power-wielding individuals or factions among the Afghan Taliban would prove counterproductive. For example, many participants wondered how the United States plans to negotiate with the "Quetta Shura" Taliban or the Haqqani network if it was intent on isolating, or even targeting, Mullah Omar and the Haqqani network leadership. Pakistani foreign policy elite also warn against the imposition of multiple preconditions for political reconciliation, arguing that the United States would have to remain flexible in order for negotiations to succeed. Finally, Pakistani opinion makers are unconvinced that the United States has the patience to work through a challenging and uncertain reconciliation process; they therefore seek reassurances that Washington will not abort the plan midway if things do not seem to be progressing towards a smooth linear transition.

(iv)   The United States would have to concretely address the issue of its long-term security presence in Afghanistan, and explain what future role it envisions for its military bases. In addition to articulating what a bilateral strategic partnership with Afghanistan would entail,[21] the United States should take all regional stakeholders into confidence regarding its long-term physical presence.

(v)   The state of the U.S.-Pakistan bilateral relationship was seen as intrinsically linked to the two countries' ability to cooperate on Afghanistan. Pakistanis wish to see a more consistent and dependable partnership which ceases to view Pakistan solely from a terrorism prism. Continued mistrust, participants feared, may well force both sides to overlook a convergence of interests on certain aspects of reconciliation in Afghanistan.

Pakistan

(i)   Pakistan's own policy requires coherence and clarity. While U.S. strategy in Afghanistan will affect how the Pakistani strategic establishment behaves, a purely reactive policy has severe demerits in terms of negative backlash in Pakistan and continued uncertainty within the country.

(ii)   Pakistan and the United States need frank and candid discussions on the reconciliation phase in Afghanistan; each other's expectations need to be fully comprehended and reservations expressed to avoid a constant blame game and fear on Pakistan's part that it may be sidelined in the reconciliation negotiations.

(iii)   Internally, there needs to be clarity on what role the security establishment is able and willing to play in terms of bringing the Afghan Taliban factions to the negotiating table. It may be dangerous for Pakistan to commit too much and then fail to deliver. Conversely, continuing to insist on a role without articulating what specific support the Pakistani security establishment can offer in reconciliation will only force outside actors to seek a course that is less dependent on Pakistan.

(iv)   In terms of the regional framework, Pakistani opinion makers involved in the discussions were partial towards a post-2014 security presence led by Muslim countries. A greater role for the Organization of the Islamic Conference (OIC) and countries like Turkey was mentioned, as was the need to acknowledge the Saudi and Iranian influence in Afghanistan. In general, there was support for Pakistan reaching out more actively to regional countries like Iran and the Central Asian Republics along with China to generate regional activism.

(v)   A prerequisite for a healthy regional process, however, is greater trust and collaboration between Kabul and Islamabad. Increased and sustained diplomatic contact, participants believed, would help Kabul and Islamabad reach a consensus on the shape and outcomes of the reconciliation dialogue. The need to engage Kabul continuously was stressed; Pakistan's civilian leadership is believed to be best placed to do so even as the security establishment takes the lead on implementing Pakistan's Afghanistan strategy.

(vi)   Participants had an interesting take on the Durand Line.[22] While some vehemently disagreed, most argued that this border would remain porous and un-policed even if it were formalized owing to the close ties between Pashtun communities on both sides. And while formalization is seen as being in Pakistan's interest, there was little support for making this a major hurdle in the reconciliation talks. The status quo is considered to be a fait accompli for the time being. Without disagreeing with this contention, those who stressed the economic dimension of the relationship nonetheless suggested the need for relatively better policing of trade activity to curtail the massive smuggling and drug trafficking that takes place across the border, with its attendant damaging effects on the Pakistani economy and society.

(vii)   As a long-term vision, Pakistan needs to aggressively pursue policies of inclusion in Afghanistan and terminate its continuing preoccupation with maintaining exclusively Pashtun ties. Even in the reconciliation phase, Pakistani policy may gain by increasing efforts, thus far marginal, to engage non-Pashtun factions in Afghanistan to assuage their concerns about Pakistani designs. There is a desire to see Pakistani policy move over time from one of interference to neutral support for intra-Afghan dialogue and peaceful co-existence.

(viii) The civilian government in Pakistan does not escape criticism from the policy elite for what is seen as a virtual abrogation of its responsibility to deal with tough foreign policy questions. Civilians need to take owner-ship and reclaim some of the space from the security establishment since it is politicians and diplomats who are best placed to bring about the 'de-securitization' of Pakistan's Afghanistan policy, a long-term vision which receives across the board support.

India

(i)   From a Pakistani perspective, India-Pakistan competition in Afghanistan can best be avoided if there is greater transparency regarding India's activities in Afghanistan.

(ii)   The two countries need to develop bilateral mechanisms to keep Islamabad informed about New Delhi's interests in Afghanistan and clear misperceptions about the nature and intent of specific activities: for example, a regular exchange of a fact-sheet on India's presence and actions in Afghanistan with Islamabad will be helpful. There was a specific call for closer intelligence sharing with regard to Indian activities in Afghanistan, and even to address Indian concerns about anti-India militants based in Pakistan.

(iii)   Some participants were of the view that discussions on Afghanistan should necessarily be seen as part of a broader India-Pakistan dialogue on bilateral ties. Those who proposed this tended to see collaborative initiatives and dialogue on Afghanistan as a confidence building measure which could help move overall bilateral ties forward.

Iran

(i)   U.S.-Iran tensions are another stumbling block in the endgame in Afghanistan. Pakistani policy elite are willing to recognize Iran's legitimate interests in Afghanistan and also admit that Iran's preferred outlook is a moderate, inclusive government, but one that is not Pashtun-dominated or with excessive Taliban presence. This position is fairly close to Washington's except that bilateral tensions between these two countries have masked this obvious convergence. A need to rectify the situation through quiet dialogue on the issue found support in the project discussions.

(ii)   Pakistani policy elite also see a need for Iran and Pakistan to engage more actively on the issue of Afghanistan and to identify the overlap in their positions. Iran's lingering concern that Pakistan may end up backing the Taliban to rule Afghanistan again needs to be assuaged through proactive diplomacy.

Postscript: Does Osama bin Laden's Killing Impact the Afghanistan Calculus?

On May 2, 2011, Al Qaida leader Osama Bin Laden was killed in a U.S. raid in Abbottabad, Pakistan. The unilateral raid was conducted by U.S. Special Operations Forces, led by the Navy SEALs in the early hours of May 2. The assault teams flew in from Afghanistan, conducted a successful 45-minute operation, and returned swiftly. Bin Laden was subsequently buried at sea. The Pakistani civilian and military leadership was uninformed about the raid.

The roundtable discussions and most of the interviews conducted during this project were completed before the May 2 episode. However, given the enormity of this development and the potential for it to impact American and Pakistani policy towards Afghanistan, the project team reached out to the roundtable participants and requested them to reflect on the implications of bin Laden's killing. A response to the following two questions was elicited (between June 1 and June 18) via email:

(i)   How do you think bin Laden's death will change the U.S.'s endgame in Afghanistan?

(ii)   Will bin Laden's killing change Pakistan's strategy vis-à-vis Afghanistan?

We received responses from 17 of the 39 roundtable participants and thus these observations are not necessarily representative of the views of all those who participated in the roundtable discussions.

The impact of bin Laden's death on U.S. strategy in Afghanistan

Respondents to these questions suggested that Osama bin Laden's killing will not fundamentally alter the U.S. endgame in Afghanistan, as the goal of denying sanctuary to Afghanistan—and Pakistan–based militant outfits plotting to strike American targets has yet to be achieved.

Most respondents however, expected the Obama administration to use bin Laden's killing to its political advantage. One of America's stated goals in

Afghanistan is to "defeat and dismantle Al Qaida," and bin Laden's killing, most respondents felt, helps achieve this in a symbolic, if not operational, context. Therefore, President Obama could now reduce a substantial number of troops before the next U.S. presidential elections; troop withdrawal commensurate with this perceived success will give him additional political mileage during his re-election bid.[23]

Moreover, the impetus for U.S. troop withdrawal will gradually shift the emphasis to a negotiated political solution. With Al Qaida significantly weakened—bin Laden's death will be capitalized to underscore how severely Al Qaida has been dented—the United States will reemphasize that it is willing to negotiate with the Taliban who accept Washington's red lines. These demands may be more seriously entertained as bin Laden's killing has given the Obama administration an opening to create a narrative of victory that can counter perceptions that the U.S. military envisions an open-ended war in Afghanistan.

On the other hand, respondents were also concerned that Washington may overcompensate and, for political reasons, seek to rapidly broker an agreement in Afghanistan without laying the necessary groundwork. Some worried that this may lead the United States to conduct talks with low-level Taliban who are not truly representative of the core of the insurgency. Not only will such a deal be unsustainable, but it will also cause the leadership of the main Taliban factions to continue perpetrating violence.

In the near future, in order to facilitate the dual goals of hastening a political solution and accelerating troop withdrawal, most of the responses predicted that the United States will increase pressure on Pakistan to crack down on groups that continue to launch attacks against ISAF and Afghan forces from Pakistan's tribal belt.

The U.S.-Pakistan relationship after bin Laden

The discovery of bin Laden in a garrison town in Pakistan put the state on a diplomatic defensive. Responses reflected an acute awareness that the Pakistani state had been embarrassed and cornered, with the world viewing bin Laden's presence in Pakistan as proof that it is Pakistan, not Afghanistan that remains the center of gravity of the problem. This has enhanced concerns that the United States, while putting pressure on Pakistan to "do more," will also seek to hold out the option of sidelining Pakistan during the negotiations. Islamabad is increasingly suspicious about Washington's intentions regarding Pakistani involvement in the Afghan reconciliation process. The mutual mistrust between the ISI and the U.S. Central Intelligence Agency (CIA) and between the two militaries, exposed as it was during the May 2 raid,[24] has raised doubts about whether the United States and Pakistan can collaborate towards a solution in Afghanistan. Respondents were also cognizant that the ISI is widely reviled by foreign actors and that it is seen as holding up progress on an Afghan settlement. Should the status quo persist, the blame would continue to fall on the ISI and it will make the United States even more adamant on sidelining the Pakistani security establishment. In essence then, the state of the bilateral relationship is being seen as an impediment to allowing the two sides to work together in the Afghan reconciliation process.

The anticipated pressure on Pakistan to "do more" is seen as an additional cause for bilateral tensions in the coming months. Responses pointed to renewed pressure on Pakistan to launch a major military operation in North Waziristan—being built up at the time most of the responses came in—and to cooperate with the United States to eliminate other militant leaders such as Ayman al Zawahiri as a trend that will continue. Some believed that the United States may even use the opportunity to underscore the importance of a broader counterterrorism approach which targets all militant groups that threaten the West. This would include not only the Taliban but also groups like Lashkar-e-Tayyaba. Worse yet, some feared that the United States will gradually turn its attention to Pakistan itself and bank heavily on unilateral measures such as drone strikes and intelligence presence in Pakistan to go after high-value targets in the country. Pushing Pakistan to act against the whole gamut of terrorist groups, let alone greater reliance on unilateral actions, will, however, strain bilateral ties further and may impact Pakistan's ability and willingness to play a positive role in the Afghan reconciliation process. The result, as seen by most respondents, would be a more challenged negotiation process and continued instability in Afghanistan, and indeed, Pakistan.

Notably, there are views which disagreed and suggested that despite growing mistrust, the United States realizes the importance of the Pakistani security establishment in achieving peace in Afghanistan. Suspicions aside, they argued, the Obama administration will continue to reach out to elicit Pakistan's support in nudging the Afghan Taliban to the negotiating table.

Bin Laden's influence on Pakistan's security calculus in Afghanistan

Respondents suggested that bin Laden's death had no bearing on Pakistan's national interests in Afghanistan. Islamabad would continue to seek an inclusive government in Afghanistan that has adequate Pashtun representation and cedes some power to the Afghan Taliban. To this end, Pakistan will continue to support a political process that leads to a representative regime in Kabul. Strained ties with the United States will however strengthen the voice of those who back a more proactive regional approach without the United States.

Separately, a few respondents pointed out that bin Laden's presence in Pakistan and retaliatory terrorist attacks within the country following his killing have exposed domestic fault lines in Pakistan's national security strategy. In the run-up to the 2014 Afghanistan transition, the Pakistan Army and intelligence agencies will have to address homegrown militant networks and the threat posed by militant infiltration into the security apparatus. Internal threats will further strengthen Pakistan's desire to see a stable Afghanistan that cannot be used by militant outfits as a launching pad for attacks against the Pakistani state.

That said, there is still a belief that Pakistan cannot afford to follow U.S. dictates in terms of opening new military fronts. An all out operation in North Waziristan continues to find opposition. Lack of capacity and the high likelihood of a serious backlash in Pakistan from the Afghan Taliban-TTP combine worried most of the respondents. Further, as the United States renews efforts to broker a political solution in Afghanistan, groups like the Haqqani network will be approached for negotiations. Pakistan's ability to bring them to the table will be dented if an offensive is launched against them. Also, as discussed at length, these groups provide Pakistan leverage in the endgame and are still Pakistan's friendliest option in Afghanistan in any post-transition scenario.

The impact of bin Laden's death within Afghanistan

Respondents also reflected on the impact bin Laden's departure would have on the Afghan Taliban and within Afghanistan. Judging by the responses, it is clear that bin Laden's killing is not synonymous with the demise of Al Qaida, let alone the Taliban factions. Moreover, some Taliban groups like Mullah Omar's no longer had as active a funding and training relationship with Al Qaida as it did once or as the Haqqani network may have even today. In essence, the Afghan Taliban's operational capabilities will remain more or less intact. However, symbolically, the killing is a blow to the insurgency. There was a sense that bin Laden's removal and the subsequent narrative of victory against Al Qaida may make it easier for the Afghan government and/or the United States to negotiate directly with Afghan Taliban leaders. A greater emphasis may be laid on distinguishing Al Qaida from the Taliban to facilitate the process further—a welcome step from the Pakistani perspective.

In terms of the Afghan government in Kabul, the bin Laden episode was seen as having provided President Karzai and his beleaguered security forces the opportunity to blame their failures against the insurgency on Pakistan's security policies. At the same time however, President Karzai is believed to realize Islamabad's importance in ensuring stability in Afghanistan and the futility of attempting to isolate Pakistan from the scene. His efforts to improve bilateral ties with Pakistan in recent months, the desire to work towards a bilateral and regional solution to the conflict (manifested by multiple official visits to Islamabad and efforts to invigorate the Afghanistan-Pakistan Joint Commission for Reconciliation and Peace), and to give shape to a power-sharing arrangement are seen in this stead. That said, some of the respondents also acknowledged that tensions remain in the relationship nonetheless, and that there is still a long way to go before Kabul and Islamabad could fully coordinate efforts to bring about an acceptable negotiated settlement, and in turn, relative stability to Afghanistan.

Notes

1. In this phase, we also held conversations with the military's official spokesperson and at the Ministry of Foreign Affairs to better understand the Pakistani state's official position on the subject.
2. The roundtable in Lahore was held on March 2, 2011, the one in Peshawar on March 5, and the four in Islamabad on March 8–10.
3. We requested Lt. Gen. (Rtd.) Asad Durrani, Ejaz Haider, Dr. Rifaat Hussain and Amb. Humayun Khan to serve as the "cross-checkers."
4. Historical data reflects official Pakistani figures (converted from Pakistani Rupees) released for the cited years by the Federal Bureau of Statistics (Government of Pakistan). There is a discrepancy in the current trade figures released by various governments and international sources but all approximate the cited figure.
5. Mullah Omar's group of Taliban is popularly referred to as "Quetta Shura" in recent literature and by the international media due to the outfit's alleged presence in the Pakistani western city of Quetta. Our use of this term is merely driven by the desire to maintain consistency with existing literature and for the ease of readers familiar with it.
6. For the purposes of this report, "Afghan Taliban" refers to all major and minor insurgent factions fighting under the Taliban moniker, including Mullah Omar's "Quetta Shura" and the Haqqani network. Specific groups are referred to individually where a distinction is sought between the various Afghan Taliban factions.
7. The general sense is that the U.S. military has usurped significant policy space on the "Af-Pak" question in Washington. Some participants even drew parallels between the U.S. military's current clout in this context and the Pakistan military's hold over its country's security policy.
8. See "Clinton to Taliban: Dump al-Qaida or 'Face Consequences'," Inaugural Holbrooke Lecture, *Asia Society*, February 18, 2011, http://asiasociety.org/policy/strategic-challenges/us-asia/clinton-taliban-dump-alqaida-or-face-consequences.
9. These views were shared in March 2011, before U.S. President Barack Obama announced a withdrawal timetable for U.S. forces from Afghanistan on June 22, 2011. According to the plan, 10,000 U.S. soldiers will be withdrawn from Afghanistan by the end of 2011, and a total of 33,000 will exit by summer of 2012. A steady decrease in numbers will continue thereafter till the transition is complete in December 2014.
10. One participant suggested that this lack of clarity was intentional and was meant to provide U.S. decision makers flexibility in changing the future course if needed. This view however did not resonate with the others.
11. After Osama Bin Laden's killing, a period not discussed in this part of the report, there has been fresh debate on this issue with some in Pakistan contending that bin Laden's departure makes it easier for the U.S. to define its mission as Al Qaida-centric.
12. General David Petraeus has since been appointed the Director of the American Central Intelligence Agency (CIA).
13. Some participants saw the United States as having an eye on the Afghan mineral wealth and as having an interest in using its presence in Afghanistan to counter Iran and the expansion of Chinese interests into West Asia.

14. A mention was made of the possibility of a de facto north-south division of Afghanistan in line with former U.S. Ambassador Robert Blackwill's proposal (See Robert D. Blackwill, "Plan B in Afghanistan: Why a De Facto Partition is the Least Bad Option," *Foreign Affairs*, Vol. 90, No.1 (January/February 2011)). However, participants dismissed this as unrealistic and unacceptable to the Afghan people and key regional actors.

15. These views predate Afghan President Hamid Karzai's statement of June 18, 2011 confirming that there have been direct political contacts between the United States and the Taliban. The then U.S. Defense Secretary, Robert Gates subsequently confirmed these contacts. Although the contacts were characterized as preliminary, Pakistan expressed its displeasure at being kept out of the loop by the United States. See Emma Graham-Harrison and Hamid Shalizi, "U.S. in Peace Talks with Taliban, Karzai Confirms," *Reuters*, June 18, 2011, http://www.huffingtonpost.com/2011/06/18/us-taliban-peace-talks_n_879680.html; and "Pakistan Upset at Being Left Out of US-Taliban Peace Talks," *Press Trust of India*, June 27, 2011, http://www.ndtv.com/article/world/pakistan-upset-at-being-left-out-of-us-taliban-peace-talks-115094.

16. Participants holding this view believed that it was their state's obsession with treating the Taliban government in Kabul during the 1990s as a mere proxy which allowed the latter to penetrate Pakistani society and to run a number of its fund-raising and ideological campaigns from Pakistan itself. The implications for Pakistani society in terms of greater susceptibility to radical Islamist ideologies were immense according to this narrative.

17. For the purposes of this report, the ANSF refer to all civilian and military forces, including the Afghan National Army (ANA), the Afghan National Police, and all the branches that fall under these.

18. Bilateral exchanges between Pakistan and Central Asian countries took place in spring 2011. On March 7–10, 2011, Tajikistan's President Emomali Rahmon met his Pakistani counterpart Asif Ali Zardari in Islamabad. Soon after, on March 15–16, 2011, Pakistani Prime Minister Yousaf Raza Gilani visited Kyrgyzstan. President Zardari also visited Turkey on April 11–14, 2011 and met with the Turkish leadership.

19. President Zardari visited Moscow on May 11–12, 2011, where he met with Russian President Dmitry Medvedev and signed agreements on agriculture, aviation, and energy cooperation. The visit was Zardari's first high-profile foreign trip after the killing of Al Qaida leader Osama bin Laden in Pakistan by U.S. Special Forces on May 2, 2011. The following week, on May 17–20, Prime Minister Gilani visited China to seek stronger support from Beijing. The trip was significant, and controversial from a U.S. perspective, because it came at a time when already strained U.S.-Pakistan ties were being further tested by the bin Laden episode.

20. Ben Arnoldy, "Can Afghanistan Economy Thrive Without Poppy?" *Christian Science Monitor*, March 5, 2010, http://www.csmonitor.com/World/Asia-South- Central/2010/0305/Can-Afghanistan-economy-thrivewithout-poppy.

21. Kabul and Washington had already initiated conversations about a bilateral strategic partnership when the roundtable discussions were held. The strategic partnership seeks continued U.S. access to some military bases in return for a U.S. commitment to continue providing assistance to the Afghan government.

22. The Durand Line is the 1610-mile-long contested border between Afghanistan and Pakistan. Marked by the British colonial rulers in 1893, the Durand Line was declared invalid in 1949 by the Afghanistan Loya Jirga as they saw it as ex-parte on their side. Kabul still claims the Pashtun territories in Pakistan that comprise FATA and parts of KPK province. Pakistan, however considers the Durand Line as an international border. In practice, the border remains porous owing to ancient tribal connections between Pashtuns that transcend the Line. Thousands cross over every day, both legally (tribes divided by the Line have Easement Rights) and illegally. In recent years, the Pakistan military has blamed part of its counterterrorism shortcomings on lack of support for its proposal to fence the Durand Line and install biometric facilities to keep better track of cross-border movement.

23. These responses were received before June 22, 2011, when President Obama announced his withdrawal timeline for U.S. troops in Afghanistan (see footnote 9).

24. The unilateral strike by the United States against Al Qaida leader Osama bin Laden's compound in Abbottabad heightened concerns within Pakistan about a growing U.S. intelligence footprint within its territory and consequent threats to its national sovereignty. This friction manifested itself on May 14 2011, when, in response to the raid, a joint session of both houses of the Pakistani parliament passed a unanimous resolution to defend Pakistan's sovereignty, security, and territorial integrity against U.S. military actions. For the past few months, the U.S.-Pakistan relationship, particularly ties between the countries' powerful intelligence agencies, the CIA and ISI, had been in a downward spiral: in December 2010, the name of the CIA station chief in Islamabad was leaked; in March 2011, Pakistan's army chief General Kayani condemned a drone attack that reportedly killed 41 people—he also hinted that his force could shoot down drones in Pakistani territory, suggesting that CIA-ISI cooperation in the drone program has been reevaluated; in April 2011, Director General of the ISI, General Ahmed Shuja Pasha, met with CIA Director Leon Panetta in Washington to demand more control over U.S. spy programs within the country; more recently in May–June 2011, Pakistan decided to expel U.S. military trainers from the country, only to see Washington hold back monetary assistance earmarked for the training program and related activities.

8

Regional Politics and the Prospects for Stability in Afghanistan

Sunil Dasgupta

T his chapter, written in 2013, brings India fully into the regional equation. It examines the effects of recent developments in Afghanistan—particularly the impending U.S. withdrawal—on regional stability, defined predominantly by the relationship between India and Pakistan—the "central fault-line in regional politics affecting Afghanistan."

It took some time for the India-Pakistan relationship to be placed at the center of U.S. policymaking regarding Afghanistan. Previously, Washington had adopted a policy of "de-hyphenation," treating each country separately; the effect of Afghanistan on the India-Pakistan rivalry was deemed to be minimal. This partly changed with the Obama administration and the creation of the "Af-Pak" structure. The academic thinking behind Af-Pak—advanced in an article by Barnett Rubin and Ahmad Rashid in 2008—initially placed India in its conceptual structure, but India reacted strongly and successfully against being included in practice.

Dasgupta's analyses of three scenarios for India's role in Afghanistan are all fairly pessimistic. First, India and Pakistan could maintain a proxy rivalry in Afghanistan, with India expanding its presence short of using troops and Pakistan reacting by strengthening pro-Pakistan groups. This dynamic, Dasgupta writes is, "a recipe for civil war." Second, India and Pakistan could cooperate in Afghanistan, particularly on trade and economic infrastructure, but this is only likely if the United States maintains a strong troop presence in Afghanistan "to mitigate the stark prisoner's dilemma game unfolding in the region." Third, India could essentially cede Afghanistan to Pakistan. This would perhaps improve the chances for stability in Afghanistan, but it is also unlikely to occur: It goes against what Dasgupta describes as the "Delhi consensus,"

Originally published as Sunil Dasgupta, "Regional Politics and the Prospects for Stability in Afghanistan," Peaceworks 86 (Washington, DC: USIP, 2013).

which posits that Afghanistan's mineral wealth and geographical location on the road to Central Asia make it vitally important to India.

Dasgupta argues that the need for regional stability justifies a sufficiently robust U.S. troop presence and has nothing to do with antiterrorism capabilities, counterinsurgency requirements, or even U.S. domestic political considerations. Relying heavily on Anatol Lieven's Pakistan: A Hard Country, *Dasgupta also suggests that, contrary to the assumptions of many analysts in Delhi and in Washington, Pakistan is not on the brink of collapse. For Dasgupta and Lieven, the error comes from analyzing Pakistan's economic weakness based on official statistics, which fail to capture Pakistan's robust informal economy. Policymakers basing their calculations on what they believe is a fragile political order would do well to take Dasgupta seriously on this point.*

Introduction

As the United States plans its withdrawal from Afghanistan, the country faces three interrelated challenges: a weak national state, rising Islamic radicalism based in Pakistan's tribal belt, and zero-sum regional politics that could fuel another civil war in the country. The first two issues have received considerable political and scholarly attention, but the problems of regional politics remain less explored, in part because of the difficulties involved in drawing the region's governments into a broad grand bargain.

Afghanistan's political problems have always been rooted in regional politics. British and Russian campaigns in the past had to deal with tensions between domestic Afghan and regional politics; regional politics have also shaped the U.S. strategy from the start of its Afghan campaign. U.S. officials' confrontation of the Pakistani government after the attacks of September 11, 2001, carried the implicit threat that the United States could join forces with India against Pakistan. In December 2001, India accused Pakistani groups of planning a terrorist attack on its parliament and threatened military reprisal. Pakistan's army responded in the east, diverting its attention from apprehending Taliban and al-Qaeda fighters escaping from Afghanistan into Pakistan.[1]

Over the past decade, both the George W. Bush and Barack Obama administrations have sought to rally the region's other governments to help stabilize Afghanistan, but these efforts have come up short. With the United States planning to draw down its troop presence by 2014, the search for a regional settlement has intensified. As the chances of a broadly inclusive political settlement with the Taliban are diminishing, the worsening security situation in Afghanistan risks another civil war that could allow al-Qaeda and other extremists to return and regroup amid the chaos. Most significantly, India and Pakistan would likely take opposing sides in such a conflict, raising the possibility of the civil war metastasizing into a "dirty little cold war,"[2] with consequences reminiscent of the 1990s.

All the state actors involved—Afghanistan, Pakistan, India, and the United States—have acknowledged that another civil war would be disastrous, but none of them appears able to mitigate the structural conditions in place. The expectation in Pakistan is that the successor to the government of President Hamid Karzai will not survive the challenges of the international drawdown in military and financial assistance. The heavily Tajik and Uzbek composition of the Afghan National Army is likely to exacerbate ethnic tensions and compel Pakistan to support Pashtun groups, including the Taliban. Recognizing Pakistan's inevitable involvement in Afghanistan, India has been cementing its relations with the Karzai government and the Tajik and Uzbek groups with whom it shares a common distrust of Pakistan. This makes for a starkly drawn prisoner's dilemma, with Afghanistan's and the region's future hanging in the balance.

This report investigates the unfolding power contest between India and Pakistan in Afghanistan as regional actors prepare for reduced U.S. presence after 2014. The Central Asian states, Iran, China, and Russia all have important interests in Afghanistan, but the India-Pakistan rivalry is the central tension that any regional solution must address.[3] This report explores three scenarios. The first makes a straight-line prediction from extant structural conditions of a balance-of-power contest after 2014. The second and third scenarios explore the possibilities for altering these structural conditions to change the nature of the contest. The second scenario examines the requirements for India-Pakistan cooperation in Afghanistan, and the third scenario explores the prospect of relieving the regional tensions through unilateral disengagement.

It may turn out to be impossible to prevent another civil war in Afghanistan. But not trying to mitigate the balance-of-power contest in the country would be misguided. The consequences of intensified rivalry between India and Pakistan would be dramatic, diminishing the prospect of peace in Afghanistan and disrupting broader regional stability.

Regional Approaches to the Afghan War

When General Pervez Musharraf, Pakistan's former president, spoke to his people on September 20, 2001, about his decision to abandon the Taliban and work with the United States in fighting terrorism, he had been worried about the possibility of a U.S.-India alliance aimed at Pakistan.[4] Less than two months later, as India mobilized its armed forces in response to the December 13 terrorist attack on the Indian Parliament, Pakistan redeployed large numbers of troops from the Afghan border to the Indian border, undercutting the objective of cutting off al-Qaeda's escape from Afghanistan into Pakistan.[5] The Pakistan Army's inability to cut off their flight was one of the greatest failures of the Afghan war.[6] The Taliban regrouped in the mountains straddling Afghanistan and Pakistan and have since turned the conflict into America's longest war.

To mitigate the consequences of the zero-sum nature of regional politics, the Bush administration pursued a policy of "de-hyphenation," so called because the United States saw the region mainly through the lens of the India-Pakistan rivalry and was seeking to put its bilateral ties with each country on separate tracks to minimize the effects of their mutual animosity toward U.S. foreign policy.[7] Thus President Bush extended military and economic assistance to Pakistan and designated that country a major non-NATO ally. At the same time, he boosted India as a rising power in Asia, calling it a natural ally of the United States. The U.S. ambassador in New Delhi openly referred to India as a potential balance to China.[8] India took the opportunity to escape its longstanding strategic parity with Pakistan, welcomed the notion of equivalence with China, and secured a civilian nuclear deal that legitimized India as a nuclear power. Meanwhile, though the Pakistan government under Musharraf acquiesced to the United States after September 11, supporting the U.S. war effort with transit access, logistics, and intelligence cooperation, there has been a continuous deficit of trust ever since— in part because Washington has implicitly threatened to ally more closely with New Delhi if Pakistan does not cooperate.

Nonetheless, de-hyphenation encouraged India-Pakistan détente. Under U.S. (and Western) pressure to show itself as credible partner in countering Islamic terrorism, Islamabad reduced its support for the Kashmir insurgency and redirected its military resources to fighting growing radicalism at home as a new movement of indigenous Taliban was emerging to threaten the state. Competition between India and Pakistan to sway U.S. support was reduced as the United States set its relations with each country on separate tracks. For a number of years thereafter, India-Pakistan relations improved, and the two sides almost reached a peace deal ending the Kashmir dispute in 2007.[9]

The de-hyphenation policy also overcame key U.S. differences with India and Pakistan. The United States saw—or hoped to see—reform-minded Pakistanis as willing and able to carry the fight to radical Islamists in Afghanistan and Pakistan. In the aftermath of the September 11 attacks, the United States depended on the Pakistan Army (President Musharraf was also its chief) to support the Afghan war and perhaps transform Pakistan itself. When Musharraf proved unable to win over the radicals and alienated Pakistan's general populace, Washington placed similar hope in Benazir Bhutto. After her assassination, the new government under her husband, Asif Ali Zardari, agreed to do what she had promised, and Washington kept in place a foreign aid package designed to strengthen Zardari and his allies.

In the Indian view, however, the Pakistan Army and the country's elite more generally were responsible for the region's problems with Islamic radicalism. When Pakistan was able to install an aligned regime in Afghanistan in the 1990s, that country became the epicenter of international terrorism. The Pakistan-backed Taliban allowed terrorist groups—not only al-Qaeda but also anti-Indian outfits such as Lashkar-e-Taiba—to openly expand training camps in the country. Indian armed forces saw a rise in the number of Afghan-trained terrorists in Kashmir. In 1999, terrorists hijacked an Indian Airlines flight with 178 passengers to Kandahar. Taliban protection for the hijackers precluded an Indian special forces rescue, and New Delhi was forced to free three jailed terrorists—including Ahmed Omar Saeed Sheikh, who was later accused of killing *Wall Street Journal* reporter Daniel Pearl in Pakistan—to secure the release of the aircraft and its passengers. To Indians, preventing Afghanistan from becoming a terrorist state once again meant preventing Pakistan from dominating Afghan politics. Most of India's strategic community still sees no difference between the two objectives.

Pakistan has remained ambivalent in its support for U.S. goals in Afghanistan (and Pakistan) given its concerns about the long-term prospects of ties with the United States. Most Pakistanis believe that the United States will walk away from Pakistan once the Afghan war is over, just as it did in 1965, 1971, and 1990. All three times, the United States left Pakistan in the lurch—in 1965 and 1971, in the middle of wars with India, and in 1990, holding the bag on Afghanistan. In the past decade, Pakistanis have generally viewed the U.S. de-hyphenation policy, and especially the U.S.-India nuclear deal, as evidence of Washington's real preferences in South Asia, where Pakistan is an ally of convenience in the war against al-Qaeda and expendable thereafter, while India is the true friend of the future. In response, Pakistan reportedly has expanded its fissile material production, seeking a nuclear off set against India's conventional superiority.[10] Pakistan's security establishment also has held the view that radical groups, such as Lashkar-e-Taiba, are effective instruments to coerce India and any unfriendly Afghan government.[11] Steve Coll, the author of *Ghost Wars*, has argued that the Pakistani security services began to turn away from radical groups after the Lal Masjid siege in 2007 but concludes that there is still "no one view" about their utility.[12] Pakistan's security establishment has distinguished between "good" and "bad" Islamists by targeting, for example, the Pakistani Taliban but not the Taliban groups fighting in Afghanistan. Lashkar-e-Taiba remains unfettered even after it was implicated in the 2008 Mumbai terrorist attack and is now known to be sending fighters to the Taliban's aid in Afghanistan.[13]

De-hyphenation was the first serious regional approach to the Afghan problem during the U.S. epoch in the country. The policy allowed the United States to fight the Afghan war with reasonable cooperation from Pakistan by seeking to alter the nature of the India-Pakistan relationship. India was conspicuously absent in formal political negotiations, such as the Bonn Conference, despite its strong interest in preventing Pakistan from installing another allied regime in Afghanistan. In choosing to work quietly, New Delhi was being mindful of Pakistani sensitivities and the complications it could cause for the United States. The de-hyphenation policy finally ran aground after the terrorist attacks in Mumbai in November 2008. Where the policy had sought to keep the two countries separate and allow détente to emerge, the attacks brought the two countries right back to distrust and hostility. The Pakistani government even admitted the involvement of Lashkar-e-Taiba in the attacks.[14] India captured one of the attackers and was able to track down telephone conversations between the attackers in Mumbai and their handlers in Pakistan. The United States later arrested a U.S. citizen of Pakistani origin who had scouted the attack locations. The Pakistani state had long tolerated Lashkar-e-Taiba. The only question then was the degree to which Pakistani intelligence agents were actively involved in the attacks.

By the time Obama became president in January 2009, the situation in Afghanistan had deteriorated considerably. The Taliban had been making a comeback in Afghanistan since 2005. The Karzai government, significantly dependent on the cooperation of regional warlords, seemed unable to prevent—or, many argue, was complicit in—the country slipping into corruption and violence. Meanwhile, the Taliban enjoyed safe havens among Pashtun tribes on the Pakistani side of the border with Afghanistan. Starting in 2004, following a punitive foray into the Federally Administered Tribal Areas (FATA) in 2003 and assassination attempts against President Musharraf, the Pakistan Army made several peace deals with Pashtun tribes that allowed Afghan Taliban to find shelter in the FATA population. These deals distinguished between the local Taliban and "foreign fighters," the mostly al-Qaeda militants from outside the region. Redirecting state priorities away from conflict with the Taliban effectively meant that those who were ideologically predisposed had some leeway to support the Taliban once again. Since the 2007 Lal Masjid siege in Islamabad, the Pakistan Army has further distinguished between the Afghan Taliban, who have been left undisturbed, and the Pakistani Taliban and other radical groups that have broken away from the state, who it continues to target.[15] This distinction has increasingly infuriated U.S. officials and led to the concerted campaign of drone strikes inside Pakistan that began in 2007, which has further soured U.S.-Pakistan relations.

President Obama's first move in the region was to refocus U.S. attention on the Afghan war. He saw Pakistan as central to the war in Afghanistan, creating the moniker "Af-Pak" to capture the inseparability of the Taliban across the Durand Line, the formally disputed border between Afghanistan and Pakistan. The president's designated new special representative, the late Richard Holbrooke, took this logic further when he argued that a political settlement from Pakistan's perspective required Indian concessions in Kashmir.[16]

India rejected this out of hand, leaving Holbrooke with no option but to narrow the regional approach to Pakistan alone. In 2009, Obama decided to send thirty thousand more troops to Afghanistan and pushed Karzai to reform his administration, root out corruption, and deliver services. Most important, he announced that the United States would begin the process of withdrawing from Afghanistan in July 2011, though he kept open the possibility of continued U.S. military presence in the country if necessary and at the request of the Afghan government.

With Pakistan, Obama has emphasized counterterrorism while backing strategic dialogue and supporting the Kerry-Lugar-Berman foreign aid package. He vastly expanded the drone program inside Pakistan, and his efforts to find Osama bin Laden finally bore fruit in May 2011. But U.S.-Pakistan relations, already under pressure from the drone strikes and intelligence-gathering efforts, have plummeted since the Abbottabad raid. Following a November 2011 border incident in which twenty-four Pakistani troops died in U.S. fire, Pakistan suspended NATO resupply convoys from the port city of Karachi going to Afghanistan. The supply routes were reopened after a great deal of bargaining, but U.S. officials now openly accuse Pakistan's Inter-Services Intelligence (ISI) of helping the Haqqani Network, a Taliban army operating out of Jalalabad in eastern Afghanistan. Recently, U.S. counterterrorism experts have been calling for the containment of Pakistan, with Indian help if necessary.[17]

Rather than turning Pakistanis against radicalism, the Obama strategy has increasingly put many Pakistanis on edge. According to cross-national polling by Pew and others, Pakistan remains one of the countries most hostile towards the United States. The rank and file of the Pakistan Army appears to be more enraged at the United States—and failures of its own political and military leaders—over the Abbottabad attack than they are about bin Laden's presence in their country and the possibility that parts of the Pakistani state may have been complicit. The doctor who assisted the United States in finding bin Laden is being tried for treason against Pakistan, as if he had done anything but follow the explicit statements of his country's leaders to fight against terrorists.

Although a negotiated end to the Afghan war may be possible, publicly available reporting on the political process is pessimistic about the chances of bringing to power a reconciliation government in Kabul at this point. Although the Obama administration has attempted to establish a negotiating channel with the Taliban, Ryan C. Crocker, who as the U.S. ambassador to Afghanistan was one of the officials tasked with pushing for talks, has spoken against inviting the Taliban back into power. "[If the] Taliban get back, stand by for al-Qaeda," he told an audience at a Washington think tank in September 2012 after he returned home from his post.[18]

The strongest of the Afghan factions—among the Taliban as well as Tajik, Uzbek, and Hazara groups—have not been willing to compromise. To the

Taliban, Karzai and his allies are corrupt and incompetent collaborators of the West who can be swept away quickly once foreign troops depart. Karzai himself is term-limited to 2014, and the political contest over who will become part of the new government could destabilize the ruling coalition itself, though it also presents an opportunity to accommodate the warring parties.

In a September 2012 Carnegie report, Gilles Dorronsoro predicted that the Taliban will launch a full-scale offensive in the Kabul region and to the east of the country as early as spring 2013.[19] In November 2012, Ismail Khan, a Herati warlord, broke publicly from the ranks of the ruling coalition supporting Karzai by asking his followers to rearm for another war.[20] "If the Afghan security forces are not able to wage this war, then call upon the mujahedeen," First Vice President Mohammed Fahim, himself a powerful Tajik warlord, is reported to have said.[21] The U.S. Department of Defense reported in December 2012 that the number of insurgent attacks did not fall in 2012, after an appreciable decline in 2011. Instead, a rise in so-called "green-on-blue" attacks, in which Afghan security forces have opened fire on their international trainers, has become a concern, in some cases forcing the U.S. military to reduce training activities for the Afghan forces.

Pakistan has taken limited steps to support U.S. efforts to engage the Taliban, recently releasing Taliban prisoners so they can participate in settlement talks. Though many Taliban leaders live in Pakistan, holding talks in the country has proven impossible. According to some reports, Taliban leaders in Pakistan willing to talk to U.S. officials have been detained and, in some cases, killed. The United States itself has not met one of the Taliban's key demands regarding the release of prisoners from the Guantanamo Bay facility.

The pressure of the 2014 pullout has prompted renewed efforts toward a regional solution. There have been growing calls for increased Indian involvement in Afghanistan.[22] Larry Hanauer and Peter Chalk of RAND have argued that the United States should encourage India to develop even closer ties with Afghanistan, as India's goals of denying safe havens to terrorists, projecting power in South and Central Asia, and securing access to new trade and energy resources in Afghanistan are consistent with Washington's objectives and superior to Pakistan's narrow security-related goals.[23] On a visit to New Delhi in June 2012, former defense secretary Leon Panetta urged "India's leaders to continue with additional support to Afghanistan through trade and investment, reconstruction and help for Afghan security forces."[24]

Scenario 1: A Balance-of-Power Contest in Afghanistan

India and Pakistan are both poised for a balance-of-power competition in Afghanistan. Indians have responded to calls for greater participation in Afghanistan with enthusiasm.[25] Even as India stayed away from the post-Taliban political process in Afghanistan, it quietly offered economic and technical assistance almost as soon as Karzai assumed leadership of the country in 2001. Karzai had ties in India; he attended university there. Key members of his government were Tajik, Uzbek, and Hazara leaders who had been part of the Northern Alliance,[26] which India supported during the 1990s civil war that brought the Taliban to power. The new Afghan government was suspicious of Pakistan for its support to the Taliban, and India had an interest in checking the return of Islamabad's influence in Kabul.

The Indian government has persisted in Afghanistan despite being targeted by the Taliban. In 2005, the Taliban kidnapped and killed an Indian official, which led New Delhi to send two hundred armed police to provide perimeter security to Indian missions in Afghanistan. In 2007, one police officer died in a grenade attack in Jalalabad. In July 2008, a suicide car bomber struck the Indian embassy in Kabul, killing fifty-five people, including senior Indian officials, though most of the casualties were Afghan. Indian, Afghan, and U.S. officials have said that the ISI was complicit in these attacks, but Islamabad has denied involvement.

Indian diplomacy intensified further following Obama's announcement of a definitive U.S. drawdown. In October 2011, New Delhi signed a strategic partnership agreement with the Karzai government, opening the door for security cooperation between the two countries. By 2012 India had spent $1.5 billion, pledged another $500 million, and sent nearly three thousand people to Afghanistan to help build roads, railways, power lines, schools, and hospitals. In the summer of 2012, an Indian consortium of private and state-owned companies bid $6 billion for mining rights in Afghanistan. New Delhi has expressed interest in reviving the natural gas pipeline project from Turkmenistan to India and sponsored Afghanistan for membership in the South Asian Association for Regional Cooperation (SAARC). India also has proposed an alternate trade route to Afghanistan through Iran, causing consternation in Pakistan and the United States.

The New Delhi Consensus

The general thrust of Indian policy toward Afghanistan has remained unchanged since the U.S. war in Afghanistan began in 2001. This policy continuity is the outcome of an Indian consensus, which Shekhar Gupta, the editor of the *Indian Express*, has described below:

> Today, everybody seems to be accepting the idea that Afghanistan is of great strategic significance to India, and we can neither cede it to Pakistan, nor leave them to fill the power vacuum that the Americans will leave behind. Similarly, that this is the Great Game country, and we are back to the Great Game, somehow inheriting the mantle of the British power in the 19th century, except that we might have to deal with an additional distraction called Pakistan. Further, that Afghanistan

is a resource (mineral)-rich land where we have future commercial
stakes, and is a gateway to Central Asia, making transit rights of such
paramount importance for us.[27]

Gupta rejects the consensus, but it is worth exploring the breadth and scope
of Indian agreement on Afghanistan policy. First, Indian desire for a more assertive foreign policy in Afghanistan is surprising, as it breaks from the doctrine of strategic restraint that has driven the country's foreign policy since its
independence in 1947.[28] The nuclear tests, a new strategic partnership with the
United States, and rapid economic growth raised the prospect of New Delhi
moving toward a more assertive foreign policy, but India's leaders have held
off from becoming too ambitious in the region. Indian thinking on Pakistan,
the country's most urgent security concern, is highly divided, ranging from
unilateral accommodation to the destruction of Pakistan, with deterrence as
the median policy position in the strategic community.[29]

Second, the military strategic reasons for India's foreign policy activism in
Afghanistan seem self-evident. India does not want to see Afghanistan return
to the 1990s, when the Pakistan-backed Taliban regime turned the country
into a haven for anti-India terrorist groups — quite apart from al-Qaeda. To
the extent that Pakistan seeks to push its influence in Afghanistan, India has
incentive to preclude Pakistan's ability to sway outcomes in Kabul. Further, if
Indian presence in and assistance to Afghanistan keeps Pakistan focused on
the west, including keeping a large number of its forces on the Afghan border,
then Islamabad will have fewer troops to use on the Indian border.

Third, the most ambitious Indian analysts see in Afghanistan an opportunity
for New Delhi to begin behaving like a great power—that is, breaking out of
its decades-long strategic parity with Pakistan and projecting power in the
region, eventually to counter growing Chinese influence there.[30] They argue
that India must advocate its own doctrine of regional hegemony, similar to the
Monroe Doctrine that the United States espoused in the nineteenth century.
Afghanistan's abundance of natural resources and the longstanding promise
of an oil and gas pipeline from Turkmenistan to India—called the TAPI—are
reasons to hold Indian interest, especially since China is also interested in Afghan mining treasures and Central Asian energy.

Lastly, the consensus goes beyond the realist case; the power behind the
consensus has come from Indian liberals who have been in power for a decade.
Indian liberals, especially in the upper echelons of the Congress Party, remain
fundamentally Nehruvian in character: They are liberals with strong beliefs in
national sovereignty.[31] They see trade, investment, energy, and access not only
as primary drivers of international relations but also as activities that countries
have the right to pursue without opposition from third countries. They find
offensive and illegitimate the Pakistani view that Indian economic and technical assistance to Afghanistan is of itself threatening, and they attribute it not

to the Pakistani public but to a self-serving security establishment in Pakistan wanting to preserve its position of privilege using the bogey of an Indian threat.

Indian liberals would have no problem including Pakistan as part of Indian projects in Afghanistan. In addition to the TAPI, which would run through Pakistan, another Indian project proposes that India build a railroad network connecting Pakistan and Afghanistan.[32] Since these projects would help Pakistan as well, Indian liberals cannot understand or accept Pakistani objections to India-Afghanistan relations. Mani Shankar Aiyar, an outspokenly liberal Indian member of parliament and onetime minister of petroleum, has forcefully argued that the gas pipeline from Turkmenistan to India would bring about regional peace.[33]

The New Delhi consensus suggests that India will not cede Afghanistan to Pakistan without a fight, especially when Kabul is reciprocating. The Karzai government clearly sees India as a friend and Pakistan as a threat. Karzai has already made a concerted effort to secure Indian support to off set Pakistan pressure. Recently, Shaida Mohammed Abdali, a former national security official and one of Karzai's closest advisers, became ambassador in New Delhi. Following up from the 2011 strategic partnership agreement, Karzai himself visited New Delhi to sign agreements on military training and mining rights in November 2012.

The New Delhi consensus may be broad, but it is also shallow. Hanauer and Chalk have argued that India's larger goals in Afghanistan—embedding the nation in the regional economy, consolidating the state in Afghanistan, and marginalizing the Taliban—are superior to Pakistan's narrow security objectives,[34] but the disparity also implies that Islamabad is more motivated than New Delhi to prevail. India's liberals have supported a forward policy in Afghanistan but are also the strongest advocates of the country's strategic restraint, the great Indian hesitation to use force in pursuit of political goals.[35] Indian leaders have avoided loose talk about the possibility of using military force in Afghanistan. Not even the Bharatiya Janata Party (BJP), the right-wing nationalist political party, has suggested that an Indian military campaign in Afghanistan is feasible. The Indian armed forces do not appear to be reorganizing for a mission outside the national borders. The military and police training programs in the India-Afghanistan strategic partnership agreement envision training in India, not in Afghanistan. Whatever training India might do will be limited to relatively small numbers, not comparable to the scope of the current U.S. effort to stand up an army in Afghanistan. India is sending a clear signal regarding its hesitation to use military force.

By limiting its options in Afghanistan to the use of soft power, India can only hope to influence Afghan domestic politics marginally.[36] Although India has close ties with the Tajiks in the north and good relations with a few Pashtun groups as well—especially the Karzai faction—New Delhi does not have the means to build a larger political coalition that can hold power in Kabul. India may be able to put together a military coalition led by Tajik militias, but the Tajiks do not operate in southern and eastern Afghanistan, which means realistically that India must limit its Afghan involvement to the safe areas of the north and the west, provoking the Pashtuns and their Pakistani backers. In reality, for India to realize the strategic value in Afghanistan, the Indian government would have to send troops to "the graveyard of empires," as Afghanistan has been called so often; and afterward, New Delhi would find it hard to limit the ensuing conflict to its own terms.

New Delhi may still choose to expand its presence in Afghanistan, knowing that its options are limited but hoping that it is better to try stanching or drawing out Pakistan than giving up now. This argument is a recipe for civil war because there is an implicit belief that India's growing soft power can match Pakistan's demonstrated ability to defend its interests in Afghanistan militarily. It generates false hope in India's ability to influence outcomes in Afghanistan, when in fact this approach is viable only if Pakistan does not put up a fight.

Pakistan Is Not a Failing State

The strongest argument for a greater role for India in Afghanistan is predicated on a declining Pakistan not being able to sustain another round of competition after 2014. To think about what might happen in Afghanistan, therefore, we need to examine the health of the Pakistani state and society.

Ahmed Rashid writes that the twin embarrassments of Osama bin Laden living secretly in a garrison town and U.S. special forces breaching national defenses—heaped on the accumulation of misgovernance, illegitimacy, defensiveness, extremism, violence, ethnic separatism, external interference, and war in Pakistan—have brought the country to the very edge.[37] The long-term trends appear tragic: Pakistan has a rapidly expanding population with little means of supporting this growth. The country is running out of water, food, and land. Only 57 percent of the population can read and write, and half of its children do not go to school, in a country where 37 percent of the population is below the age of fifteen.[38]

The Afghan war has generated some real setbacks for Pakistan. The rise of the Pakistani Taliban has spread the extremist challenge to well beyond the Pashtun parts of the country and into the Punjabi heartland, becoming the most serious threat to the polity since the 1971 civil war that ended in the secession of East Pakistan as Bangladesh. Ashley Tellis of the Carnegie Endowment for International Peace predicts that "every foreseeable ending to the Afghan war today—continued conflict with the Taliban, restoration of Taliban control in the southern and eastern provinces, or a nationwide civil war—portends nothing but serious perils for Islamabad."[39]

Most external predictions about Pakistan, including those from India, do not see the full picture of an extraordinarily diverse and variegated society. Those who visit Pakistan consistently report that on most days it is a normal functioning society. Karachi is a difficult city to live in, with political violence a recurrent threat, but in most respects it is not unlike other developing-country megacities. The war against terrorism is often distant, confined to FATA, Balochistan, and sometimes Peshawar. The state has pushed back energetically against terrorism, especially since the 2007 Lal Masjid siege in the middle of official Islamabad. Terrorism pierces the humdrum but narrowly targets symbols of Western power and local collaboration.

Even the picture of the formal state teetering from one crisis to another is not quite true. Pakistan's formal institutions of governance have performed poorly in many areas but have done well in others. The current national assembly has passed more laws than in past sessions, in particular those protecting women and human rights. It also has passed constitutional amendments devolving power to the provinces, a longstanding demand. An independent election commission effectively vets electoral rolls in many parts of the country. The State Bank of Pakistan, the country's central bank, functions with independence in setting monetary policy. The Motorway Police in Pakistan is widely seen as a model police force in the developing world. Certainly, the Pakistani press has been a robust check on the malfunctioning of government: The victory of the lawyers' group protesting Musharraf's suspension of Judge Iftikhar Muhammad Chaudhry in 2007 would not have been possible without an oppositional media. Perhaps most important, Pakistan's economy grew at 7 percent a year between 2003 and 2007, suggesting that the economic downturn since 2008 has more to do with the decline in the international economy rather than any endogenous weakness.

British journalist Anatol Lieven correctly argues that Pakistan looks very much like its counterpoint, India: "If Pakistan was an Indian state, then in terms of development, order, and per capita income it would find itself somewhere in the middle, considerably below Karnataka but considerably above Bihar."[40] Pakistan's literacy rate has been rising roughly at the same pace as India's for a few decades (though India's literacy rate is higher at 74 percent).[41] Similarly, the youth bulge in Pakistan is not a recent phenomenon.

More generally, Pakistan's ability to support the Taliban and provide drinking water might be associated but are not directly correlated. Scholars of Pakistani civil-military relations have argued that the country's many domestic failures stem from the diversion of resources from development to defense.[42] If that is the case, then Pakistan's domestic failures have allowed the country to enjoy external success, especially in defending its strategic parity with India for more than six decades. Both Rashid and Lieven report that the Pakistan Army's counterinsurgency operations in Swat were reasons for hope.

Whether Pakistanis should feel threatened by India is beside the point. Pakistan's military says it feels insecure and has reacted in ways that are entirely consistent with the predictions of the predominant school of international relations thinking. Realist theory places greater salience on security imperatives than on less urgent drivers, including economic development and institution building. The theory also prioritizes immediate over long-term security threats. By that measure, Pakistan has responded as expected and with relative effectiveness. In this view, Pakistan's narrow and security-related interests in Afghanistan should overmatch India's broad and diff use interests. Pakistan may be a weak state by some measures, but it is not about to fail and will remain capable of mounting a military campaign.

The real problem in Pakistan is not state failure but the balance in the relationship between the state and civil society. Since Max Weber, the state has been defined by its ability to impose itself on society, but the modern state has had to combat pluralism, which decries the grand autonomy of the state in exercising its monopoly on the legitimate use of violence. Pluralism demands that this monopoly be earned and remain contingent on the state providing public goods. In Pakistan, the state is pluralistic—or at least oligopolistic—and decisions about public goods are made outside the Weberian hierarchy of the state, both in society and the factions within the state apparatus.

The clearest example is Pakistan's informal economy, which has continued to grow even as the official economy has hit the skids. The informal economy has been estimated to be as large as 50 percent of the official GDP, employing three times as many workers as the formal sector. In 2011, while the official economy grew at a sluggish 2.4 percent, demand for cars, cement, and other goods sharply increased, indicating sources of demand outside the documented economy.[43] Meanwhile, Pakistan's tax collections languish at less than 9 percent of its GDP, and no more than one million people pay income taxes.

The Pakistan Army has been called the state within the state,[44] but it is not so much a hidden government as it is a part of a fragmented and variegated structure of power and authority that spans the country's political system. Civil society groups and government agencies can make and pursue their own policies, leaving the formal hierarchy of the state to follow, justify, and sometimes recant their actions. While outsiders despair at the country's dismal civil-military relations record, Pakistanis see the army as another political party, somewhat more honest than the civilian parties but also heavy-handed. When the military has failed, Pakistanis have protested that failure in the same way that they have protested the failures of the Pakistan Muslim League and the People's Party of Pakistan.

No regime in Pakistan, not even its military, has been able to impose broad state control over society. Unlike the South American military dictatorships, Pakistan's episodic military rulers have never been able to slip into totalitarianism, capable of shutting down all dissent. The chilling quietness of Pinochet's Santiago that Gabriel García Márquez describes in *Clandestine in Chile* is impossible to find in Pakistan.[45] The Pakistani media's extraordinary position can only be understood in the context of a robust civil society that the state has not been able to repress. The final triumph of illiberalism occurs when opposition becomes quiescent without the government needing to shed blood. Saleem Shehzad, a Pakistani journalist whose reporting had cut too close to heart of the ISI's relationship with radicals, was murdered because he could not be silenced.[46] Shehzad's murder resulted in even greater protests and the pursuit of the causes of his death, not the firming up of lines journalists could not cross.[47]

When cohesion does not come from the state, it comes from society. Lieven writes of Pakistan's weak government but strong civil society. The imbalance in state-society relations in Pakistan has meant that the state cannot consolidate, but the prospect of state failure is less significant in a country where the government is less central to the health and functioning of the society. The country may be unable to achieve goals that only states can—legitimate the leviathan, for example—but the absence of the state has allowed Pakistani society to develop privately.

The fragmented political system, rooted in the state-society imbalance, allows contradictory policies to coexist in parallel even on national security issues. It is not surprising that Pakistan fights terrorism and supports radical groups at the same time. The country can react with outrage at the attack on Malala Yousafzai but also allow the structure of extremism to continue to exist and believe that it exists mainly to fight against external threats. The simultaneous occurrence of the Lahore Declaration and Kargil War preparations are a case in point.[48] Today, there are those who have pushed for open trade with India, a major step in India-Pakistan rapprochement, but there are others who fear active Indian presence in Afghanistan.

Pakistan is neither about to collapse nor is it likely to be amenable to the kind of containment strategy being proposed against it. Pakistan's foreign policy masters have demonstrated great ability to outmaneuver external pressure—unlike the leaders of North Korea and Iran, who have had greater difficulty in managing foreign demands. As a country, Pakistan is integrated in the international system in a way North Korea never has been. Millions of Pakistanis live outside the country, especially in the Persian Gulf, and unlike most expatriate Iranians or Iraqis from Saddam Hussein's regime before 2003, most Pakistanis on foreign soil are not disaffected exiles with minimal ties back home but strong nationalists with continuing ties inside Pakistan.[49]

In the mid-1990s, the United States backed Pakistani assistance for the Taliban campaign in Afghanistan, and Pakistan had the support of the moneyed Saudi government.[50] This time Pakistan is more isolated. This loss of external support is at the bottom of the direst predictions of state collapse in Pakistan.

But even as the United States, Saudi Arabia, and others stand apart from Pakistan, they are unlikely to abandon the country entirely or be in a position to restrain reenergized anti-India radicalism. The lessons of abandonment from the 1990s are still vivid. Pakistan today has nuclear weapons, which must be secured above all else, and there is no serious expectation that Pakistan can be changed from outside. It also is unrealistic to expect that Pakistan's army will surrender what it thinks are its national interests by accommodating India's objectives in Afghanistan. Pakistan has a clear military advantage in Afghanistan through its relationship with the Taliban. It could strike Indian interests there almost at will. If these attacks occur, India will not have any real means to defend its interests, especially with U.S. capacity to provide security diminishing after 2014.

In effect, India can only hope to stretch Pakistan's commitment in Afghanistan, perhaps pulling Islamabad further into Afghanistan. The New Delhi consensus and the continued viability of Pakistan's security apparatus suggest a balance-of-power contest between the two countries and carry the risk of igniting the civil war in Afghanistan that all parties want to avoid. As Shekhar Gupta writes, contesting Afghanistan will put India "permanently and, inevitably, violently at odds with the Pakistanis."[51] With Afghanistan as the new point of acute India-Pakistan competition, the proxy war might widen. The Pakistan Army could decide to respond by renewing support to Kashmir separatists. The result could be increased cross-border shelling and perhaps another nuclear crisis. An Indian threat could also bring the radicals and the Pakistan Army back together after some years of a frayed relationship.

Scenario 2: A Regional Peace Plan

Though current developments point toward an India-Pakistan balance-of-power contest, the resulting proxy war is not desirable for any of the players. From the perspectives of Washington and the Afghan government, the most preferred outcome is for India and Pakistan to cooperate in Afghanistan.

Potentially, India-Pakistan cooperation could range from the maximalist—the two states working together to bring peace and development—to the minimalist—a limited agreement not to foment another proxy war directly. At the maximalist end stands a project like TAPI. At the minimalist end, India could consult with Pakistan on its economic and technical assistance programs in Afghanistan, and Pakistan might agree to refrain from planning and assisting in attacks on Indian facilities in Afghanistan. In between are a number of cooperation opportunities: joint training of Afghan military and police, India limiting its Afghan engagement to the Northern Tajik and Uzbek areas, non-security assistance, or transparent cash assistance programs, while Pakistan provides verifiable assurances on security.

The trouble with India-Pakistan cooperation, however, is that the minimalist opportunities are no more likely than the maximalist ones. Without some form of verifiable security assurances from Pakistan, the Indian government is unlikely to want to limit its current level of engagement, especially since the Afghan and U.S. governments have been encouraging greater Indian involvement in Afghanistan. On the Pakistani side, accepting increased Indian presence in Afghanistan without a compensating improvement in its long-term security and political concerns is tantamount to surrender. Even if a Pakistani government were willing to accept this loss, key factions in the society and the state might not be willing to do so, especially if it hurts their parochial interests.

The history of India-Pakistan peace efforts shows that incremental steps to build trust, such as bus and train transport links or Pakistan according most-favored nation status to India, have not accumulated. The few instances of progress have come from breakthroughs at the top—no one else seems to have the authority to conclude meaningful agreements—but these high-profile initiatives have been vulnerable to violence on both sides of the border. The Kargil War and the Mumbai attacks were dramatic examples of how India-Pakistan peace processes could be derailed. In Pakistan, the continued problems in Kashmir and Gujarat have fed beliefs about India as an anti-Muslim Hindu state that must be fought.

India and Pakistan could agree on a degree of cooperation only if the United States decided to remain in Afghanistan with numbers of troops large enough to mitigate the stark prisoner's dilemma game unfolding in the region. Significant numbers of U.S. troops remaining in Afghanistan well into the future would tamp down regional competition in Afghanistan, give the Afghan government time to consolidate, and allow India and Pakistan to restart their peace process. The U.S.-Afghanistan strategic agreement holds open the possibility of continued U.S. military presence, but the United States is war weary. Anything more than a token presence after 2014 will be hard to justify absent a major reversal.

Obama and Karzai met in Washington in January 2013 to discuss a residual U.S. troop presence, but no announcement has been forthcoming. Politically, the 2012 presidential campaigns showed bipartisan support for bringing the troops back home by 2014, although some professional foreign policy and military circles appear to favor staying on.[52] Kimberly Kagan and Frederick W. Kagan argue that the United States should keep as many as thirty thousand troops in Afghanistan.[53] General John Allen, the departing Afghanistan theater commander, proposed three scenarios with a maximum of twenty thousand troops.[54] General David Barno (a former U.S. commander in Afghanistan) and Matthew Irvine have written that the United States could protect its interests with ten thousand troops or less.[55] In his 2013 State of the Union address, Obama said that another thirty-four thousand troops will leave Afghanistan in

February 2013 but made no mention of how many troops are likely to remain behind. *The New York Times* and *The Washington Post* have reported independently that the Pentagon is now considering eight thousand troops, but the White House is thinking of numbers as low as three thousand, dropping to one thousand by 2017.[56]

Continued U.S. presence in Afghanistan is probably the best outcome for India and, arguably, for Pakistan as well. U.S. presence would provide the security umbrella under which New Delhi could continue to pursue its relations with Kabul without having to worry about confronting Pakistan directly. India's return to Afghanistan in 2002, and the subsequent expansion of Indian diplomacy in Afghanistan, occurred under the protection of U.S. military presence. Pakistan would favor continued U.S. presence in Afghanistan if it could get Washington to curtail the drone strikes to the targets it wants and the recriminations about ISI support for the Haqqani Network. Ideally, for Pakistan, continued U.S. presence in Afghanistan would spare it the security burden of fighting radicalism. In a post-U.S. Afghanistan, if the Taliban consolidated itself, Pakistan would be the next target for radicalism. Perhaps the Afghan government itself would see the most benefits from continued U.S. presence; whether or not this might change Karzai's willingness to accommodate challengers, it would certainly mean a smoother succession in Kabul, reducing the likelihood of Karzai following Najibullah to the end.

Scenario 3: Could India Stay Out of Afghanistan?

If the United States does not stay on, the prospect of a balance-of-power contest and possibly a proxy war similar to that of the 1990s rises.[57] The only option left under these conditions might be to ask India to stay out of Afghanistan in an effort to assuage Pakistan's security concerns and bring it into a peace process that allows a modicum of peaceful withdrawal for the United States while altering the nature of the India-Pakistan rivalry.

New Delhi wants to be involved in Afghanistan precisely to undermine Pakistani influence and thereby break out of its rivalry with Pakistan. Pakistan impedes India's access to Central Asian energy sources, since any pipeline must pass through that country, and the only other route for the gas—through Iran and then shipped in container ships to India—is subject to U.S. sanctions on foreign investment in Iran. That India has benign goals in Afghanistan, therefore, should hardly matter to Pakistan. If the consequence of India's policy in Afghanistan is to mitigate Pakistani influence in that country, no matter what the intent, why should Islamabad support the effort?

Gupta argues that Afghanistan is strategically more important for Pakistan than for India. Pakistan has a long and troubled border with Afghanistan. The movement of refugees and goods as well as drugs and guns makes the region restless where the Pakistan Army is fighting a full-on counterinsurgency campaign. In contrast, he writes, Afghanistan is not an important trade partner of India. Afghanistan has never sent terrorists to India. No Afghan ethnic group has mounted an attack on India, nor has the Pashtun belt in Afghanistan and Pakistan been used to plan any attack on India.[58]

As the United States withdraws, and in the absence of any regional understanding, India's aid projects in Afghanistan will become vulnerable to attack by Pakistan-backed Taliban. New Delhi has deployed small numbers of paramilitary forces purely for perimeter defense of a few key installations in Afghanistan, but there are no indications that the Indian government will send more troops to the country.

India's withdrawal from Afghanistan would not be without risk. It would embolden the Taliban and, more important to India, embolden Pakistan, potentially encouraging Pakistan to pursue aggressive gains. The greatest danger for the United States is the return of the Taliban, bringing al-Qaeda in its wake; for India, the Taliban's return to power, with or without al-Qaeda, is cause for concern given the Lashkar-e-Taiba's reported ties with the Taliban.[59] Inside Afghanistan, Tajik, Uzbek, and Hazara political leaders are likely to object violently to the return of the Taliban on Pakistan's back, potentially resulting in the civil war that, again, all actors want to avoid.

Some of the risks are unavoidable or no worse than what the current trajectory suggests, but India withdrawing from the situation in Afghanistan could alter a key structural condition in Afghanistan. If Pakistan's Afghan policy is refracted through its India lens, then Islamabad should welcome removing the prism. The Pakistan Army then may not want the Taliban to take power in Afghanistan, fearing the emboldening effect it might have on the Pakistani Taliban.[60] Conversely, growing Indian presence in a post-U.S. Afghanistan would offer the Pakistan Army and radical groups another cause to energize their alliance.

Pakistan's direct interest, relations, and leverage in Afghanistan surpass that of every other country except the United States. With U.S. troops withdrawing, Pakistan is poised to be the most powerful external actor in Afghanistan. Pakistan has now won three victories against the former Soviet Union, the Iran-Russia-India combination backing the Northern Alliance, and now, the United States. These victories have come at a tremendous cost. Pakistan itself has become more violent and less stable, though not to the point of failure. Pakistan's rivalry with India has remained largely in place as past peace efforts have failed. These structural imperatives are unlikely to change soon, but as Afghanistan slides into another civil war and India-Pakistan relations worsen as a result of their competition there, the possibility of an Indian withdrawal should be considered as one way of defusing the rising tensions.

As New Delhi is likely to resist a policy of surrender to Pakistan, the United States should return to its de-hyphenation policy from the mid-2000s that emphasized Indian acquisition of U.S. technology. The U.S. Defense Department has been working with the Indian government to develop closer ties, but the initiative requires presidential and congressional guidance, especially on export controls, about which India is particularly sensitive. An emphasis on code-velopment of new weapons systems could reduce the effects of the technology export controls. A significant part of the problem lies in India, where broken military research and development and procurement systems stymie progress.

For their part, the Afghans are likely to resist being left to Pakistan. Karzai has assiduously cultivated a relationship with India, and New Delhi has close ties to Tajik leaders, who are unlikely to see intervention against India's engagement in benign terms. However, if Pakistan can be convinced of an Indian withdrawal or even limited disengagement, it could be the best hope that the Taliban will not receive direct ISI assistance should it launch offensives northward. The different groups within Afghanistan might be more well balanced in that case, and with the benefit of continued Western financial assistance, the Afghan government can have some hope of outmatching the resources available to the spoilers.

Conclusion

If the United States continues its drawdown in Afghanistan without addressing the structural challenges stemming from the India-Pakistan balance-of-power contest, a new civil war is all too likely. There are generally two ways to alter this structural reality: Pakistan could agree to expanded Indian presence in Afghanistan as part of a regional peace plan, or India could withdraw from Afghanistan to assuage Pakistan's security concerns. There are other variations on these two themes, but any real effort to resolve the problem must embrace the logic of one of the two choices.

The possibility of a regional peace plan currently looks slight but potentially promising in the context of the debate over how many U.S. troops will remain in Afghanistan after 2014. If Washington and Kabul agree on a relatively larger troop presence, India and Pakistan would have more time to build on their own bilateral peace process, which could include an arrangement on Afghanistan. One possibility is that India could restrict itself to the Northern non-Pashtun areas, leaving southern and eastern Pashtun regions as a Pakistani sphere of influence. In this scheme, Kabul, secured by an international force, could serve as a buffer. If Washington and Kabul agree on keeping only a small contingent of U.S. troops in Afghanistan, we should expect minimal cooperation.

The problem is that the chances of the United States agreeing to have its troops stay on in significant numbers are diminishing. Though there is growing belief among professional foreign policy and military experts that the United States may have to remain longer in Afghanistan, Obama seems politically and personally committed to bringing home all but a handful of troops. Public opinion polling on the subject widely backs withdrawal. The polling numbers may change if U.S. leaders make the case that the situation has changed and a longer stay is warranted, but such appeals have been rare. The dissolution of the "Af-Pak" office will present additional bureaucratic challenges as the State Department absorbs its functions. With responsibility for India and Pakistan in the Defense Department separated into the Pacific and Central Commands, policy coordination will be difficult to maintain.

A reduced U.S. presence and lack of India-Pakistan agreement will require a significant shift in thinking in Washington and New Delhi. An attempt to balance India's and Pakistan's engagement in Afghanistan is not likely to lead to peace, because there is no balance: India has superiority in soft power, and Pakistan has clear military advantage. A direct confrontation between soft and hard power results in only one outcome—military victory—which is why advocates of soft power see it as working in the background, as an embedded rather than instrumental capacity.[61]

The Indian consensus on Afghanistan is limited; there is no mainstream support for Indian military intervention in the country. Without military force—in the absence of U.S.- provided security—the Indian presence in Afghanistan remains vulnerable to Pakistan-backed Taliban attacks. India's Afghan allies might be able to provide some security, and New Delhi may boost these efforts by supplying weapons, but this leads to the civil war no one wants. The United States taking the lead in developing a new Afghan policy, however, is tantamount to a U.S. return, which the American public does not want. Without continued American support, though, the Indian position in Afghanistan is tenuous.

A clearer vision in Washington could change the situation. The problem in Afghanistan has changed. Al-Qaeda, as an organization, has transformed from a centrally controlled unit to a networked enterprise with different groups aligning themselves to it from time to time. Its members no longer seek to congregate in Afghanistan; al-Qaeda has a center of gravity—it is in Pakistan.[62]

The United States is shifting its focus from Afghanistan to Pakistan, but without resolving the structural conditions in Afghanistan, it is likely to have to return. Today, the situation in Pakistan is the most difficult foreign policy challenge a U.S. president has faced since the 1962 Cuban Missile Crisis because external actors—the United States, the United Nations, Europe, Saudi Arabia, China, Israel, and certainly India—have very little leverage in the country. Outsiders can get Pakistan to deliver on short-term objectives, such as allowing NATO convoys to transit, but only Pakistanis can bring about long-term change in the nature of the state and national identity—and

Pakistanis, for their own and sometimes understandable reasons, do not want to do it yet.

Notes

1. There are other reasons for Osama bin Laden's escape from Tora Bora into Pakistan. U.S. military commanders have been criticized for using Afghan militias in the battle of Tora Bora, as the militias have been accused of incompetence and corruption. See "Tora Bora Revisited: How We Failed to Get Bin Laden and Why It Matters Today: A Report to Members of the Committee on Foreign Relations United States Senate," 111th Congress, November 30, 2009, available at www.foreign.senate.gov/imo/media/doc/Tora_Bora_Report.pdf (accessed March 10, 2013).

2. The term is from Shekhar Gupta, "Get Out, Leave Af to Pak," *Indian Express*, November 21, 2011, available at www.indianexpress.com/news/get-out-leave-af-to-pak/877841/0 (accessed March 10, 2013).

3. Other regional approaches include the Istanbul Process led by Turkey, the New Silk Road Initiative launched by the United States under the leadership of Secretary of State Hillary Clinton, and a proposed Six Power Dialogue, which would include Pakistan, India, Iran, China, Russia, and the United States. Lakhdar Brahimi, the UN secretary-general's special representative to Afghanistan and one of the key architects of the Bonn Conference in December 2001 that chose Hamid Karzai as the new leader of Afghanistan, has emphasized repeatedly the importance of regional approaches to stabilizing Afghanistan.

4. Pervez Musharraf, *In the Line of Fire: A Memoir* (New York: Free Press, 2006), 203. See also Associated Press, "Musharraf's Book Says Pakistan Faced U.S. 'Onslaught' If It Didn't Back Terror War," *USA Today*, September 26, 2006, available at http://usatoday30.usatoday.com/news/world/2006-09-25-pakistan-memoir_x.htm (accessed March 10, 2013).

5. Polly Nayak, "Reducing Collateral Damage to Indo-Pakistani Relations from the War on Terrorism," Policy Brief no. 107, The Brookings Institution, Washington, DC, September 2002, available at www.brookings.edu/research/papers/2002/09/southasia-nayak (accessed March 10, 2013).

6. See "Tora Bora Revisted."

7. See Ashley J. Tellis, "The Merits of Dehyphenation: Explaining U.S. Success in Engaging India and Pakistan," *Washington Quarterly*, vol. 31, no. 4 (2008), 21–42, available at http://csis.org/files/publication/twq08autumntellis.pdf (accessed March 10, 2013). President Clinton initially began the process of decoupling U.S. relations with India and Pakistan in 1998; see Strobe Talbott, *Engaging India: Diplomacy, Democracy, and the Bomb* (Washington, DC: Brookings Institution Press, 2004).

8. Robert D. Blackwill, "Why is India America's Natural Ally?" *The National Interest*, December 3, 2004, http://nationalinterest.org/article/why-is-india-americas-naturalally-2764 (accessed March 10, 2013).

9. The chronology here is collapsed for the purposes of this report, but the India-Pakistan rapprochement occurred between 2004 and 2007, and it was only after the Lal Masjid siege in July 2007 that the Pakistan government finally became serious about fighting radicalism at home. However, the planners of the Mumbai attacks in November 2008 did not stop. On India-Pakistan rapprochement and its failure, see Steve Coll, "The Back Channel," *The New Yorker*, March 2, 2009. On Pakistan's counterterrorism efforts, see John Schmidt, *The Unraveling: Pakistan in the Age of Jihad* (New York: Picador, 2012).

10. Shakil Sheikh, "Pakistan Vows to Maintain Credible N-Deterrence," *The News*, April 13, 2006.

11. See Stephen Tankel, *Storming the World Stage: The Story of Lashkar-e-Taiba* (New York: Columbia University Press, 2011), chapter 3.

12. See interview with Steve Coll by *Indian Express* editor-in-chief Shekhar Gupta on NDTV 24x7's *Walk the Talk*, May 17, 2012, available at www.indianexpress.com/olympics/news/ -india-s-security-problems-aregraver-than-america-s-in-relation-to-jehadi-terrorism-/ 573089/1 (accessed March 10, 2013).

13. Tankel, *Storming the World Stage*, chapters 8 and 9.

14. The Pakistani government has charged seven persons, including the Lashkar operations commander, Zaki-ur Rahman Lakhvi, for the Mumbai attacks, but the judicial process remains stalled.

15. Coll interview, May 17, 2012.

16. Holbrooke's logic is evident in Barnett Rubin and Ahmed Rashid's argument that Pakistan's Afghan and Kashmir border problems had to be tackled together. See Rubin and Rashid, "From Great Game to Grand Bargain," *Foreign Affairs* (November/December 2008), available at www.foreignaffairs.com/articles/64604/barnett-r-rubin-and-ahmed-rashid/ from-great-game-to-grand-bargain?page=show (accessed March 10, 2013).

17. Bruce Riedel, "A New Pakistan Policy: Containment," *New York Times*, October 14, 2011, available at www.nytimes.com/2011/10/15/opinion/a-new-pakistan-policy-containment. html (accessed March 10, 2013).

18. Ambassador Ryan C. Crocker's speech on Afghanistan at the Carnegie Endowment for International Peace, Washington, DC, September 17, 2012, available at www.carnegieendowment.org/files/091712_transcript_crocker1.pdf (accessed March 10, 2013).

19. See Gilles Dorronsoro, *Waiting for the Taliban in Afghanistan* (Washington, DC: Carnegie Endowment for International Peace, September 2012), available at www.carnegieendowment.org/files/waiting_for_taliban2.pdf (accessed March 10, 2013).

20. Graham Bowley, "Afghan Warlord's Call to Arms Rattles Officials," *New York Times*, November 12, 2012, available at www.nytimes.com/2012/11/13/world/asia/ismail-khan-powerful-afghan-stokes-concern-inkabul.html?pagewanted=all&_r=0 (accessed March 10, 2013).

21. Graham Bowley and Jawad Sukhanyar, "Bomber Strikes Near NATO Office in Afghanistan," *New York Times*, September 8, 2012, available at www.nytimes.com/2012/09/09/ world/asia/in-kabul-suicide-bomberstrikes-near-nato-headquar ters.html (accessed March 10, 2013).

22. See Richard Fontaine, "We Need an Indian Civilian Surge," *Foreign Policy*, November 4, 2010, available at www.foreignpolicy.com/articles/2010/11/04/we_need_an_indian_ civilian_surge?page=0,0 (accessed March 10, 2013).

23. Larry Hanauer and Peter Chalk, "India's and Pakistan's Strategies in Afghanistan: Implications for the United States and the Region," Occasional Paper, RAND Corporation, Center for Asia Pacific Policy, Santa Monica, CA, 2012, available at www.rand.org/content/dam/ rand/pubs/occasional_papers/2012/RAND_OP387.pdf (accessed March 10, 2013).

24. U.S. Secretary of Defense Leon E. Panetta, "The U.S. and India: Partners in the 21st Century," speech at the Institute for Defense Studies and Analyses, New Delhi, India, June 6, 2012, available at www.defense.gov/speeches/speech.aspx?speechid=1682 (accessed March 10, 2013).

25. Government of India, Ministry of External Affairs, "Remarks by Foreign Secretary at a Round Table during a Regional Conference on 'Peace and Stabilization in Afghanistan: What Can Neighbours Contribute?' Organised by Delhi Policy Group," July 19, 2012, available at http://202.131.117.199/MEAFinal/Speeches-Statements. htm?dtl/20250/Remarks+by+Foreign+Secretary+at+a+Round+Table+during+a+ regional+conference+on+Peace+and+Stabilization+in+Afghanistan+What+can+neighbo urs+contribute+organised+by+Delhi+Policy+Group (accessed March 10, 2013).

26. For a good description of the Northern Alliance, see Ahmed Rashid, *Taliban: Militant Islam, Oil and Fundamentalism in Central Asia*, 2nd ed. (New Haven: Yale University Press, 2010).

27. Gupta, "Get Out."

28. Stephen P. Cohen and Sunil Dasgupta, *Arming without Aiming: India's Military Modernization* (Washington, DC: Brookings Institution Press, 2010).

29. Stephen P. Cohen, *Shooting for a Century*, forthcoming manuscript, Chapter 3.

30. Harsh V. Pant, "India's Changing Role: The Afghanistan Conf lict," *Middle East Quarterly* (Spring 2011), 39, available at www.meforum.org/meq/pdfs/2895.pdf (accessed March 10, 2013).

31. For an update of Nehruvian foreign policy, see Sunil Khilnani, Rajiv Kumar, Pratap Bhanu Mehta, Lt. Gen. (Retd.) Prakash Menon, Nandan Nilekani, Srinath Raghavan, Shyam Saran, and Siddharth Varadarajan, "Nonalignment 2.0: A Foreign and Strategic Policy for India in the Twenty-First Century," Center for Policy Research, New Delhi, available at www.cprindia.org/sites/default/files/NonAlignment%202.0_1.pdf (accessed March 10, 2013).

32. Heather Timmons, "Can India 'Fix' Afghanistan?" India Ink, NYTimes.com, June 7, 2012, available at http://india.blogs.nytimes.com/2012/06/07/can-india-fix-afghan istan/ (accessed March 10, 2013).

33. F.S. Aijazuddin, "The Uninterruptible Spokesman," Dawn, May 31, 2012, available at http://dawn.com/2012/05/31/the-uninterruptible-spokesman/ (accessed March 10, 2013).

34. Hanauer and Chalk, *Strategies in Afghanistan*, xi.

35. Cohen and Dasgupta, *Arming Without Aiming*. See also Sunil Dasgupta, "The Fate of India's Strategic Restraint," Current History, April 2012, available at www.brookings.edu/~/media/research/files/articles/2012/4/india%20dasgupta/04_india_dasgupta (accessed March 10, 2013).

36. Pant, "India's Changing Role," 33–36.

37. Ahmed Rashid, *Pakistan on the Brink: The Future of America, Pakistan, and Afghanistan* (New York: Viking, 2012), chapters 1 and 2.

38. Ibid, 13.

39. Ashley J. Tellis, "Pakistan's Impending Defeat in Afghanistan," Commentary, Carnegie Endowment for International Peace, June 22, 2012, available at http://carnegieendowment.org/2012/06/22/pakistan-simpending-defeat-in-afghanistan/c6sn (accessed March 10, 2013).

40. Anatol Lieven, *Pakistan: A Hard Country* (London: Allen Lane, 2011), 21.

41. Munir Ahmed Choudhry, "Pakistan: Where and Who Are the World's Illiterates?" background paper prepared for *Literacy for Life*, UNESCO Education for All Global Monitoring Report 2006, 2006/ED/EFA/MRT/PI/22, available at http://unesdoc.unesco.org/images/0014/001459/145959e.pdf (accessed March 10, 2013). On Indian literacy, see Census India 2011, "State of Literacy," available at www.censusindia.gov.in/2011-prov-results/data_files/india/Final_PPT_2011_chapter6.pdf (accessed March 10, 2013).

42. Ali Cheema, Presentation at the Fifteenth Sustainable Development Conference, Panel on Civil-Military Imbalance and Its Policy Implications. Islamabad, Pakistan, December 11, 2012.

43. Naween Mangi, "The Secret Strength of Pakistan's Economy," *Bloomberg Businessweek*, April 5, 2012, available at www.businessweek.com/articles/2012-04-05/the-secret-strength-of-pakistans-economy#r=auth-s (accessed March 10, 2013). There are other estimates of the informal economy as well: The Asian Development Bank estimates it to be larger than a third of the country's official GDP, which is also reported in the Mangi story. Economists at the State Bank of Pakistan estimate the informal economy has been shrinking from a high point in the 1990s and is today less than 30 percent of the official economy. Muhammad Farooq Arby, Muhammad Jahanzeb Malik, and Muhammad Nadim Hanif, "The Size of Informal Economy in Pakistan," Working Papers no. 33, State Bank of Pakistan, May 2010.

44. The term is widely used in academic literature. See Ayesha Siddiqa, *Military Inc.: Inside Pakistan's Military Economy* (London: Pluto Press, 2007). Former Pakistani prime minister Yousaf Raza Gilani used the term in a December 2011 speech. See "Pakistan: PM Gilani Denies He Is to Sack Army Chief," *BBC News*, December 26, 2011, available at www.bbc.co.uk/news/world-asia-16334437 (accessed March 11, 2013).

45. Gabriel García Márquez, *Clandestine in Chile: The Adventures of Miguel Littín* (New York: New York Review Books Classics, 2010).

46. Jane Perlez and Eric Schmitt, "Pakistan's Spies Tied to Slaying of a Journalist," *New York Times*, July 4, 2011, available at www.nytimes.com/2011/07/05/world/asia/05pakistan.html?pagewanted=all&_r=0 (accessed March 10, 2013). Although the Committee to Protect Journalists reports that Pakistan was one of the ten deadliest countries for journalists in 2012, there does not seem to have been a let-up in the journalistic vigor in spite of the dangers. See Committee to Protect Journalists, "Pakistan," available at www.cpj.org/asia/pakistan/ (accessed March 12, 2013).

47. Media protests forced Prime Minister Gilani to set up a judicial commission to investigate Shehzad's death.

48. On concurrence, see Jyoti Malhotra, "Atal to Nawaz—Why Kargil after Lahore?" *Indian Express*, August 27, 1999, available at www.expressindia.com/news/ie/daily/19990827/ige27001.html (accessed March 10, 2013).

49. Udo Kock and Yan Sun, "Remittances in Pakistan—Why Have They Gone Up, and Why Aren't They Coming Down?" Working Paper WP/11/200, International Monetary Fund, August 2011, www.imf.org/external/pubs/ft/wp/2011/wp11200.pdf (accessed March 10, 2013).

50. Rashid, *Taliban*.

51. Gupta, "Get Out."

52. President Obama campaigned on bringing the troops back home by 2014, and Mitt Romney agreed with the timetable, despite some of his foreign policy advisers having advocated against an early pullout. For the views of professional diplomats, see Crocker's speech, September 17, 2012.

53. Kimberly Kagan and Frederick W. Kagan, "Why U.S. Troops Must Stay in Afghanistan," *Washington Post*, November 23, 2012, available at http://articles.washingtonpost.com/2012-11-23/opinions/35511014_1_eastern-afghanistan-predator-drones-special-mission-units (accessed March 10, 2013).

54. Elisabeth Bumiller and Eric Schmitt, "Afghan War Commander Gives Options for After '14," *New York Times*, January 2, 2013, available at www.nytimes.com/2013/01/03/world/middleeast/afghan-warcommander-gives-options-for-after-2014.html (accessed March 10, 2013).

55. David Barno and Matthew Irvine, "How to Fight in Afghanistan with Fewer U.S. Troops," *Washington Post*, November 30, 2012, available at http://articles.washingtonpost.com/2012-11-30/opinions/35585449_1_afghan-troops-afghan-force-afghanistan (accessed March 10, 2013).

56. Michael R. Gordon and Mark Landler, "Decision on Afghan Troop Levels Calculates Political and Military Interests," *New York Times*, February 12, 2013, available at www.nytimes.com/2013/02/13/us/politics/obama-to-announce-troops-return.html?_r=2& (accessed March 10, 2013); Rajiv Chandrasekaran, "Obama Wants to Cut Troop Level in Afghanistan in Half over Next Year," Washington Post, February 12, 2013, available at www.washingtonpost.com/world/national-security/official-obama-to-cut-trooplevel-in-afghanistan-in-half-by-next-year/2013/02/12/63a044c8-7536-11e2-8f84-3e4b513b1a13_story.html (accessed March 10, 2013).

57. For a discussion of the consequences of the United States leaving Afghanistan early, see Frederick W. Kagan, "A Case for Staying the Course," in Hy Rothstein and John Arquilla, eds., *Afghan Endgames* (Washington, DC: Georgetown University Press, 2012), 97–100.

58. Gupta, "Get Out."

59. As Ambassador Crocker points out, the real danger is the Taliban and al-Qaeda returning together. See his speech, September 17, 2012.

60. Bruce Riedel, "A New Pakistan Policy: Containment," *New York Times*, October 14, 2011, available at www.nytimes.com/2011/10/15/opinion/a-new-pakistan-policy-containment. html (accessed March 10, 2013).

61. See Joseph S. Nye, Jr., "Soft Power," *Foreign Policy*, no. 80 (Autumn 1990), 153–171, available at www.jstor.org/stable/1148580 (accessed March 10, 2013).

62. Yemen and Mali are other countries in which the United States believes al-Qaeda members are congregating.

9

Thwarting Afghanistan's Insurgency
A Pragmatic Approach toward Peace and Reconciliation

Mohammad Masoom Stanekzai

S tanekzai was a USIP senior fellow on Afghanistan from 2007 to 2008. He later became an adviser to President Hamid Karzai and chairman of Afghanistan's High Peace Council's joint secretariat, where he had a chance to begin implementing some of the ideas developed at USIP and presented in this chapter, written in 2008.

Stanekzai's analysis picks up on a number of points from earlier chapters. The insurgency has expanded year after year, U.S. policy has been reactive, and the evidence of recent trends raises "serious doubts about whether military solutions alone will be able to defeat the insurgency and stem the expansion of terrorism." Despite this pessimistic starting point, Stanekzai sees an opportunity to embark on a reconciliation process. Popular dissatisfaction with the Taliban has grown, and Afghan security forces have improved. There has been robust economic growth, amid continued demonstrations of strong international commitment to Afghanistan.

Stanekzai's framework for peace and reconciliation works at the national, community, and individual levels. The national level focuses on the diplomatic effort of securing cooperation from neighbors to close insurgent sanctuaries and promote reconciliation. The community level taps the proven ability of communities to exercise leverage over young men who have joined the insurgency to hand in their weapons. At the individual level, Stanekzai proposes reaching out to fighters and commanders who are no longer interested in fighting for the Taliban but fear arrest if they attempt to return to normal life.

Originally published as Mohammad Masoom Stanekzai, "Thwarting Afghanistan's Insurgency: A Pragmatic Approach toward Peace and Reconciliation," Special Report 212 (Washington, DC: USIP, 2008).

While being pragmatic, Stanekzai argues for adhering to certain principles, including Afghan ownership of the process and the need for wide public support. His views are informed by a historical understanding of previous attempts at reconciliation and a precise classification of the components of the ongoing insurgency and the sources of conflict, which remain essential starting points for understanding events in Afghanistan. Stanekzai's argument for opening a reconciliation process presumes a position of strength that the military surge, announced in 2009, was designed to obtain, though Stanekzai also suggests a temporary increase in ISAF troops in light of the upcoming election and the need to frame the environment for reconciliation.

Introduction

Afghanistan is at a crucial stage of transition. The Taliban, with sanctuaries and a support base in Pakistan's Federally Administered Tribal Areas (FATA), has grown stronger, relying on a wide network of foreign fighters and Pakistani extremists who operate freely across the Afghan-Pakistani border. As a result, violence in Afghanistan has been escalating for the past two years. More than 14,500 people, including hundreds of foreign troops, have been killed there since the Taliban began its comeback in 2006. Recent statistics suggest that the situation is only getting worse. June 2008 represented the deadliest month for foreign troops in Afghanistan since the 2001 fall of the Taliban and the second month in which casualties exceeded those in Iraq.

Complicating matters, the insurgency is not a pure, genuine national insurgency that is simply fighting against occupying forces or the government, and the Taliban is not the only source of violence and unrest. Other groups, including Hizb-i Islami, armed criminals, and drug networks linked closely with illegal armed groups, as well as corrupt elements inside and outside the government, contribute to the country's security concerns. Additionally, a record increase in opium production provides up to 40 percent of the Taliban's total financial support and contributes dramatically to corruption. If the current levels of violence and poppy production are not contained, both the government and international security forces will lose further support among the people, providing more space for the insurgents and terrorist groups to operate (see figures 1 and 2).

The Afghanistan government and the international community have typically responded to the violence by being reactive rather than proactive, as evidenced by the gradual increase of the International Security Assistance Force (ISAF) in Afghanistan in response to rising security threats and a general lack of contingency planning. Although military and peacekeeping operations are absolutely vital for creating a secure environment conducive to state building and reconstruction, present trends raise serious doubts about whether military solutions alone will be able to defeat the insurgency and stem the expansion

Figure 1. Average number of violent incidents per month, 2003–2008

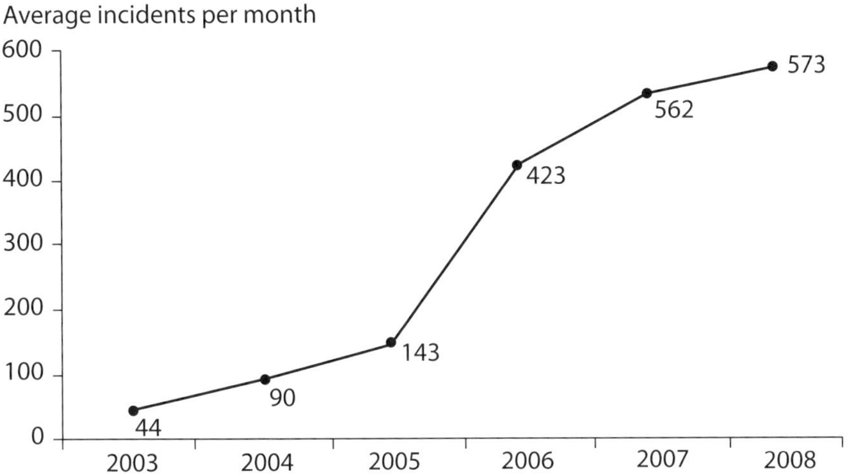

Average incidents per month

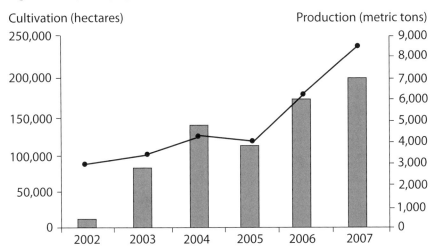

Sources: Afghanistan's Ministries of Defense and Interior, the National Directorate of Security, and the UN Department of Safety and Security

Figure 2. Opium poppy cultivation and production levels, 2002–2007

Sources: UN Office of Drungs and Crime and Afghanistan's Ministry of Counter Narcotics

of terrorism. In short, reconciliation must also be a key element of stabilization operations in Afghanistan.

Although the danger that Afghanistan could once again become a failed state is real, the chance to stabilize Afghanistan is not lost: broad support is emerging for an effective national reconciliation and negotiation program that will end the bloodshed. But what might such a program look like, and how might it succeed when past attempts have failed? This report represents an attempt to answer these important questions and to provide an approach for encouraging reconciliation among Afghans in the name of stabilization and peace. It begins by arguing that an opportunity exists for reconciliation and then explores the various challenges to reconciliation, including Afghanistan's unique sources of conflict and wide spectrum of insurgent, terrorist, and criminal groups. Next, it briefly examines the government's past attempts at reconciliation with the Taliban and then offers a pragmatic framework for overcoming the country's various sources of conflict and promoting reconciliation among the conflict's key actors. The report concludes with a series of recommendations for the Afghan government and its international partners acting in support of the country's peace and reconciliation.

An Opportunity for Reconciliation

Although Afghanistan's insurgents have proved adept at exploiting local fissures, creating horror, and attacking high-value targets, Afghanistan has witnessed positive progress on numerous fronts since 2002. At present, multiple factors suggest that the time is ripe for a reconciliatory process to begin (see table 1).

First, Afghans are tired of long years of conflict and the majority are willing to support a peace process, but they are uncertain and afraid due to past experience. If reassured and mobilized, they will stand firmly and support the current democratic process as they did when the Taliban was first ousted. Indeed, Afghans prefer the current democratic process over Taliban rule, but they are frustrated by the government's corruption and incompetence in delivering basic services, especially security, jobs, and justice.

Second, the Taliban is not enjoying the same level of support that it enjoyed when it first emerged as a political and military power. This is partly because of the Taliban's increasing indifference to civilian casualties and partly because Afghans are once again getting frustrated with its free-market approach to war in which it enlists criminals to conduct operations in its name.

Third, Afghan national institutions, especially the Afghan National Army (ANA), are gaining in strength and slowly becoming trusted. If further strengthened, the army has the potential to gradually replace ISAF. Such a strategy will put an end to widespread speculation about a long-term Western occupation that insurgents presently use to advantage in their propaganda.

Fourth, for more than six years Afghanistan's average annual economic growth rate has been above the ten-year annual target of nine percent recommended in the report Securing Afghanistan's Future, which was presented at the 2004 Berlin Conference on Afghanistan (see figure 3). This is welcome news

Table 1. Progress achieved in Afghanistan (2002–2008)

S/No	DESCRIPTION	2002	2008	Notes
1	Afghan National Army	1700 (estimate)	70,000	Field strength of 50,000
2	Afghan National Police	50,000	79,910	In 2002, none were properly trained, equipped, or paid. At present, 20,000 are properly trained and paid, and are better equipped but still lagging behind the army
3	Afghan Military Forces	100,000	Decommissioned	64,000 ex-combatants reintegrated
4	International Security Forces and Provincial Reconstruction Teams	1 PRT 4,900 ISAF troops	52,700 ISAF troops 26 PRTs	Deployment has been expanded to all regions with 26 PRTs now covering all 34 provinces
5	Illegal Armed Groups	1,800 groups (estimate)	342 groups disbanded	64,000 weapons and 27,000 tons of ammunition have been collected.
6	Access to Health Care	9%	85%	Percentage of the population covered by basic services
7	Education	3.7 million children enrolled	5.7 million enrolled	In 2005 there were almost 11.8 million children under the age of 15
8	Rural Development	0	32,000	Number of villages that have benefited from development projects
9	Infrastructure development	Mostly destroyed	13,150 km	Combined length of roads that have been rehabilitated, improved, or built
10	Natural Resources Management	13% and 8%	23% and 12%	Percentage of population with access to safe drinking water and adequate sanitation facilities, respectively. Three million citizens have benefited from rural water and sanitation projects. Sanitation facilities in urban areas are provided by connections to public sewers or by household systems. In rural areas, pit privies, pour-flush latrines, septic tanks, and communal toilets are considered adequate.
11	Economy and Trade		70%	Percentage increase in income per capita
12	Media and Telecom	5%	75%	Percentage of the population that has access to communication

Sources:
1. UNAMA, "International Conference in Support of Afghanistan: Paris, 24 May, 4 June, 12 June 2008," www.unama-afg.org/news/_londonconf/_factsheet/paris-con-factsheet.pdf.
2. Ibid.
3. *Afghanistan: Getting Disarmament Back on Track*, Asia Briefing No. 35 (Kabul/Brussels: International Crisis Group, February 23, 2005), www.crisisgroup.org/home/index.cfm?id=3290.
4. U.S. Department of State, "Afghanistan: Provincial Reconstruction Teams," January 27, 2006, www.state.gov/p/sca/rls/fs/2006/60031.htm; NATO, "ISAF Regional Commands and PRT Locations," June 20, 2008, www.nato.int/isaf/docu/epub/pdf/isaf_placemat.pdf; and Kenneth Katzman, Afghanistan: Current Issues and U.S. Policy, Rep. No. RL30588 (Washington, DC: Congressional Research Service, December 3, 2002), available at http://digital.library. unt.edu/govdocs/crs/.
5. UN News Centre, "Afghanistan: More Illegal Armed Groups Disbanded with UN Help," July 24, 2008, www.un.org/apps/news/ story. asp?newsid= 7472&cr=afghanistan&cr1=.
6. U.S. Agency for International Development, "USAID Assistance to Afghanistan, 2002–2008," March 27, 2008, www.usaid.gov/press/ factsheets/2008/fs080327.html.
7. UNAMA, www.unama-afg.org/news/_londonconf/_factsheet/paris-con-factsheet.pdf; and UN Development Programme (UNDP), *Afghanistan: National Human Development Report 2004—Security With a Human Face. Centre for Policy and Human Development (UNDP, 2005)*, available at www.cphd.af/nhdr/nhdr04/nhdr04.html.
8. UNAMA, www.unama-afg.org/news/_londonconf/_factsheet/paris-con-factsheet.pdf.
9. Ibid.
10. UN Children's Fund (UNICEF), "Annex 3: Progress on Access to Clean Drinking Water, 2002), www.unicef.org/media/files/progesscleanwater.doc; UNAMA, www.unama-afg.org/news/_londonconf/_facsheet/paris-contactsheet.pdf;Worldwater.org, "Table 4. Access to Sanitation by Country, 1970 to 2002," www.worldwater.org/data20062007/Table4.pdf;UNICEF,"UNICEFHumanitarianActionUpdateAfghanistan,17January2008,"availableatwww.reliefweb.int/rw/rwfiles2008.nsf/filesbyrwdocunidfilename/ammf-7axh7nfull_report.pdf/$file/full_report.pdf.
11. UNAMA. www.unama-afg.org/news/_londonconf/_factsheet/paris-con-factsheet.pdf.
12. Ibid.

Figure 3. Annual economic growth rate, 2002–2008

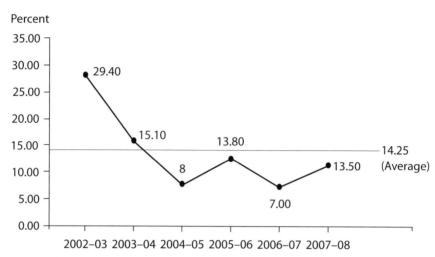

Sources: Afghanistan's Ministry of Finance, Afghanistan National Development Strategy, and World Bank

given that more than 60 percent of the Afghan population is below twenty years old, comprising a generation that lost virtually all opportunity for education and risks suffering from massive unemployment.

Fifth, growing regional fears about the threat posed by extremist militants means it may now be possible to develop a region-wide consensus for dealing with the threat: China is worried about the Uighurs; Uzbekistan about the Islamic Movement of Uzbekistan (headed by Namangani); Russia about Chechen rebel groups (all linked with al Qaeda); Iran about the Taliban and al Qaeda; and Pakistan about the expansion of criminality and insecurity and the further loss of control over its border areas.

Sixth, although members of Pakistan's Directorate for Inter-Services Intelligence (ISI) and military continue to support the Taliban and al Qaeda, Pakistan's recent election represented a vote of no confidence in extremist groups. Indeed, if Pakistan does not help stabilize Afghanistan by taming groups in FATA, a collection of seven agencies and six "frontier districts" that share 250 miles of mountainous border with Afghanistan, it may ultimately face the same situation that Afghanistan suffers from today. Both Afghanistan and Pakistan are increasingly burdened with security challenges that divert significant resources and energy from much-needed services and economic development initiatives.

Seventh, it was recently announced that United Front opposition leader and former Afghan president Burhanuddin Rabani was in contact with the

Taliban and wanted to negotiate with it. In the past, United Front leaders were equivocally against any negotiation with insurgents. This announcement demonstrates a growing consensus among Afghans to reach out to groups that engage in political violence against the state.

Eighth, the NATO Summit in Bucharest in April 2008 and the Paris donor conference in June 2008 highlighted the strong commitment of the international community to peace and stability in Afghanistan, sending positive signals and boosting confidence and morale inside Afghanistan.

Challenges to Reconciliation

Despite the favorable developments that may make the present an opportune moment for reconciliation, the various sources of conflict and the multitude of insurgent and terrorist groups within Afghanistan will present formidable challenges to any reconciliation process.

Principal Sources of Conflict

Conflict in Afghanistan springs from several sources and can be classified into two broad categories, the first of which can be broken down along real-world geographical lines—regional, national, and local—and the second along the more abstract lines of religion, ethnicity, and family.

Regional Sources of Conflict. Afghanistan is at the center of numerous regional disputes, including its territorial dispute with Pakistan over the Durand Line, Pakistan and India's territorial dispute over Kashmir, and potential future water-related disputes with neighboring countries. In this complex regional environment, many of Afghanistan's neighbors are trying to increase their influence in Afghanistan to promote their own security and economic interests. In the process, they have abused Afghanistan's ethnic and religious diversity by supporting one group over another for their own ends. Pakistan, for example, has used and continues to use the Taliban and the militias in FATA as a strategic asset to secure its strategic interests in Afghanistan, to help it reestablish its position as the key regional player, and to receive more aid from the United States. Similarly, Iran has supported Shia groups in Afghanistan to further its influence there.

National Sources of Conflict. Throughout Afghanistan's modern history, the conflict between modernizers—principally urban, educated elites—and conservatives—principally rural, illiterate villagers led by ulema and tribal leaders—has continually led to revolts against the state. In 1929, King Ammanullah was overthrown after embarking on a rapid modernization program based on the Turkish model. In 1979, the modernizing reforms of Communists provoked widespread revolt, ultimately leading to the overthrow of the central authority and collapse of the Communist regime in 1992. And now, today, the fundamentalist Taliban, with support from al Qaeda, is revolting against the current moderate democratic process and attempts at modernization and development.

Over the past three decades, separate power bases have emerged in Afghanistan in the form of political-military parties and networks of commanders and their followers. Fed by the illicit economy and supported by foreign powers, these parties and networks have access to vast human support and financial resources, much of which is generated by drug trafficking, illegal taxation, and customs fees, and are thus able to maintain power outside the state.

Local Sources of Conflict. Many local disputes in Afghanistan are related to conflicts over land and access to water. Such disputes are mainly between displaced persons who returned from refugee camps to their places of origin and those who either stayed in the area or returned at any earlier period. In some cases, local commanders have claimed the lands of those who were displaced; in other cases, local commanders belonging to one majority ethnic group have forced villagers belonging to a minority group to flee only to re-distribute the abandoned land to the remaining population. Such cases have mainly been registered in the northern provinces of Takhar, Mazar, and Fariba. Land has also been acquired unjustly or sold illegally through the use of fake documents or the abuse of government positions.

The destruction of water distribution systems has also led to violent conflict, as have disputes over the ownership and use of public property, such as forests and pasturages, especially between nomads (Kochies) and other tribes (mainly the Hazara residents of the central highlands). In each of the past two years, for example, fighting erupted during the seasonal movement of Kochies and their herds toward the central highlands. Fighting was over land ownership and grazing rights. Several people were injured, while others were killed. Additionally, homes were burned, and herds were taken by force. Spoilers on both sides, principally Kochie and Hazara political leaders, have exaggerated the dispute.

Religion-Based Sources of Conflict. Islam is the predominant religion in Afghanistan and is mixed with Afghan culture, making it difficult for the majority of illiterate people to make distinctions between certain aspects of Islam and their own indigenous traditions. Although moderate Islam, in particular, has deep roots in Afghan society and is the most important part of belief in the day-to-day life of Afghans, Afghans can be deeply angered by incidents that are perceived as contradictory to their Islamic belief. An overwhelming majority of Afghans reject the radical version of Islam practiced by the Taliban not only because it has caused social strife but also because it contradicts their principle understanding of Islam.

Promoting moderate Islam in Afghanistan will have a significant positive impact on the peacebuilding process and help unify and heal the country. The rule of the mullahs (traditional clergy) is dominant, particularly in the rural areas of Afghanistan. Their network is loose but pervasive throughout the country, and their decisions, in many cases, determine people's decisions and actions. Reaching out to them and using their potential for peacebuilding will be an important step that can help offset the extremists' appropriation of mosques in their propaganda campaign against the government.

Ethnic Sources of Conflict. Although Afghanistan is not ethnically homogenous and its national culture is not uniform, there is a strong collective sense of identity within the country. Most ordinary Afghans broadly believe that they will be prosperous only if they are united and live in peace with one another under a lawful and just system where they equally benefit from services. As Louis Dupree wrote in his book *Afghanistan*, "In Afghanistan, only distinctive tribal and ethnic clothing, language, religion and other cultural impediments make the difference. But like the United States, and for a much longer period, Afghanistan had been a cultural, as well as physical, melting-pot . . . the influences of many empires rose, fell and blended."[1]

The ethnic divisions within Afghanistan were deepened during the initial years of resistance against the Soviet invasion, when leaders organized jihadi parties and militia groups around networks of close friends and relatives, creating new ethnocentric power structures. As a result, militia groups on all sides were dominated by geographical location and tribal and ethnic affiliations. When these groups were threatened by a common foreign enemy, they joined together, but when the time came to share power, they fought one another with all the means at their disposal and played the "ethnic card" to mobilize support and retain power and access to resources.

The individualistic approach of these groups created an environment in which each group put its own interests over national interests. During the civil war in Kabul, for example, these groups banned the movement of ordinary Afghans and contact between Afghans belonging to different ethnic groups. They also tortured members of other groups to create hate and dependency and to force people to follow them out of fear. None of the ordinary Afghans interviewed by me during the past ten years approved of what their respective leaders and commanders had done in the name of ethnicity. Hence, Afghans did not necessarily follow the leaders and militia commanders because of their inherent ethnic interests or loyalties; rather, they were forced to because of fear and a need to protect themselves and their families.

Familial Sources of Conflict. Family disputes and feuds are an additional cause of conflict in Afghanistan and mostly involve issues of marriage and shared property. In some cases, ISAF has been intentionally misled by locally hired individuals in the middle of a personal or familial dispute. For example, such individuals have been known to falsely accuse their rivals of having links with al Qaeda, knowing that their homes will be searched or that they will be arrested. Such circumstances in which innocent parties are treated unjustly or unfairly have the unintended effect of damaging the image of the international forces and government in the eyes of Afghans and creating further space for the insurgents.

Insurgent, Terrorist, and Criminal Groups

Although the nature and composition of the country's insurgent and terrorist groups change frequently and require continued assessment, the following groups are the ones that will likely present a key challenge in any reconciliation process.

The Afghan Taliban. The Afghan Taliban is currently led by two main *shuras* (councils): the Quetta Shura and the Peshawar Shura. The Quetta Shura, also known as the Leadership Council, is headed by Mullah Omar and dominated by those from Kandahar, Uruzgan, and Helmand. Most council members come from the old leadership of the Taliban. The Peshawar Shura, which is headquartered in Pakistan's North-West Frontier Province (NWFP), is composed of smaller tribes but lacks a leader with Mullah Omar's overall authority and legitimacy. There are additional differences between the Quetta Shura and the Peshawar Shura with regard to status and resources.

As a whole, the Taliban operates in small groups—from three to thirty individuals, most of whom are between the ages of seventeen and twenty-six (except for the commanders and secret operatives). Although these groups are composed of core madrassa-trained Taliban and local recruits, they also include mercenaries—criminals hired for special tasks. Each group also generally has foreign fighters and advisers, many of whom are in command positions. Support for these groups comes from the drug mafia, which not only provides financial resources but also information, linkages, and help in penetrating high-value-target areas that are under effective government control.

Of the numerous Taliban groups, one of the strongest and most active is led by Jalaludin Haqani, a member of the Taliban's Leadership Council and an experienced Afghan rebel commander from the Zadran district in southeast Afghanistan. Once trusted by the CIA, Haqani was the first Afghan leader to sponsor Arab fighters during the last years of the anti-Soviet war, establishing very close relations with wealthy Arab sheikhs and Pakistan's ISI.[2] Assisted by his son Sarajudin, he is once again proving himself to be a capable organizer, operating as a middleman between al Qaeda and the ISI from his base in Waziristan. Sarajudin has recently called for a change in the Quetta Shura leadership, arguing that a lack of leadership has led to the killings of some of the Taliban's most senior commanders.

The Hekmatyar Group (Hizb-i Islami). Based mostly in the Dir District of Pakistan's Bajaur Agency along the Afghanistan border (near Kunar and Nuristan), Hizb-i Islami is led by Gulbuddin Hekmatyar, a controversial figure who lost much of the credibility among Afghans that he had gained during the initial years of the anti-Soviet war. This was largely due to his continued rocket attacks on Kabul after the fall of the Communist regime in 1992, causing serious damage to ordinary Afghans and the new mujahidin government. As a result, his group has not been able to mobilize new recruits and instead relies on a network of former commanders and followers (some of whom maintain close links with their old ISI friends). Many members have already left him, with some joining the government in senior positions. Although they have broken off from the group and separated themselves from its current policy of fighting coalition forces, they represent potentially important points of contact between the government and Hekmatyar. Indeed, there is a growing possibility that Hekmatyar's group could, at some point, join a reconciliation process at the leadership level, although such a scenario would be very complicated because of Hekmatyar's past actions and because Hekmatyar and his group are on the UN Security Council's terrorist designation list.

Contractors and Criminals. Large networks of illegal armed groups involved with poppy production and drug trafficking exist in Afghanistan. Many young unemployed Afghans, particularly some of those who were forcibly returned from Iran, have joined their ranks as criminals and addicts. This represents another major threat to security and the rule of law and only serves to strengthen the insurgency.

Afghan criminal groups engage in a range of money-generating activities, whether its robbing and killing traders, or kidnapping children and foreign aid workers for ransom. They are also often contracted by the Taliban to carry out specific acts in return for payment or to provide protection during smuggling or kidnapping operations. Corruption in the police force has only added to the problem, further contributing to the country's instability and hurting the government's image.

Tehrik-I-Taliban Pakistan. Following the launch of Operation Enduring Freedom in 2001, the Taliban and al Qaeda fled to Pakistan. They found sanctuary in FATA, a region ruled by old tribal customs that has been the site of major guerrilla and terrorist training camps since the Soviet invasion of Afghanistan in the 1980s (many of which were established with U.S. and Saudi money under the direct supervision of the ISI). Far from Islamabad's reach, FATA currently serves as a launching pad for terrorist and cross-border attacks on Afghan and international security forces.

Established as an umbrella organization by a shura of forty senior Taliban leaders, the Tehrik-I-Taliban Pakistan (PTT) quickly and effectively established itself in FATA, killing more than 300 tribal elders. Militia leader Baitullah Mehsud, who once operated under Sarajiden Haqani, was appointed as the group's *amir* (leader) in 2007, while Mulana Hafiz Gul Bahaddur of North Waziristan and Mulana Faqir Muhammad of Bajaur Agency were appointed as the second and third in command.

As a syndicate, the PTT is composed not only of Taliban but also of groups such as Lashkar-e-Taiba (LET), Tehreek-Maram-Shariya Mohammadyah (TNSM), the Harkatul Mujahideen al-Aalmi (HMAA), the Harkatul Ansaar (HA), the Harkat-i-Jehad-i-Islami(HJI), the Ansaru Sunnah (AS), and the Ansarul Muslimoon (AM). These groups have concentrated their human and material resources in Waziristan in preparation for renewed attacks on international and Afghan security forces. Most of these groups were formed in the late 1990s by the ISI as a proxy force of jihadists to fight the Indian government in Kashmir. Each of these organizations has independent weapons stockpiles, millions of dollars in funds, and hundreds of fighters.

Foreign Fighters and al Qaeda. With its ability to mobilize foreign fighters and its access to financial resources, al Qaeda represents one of the most sophisticated networks of terrorists capable of attacking targets on a global level. It has played a central role in spreading militancy in the region, providing the insurgency with strategic communication and planning, financing, and networking opportunities. In addition, it brings recruits to Afghanistan not only from Arab countries but also from Chechnya, Uzbekistan, and China's Xinjiang province.

Relations among al Qaeda, the Taliban, and other extremist groups are very complicated. They can be direct or indirect and are characterized by a combination of hostility and friendship. They need one another for survival, but sometimes they have conflicts of interests. What is clear is that the Taliban and extremist groups need al Qaeda's money, brains, and experienced fighters, while al Qaeda needs safe havens from which it can operate worldwide.

With multiple sources of conflict and numerous destabilizing forces in Afghanistan, it is clear that developing a successful reconciliation program and building durable peace will not be an easy task. But before a framework to address the problem can be designed, past and present attempts at reconciliation must be examined and their shortcomings understood.

Past Attempts at Reconciliation

Following the Taliban's removal from power by the United States, the Bonn Agreement provided an opportunity to not only recreate the State of Afghanistan but also to end conflict there by developing a road map for peace. It recognized the need to ensure broad representation in the interim arrangement and to include those groups that have not been adequately represented at the UN-sponsored talks on Afghanistan. Although the Taliban had been defeated, was seeking amnesty and personal safety, and had no significant political ambitions, the political environment at the time made it difficult to accommodate them, leaving an opportune moment for reconciliation to be lost. As Lakhdar Brahimi, the United Nations special representative of the secretary-general, publicly stated, "The Bonn talks were dominated by one group and at that time nobody was ready to consider the partly defeated side of the conflict; therefore, the Taliban were left by themselves, which gave an opportunity to spoilers to regroup."

President Hamid Karzai first announced plans for a reconciliation policy in a speech before a gathering of ulema in Kabul in April 2003. He stated that "a clear line has to be drawn between the ordinary Taliban who are real and honest sons of this country, and those who still use the Taliban cover to disturb peace and security in the country. No one has the right to harass/persecute any one under the name of Taliban." He added that all those who were active within the ranks of the Taliban—and who were not among those known to have committed crimes against the Afghan people—could begin living as normal citizens of Afghanistan by denouncing violence.

In early 2005, the government established the Independent Peace and Reconciliation Commission (PTS) to facilitate the reconciliation process. Shortly thereafter, commission chairman Hazrat Sebghatullah Mojaddedi announced that the amnesty offer from Karzai was being extended to all Taliban leaders, including the regime's former head Mullah Omar. Although the U.S. military supported the Afghan government's general reconciliation policy and the commission, it stated unequivocally that those guilty of terrorism or other serious crimes would not be allowed to join the amnesty. Resistance to such an idea came not just from the United States: Mojaddedi's announcement was in direct contradiction of two UN Security Council Resolutions (UNSCR 1267 [1999] and 1735 [2006]) that sanctioned those very leaders.

On December 12, 2005, the Afghan Cabinet formally adopted the Action Plan on Peace, Justice, and Reconciliation in Afghanistan. The action plan focused mostly on the past and not on how to end the current violence. Then, on January 31, 2007, the lower house of the Afghanistan National Assembly approved a controversial draft amnesty bill that would provide amnesty to war criminals of the past three decades (from 1979 to 2001). An amended version, which was approved in March 2008, notes specifically that "the law does not include those who are wanted for internal and external charges against the security of the country." It further adds that "[the bill] will not cover those who do not accept the constitution of Afghanistan and the present government." Although the bill also recognizes the right of direct victims to appeal for justice, it states that in the interest of "stability and peace," those who fought against one another for the independence of Afghanistan would be granted amnesty.

Aside from these broad national initiatives at reconciliation with the Taliban, attempts at outreach and reconciliation on a more local level have been initiated with modest success by a number of actors—namely, the Afghan government, nongovernmental organizations, and the international community.

The Afghan Government

Although the Afghan government's primary focus has been on reaching out to individual members of the insurgency and to midlevel leaders, the Independent Department of Local Governance (IDLG) recently began to reach out to community leaders, commanders, and mullahs. It is trying to engage and encourage them to actively improve security in their districts. These initiatives are not well coordinated, however, and there is a gap between strategic focus and tactical approaches. Further, local insurgent leaders occasionally engage with the government to gain its trust and receive compensation only to continue with their illicit and antigovernment activities. Making such attempts at reconciliation more difficult still is the sheer number of Afghan governmental departments either directly or indirectly involved in outreach and reconciliation initiatives:

- the Office of National Security Adviser to the President
- the National Department of Security
- the Independent Peace and Reconciliation Commission (PTS), which has nine offices in the most violent provinces of the south, southeast, and west of the country
- the Independent Commission of Human Rights
- the Ministry of Interior Departments of Intelligence
- the Ministry of Defense Department of Intelligence
- the newly established Independent Department of Local Governance
- individual members of parliament, provincial councils, and provincial governors

Nongovernmental Organizations

Recently initiated by the IDLG and the Ministry of Rural Rehabilitation and Development (MRRD), the Community Based Development Councils are created through the National Solidarity Program and tasked with directly supervising and managing the implementation of rural development projects together with the district councils. Their mission is to mobilize communities for active participation in local security and stabilization and in the disbandment and demobilization of illegal armed groups.

The Afghan Civil Society Forum and a number of national and international nongovernmental organizations, such as Oxfam, the Tribal Liaison Office, and the Cooperation for Peace and Unity in Afghanistan, are also engaged in peace-building and conflict resolution training and initiatives at community levels. The Afghan National Solidarity Plan (NSP), created in 2003 to develop the ability of Afghan communities to identify, plan, manage, and monitor their own development projects, provides a unique opportunity for reconciliation at the community level through its wide network of more than 21,000 village development councils. However, this capacity is not yet fully utilized at the local level.

Supported by the Ministry of Religious Affairs, the Ulema Shura (Council of Islamic Scholars) meets on a bimonthly basis with the president to exchange views and advise the government on religious matters, but unfortunately the insurgents' outreach to the mullahs is currently more robust than that of the government.

The International Community

The United Nations Assistance Mission Afghanistan (UNAMA) is engaged in political outreach and supports the reconciliation efforts of the PTS and the Afghanistan Independent Human Rights Commission (AIHRC). Its mandate is to "provide good offices to support, if requested by the Afghan Government, the implementation of Afghan-led reconciliation programs, within the framework of the Afghan Constitution and with full respect of the implementation of measures introduced by the Security Council in its resolution 1267 (1999), and other relevant resolutions of the SC." With eight regional offices and ten provincial offices, UNAMA has significant capacity at the field level, but this capacity needs to be more effectively and strategically utilized in support of government-led initiatives.

Diplomatic missions, mostly through the development agencies of major donor and troop-contributing countries, generally focus on areas where troops are deployed and on supporting PTS, civil society organizations, and AIHRC through financial and technical assistance at the local level. Some missions even have their preferred local tribal and warlord contacts and use their network to reach out to local members of the insurgency to negotiate deals or at least reduce pressures on their military outposts. All forty-seven troop-contributing countries have their own small cells of outreach and intelligence.

Provincial Reconstruction Teams (PRT), set up by the U.S. military and NATO coalition forces, reach out to Afghans through the provision of development projects. In cases where they work closely with provincial governors, they make better contributions and help in improving the reach of local governors.

Through the combined efforts of the government and its partners, especially the PTS, some progress has been made to date, but the results have been modest. Due to organizational weakness and the general political climate, the process has never been able to get sufficient political or financial support, nor has it been able to make any headway toward breaking the insurgency and generating momentum for sustained peace and stability.

A full review of past efforts at reconciliation with the Taliban reveals that the process has lacked consistency. The government and its international partners offer conflicting messages, and no agreed-upon policy framework exists to pursue reconciliation in a cohesive manner. Additionally, an incomplete understanding of the Taliban and other groups engaged in violence further contributes to a lack of serious progress. Nevertheless, although attempts at talks have not been successful, experience shows that the Taliban can be engaged and, in fact, are willing to engage in negotiations. Experience also shows that when the government negotiates from a position of strength and has something to offer (e.g., security and economic development), negotiations are more likely to lead to a successful outcome. Based on this knowledge and the preceding analyses, one can begin to construct a pragmatic framework for peace and reconciliation in Afghanistan.

A Framework for Reconciliation

The goal of reconciliation in Afghanistan must be to achieve peace and long-term stability under the Afghan Constitution with full respect for the rule of law, social justice, and human rights. To successfully meet this goal, Afghanistan's reconciliation program needs to be carefully targeted and guided by a clear set of principles.

The Targets of Reconciliation

To be all inclusive and comprehensive, reconciliation in Afghanistan must take place on the national, community, and individual levels.

The National Level. Reconciliation efforts on the national level should focus on building trust with neighboring countries through active diplomacy and on ending sanctuaries and support to the insurgency leadership. They should also focus on providing senior-level rebel commanders with an alternative way out of the violence by offering them opportunities to participate in the political system and by guaranteeing them and their families safety from harassment by the Taliban and coalition forces and safety from national and international prosecution. These efforts will require clarity and dedicated government leadership and must be attempted from a position of strength to make them credible. They will also require the support of the international community and an active role from the United States (under the lead of the Afghan government) and the United Nations in fostering regional cooperation, implementing Security Council resolutions, and helping end the Taliban sanctuaries in Pakistan.

The Community Level. Promoting community-based peacebuilding initiatives and tapping their full potential will be key components of encouraging reconciliation from the ground up. Organized communities have a demonstrated ability to pressure insurgents into joining a peace process and have already proven to be instrumental in weapons collection at the district level and in providing security during elections. For example, district councils successfully helped pressure commanders of illegal armed groups to cooperate in the disarmament process. This generated positive momentum in more than seventy-one districts and resulted in the collection of thousands of weapons and tons of ammunition.

There is great potential for further initiatives on the community level, but it is thus far largely untapped. The NSP of the MRRD, the IDLG, nongovernmental organizations, development agencies, members of Afghanistan's parliament, provincial councils, the Ulema Shura, the private sector, women's groups, and other civil society organizations are all involved on the community level but not in a structured and coherent way. They lack effective strategic communications and require a framework of support and interaction. Thus, positive results are not visible at large. Initiatives at the community level will be most effective if they are well connected with initiatives on the national and individual level through an effective support and monitoring mechanism.

The Individual Level. Reconciliatory efforts in the form of covert negotiations and invitations to join the peace process are currently focused on individual and midlevel commanders, particularly those who do not want to be part of the neo-Taliban movement but who otherwise fear arrest or harassment. Efforts have also been made by U.S. and coalition forces to release certain prisoners so that they can rejoin their families and communities. They are provided with amnesty letters by the chairman of the PTS. In return, community and tribal elders guarantee that these newly released individuals will no longer engage in violence. Included among these released prisoners are some former high-ranking Taliban officials: Mullah Zaief, Mullavai Wakil Ahamad Mutawakel (the foreign minister under the Taliban), the director of Radio Sharia, and Mullah Abdul Salaam (the current governor of Mossa Qala). Although this initiative represents visible cooperation between the PTS and a number of national and international partners, the program requires a full review and redesign and needs to be partnered with broader stabilization initiatives. To make it fully effective, greater focus is needed on the political level to better guide the process.

Principles of Engagement

Based on the analysis herein and work already being done by members of the Policy Action Group (PAG) in Kabul, a group of senior Afghan government officials and representatives from the international community, the following series of principles should guide Afghanistan's reconciliation program:

Fundamental Principles

Afghan ownership. All reconciliation initiatives must be led by Afghan government mechanisms and institutions.

- The Afghan government may ask the United Nations and other international actors to provide support to Afghan-led reconciliation programs.
- International military forces, including ISAF, should respond expeditiously to any Afghan government request to suspend military action against specific individuals or groups identified as prospective insurgent "reconcilees" for the duration of any future reconciliation talks and against those individuals or groups whom the Afghan government identifies as reconciled.
- The international community should coordinate its efforts and avoid actions that discredit the Afghan government in the eyes of its people and damage the process of reconciliation.
- International military forces, including ISAF, and the Afghan government should notify each other, at the earliest possible opportunity, of talks by their representatives or agents with prospective insurgent "reconcilees" to avoid any damage to reconciliation proceedings and to link the talks with broader initiatives.

Compliance with national and international law. Reconciliation efforts will be guided by (and should be in compliance with) the Afghan Constitution, sharia law, and UNSCR 1267 (1999), 1735 (2006), and 1820 (2008). The Afghan government will seek international agreement for measures that may contradict certain resolutions but have significant promise for stabilization and reconciliation.

Control over territory. The Afghan state is one and reconciliation initiatives should not allow discussions that call for concessions with regard to control over territory.

Flexibility. The reconciliation process should be tailored to allow some level of flexibility to facilitate reconciliation on a case-by-case basis.

Renunciation of violence. Reconciliation with individual insurgents or insurgent groups contributes to the goal of long-term stability only if prospective interlocutors comply with constitutional disarmament requirements and renounce violence.

Rights of individuals. The rights of individuals who suffered as a direct result of atrocities and criminal acts should be recognized. The existing legal framework, including sharia law, provides provisions on the rights of individuals to register criminal cases against those who have committed crimes. Although no one has the right of forgiveness (Haquall Abde) except the victims, all reconciled individuals should enjoy the full rights and protections of citizens of Afghanistan as ensured by law.

Process-related Principles

Confidentiality. The details of negotiations between the government and insurgents should be accessible only to a limited number of responsible people. There should not be a release of information too early in the process.

Monitoring and accountability. A mechanism of individual accountability should be put in place that allows room to maneuver when prompting reconciliation, but not at the cost of the rights of individual victims who may wish to take future legal actions. The reconciliation program and reconciled individuals should be carefully monitored to (1) verify that the behaviour of individuals who are protected by their reconciled status is in line with the Afghan Constitution and the agreed-upon legal framework and (2) ensure that reconciled individuals are not harassed by government or international security forces without a genuine legal reason and are being fully reintegrated.

Power sharing. Decisions on power sharing should be made on the basis of the constitution and in accordance with the democratic process.

Organizational and Institutional Principles

Organizational arrangement. Based on an initial review of the structure of PTS, the following is needed:

- a senior focal point with a small secretariat who presides over a small committee of authorized professionals, including senior representatives of the international community, that helps coordinate the range of actors and activities at the highest levels of the government and international community;

- new PTS members with strong and respected personalities, skills, and talents and credible influence in the local politics of areas under the control of the insurgents;
- reorganized PTS operational, managerial, and financial systems.

Strategic coordination. A direct channel of communication should be maintained at all times between those engaged in reconciliation and those providing security services. The government should also coordinate with all organizations authorized to engage prospective reconcilees. The senior focal point should be responsible for the strategic coordination of reconciliation efforts. This individual should report directly to the president. The senior focal point should also be responsible for coordinating between reconciliation processing offices and Afghanistan National Security Forces (ANSF) and international military forces and for ensuring that the Afghan government and international community avoid any contradictory statements that could destroy dialogue or the credibility of the reconciliation process.

The senior focal point should also seek verifiable confirmation that reconciled individuals are contributing to peacebuilding and adhering to the Afghan Constitution. Additionally, this individual should also be notified of all reconciliation efforts, including those by members of parliament, Afghan national security organizations, the PTS, and international partners. This will help avoid confusion and ensure that no individuals or organizations engage in any kind of political negotiation with insurgents on behalf of the government without proper authorization.

Strengthen local capacity. The government should support community-based peacebuilding initiatives and strengthen capacity at the subnational level to promote and support reconciliation at the local level, especially to prevent violent conflict over land and pasturage disputes and to gain commitments for full disarmament.

Outreach-related Principles

Generate public support. A robust public relations campaign should be implemented that works in concert with Afghanistan's civil-society organizations, ulema, tribal leaders, and political groups to establish contacts and mobilize people in support of peace and stability. The role of political parties and nongovernmental actors at the community level will be crucial. Community-based organizations, elders, mullahs, the private sector, and women should be effectively utilized and their positive role in promoting reconciliation and strengthening democratic principles should be supported.

Outreach. Efforts must be made to communicate with and involve individuals and groups engaged in political violence against the state.

Support reconciled individuals. The experience and resources of the Disarmament and Reintegration Commission and Afghanistan's New Beginnings Program are invaluable and should be drawn on in developing reintegration and support networks for reconciled individuals.

First Steps. While most key actors in Afghanistan would welcome reconciliation, much skepticism exists. Some critical questions need to be answered and clarified before moving full speed toward reconciliation. Specific questions remain about who should negotiate with whom and under what conditions negotiations should occur. First steps should be geared toward addressing this skepticism and answering these outstanding questions.

To this end, an advisory team composed of experienced, senior-level international and Afghan diplomats and experts should be established with UNAMA support to help the government and the Special Representative of the United Nations Secretary-General develop a precise program document, which would include details on reorganization, outreach, reintegration implementation, monitoring, and management support. Such a team would undoubtedly be invaluable in devising a strategy geared toward building regional consensus, putting an end to the Taliban sanctuaries, promoting reconciliation, and developing trust at the national level. It would require not only the support of the Afghan government and the United Nations but also the full support of NATO, major donor countries, and the United States. The program document itself must outline a clear division of labor among the key parties and be agreed to by the principles in Kabul. The United States Institute of Peace, with its links to Afghanistan and expertise in post-conflict stabilization and peacebuilding, could help in the design, training, and mentorship of such an initiative.

Conclusions and Recommendations

In order to move forward in Afghanistan, a comprehensive and coordinated political reconciliation process must be started. At the same time, significant progress must be made on the security front and on the international (regional) front. Without security, stability, and cooperation from Afghanistan's neighbors, reconciliation will not occur. This report outlined the contours of a reconciliation process, but a number of actions will be critical to creating an environment conducive to reconciliation.

First, ISAF/NATO should temporarily increase the level of troops, which is justifiable since preparation for next year's election should start now. In the absence of such a surge, the cost of security over the long term will be intolerably high. The United States and other NATO member countries should act now.

Second, the Afghan government should accelerate security-sector reform, paying particular attention to the Ministry of Interior and police. It should also increase the ceiling of the ANA up to at least 220,000. This increase should be in the form of reserve or National Guard so that they can replace the international troops after the troop surge is over. As soon as the security threats are reduced to a manageable level, the number can be brought back to the original ceiling to ensure the sustainability of ANA.

Third, in order to prevent social unrest, political and military measures need to be complemented with substantive efforts to accelerate reconstruction, generate good governance, and overcome the food crises.

Fourth, the time has come for the United Nations and the international community to enter into serious discussions with Pakistan about cooperative measures to end Taliban sanctuaries and the cross-border insurgency. The UN Security Council should start immediate discussions on improving the implementation of its resolutions and decide on additional measures against those who continue to support the Taliban, harbor its leadership, or provide it with logistical, training, and planning support. The leadership of both Afghanistan and Pakistan should be helped and pressured to put their differences aside and cooperate seriously and sincerely with mutual respect for each other's territorial integrity and sovereignty and to work toward improving security for both countries. This engagement should build upon the concrete steps agreed to in the Peace Jirgah, which was organized jointly by Afghanistan and Pakistan in 2007 to build peace along their common border areas.

Fifth, India, Pakistan, and Afghanistan should engage in a direct dialogue with the United States as mediator in an attempt to end the use of Afghanistan soil as a proxy Indo-Pakistani battleground. Although such a dialogue has never been tried before, building confidence and providing security guarantees would reduce tensions and help stabilize Afghanistan.

Sixth, the Afghan government and the international community must invest in a state that is functional and able to provide basic services so that the Afghans themselves can take charge without relying on others. Investment in education, media, and civil society is the only way to help overcome extremism. Promoting moderate Islam is a key unifying factor. The positive role of Islam in promoting peace and reconciliation must be recognized. Copying models from the outside will not work in Afghanistan. Building functional state institutions and ensuring equal social and economic opportunities as well as justice are fundamental to building national unity. Such an approach will help transform ethnic diversity from threat to asset.

Seventh, the government should intensify its fight against corruption and drug trafficking. Continuation of the status quo will not help rebuild public confidence.

Eighth, the Reconstruction Opportunity Zones initiative of the United States and the decision of the G-8 in Japan to invest in tribal areas on both sides of the Afghan-Pakistani border represent important steps toward stability in the region. Resources must be made available in a timely manner and spent effectively in order to generate results that promote peace. This requires a comprehensive program for investment that should be developed by a joint team of Afghan, Pakistani, and international experts.

Ninth, the current reactive approach toward the stabilization of Afghanistan has not proven productive. Further, hesitation by NATO and other troop-contributing countries to address the needs of international field commanders in Afghanistan and restrictions on troop deployment undermines the struggle against terrorism, prolongs the mission, and ultimately weakens the Afghan government's position in any reconciliation effort. It is very important that ISAF works to lower civilian casualties and avoids any incidents in which religious and traditional Afghan values are demeaned. In addition, the international community must now deliver on the commitments it made at the Bucharest and Paris conferences.

Notes

1. Louis Dupree, *Afghanistan*, (Princeton: Princeton University Press, 1980), 55.
2. Steve Coll, *Ghost Wars: The Secret History of the CIA, Afghanistan, and Bin Laden, from the Soviet Invasion to September 10, 2001* (Boston: Penguin, 2004), 201.

10

Impact or Illusion?
Reintegration under the Afghanistan Peace and Reintegration Program

Deedee Derksen

I n 2008, Mohammad Masoom Stanekzai suggested that reconciling with insurgents can contribute to long-term stability only *"if prospective interlocutors comply with constitutional disarmament requirements and renounce violence"* (see chapter 9). Between 2008 and 2011, an Afghan program was designed (largely under Stanekzai's influence), funded, and implemented to secure precisely that disarmament. The results of the Afghan Peace and Reintegration Program (APRP) in its first year of implementation are the subject of Derksen's critique, published in 2011.

Derksen highlights two issues that students of the international intervention in Afghanistan may recognize from many other programs. While each setback in Afghanistan has resulted in new strategies, policies, frameworks, and other visions and designs, there has been a consistent failure of implementation—either the design has been inappropriate to what is possible locally or the implementers have gotten in each other's way. Regarding the APRP, Derksen notes delays in establishing the program's infrastructure (e.g., bank accounts, safe houses), the lack of jobs, and the inability of Afghan forces to protect insurgents being reintegrated into society.

The obstacles were predictable, and given that the success of the project depended on a positive initial demonstration effect, the greater failure is perhaps at the strategic level. Stanekzai envisioned the reintegration program taking place alongside a larger reconciliation program with the insurgent's leaders. Derksen reports that, from the beginning, *"international actors and the Afghan government have disagreed on the sequence of both. ISAF and donors hoped that the reintegration of low- and mid-level*

Originally published as Deedee Derksen, "Impact or Illusion? Reintegration under the Afghanistan Peace and Reintegration Program," Peace Brief 106 (Washington, DC: USIP, 2011).

fighters, combined with the pressure of kill-capture campaigns, would force insurgent leaders to negotiate." Derksen argues that this fundamentally misreads why fighters join insurgent movements. The analyses by Stanekzai and others of the conflict's dynamics were ignored to secure what appeared to be an easy win. But there are few easy wins in counterinsurgency. One of Derksen's final recommendations is to "focus on quality not speed." It may be too late for that.

Why the APRP Developed

Since late 2010 the Afghan government, supported by its international partners, has tried to reintegrate insurgents under the APRP. The program aims to entice fighters to leave the battlefield in return for security, jobs and other incentives—provided they renounce violence, respect the Afghan constitution and cut ties with al-Qaida.

The program, authorized by President Karzai in June 2010, proposes parallel processes of reintegrating lower-level fighters and reconciling with higher-level insurgent commanders through political dialogue. At the London Conference six months earlier, donors pledged $140 million for reintegrating these commanders and foot soldiers. Western governments, hoping to withdraw troops amid deteriorating security, increasingly favor a political solution. The Afghan government envisaged reintegration accompanied by talks with insurgent leaders. But the International Security Assistance Force (ISAF) saw it as part of a military strategy that would force the leadership of the insurgency to the table. As a result, ISAF pressed for its quick implementation.

The program is led by a 70-member High Peace Council (HPC) created in September 2010, and implemented by a Joint Secretariat (JS) in which ISAF and the United Nations mission participate with the government. It intends to offer not only employment to former fighters, but protection and grievance resolution in their communities.

APRP is being rolled out in a challenging context. Progress on high-level dialogue among the parties is fitful at best, while the government is perceived as corrupt and weak. NATO tactics are heightening tensions and public commitments to withdraw international troops are raising fears that it could be unwise to reintegrate and side with an Afghan government that may not have a strong partner to back it up.[1]

Unsurprisingly, in this context there have been few takers for reintegration.

Implementation: the Devil's in the Details

Establishing the local infrastructure (bank accounts, provincial peace councils and support teams) has taken longer than the ambitious schedule demanded.

By the end of May 2011, the Afghan government had received $133.4 million of the committed funds for reintegration, but spent only $7.7 million. Instead, ISAF has assumed many responsibilities, reinforcing the perception that APRP is driven by the international military.

Although the APRP promises to address grievances in communities and support an amnesty policy consistent with Afghanistan's constitution and treaty obligations, few concrete steps have yet been taken. JS and the HPC officials have visited several provinces, but delays in establishing APRP provincial infrastructure and providing guidelines for governors have meant little outreach at local level. Nor has a detailed amnesty policy been finalized, with Western and Afghan officials reluctant to tackle this politically sensitive issue.

The inability to guarantee the security of former fighters is another grave problem. All reintegrated commanders interviewed feared for their safety, with many threatened. While some commanders are in safe houses and others have returned to their villages, the program does not yet provide any systematic way to protect them. This is a major obstacle, especially in Afghanistan's South and East, where insurgents who approach local authorities are at extreme risk from both sides.

Moreover, very little has been on offer thus far in terms of employment and community rehabilitation. In theory, options include vocational and literacy training, religious mentoring, or enrollment in Afghanistan's security forces, or in a public works or agriculture conservation corps. But in reality, former fighters have been offered few civilian jobs.

Without civilian jobs or adequate security, many reintegrees are admitted into the Afghan Local Police (ALP), despite the formal independence of the two programs. Linking the APRP and ALP, however, risks additional problems. First, many reintegrees are not vetted and their enlistment has led to abuse of authority. Second, recruiting reintegrees into the ALP can perpetuate and intensify rivalries by encouraging local powerbrokers to introduce their allies into the APRP. A local official involved with APRP in Baghlan argued:

> Now there is a big problem between Tajiks and Pashtuns because of reintegration, Tajiks see Pashtuns joining the government, receiving weapons and becoming powerful locally, and they want to increase their own strength.

Questionable Reintegration Numbers and Roles

Although former fighters are supposed to be vetted and registered, their numbers and backgrounds are disputed. The JS claims all were "real Taliban," but others disagree, noting that 85 percent of reintegration has occurred in provinces where the insurgency is less intense.[2] ISAF appears to view reintegration of non-insurgents as legitimate, whereas the Afghan government views APRP as exclusively for the Taliban. According to the JS, the National Directorate of Security and the Ministries of Interior and Defense vet potential fighters to reintegrate at the provincial and national level. But as of May 2011, no finalized standard operating procedure appeared to exist and ISAF was still developing the Reintegration Tracking and Monitoring Database.

In the North and West, where the numbers of reintegrated former fighters are highest, their backgrounds appear mixed or unclear. In Baghlan, for example, Taliban commanders interviewed who had not joined the government are ideological and entrenched in the movement with ties to commanders elsewhere. In contrast, reintegrated commanders tend to present themselves as leaders of village defense forces that switched sides when the government established a presence in their area, or in response to pressure from rival insurgents. Some groups approached the police, others the NDS or provincial councilors. The "hosts" took care of vetting but neglected to share findings with other implementers.

The first group of some 100 reintegrees, who presented themselves as Hizb-i-Islami, joined in March 2010 after losing a battle against Taliban gaining strength in the area. Another group of 100–160 men represented a progovernment unit that reintegrated in order to enlist in the ALP. (It is unclear if that group is still in the program.) According to researchers familiar with the cases, in Badghis and Kunduz, only a part of those who were reintegrated were actually insurgents: others were criminal groups or members of progovernment militia.

In the East and the South, where the insurgency is fiercest, there has been little official reintegration though ISAF officials and the JS claim that insurgents are being reintegrated informally: they agree with a governor to stop fighting and go home, but are not registered for the APRP.

The Missing Political Approach

On paper, the APRP is a two-track program "aiming to promote peace through a political approach"—involving reintegration and reconciliation. In reality, international actors and the Afghan government have disagreed on the sequence of both. ISAF and donors hoped that the reintegration of low- and mid-level fighters, combined with the pressure of kill-capture campaigns would force insurgent leaders to negotiate. However, this largely military-led strategy is unlikely to fully address the ties of patronage and loyalty within the Taliban movement. Almost all active insurgent commanders interviewed argued they were not interested in reintegration unless their leaders were at the table with the Afghan government and the process addressed the core grievances of the international military presence and government corruption and predation. At the same time, many former fighters reintegrated under the program appear only loosely tied to the insurgency, if at all. All this suggests that reintegration without broader reconciliation will have limited strategic impact.

The main national and international civilian and military actors involved in APRP used a review conference in May to evaluate its progress. Their plan for the APRP now aims to put the necessary infrastructure in place quickly. But many of the people interviewed find it overly focused on economics, while overlooking other factors like the behavior of foreign forces, dissatisfaction with the Afghan government and Pakistan's influence. The emphasis on economics also ignores the destabilizing impact of development aid, which can fuel corruption and competition for limited resources.

The international community and Afghan government appear reluctant to tackle drivers of the insurgency linked to their own behavior—notably government corruption and foreign troop's tactics. Also, some interviewees noted that those who are implementing reintegration are far from neutral in that they are parties to the conflict. That has led to groups questioning the legitimacy of the HPC, for example, some of whose members have more experience waging war than making peace. Many insurgents therefore regard reintegration as surrender. As one Taliban commander from Helmand said, "This is not a reintegration process, this is an American process. With whom should we join? With this corrupt and unjust government? I will never join this process and won't let any of my friends."

Many U.N. and Afghan officials agree that significant reintegration will not occur unless insurgents see it as part of a broader, politically negotiated settlement process.

Conclusion

There is broad support among Afghans and Afghanistan's partners for a peace process. On paper, the APRP is quite comprehensive, however, to date it has yielded limited results. In rolling out the program quickly, political issues like grievance resolution and amnesty were inadequately tackled, and the lack of a political approach to reintegration embedded in a broader reconciliation process remains a fundamental flaw.

Reintegration began during an American military troop surge and was aimed by ISAF at weakening the Taliban movement before inviting them to the negotiating table. However, as troops withdraw and the Afghan government assumes increasing security responsibilities, there may be an expansion of talks with the Taliban leadership. This "transition" involves challenges, but also opportunities to tie reintegration to a broader political process. Looking ahead to this process, the international community and the Afghan government should:

- *Link reintegration with reconciliation.* Situate reintegration of low- and mid-level commanders within a broader reconciliation process aimed not only at insurgent leaders, but also disenfranchised groups. Prepare for scenarios under which reintegration supports the implementation of a peace settlement, potentially including a broader based Afghan management mechanism acceptable to settlement parties, or management by a third party implementer.
- *Focus on quality not speed.* Afghanistan will require a robust reintegration infrastructure able to handle large numbers to secure a sustainable peace. Instead of trying to quickly reintegrate the highest numbers possible, concentrate on establishing effective institutions, particularly political and judicial, and manage expectations through clear communication of program goals and features.
- *Support local processes.* Expand administrative, financial and moral support for local officials involved in implementing APRP, coupled with monitoring of the use of resources and community vetting of reintegrees.

Notes

1. On Afghan stakeholder perceptions, see Hamish Nixon, *Achieving Durable Peace: Afghan Perspectives on a Peace Process*, Oslo/Washington D.C.: CMI, PRIO, and USIP.
2. Afghan government documents in May 2011 showed 1,571 of 1,809 reintegrees were in northern and western provinces.

11

Designing a Comprehensive Peace Process for Afghanistan

*Lisa Schirch**

Schirch's chapter, originally published in 2011, addresses a point raised but not always developed in other chapters: A negotiated agreement must be inclusive to lead to sustainable peace, but the nature of political negotiations requires that they also be discreet. Schirch unravels this tension to show how a peace process can be structured, such that discretion and inclusion are not mutually exclusive. Drawing on lessons from other countries that achieved stability after long years of conflict, Schirch makes a detailed argument for a comprehensive and inclusive peace process.

Schirch places a great deal of importance on including civil society, providing examples and models of how other countries have been successful in this area. Afghans see civil society as citizens concerned about the public good rather than groups that promote private or sectarian interests, as is often the case in other countries. Thus village elders and religious scholars can be considered civil society members if they have demonstrated that commitment to the public good.

The chapter maps the who, what, and how of a potential peace process, using a number of hypotheticals without being overly prescriptive. The section on how to develop a peace process details possible ways to involve civil society without jeopardizing the need for discretion.

Schirch echoes Stanekzai's recommendation for patience, arguing that a peace process should "go slow to go fast." Behind this recommendation is the idea that the process (the how) is as important as the outcome (the what). A flawed process leads to a flawed outcome.

Originally published as Lisa Schirch, "Designing a Comprehensive Peace Process for Afghanistan," Peaceworks 75 (Washington, DC: USIP, 2011).

* With contributions from Aziz Rafiee, Nilofar Sakhi, and Mirwais Wardak.

From "Peace Talks" to a "Comprehensive Peace Process"

The transition from war to peace in Afghanistan requires much more than high-level negotiations and low-level reintegration efforts. The current negotiation agenda between U.S. and Taliban representatives holds potential for establishing conditions for an end to the war. Yet it does not lay a foundation for a sustainable peace. The current approach muffles other critical conflicts that are obstacles to peace in Afghanistan and the region and overlooks Afghan civil society's capacity to support a national peace process. The June 2010 National Consultative Peace Jirga called for the creation of a National Peace Council and a redesign of reintegration efforts in the new Afghan Peace and Reconciliation Program (APRP). Noting concerns about the lack of democratic representation first in the Peace Jirga and later in the National Peace Council, civil society leaders continue to flag the exclusion of public interests in current peace talks.[1] Public participation in a comprehensive peace process is an essential component for successful transition from war to a stable peace.[2]

Half of all peace agreements fail—and once they fail, the underlying conflicts have an even greater chance of becoming intractable. In the history of successful transitions from war to peace, one lesson is clear: go slow to go fast. Rushed peace processes that limit or exclude public participation and interests are more likely to fail than those that build a solid foundation for a sustainable peace. Too often international diplomats seem to throw all of their eggs in one basket with high-level peace negotiations to achieve a quick settlement. When these efforts fail to produce immediate outcomes, the stakeholders return to the battlefield convinced that diplomacy was tried and exhausted. Peace agreements thrown together quickly often unravel in a way that results in an even longer process, less trust among key stakeholders, more costs to the international community, and more death and destruction on the ground.

The jumble of terminology in Afghanistan fogs the complicated landscape of peace efforts. (For purposes of this report, the definitions found in box 1 are used.) In Afghanistan, the concept of "reconciliation" often refers to high-level negotiations between the Taliban, Karzai government, and international forces.[3] But in other contexts, such as in South Africa, reconciliation has traditionally referred to a national civil society–led process following official, political negotiations. More recently, media reports signal that there are high-level "peace talks" under way. Peace talks aim to reach a "peace agreement," a statement that would lay out the conditions and steps for a transition from armed struggle to a politically negotiated process. The term "reintegration" refers to low-level disarmament efforts to entice foot soldiers with jobs programs and other economic incentives. And at the same time, Afghan civil society calls for

Box 1. Definition of Terms

> Reintegration refers to low-level efforts to offer incentives to disarm and return armed individuals to community life.
>
> Reconciliation refers to a process between conflicting groups to understand core grievances and identify mutually satisfying solutions with the goal of ending fighting and normalizing political relationships.
>
> Transitional justice refers to a process of building a culture respectful of human rights by repairing justice systems, healing social divisions, and building a democratic system of governance.
>
> Peace negotiations or "peace talks" refer to discussions aimed at reaching both reconciliation and a peace agreement.
>
> A peace agreement is a negotiated cease-fire and road map for participatory governance in a divided country.
>
> A peace process is a multilevel, multiphased effort involving armed and unarmed stakeholders in a conflict to both bring an end to armed fighting and lay out a sustainable political, economic, security, and territorial agreement. It involves top-level negotiation between the armed groups, plus diverse forums for public dialogue and engagement to foster a broad consensus on the future direction of the country.

a national "transitional justice process" with an agenda contrasting from that found in the formal peace talks. All of these terms and processes have a place within an Afghan *comprehensive peace process*.

A "comprehensive peace process" is distinct in that it includes a much wider array of activities, actors, and forums aimed at achieving peace.[4] Comprehensive peace processes are multilevel, dynamic efforts to build a public consensus around a shared future. A peace process may or may not lead to a peace agreement. In Afghanistan, for example, a comprehensive peace process could help address root causes of the conflict whether or not a peace agreement between the country's armed, political, and ethnic groups ever materializes. Building a national consensus on the country's future among civil society could aid in achieving a political settlement between armed groups. A comprehensive peace process requires a careful look at *who* participates in a peace process, *what* issues are on the table, and *how* the process is structured. In short, a comprehensive peace process requires creating structures for wide participation and deep discussion of underlying interests and grievances that fuel conflict. Only a *wide* and *deep* multilevel, sequential process, using principled negotiation techniques, will enable the country to build a national consensus on the way forward.[5]

The pool of human experience in fostering national peace processes in divided countries is still shallow. Not enough people are thinking through what a comprehensive Afghan peace process, based on lessons learned in other countries, could or should look like. This report seeks to fill that void by distilling key elements of designing peace processes from historical case studies, and looking at the unique challenges and opportunities for a culturally attuned, comprehensive peace process in Afghanistan. This report first makes the case for a comprehensive peace process. It then examines who should be involved in a comprehensive peace process, what types of incentives, negotiation strategies, and issues should be brought to negotiation tables, and how inclusive mechanisms for public input and mediation, technical support, and coordination teams can structure a comprehensive peace process. The final section of the report provides policy recommendations for Afghan civil society, the Afghan government, and the international community.

The Case for a Comprehensive Peace Process

Research comparing attempts to transition from war demonstrates the difficulties facing all routes to peace. A military victory leading to a durable peace in Afghanistan is extremely unlikely. Only a small percentage of wars end because one side wins and another loses. Most wars end in stalemate, with neither side claiming victory.[6] And of those wars that are won, those with a rebel or insurgent victory tend to have more stable outcomes than others.[7] Moreover, attempts to end wars by inflicting pain on opponents require a great deal of time and destruction of relationships, lives, and infrastructure thereby making it all the more difficult to build a sustainable peace after attempts at such an unlikely victory. A survey of research on war termination concludes external efforts to push stakeholders to negotiate through violent punishment or war rarely work if the stakeholders believe they will not achieve their goals through negotiation.[8]

Current enemy-centric "kill-and-capture" International Security Assistance Force (ISAF) policies endanger negotiation by removing leaders who have a political agenda and maturity to make deals. The remaining lower-level leaders of armed insurgent groups tend to be more extremist in their views and are more likely to continue fighting at any cost.[9] Attempts for the international community to financially buy their way out of the war by supporting the Afghan and Pakistani governments look equally doomed to fail. Ironically, the international community's greatest leverage in Afghanistan lies neither in imposing a hurting stalemate onto armed insurgent groups nor making military and financial commitments to prop up the Afghan government and Pakistani military and intelligence agencies that the public widely sees as illegitimate. The military and financial "intravenous drip" keeps the current dysfunctional system in place, allowing these governments to forgo the hard work of earning public legitimacy and consent to govern while simultaneously providing financial incentives for many stakeholders to perpetuate the war for their own financial gain. Rather, an international military and financial drawdown from Afghanistan may be the greatest leverage available to the international community. A political and financial "hurting stalemate" may be far more effective at creating incentives for all sides to enter into earnest negotiations to end the war and to build a durable peace than what is achieved by flexing military might.[10]

Most wars end through peace agreements, but half of these also fail and there is a return to war.[11] Most of the peace processes in recent history have been deeply flawed in a variety of ways, such as excluding all but certain armed groups, failing to make needed structural changes, lacking necessary international support, or insufficient attention to the challenge of implementing agreements. Comprehensive peace processes that include international security guarantees, investments in economic development, demilitarized zones, and robust mechanisms for addressing conflicts at all levels of society through principled negotiation and mediation have a more successful track record.[12] Comprehensive peace processes are more likely to lead to positive outcomes than their noncomprehensive counterparts.[13] Comprehensive peace processes more often lead to these interrelated positive outcomes:

- *Public support.* One of the reasons that half of all peace agreements fail is that too few people support them. The more people a peace process includes, the more people that may support an agreement.
- *Legitimacy.* Peace negotiations that include only armed actors inadvertently legitimate the use of arms to achieve political power. A comprehensive and inclusive peace process creates a more legitimate outcome and builds public consent for the national government.
- *Sustainability.* Comprehensive peace processes more often address a range of driving factors fueling conflict and thus help to prevent the causes of recurring violent conflict. Unarmed groups including religious and ethnic or tribal leadership, women, labor unions, educators, youth, and other elements of civil society play important roles in ensuring that peace agreements address critical issues fueling ongoing violence, such as reforming state institutions, and deep-seated public grievances.
- *Democratic governance.* A comprehensive peace process is an exercise in participatory deliberation and intergroup dialogue and negotiation. With the help of facilitators and mediators and the support of widespread training via local civil society institutions such as media programs and religious centers, a comprehensive peace process can teach skills of how to identify differences and build on common ground. Dialogue models used in a comprehensive peace process are strikingly different than those employed in Western-style democracies' competitive politics and hard-fought elections, which have been found to exacerbate

social and political conflict in divided societies.[14] While it may take more time to structure a participatory process, the long-term payoff for this participation is that the peace process can lay the groundwork for democratic governance.

These outcomes are directly related to the inclusion of a wide range of stakeholders who raise a wide range of issues via a series of interrelated mechanisms for structuring public participation in a peace process. The next three sections of this report detail the *who*, *what*, and *how* of an Afghan comprehensive peace process.

The "Who" of an Afghan Peace Process: Key Stakeholders

An exclusive peace agreement reached only between certain armed groups at the top of society is insufficient. A sustainable peace requires building a national consensus on how to move the country forward. Research comparing successful and unsuccessful peace agreements illustrates that civil society engagement is often the critical ingredient to a successful peace process.[15] Engaging with armed actors who want to be included in a peace process is also essential, as excluding them cements their commitment to using violence as the only communication channel.[16] Peace processes that include a wider range of voices are more likely to lead to success, legitimacy, sustainability, and democratic governance. A tipping point or critical mass of people supporting a peace process for a war-to-peace transition is essential, particularly in countries with a weak central government, like Afghanistan. Figure 1 illustrates the key leadership at all levels of the pyramid that must be engaged to build a public consensus.[17]

Policymakers looking for a quick fix or "good enough" solution face temptations to shortcut the process. A desire for confidentiality, manageability, and security lead some to conclude that peace talks require only private negotiation spaces for moderate leaders of armed groups. These concerns are valid. A comprehensive peace process should include a track for confidential discussions and should have a design that is both realistic and flexible. Achieving cease-fire agreements and developing security arrangements often requires secret negotiations outside of the public eye. However, shortcuts cannot build sustainable peace.

Comparative case studies of public peace processes in Guatemala, the Philippines, Mali, and South Africa illustrate that manageable mechanisms and models for public input exist. A later section of this report details five broad models of public participation in peace processes and their relevance for Afghanistan.

Figure 1. Pyramid of Afghan Stakeholders

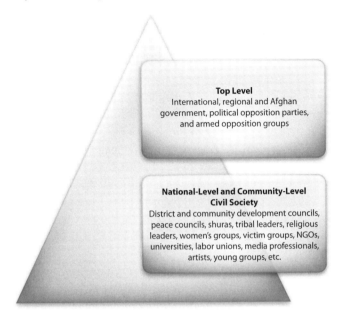

Including "Spoilers" and "Terrorists"

It is routine for governments and groups engaged in armed conflict to refuse to negotiate with each other and to conclude that "violence is the only language" understandable to their opponents. Yet the history of the post–Cold War era shows most wars end in agreements and at some point all sides come to see that negotiation is the only viable option.[18] Nelson Mandela and the African National Congress, and armed insurgent groups in Guatemala, El Salvador, Mozambique, Cambodia, and numerous other countries, were once thought to be parties that could not be negotiated with. Yet today there are viable peace agreements in each of these countries. Engaging with armed groups is not equal to legitimating their cause.[19] Negotiation processes can uncover legitimate grievances buried beneath a group's radical rhetoric. Addressing these legitimate grievances, which often center on a desire for respect and dignity, is far less expensive and more effective than the fantasy of firepower solutions aimed at eradicating the group or its ideas.

Strategies for managing potential spoilers of a peace agreement are necessary. "Spoilers" are groups that aim to disrupt any peace agreement either because their interests were not represented or included in the negotiations or because they perceive themselves to benefit more from ongoing violent conflict.[20] Peace processes often exclude spoilers because they do indeed aim to disrupt efforts toward peace.[21] The dilemma in any high-level negotiation is whether to include potential and manifest spoilers. If the process includes both spoilers, they may make it impossible for moderates to make progress in areas where they find common ground across the lines of conflict. On the other hand, a peace process that excludes all potential spoilers may not have anyone around the table. If so-called spoilers are left out of the process because they are more difficult to work with, then they often come back later to disrupt the implementation of an agreement. Excluding potential spoilers can increase their commitment to violence by removing viable political alternatives.

Managing spoilers means preparing for the reality that certain stakeholders, including some participating in a peace process and those left out of the process, will either not follow through on implementation of agreements or will actively attempt to sabotage agreements. Developing plans for managing spoilers requires actively engaging with their interests so as to shift their perception of the costs of spoiling the process and the benefits from allowing a peace process to move forward.

The 2001 Bonn Agreement on Afghanistan excluded key civil society interests and the Taliban. The process rewarded some warlords from the Northern Alliance with political authorities and impunity for their crimes, which some deem as on par with crimes by the Taliban. Many scholars noted the exclusion of Taliban leaders in the Bonn Agreement led to missed opportunities for finding a political solution.[22]

Current negotiations threaten to repeat these mistaken calculations of who to include or exclude in discussions about Afghanistan's future, as they focus on high-level stakeholders in the international community, neighboring countries, the Afghan government, and moderate, politically minded Taliban representatives from Quetta Shura. These negotiations exclude some armed groups such as the Haqqani network, deemed too extremist for the process. While secret talks between certain politically minded stakeholders may be appropriate at early stages, an ongoing process that excludes the voices and interests of potential spoilers lessens the chances for achieving a sustainable peace.

Involving Civil Society

Including only certain armed stakeholders in a peace agreement creates long-term problems. First, it rewards groups who use violence with political influence and even positions of power. Second, a peace agreement that excludes public input leaves out the interests and needs of other key stakeholders in a society required to achieve a sustainable solution to underlying issues. If key stakeholders are left out, they will lack ownership of the agreement and the political will required to implement it. Successful and sustainable peace processes find ways to engage both armed groups deemed too extreme for negotiation and unarmed civil society deemed irrelevant or unwieldy.[23]

In addition to those at the top of the pyramid in figure 1, national-level and community-level civil society leaders and the general public at the bottom of the pyramid also need spaces to represent their interests in a comprehensive Afghan peace process. Civil society organizations (CSOs) are groups of citizens not in government that organize themselves on behalf of some public interest. CSOs face many of the same challenges as government, such as corruption, lack of capacity, and inadequate funding to achieve their goals. As opposed to elements of "uncivil society that fuel violence," CSOs foster democratic dialogue, tolerance, and trust between groups, work in partnership with the state to carry out important public services, and hold the state accountable for its responsibilities to citizens and transparent governance. Stable governance and a durable peace require a citizen-oriented state working in partnership with an active civil society that has adequate space to hold government to account.[24] Civil society organizations (CSOs) are groups of citizens not in government that organize themselves on behalf of some public interest. As opposed to elements of "uncivil society that fuel violence," CSOs foster democratic dialogue, tolerance, and trust between groups. Civil society works in partnership with the state both to complement and supplement its capacity and to hold the state to account for its responsibilities and transparent governance. An active local civil society at the national and community levels is an indicator of a functioning and democratic state.[25] Given this broader understanding of civil society–state relations, the role of CSOs in a peace process is more obvious.

Generating and consolidating a new national narrative or story about a country's future is an essential element of a sustainable peace process. Public dialogue can help to create this national consensus on what a shared future looks like. When the public believes that its individual identity, economic, political, and security interests are supported by the nation at large, it will support a peace process to make that new reality possible. Media campaigns using television, radio, billboards, and posters to generate public support have been a component of a number of successful peace processes.

During the U.S. civil rights movement, those wanting a more inclusive, respectful society did not set out to kill or wage war against the intolerant Ku Klux Klan (KKK)—a once widespread violent white supremacy movement. Instead, Americans prosecuted KKK crimes while working to build a national consensus that rejected the ideology of racism, intolerance, and violence. While KKK groups still exist today in some areas of the U.S. and racism is still widespread, Americans created a strong enough national consensus—from Washington down to small towns in middle America—to push the KKK to the margins. The civil society movement, supported by institutions enforcing rule of law, defeated the *ideas* of the KKK through the media, public discussions, and peaceful protest.

An Afghan peace process cannot accomplish in a few years the kind of social change that takes decades or generations, especially without a functioning judicial system to support rule of law. The ideas driving the Taliban and other armed Afghan opposition groups, and the culture of impunity and corruption in Afghanistan, will take generations to change. However, a comprehensive peace process can build a national consensus to point Afghan society in a direction where most stakeholders believe they will achieve more through the political process than the battlefield. A comprehensive Afghan peace process could blend models used in other countries with Afghan peacebuilding traditions to create an inclusive national agenda to move forward collectively and peacefully.

Afghan civil society is complex. In addition to traditional or tribal structures such as *jirga*s (assemblies) and *malik*s (leaders), religious leaders and structures such as the Shura-e-Ulama (council of religious scholars) play important roles in mediating local conflicts.[26] Afghan civil society also includes trade unions, universities, artists, media professionals, women's groups, youth groups, and other forms of social structure outside of the state, including local Afghan nongovernmental organizations (NGOs) and Community Development Councils (CDCs). All of these civil society sectors have roles to play in fostering durable peace in Afghanistan.

Researchers on Afghan civil society consistently find that locals define civil society broadly as citizens "concerned about the public good as opposed to private or sectarian interests."[27] Afghan civil society plays active roles in fostering participatory governance and peace, including "breaking through client networks, solving local problems, and creating constituencies for peace."[28] Yet civil society activists describe a "war on civil society" carried out by armed opposition groups, the Afghan government, and NATO forces, each of which they say further disenfranchises the interests of average Afghans.[29]

Shallow definitions and understanding of the concept of civil society plague international policy. Historically, counterinsurgency manuals advised on how to "pacify" civil society so that it withdraws support from armed opposition groups and accepts government authority. Remnants of pacification strategies linger on while newer counterinsurgency guidance in Afghanistan asserts the need for military forces to gain public support and use civil society as "force multipliers," service providers, or implementing partners for donor-designed projects. Citing an important surge in Iraqi civil society opposition to armed groups independently accompanying the military surge, U.S. military leaders in Afghanistan look for an Afghan civil society equivalent to reduce violence.

> Premised on the belief that tribesmen living in the Pashtun belt make up the majority of the insurgency's recruits, the tribal elder is posited as Afghanistan's equivalent of an ... awakened Iraqi chieftain. It is to him that policymakers will turn when looking to consult ordinary Afghans on plans for reconciliation.[30]

There are several problems with this tribal strategy. First, tribal leaders are not eager to join forces with "a collateral damage prone International Security Assistance Force (ISAF) trumpeting a corrupt central government and a circus of intrusive development projects."[31] Second, tribal groups sway back and forth between competing external forces and the Afghan government, depending on rapidly shifting short-term assessments of what is in their interest.[32] Finally, Afghan civil society is much more diverse and complex than suggested by this tribal strategy.

Afghan civil society will best contribute to an Afghan peace process when it is allowed space to act independently and when there are adequate civil freedoms to discuss key issues driving the conflict in Afghanistan.

The "What" of an Afghan Peace Process: A Negotiation Framework

All stakeholders calculate their interests in supporting continued war versus a negotiated solution—that includes armed groups and government but also business leaders, farmers, drug traffickers, military contractors, and ordinary citizens in Afghanistan and in those countries supporting international forces. A successful peace process is one in which all stakeholders are satisfied that the outcome is better than the alternative of continuing to fight. Stakeholders assess their "best alternative to a negotiated agreement" (BATNA) to determine whether to continue fighting.[33] If stakeholders believe they can achieve more on the battlefield, through other means of coercion, or by the continuation of the status quo, they will not negotiate in good faith. Stakeholders calculate their BATNA depending on the calculus of the costs and benefits, incentives and sanctions for participating or not participating. The "ripeness" of a peace process centers on whether the groups in conflict believe they have more to gain from peace or continued fighting.[34] There is no easy calculus to determine when a group may decide to devote energy to a negotiated outcome.[35]

Box 2 summarizes some of the dilemmas of negotiation.[36] The dangers of a negotiated agreement in Afghanistan can be significantly reduced with the design of a comprehensive peace process involving a more strategic set of incentives, a principled negotiation approach, and a wider negotiation agenda. Internationals pushing a settlement may craft an agreement that looks good from an outsider's point of view. Countless think tanks in foreign capitals have put forth solutions to Afghanistan's challenges but the long and messy process of all stakeholders coming to understand each other's underlying interests through wide consultations and public dialogue is necessary for all sides to understand why certain provisions in an agreement may be the best possible outcome.[37]

Box 2. Dangers of Negotiating versus Not Negotiating

Dangers of Negotiating	Dangers of Not Negotiating
A negotiation between armed opposition groups could	*Continued attempts to solve the conflict on the battlefield could*
endanger progress on human rights and women's empowerment, particularly if the negotiations exclude women and minorities;	perpetuate further suffering of civilians in a war with no end in sight;
foster a culture of impunity by allowing perpetrators to go free without accountability for their crimes;	increase the possibility that the insurgency will grow stronger over time, making negotiation more difficult in the future;
increase the tensions between ethnic groups if power sharing is perceived as consolidating Pashtun dominance and excluding other ethnic groups from political power;	increase the tensions between ethnic groups if the war overshadows efforts to address interethnic conflict and/or if the Taliban gains territory;
pose challenges in monitoring the relationship with al-Qaida;	lead to a missed opportunity to brainstorm options and conditions for ending the war.
lead to further control by Pakistan over Afghanistan, since it is widely believed that elements within Pakistan control the Taliban.	

Negotiation efforts fail in many peace efforts because mid-level diplomats, without comparative experience in successful peace processes, use coercive bargaining to battle and seek compromises on the positions of armed groups. To entice armed groups to "give up" their fight, all sides continue to pound each other on the battlefield while internationals throw small financial incentives at low-level fighters. In practice, this approach does not work. It leads to compounding and lengthening the time and costs of a war. Instead, research on successful peace processes suggests the need for a more comprehensive understanding of incentives and sanctions and a principled or "interest-based" rather than coercive approach to negotiation. It also suggests the need to address a wide range of drivers of violence—not just the armed groups' stated public positions and demands—including the key issues of diverse stakeholders necessary to build a national consensus.

Using Incentives and Sanctions

It is common for groups to apply sanctions against each other to physically, economically, or politically harm the interests of others. Efforts to inflict pain to opposing groups aim to achieve victory or exhaustion in some cases. Pounding on the battlefield or on the airwaves of public opinion seeks to make opposing groups reach a "hurting stalemate" where they determine that there are more costs than benefits to fighting.

All armed groups in Afghanistan are still trying to inflict pain on others and boast that they are winning on the battlefield, indicating their own reluctance to make conciliatory moves. There are high costs to the current approach attempting to impose a hurting stalemate in Afghanistan in hopes of driving armed groups to surrender or negotiate.

In practice, the use of violent coercion does not have a successful historical track record, as detailed earlier in this report. It leads to compounding and lengthening the time and costs of a war. Faced with a "lose-lose" option of losing on the battlefield or surrendering without incentives that address their interests, many groups will choose to continue fighting. Coercive bargaining also carries a failed history. Negotiation efforts fail in many peace efforts because mid-level diplomats without comparative experience in successful peace processes use coercive bargaining to battle and seek compromises on the positions of armed groups without addressing underlying legitimate grievances or interests.

Instead, research on successful peace processes suggests the need for a more comprehensive understanding of both incentives and sanctions and a principled or "interest-based" rather than coercive approach to negotiation. It also suggests the need to address a wide range of drivers of violence—not just the armed groups' stated public positions and demands—including the key issues of diverse stakeholders necessary to build a national consensus.

Peace processes depend on a range of incentives to entice armed groups and their supporters to negotiate with their enemies. These include a range of types of intrinsic incentives generated by the stakeholders themselves as well as external incentives offered by external groups with an interest in peace.[38]

Externally generated incentives. External incentives are most effective when they work in conjunction with internal or intrinsic incentives. External stakeholders can support a peace process by assisting with the needed economic and technical elements of implementing a peace agreement. However, creating pools of money or financial incentives for key stakeholders to participate in a peace process poses a number of challenges. It can encourage local people to feel like they are participating not because they want to, but because they are getting paid to participate. This can lower their willingness to put in their own effort and make their own sacrifices to ensure that peace is sustainable. It can also lead to the idea that the peace process is externally driven and ultimately about making money, taking away local leadership and legitimacy. It can also encourage perceptions that there are unlimited funds for peace process activities and that involvement in the peace process itself is about financial gain. In communities where so-called peace dividends fund small-scale projects like building schools or health centers, local populations have in some cases come to see peace as having only a financial benefit without an inherent value. These lessons learned from other contexts should temper the international community's eagerness to bring an end to the war in Afghanistan by external incentives.

Internally generated or intrinsic incentives. When the stakeholders themselves develop their own incentives for working toward peace, these tend to be more successful and creative than outside efforts. In places where disarmament, demobilization, and reintegration (DDR) programs have been successful, local civil society helps to design, develop, and carry out internally generated incentives. For example, the Somali women of Wajir, Kenya, set up a peace prize for the clan chief contributing most to peace. After the first year's prize, other chiefs approached the women to ask for training in mediation and negotiation. These incentives represent stakeholders' efforts to address each other's core interests by, for example, agreeing to share political power or resources. In Afghanistan, internally generated incentives require local stakeholders to understand and address the grievances and interests of other groups.

Security incentives. Armed groups often continue fighting because to leave the network of their group may make them a target for all sides. Developing security guarantees for both armed individuals and groups who enter into a negotiation process can serve as a confidence-building measure to encourage others to join the process. While current external incentives in Afghanistan do include security guarantees, there is not sufficient research to determine whether armed groups trust that they will be safe if they reintegrate.

Amnesty incentives. Amnesties are another form of security incentive, insulating leaders from a justice process to hold them to account. Victims and human rights advocates note that amnesty laws such as the one in Afghanistan create new problems of impunity.

Political incentives. Individuals and groups engaged in a civil war seek political access and influence. Entering into peace processes can be risky for both groups with and without political authority; no one knows if they will come out with the same level of political influence if the process redesigns government structures. Peace agreements often result in some form of power-sharing governance to ensure that key stakeholders are content with their access to political power, economic resources, and security and maintain a sense of their identity. Power-sharing agreements can be risky if they result in forcing together groups that are not in agreement about basic principles of governance.[39]

Since the Taliban and other armed opposition groups have not yet articulated a clear political platform, it is difficult to assess the possibilities of powersharing at this stage.

Economic incentives. All sides calculate the economic costs and benefits of continuing to fight or moving toward peace. War brings cover to illicit activities and economic opportunity. A tremendous number of stakeholders on all sides of the conflict financially benefit from instability and the continuation of war in Afghanistan. Creating economic incentives for peace means making peace more profitable than war. Also, members of armed groups may benefit financially from the war, as being a soldier or insurgent is a job, a form of employment. But research in Afghanistan illustrates that relatively few insurgents operate on purely economic motives.[40] Moreover, economic incentives have been relatively small compared with the benefits of continued fighting. Efforts to use economic incentives to buy off leaders almost always turn out to be a short-term strategy that backfires. Economic incentives can work only when a peace process also addresses other core grievances.

Identity incentives. While often overlooked, all sides also assess the impact of a peace agreement on their identity and sense of dignity, self-determination, and group autonomy. Those groups that fight for identity, religion, or ideology are much more likely to accept any cost to continue fighting than those groups that fight for material resources or political power. Stakeholders often continue to fight for what they perceive is greater security, economic interests, political access, and a dignified identity long after they have felt the pain of war.

Sometimes this is addressed by allowing groups to retain a sense of ethnic or religious identity in a particular territory, which may even be marked symbolically with a separate flag, even though the territory belongs to a larger nation in a federal governance system, as with the territory controlled by the Moro Islamic Liberation Army in the Philippines.

Members of armed groups also benefit from the status of holding a gun, projecting an image of a masculine identity, and earning respect. Leaders of armed groups know they have a pathway for promotion through the ranks of their network. Armed leadership also allows them to impose order and prevent dissent in their group. Calculating how to address these ego factors via incentives that replace the respect earned from a gun with opportunities for individuals to earn respect or at least maintain dignity in another way is also important.

Comparative experiences in other countries illustrate that *internally generated incentives* are more successful and sustainable than *externally generated incentives* from the international community. At any rate, the effectiveness of any of these incentives builds on the credibility or likelihood that the incentives are valid and that others will follow through with their promises. "Changing the goal posts" can cause cynicism and detract from moderate leadership's ability to sway others to participate in a peace process. Skillful mediation is all the more crucial when orchestrating a complex set of incentives and sanctions to move groups toward the negotiation table. Ultimately incentives are only the icing on the cake. The real enticement to end war comes by addressing the root causes driving violent conflict through the use of principled negotiation.

Employing Principled Negotiation to Address Root Causes

Negotiation, unlike warfare, is not a win-lose game. Stakeholders who take a "win-lose" orientation to peace are unlikely to achieve sustainable outcomes. There are three broad approaches to negotiation. Soft negotiation assumes that reaching agreement requires the acceptance of concessions, losses, and compromise. Hard negotiation assumes that winning requires making threats, demanding concessions, and sticking to strict public positions requiring the other side to lose. Successful peace processes require principled negotiation where the goal is to solve problems by finding options that meet the basic underlying interests (not public positions) of all stakeholders. Principled negotiation aims to create a "win-win" solution that all stakeholders can accept.[41]

Principled negotiation is interest based; it requires each stakeholder to identify their core, underlying interests and needs beyond their public positions. An analysis of underlying interests of all sides, beyond their public statements, can assist in finding mutually satisfying agreements or outcomes that all sides can live with. Principled negotiation is different from positional negotiation where stakeholders make absolutist public positions that make progress difficult. Negotiations based on wholesale compliance have a high risk of failure. It is best to avoid preconditions to talks as they make it impossible to even learn about the other stakeholder's interests or to explore creative options for addressing underlying interests. Small, unilateral confidence-building measures (CBMs) build trust for more substantial negotiations and undermine antagonistic leaders. Hiding underlying interests only delays understanding or contributes to conspiracy theories. It may be very difficult for groups to use an interest-based approach to negotiation without the help of an outside mediation team coaching them to reality test their BATNA and explore their underlying interests.

For example, with the help of former president Jimmy Carter as a mediator, Egypt and Israel reached a win-win outcome to their negotiations over the Sinai Peninsula, though initially both groups had taken a win-lose approach that demanded full ownership of the Sinai for their respective sides. But through the process of principled negotiation they came to see that their underlying interests were not mutually exclusive. Israel wanted to make sure Egypt's military was not on its border. Egypt wanted to maintain its historic tie to the land. The agreement that the Sinai would be a demilitarized zone under Egyptian control met both sides' underlying interests.

In Afghanistan, negotiating on underlying interests rather than public positions is essential. For example, Taliban leaders generally talk about achieving a true Islamic and independent system but have been vague on their political platform and unclear about their underlying interests. It is impossible to negotiate or reintegrate armed opposition groups without knowing these interests. When the Taliban were in power, the expression of these interests was grave intolerance of religious and political pluralism and repression of women. It is hard to imagine any negotiation with the Taliban if their underlying interest is this type of repression. The Taliban also oppose perceived imposition of Western cultural values and development goals aimed at "modernization." The symbol of Western cultural imposition is a provocatively dressed woman on a billboard. There is a lot of room for negotiation between this extreme and the demand that women wear burqas and that girls not receive education. Many traditional Afghan religious and secular leaders do see the benefit of educating girls and including women's leadership. Taliban leaders and religious leaders have permitted development and even activities aimed at women's empowerment when they are locally led and directly benefit the community.

Likewise, the Taliban demand that the United States withdraw immediately and have no permanent bases also requires discussion of underlying interests including sovereignty and cultural integrity. Given the history of external countries besieging Afghanistan, there are legitimate and shared concerns about the level of control and presence of outsiders. Discussing these underlying interests and ways to address them with creative, mutually satisfying options is essential.

Recognizing Three Key Themes in an Afghan Peace Process

Current negotiations in Afghanistan probably focus on "talks about talks." If they go deeper than that, media reports suggest the discussions focus on gaining Taliban agreement to stop fighting, securing Taliban recognition of the Afghan Constitution, ending Taliban ties with al-Qaida on the one hand, and addressing the Taliban's insistence that the United States not set up permanent bases in the country.[42] This agenda leaves out many issues that fuel the current conflict. A comprehensive Afghan peace process would orchestrate work in three areas: developing a high-level political settlement between armed groups; increasing legitimacy for the Afghan government; and building a national public consensus on the future relations between diverse groups. A political settlement without significant progress in the two latter dimensions would be unlikely to produce a sustainable peace.[43] Figure 2 illustrates these three components of a peace process. Box 3 gives a longer list of the overlapping issues in each of these dimensions.

Figure 2. Three Central Themes of an Afghan Peace Process

Issues between armed groups. High-level reconciliation and low-level reintegra-tion are important components of an Afghan peace process. There are many contentious issues between international forces, the Afghan government, and armed opposition groups. The concept of principled negotiation and commu-nity-level peacebuilding provides a foundation for thinking through a more meaningful plan for reintegration and reconciliation between armed opposi-tion groups and Afghan society. There are many issues requiring discussion between armed groups. Those mentioned frequently include the status of forces of armed troops, whether the United States will keep permanent bases in Afghanistan, how armed groups take accountability for civilian deaths, and issues like drug trafficking and the interpretation of sharia (Islamic law) and how this impacts the rights of minorities and women.

There are significant divisions within the international community, within the Afghan government, and within armed opposition groups. The interna-tional coalition disagrees on the level of success they are achieving, with some pulling their troops out for lack of progress. Within the Afghan government, well-intentioned bureaucrats disagree with colleagues profiting from the cor-ruption, drug trade, and military conflict. Within the armed opposition groups, divisions over whether to negotiate and how to define the ideal outcome of the armed conflict are so great that groups kill each other even though they share a common enemy in the government and international forces. Armed opposition groups fight for different reasons. Some fight against repressive government warlords and government corruption. Some fight to avenge the humiliation felt as a result of foreign troops' house searches, night raids, and bombs. Some have simple economic motives to secure basic employment or more greedy, ambitious economic motives to profit from the instability.[44]

Box 3. Issues Requiring Negotiation and Discussion in a Comprehensive Peace Process

Presence of foreign troops

Presence of permanent bases and status of forces agreements for foreign troops

Process of disarmament, demobilization, and reintegration of armed opposition groups

Interpretation and versions of sharia

Accountability for civilian deaths

Presence of local militias

External interests in Afghanistan

Balance of power between the central government and the local villages and districts and between different ethnic groups to ensure minority rights and protections

Protection of constitutional rights to education, political access, and freedom of expression

Addressing war crimes through memorials to past victims, truth telling and fact gathering, accountability of offenders to victims, and victim compensation

Addressing corruption

Addressing crime and drug trafficking

Increasing sense of citizenship and citizen oversight of corruption, crime, drug trafficking, the security sector, and other areas requiring public input

Developing a national narrative that addresses diverse groups' unique historical experiences

Building trust and respect between different ethnic and linguistic groups and protecting minority rights to foster a national unity and confidence that Afghans support human rights and security not just for their own group but for all segments of the population

Respecting and protecting women's rights

When it comes to identifying government corruption or drug trafficking as a key issue in the conflict, the international community, some armed opposition groups, and Afghan civil society share many similar concerns. If negotiations continue to exclude civil society, armed opposition groups may bring this issue into formal negotiations. This is problematic because successful peace processes require structural reforms and it is civil society that can most authentically argue for these reforms. The armed opposition groups are able to appeal to Afghans precisely because locals perceive their stated grievances on government corruption and drug trafficking as legitimate. The international community and Afghan civil society, on the other hand, rightly point a finger at all those in armed opposition groups, the Afghan government, and the international community who profit from the ongoing war, recognizing that international funding channeled through corrupt hands lands in the pockets of these war profiteers.[45] Another strange alliance occurs when the Afghan government and the armed opposition groups all condemn civilian casualties caused by international forces. Official negotiations are more like a triangle rather than a line between two sides. In each corner of the triangle, groups could find strange bedfellows to address shared interests.

All sides share a concern about the influence of external interests in Afghanistan. International forces are concerned about the influence of Pakistan, Iran, China, and other countries. In repeated polls and focus groups,[46] a majority of Afghans report a perception that Pakistan plays a significant role in supporting the Taliban. The armed opposition groups share a concern with Pakistan that India is trying to win favor with the Afghan government. Informal conversations with diverse groups of Afghans and Pakistanis reveal that many believe the war in Afghanistan cannot be ended without robust regional diplomacy that also includes Pakistan, India, Iran, Tajikistan, Uzbekistan, Russia, Saudi Arabia, Yemen, China, and other countries. The public widely perceives a lack of sustained diplomatic activity or sufficient economic, political, security, and territorial incentives for countries in the region to participate in such a process. Armed opposition groups get support from external bases thus requiring that any peace process include political solutions on all sides of Afghanistan's borders.

Disarmament, demobilization, and reintegration (DDR) of armed opposition groups is also a key issue needing discussion between the leadership of armed groups. The Afghan government's reintegration program, called the Afghan Peace and Reconciliation Program (APRP), has competing goals at the local level. On the one hand, ISAF sees it as a component of counterinsurgency, to weaken or cause divisions within an insurgency.[47] On the other hand, civil society groups in Afghanistan see the legitimate role of reintegration to reduce violence and foster community reconciliation by addressing key grievances.

Civil society leaders critique reintegration efforts that rely on "buying off" or bribing armed insurgent groups rather than addressing key local grievances that fuel the insurgency, noting financial incentives address the symptoms of the disease but not the disease itself.[48] The APRP would be more likely to be successful if it focused on local grievance resolution rather than on attempts to buy off insurgents. Ideally, DDR efforts replace the economic and security value of a weapon with local security guarantees and economic opportunities. These efforts help excombatants save face and address some of their core grievances through the creation of internally generated economic, security, political, and identity based incentives described earlier in this report. Sustainable DDR requires reconciling relationships, understanding and acknowledging all stakeholder's interests and basic needs, moving together to identify mutually satisfying agreements that all stakeholders can live with, and establishing a "good enough" solution.[49]

Issues facing government legitimacy. Successful peace processes address root causes driving violence. In Afghanistan, corruption and structural problems with the current Afghan government and its approach to drug trafficking and the security sector are key driving factors fueling support for armed insurgent groups and preventing the Afghan public from supporting its government. In Afghanistan, as in many other countries, structural reforms are an essential part of a peace process. Bolstering government legitimacy in Afghanistan requires a peace process that addresses corruption, elite control over government, political exclusion of women and minorities, and the need for significant structural reforms.

Research shows that Afghans do identify with and support the concept of an Afghan state and representative democracy, though one based on local tradition, culture, and Islamic religion.[50] However, Afghans widely perceive Westernized democracy and the rest of the international project in Afghanistan as a self-perpetuating system that fuels the insurgency,[51] creates an environment for war profiteering,[52] and politically disenfranchises most Afghan citizens by rewarding warlords with illegitimate political power through armed force rather than provision of public services.[53] The challenges of nation building in Afghanistan also include significant distrust and tensions between ethnic groups that vie for political control and exclude other groups.[54] Afghan citizens point toward the inadequate quality of and widespread corruption within state institutions. Civil society fears that a political pact between warlords, a corrupt government, and armed opposition groups would pave the way for more violence and further exclude legitimate political leaders who base their support on citizen consent rather than the power of the gun.

National-level civil society organizations are increasingly vocal about their shared concerns about the current Afghan government, corruption, and the need for structural reforms. A peace process in Afghanistan that excludes civil society may not place as much emphasis on government corruption or structural reforms, as the international community supports the Karzai administration and that government has little interest in putting corruption or structural reforms on the negotiation table. While the Taliban or other armed opposition groups may bring the issue of corruption to the official negotiation table, this is unlikely to be a central concern given other priorities. Afghan civil society groups like Integrity Watch Afghanistan support communities in monitoring and reporting on corruption and promoting transparency.[55] Afghan news journalists also play an important role in exposing corruption, though threats of retaliation, night letters, and killing of journalists create a challenging environment for the news media.[56] Afghans' sense of citizenship and citizen oversight of corruption, crime, drug trafficking, the security sector, and other areas require strategies for engaging public interests.

A successful Afghan peace process will require increasing government legitimacy in the eyes of armed opposition groups and civil society by improving government performance in all areas of governance. Peace process efforts could focus on reducing widespread corruption and increasing the functioning and accountability of government ministries, particularly judiciary and police, by creating more effective checks and balances on state power via the constitution and guards against abuses of power.

A peace process also requires strengthening the constitution's protection of human rights, necessitating supervisory or monitoring bodies including civil society representatives. Countless other research reports outline these measures, but few put these issues as central to the success of a peace process. Reaching a political settlement in Afghanistan requires putting all these issues on the formal negotiation table. National civil society leaders assert "justice is as integral to sustainable peace as security."[57] National-level civil society leaders bring concerns that a peace process will undermine the Constitution, human rights, and justice. They assert that the Bonn Conference in 2001 included some individuals responsible for mass crimes against Afghan civilians while excluding others. Some of these individuals continue to experience impunity for their crimes, financially benefit from their criminal gain, and participate in government. In a joint statement about the peace process in November 2010, civil society leaders wrote, "we are concerned after listening to the speeches of High Peace Council representatives that the privileges/concessions promised to the Taliban should by no means undermine or compromise the achievements of the past nine years in terms of civic values and human rights, especially women's rights, enshrined in the Constitution."[58]

These groups expressed concerns regarding the 2007 Afghan amnesty law that protects all past and present belligerents from prosecution. They assert the international community virtually ignored the passing of the law and failed to express a commitment to transitional justice processes, such as the investigation or prosecution of war crimes, crimes against humanity, rape, and torture. In response, a coalition of twenty-four NGOs called the Transitional Justice Coordination Group organized a "victim's jirga" to provide a space for recounting personal tragedies and war crimes under various regimes.[59] These groups note that the concept of justice does not necessarily refer to public trials. At the very least, transitional justice would acknowledge, document, and verify crimes committed by all sides as a necessary part of public healing and transformation from decades of war toward a more stable and peaceful future. Justice, they say, requires developing creative mechanisms for holding perpetrators of crimes against humanity accountable, particularly ensuring that they are prevented from holding office. Transitional justice can include symbolic measures such as naming and shaming offenders for human rights violations via a truth-seeking commission, acknowledging victims through documentation, real and symbolic reparations, and efforts to foster trauma recovery, institutional reform, and reconciliation between groups.[60] Civil society advocates a process of transitional justice to address past crimes and a culture of impunity. This concept of transitional justice is missing from plans for Afghan peace talks.

Issues facing national and local civil society efforts to build a national consensus. Building a national public consensus requires a peace process design that includes public issues, represented by national civil society groups as well as local-level community input. Local-level civil society faces a different set of issues. Local-level conflicts stem from family feuds, land and water disputes, tribal and ethnic power struggles, and the impacts of national-level conflict.

A successful peace process in Afghanistan links with the process of nation building; both require addressing the significant distrust and tensions between ethnic groups that vie for political control.[61] Civil society groups assert the need to develop a national narrative that addresses diverse groups' unique historical experiences and builds trust and respect between ethnic and linguistic groups. A public discussion also needs to include issues related to protecting women's and minority rights to foster a national unity and confidence that Afghans support human rights and security not just for their own group but for all segments of the population.

Civil society also identifies the design of the peace process itself as a key issue, highlighting the key principles of transparency and inclusion that should inform peace efforts.[62] Civil society fears that government and armed actors will use negotiation to achieve narrow political goals that will benefit particular ideological, ethnic, tribal, or religious groups and leave out others, further fragmenting the country. Noting the importance of overcoming ethnic divisions and building trust, many NGOs, media outlets, journalist associations, and other forms of civil society have found ways to collaborate to raise jointly identified issues related to government reconciliation initiatives. For the public to support and trust a peace process and peace agreement, the process needs to be transparent and include civil society concerns, such as addressing impunity and transitional justice issues using restorative justice practices and building trust between ethnic groups. National-level civil society has a key role in monitoring peace efforts to ensure that they respect and do not undermine basic principles of women's rights and justice issues. Civil society leaders look for a just peace process that will uphold human dignity and include robust mechanisms for public input.

The "How" of an Afghan Peace Process: Mechanisms for Structuring Public Input, Technical Support, and Coordination

Part of the reason why half of all peace agreements fail is because of too much of an emphasis on the signed *agreement* and not on the *process*. Transitions from war to peace fail when leaders rush the delicate process or leave too many difficult issues vaguely defined. A peace process is essentially about creating structured mechanisms for participatory deliberation and decision making

Figure 3. Four-tiered Design of a Comprehensive Peace Process for Afghanistan

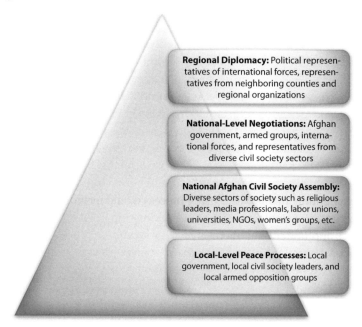

Regional Diplomacy: Political representatives of international forces, representatives from neighboring counties and
regional organizations

National-Level Negotiations: Afghan
government, armed groups, international forces, and representatives from
diverse civil society sectors

National Afghan Civil Society Assembly:
Diverse sectors of society such as religious
leaders, media professionals, labor unions,
universities, NGOs, women's groups, etc.

Local-Level Peace Processes: Local
government, local civil society leaders, and
local armed opposition groups

involving diverse stakeholders. Peace requires a multileveled process involving top, middle, and community levels of society to assess the root causes of the conflict, propose creative options for addressing these problems, address basic needs and rights, and develop a national consensus for peace. A successful peace process combines high-level negotiation with vertical processes that link high-level negotiations with public dialogue processes. Successful peace processes rely not on one negotiation table, but on the construction of a sequenced and coordinated process with multiple negotiation tables or channels feeding into a central negotiation table.

Figure 3 illustrates this four-tiered peace process including all stakeholders. Given the regional nature of the conflict in Afghanistan, a regional peace process is an essential component of an Afghan national peace process. Like the national process, the regional process should also include multiple negotiation tables for addressing the diverse interests of Afghanistan's neighbors and the international community and for creating confidence-building mechanisms and oversight to monitor illegitimate external involvement. At the national-level in Afghanistan, a peace process could include both military negotiation tables for armed groups to discuss cease-fires as well as nonmilitary negotiation tables.[63] National-level forums could provide communication channels for all armed groups, even those not willing to negotiate directly. Shuttle diplomacy and conciliation by respected peacemakers can assist this process. In addition to including the Afghan government, regional governments, and political representatives from international forces, a comprehensive Afghan national peace process should have opportunities for deliberation between national civil society organizations in Afghanistan and neighboring countries and mechanisms to include citizens in local community-level peace processes.

Successful peace processes offer opportunities for both direct participation by stakeholders and for representative participation to ensure that a process is inclusive yet manageable. Adequate sequencing and spacing of negotiation tables allow the necessary internal discussions necessary for leaders to maintain the legitimacy and consent of the people they are representing in the peace process. Where groups are not willing to participate in direct negotiation, conciliatory channels are essential for opening up communication aimed at understanding key interests and motivations driving groups that support continued fighting. In this way, a peace process would include all stakeholders, recognizing that a stable peace requires addressing at least some of the core grievances and underlying interests of all groups.

The following section describes a range of public consultation mechanisms for including diverse civil society sectors and public input into the peace process in Afghanistan. It then describes the type of mediation and technical support needed to coordinate a comprehensive peace process.

Drawing on the Five Established Models for Public Consultation

There are five broad models of public participation in peace processes. Each is relevant to the design of a comprehensive peace process in Afghanistan. Unlike many other cultures, Afghans have a long tradition of participatory deliberation and decision-making *jirga*s and *shura*s (councils) at the national and local levels and across different regions. Traditionally, these processes include male tribal and village elders and draw on customary law or local interpretations of Sharia law rather than the constitution, human rights, women's rights, or other established legal standards. But civil society activists note the need to separate the *jirga* format—a deliberative process where people gather in a circle to discuss issues—from the notion that a *jirga* by definition excludes women and democratic representatives. *Jirga* and *shura* forums can evolve to draw on broader legal standards and include more diverse stakeholders. Most of the models described below require decisions to be made through modified consensus, as in the *jirga* or *shura*, where all stakeholders have an opportunity to voice their concerns and issues and decisions are made when there is broad, but not necessarily total, agreement.[64]

Direct local peace processes and agreements. When the authority to stop a war is not centrally located, high-level negotiations cannot create a national cease-fire or political settlements. In Mali, civil society initiated direct traditional decision-making processes based on local rituals and traditions for dialogue.[65] These local processes resulted in local-level cease-fires and agreements that enabled previously stymied high-level negotiations to advance. These local-level peace processes can take place simultaneously across a country and involve thousands of people. Each locality may work through a similar agenda of issues to identify stakeholders' core grievances and develop local security guarantees, political power-sharing deals, and address economic and identity issues. Local communities then are responsible for implementing the agreements they make. These local peace processes can help create a national consensus that eventually leads to an end to the war.

Local and traditional Afghan structures for deliberation, consensus building, negotiation, and decision making could play a larger role in a comprehensive peace process based on direct local participation as was the case in Mali. Relatively new district development assemblies (DDAs), community development councils (CDCs), and peace councils complement and build on the format of traditional *jirgas* and *shuras* but often include more diverse civil society sectors. Newer structures include members trained in principled negotiation and mediation and include a wider representation of community interests by involving women and people of different ages. In some places, women's *shuras* or women-led CDCs and peace councils meet separately. The CDCs are nongovernmental, voluntary, unpaid, and democratically elected institutions operating across Afghanistan to help prioritize, design, and implement development projects such as health centers, irrigation systems, and schools with government funds. CDCs work in partnership with the Ministry of Rural Rehabilitation and Development's National Solidarity Program (NSP), blending locally owned, cost-effective development projects with efforts to increase local capacity for conflict management. Peace councils help communities find mutually satisfying solutions to key divisive issues such as corruption and ethnic divisions identified in the last section of this report.

Afghan NGOs have been carrying out peacebuilding capacity-building programs in Afghanistan for the last twenty years.[66] These programs address water and land disputes, domestic violence, and family issues, as well as conflicts within community development councils over setting development priorities. For example, in Sayedabad district of Wardak province, a local peace council mediated a dispute among four villages around a water and irrigation project. Through the process of mediation, the group agreed to finish the project to provide more effective water distribution to all four villages.[67]

Local peace councils already exist in many areas of Afghanistan to address local disputes over land, water, debts, domestic violence, and other community issues. In some parts of Afghanistan, civil society organizations are already identifying and training local peace councils in community grievance resolution processes to assist with conflicts directly related to the reintegrees and to leverage both formal and informal justice systems. As part of APRP, they help communities cope with reintegration and all of the everyday tensions that accompany real reconciliation efforts such as physical security, freedom of movement, economic well-being, and access to governance and justice, the five key areas identified as key indicators of human security in Afghanistan.[68]

For example, in a case in Helmand province, armed opposition groups agreed to stop fighting ISAF, reject out-of-area fighters, remove or show the location of planted improvised explosive devices (IEDs), allow freedom of movement to patrols, and accept ANSF checkpoints. In return, the Government of the Islamic Republic of Afghanistan (GIROA) agreed to have all Afghan leads in compound searches, to ensure that there are Afghans partnered in all patrols, and to begin short-term cash for work and long-term economic development opportunities.

These peace committees could play a central role in local-level peace processes based on addressing key grievances through principled negotiation to support a national-level process. If carried out across the country simultaneously, local-level negotiations could help build cease-fires, political power sharing, and security guarantees that would result in a more sustainable outcome and make a national peace accord possible. A comprehensive peace process in Afghanistan would view these local-level reconciliation processes as a core component of a national peace process. However, it is also conceivable that local-level deals could result in allowing armed groups to retain security responsibilities could prove problematic for a sustainable peace at the national level. Local-level peace processes thus need coordination mechanisms to ensure complementarity of local and national efforts.

Participation through consultation. In South Africa, local consultations across the country complemented and fed into high-level negotiations. In the Philippines, a National Unification Commission held local, regional, and national consultations to identify core drivers of the conflict and lay out alternatives to address them. In Guatemala, a Civil Society Assembly brought together representatives of diverse sectors such as labor and agriculture. Mayan communities played a major role, resulting in a written agreement recognizing their unique indigenous identity and rights. The agenda in the Civil Society Assembly included topics that had not been openly discussed for decades. This assembly created nearly two hundred specific commitments included in the final, formal peace agreement.[69]

These examples illustrate a model of civil society holding separate, broad consultations that run *in parallel* to official negotiations and/or are sequenced and coordinated with an official process (see figure 4). In this "accordion model" peace process, a sequence of small, private meetings and large public meetings move back and forth like an accordion opening and closing. A small,

Figure 4. Accordion Consultation Model

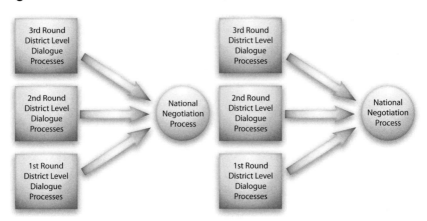

select group of key stakeholders negotiates over key issues while large, open processes seek input and creative generation of options from the public.

Civil society consultations may look at the key divisive issues, possible creative solutions, and build a national consensus. Civil society's diversity means that they may reflect the tensions evident between national political leaders. Public consultations can help make progress on difficult issues that may be blocking formal negotiation processes by allowing the public to deliberate and build consensus on them.

A number of different conferences have brought diverse Afghan civil society leaders together to discuss their shared values and concerns.[70] But these conferences are not structured as an ongoing Afghan civil society assembly tasked with representing diverse constituencies. A national-level Afghan civil society assembly, like that held in Guatemala, could play a key role in assuring that a wider set of issues makes it onto the formal negotiation agenda. An assembly could address some of the key issues affecting civil society, such as women's rights or concerns from victims and human rights organizations about past and present human rights violations and the amnesty law. It could also play a key role in a peace process to build structures for public consultations on these and other issues such as corruption, ethnic tensions, and how to address the Taliban. An Afghan civil society assembly could also serve as a monitoring body for the National Peace Council, ensuring transparency and accountability.

In Guatemala, the international community played a significant role in ensuring that the civil society process had sufficient resources both during its deliberation and in the implementation phase. Given that so many peace agreements fall apart during implementation challenges, it is important to note that a civil society assembly's work does not end with an agreement. Rather,

Figure 5. Representation Model

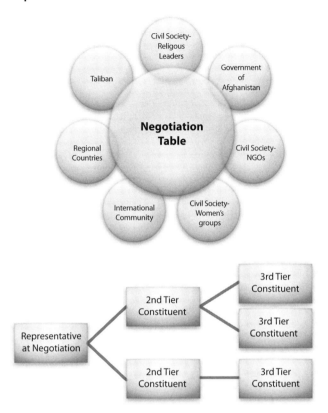

an assembly ideally continues to monitor a peace agreement and press for implementation in the postaccord phase.

Participation by representation. A third type of structure for peace processes includes a process of electing a representative group to work out the details of a peace agreement and/or a new constitution. Each group at the official negotiation table represents a group of constituents from a certain sector of society. In this type of a process, civil society sectors such as women's groups, religious leaders, human rights groups, and labor unions have a representative participating in national-level negotiations. Even in cases where there is no direct election or representatives, it is assumed that the core negotiators are representing the interests of their groups. Often there is a great deal of conflict within a group. The core negotiator then is negotiating not only with other key stakeholders at the negotiation table, but also with the second and third tiers of stakeholder constituents whom they are representing, illustrated in figure 5.

In South Africa, a national-level, elected constituent assembly negotiated a new constitution. Religious leadership played a significant role in helping to foster values in reconciliation. Human rights groups shaped many of the discussions about accountability and compensation for victims. While no side achieved all of its goals, there was a national consensus built that moved the country toward a sustainable political solution.

The benefit of this model is that the key issues of unarmed groups can be directly communicated to other key decision makers. This form of public participation can also incentivize the creation of new political parties or organizations that organize themselves to represent others' interests. In the Northern Ireland peace process, citizens elected political parties who were part of the multiparty negotiation process.

The challenge of this model is that there may be great competition for the designated seats. Elite and westernized civil society leaders may gain access to the process, but there is the question of whether they truly are in touch with diverse civil society sectors and village-level interests and perspectives. Effective representation requires agreement among civil society on a process to decide who directly represents their diversity.

After the absence of any women in a number of national peace negotiations, global women's groups mobilized to pass UN Security Council Resolution 1321, which mandates the inclusion of women's representatives in peace processes. In peace processes in Southern Sudan, for example, women's groups had a designated seat at the table. There could be a separate forum for discussion of the issues and interests important to certain groups, such as women's groups or victims' groups. These could be a formal or informal women's negotiation table and a victims' negotiation table, to help build consensus for strategies to assert their specific interests and ideas to address them. Representatives from these discussions could then articulate these interests at other negotiation tables that include representatives of other interests.

An Afghan Civil Society Assembly could elect representatives to sit on the National Peace Council and represent diverse civil society interests at formal, high-level negotiations. The current Afghan National Peace Council, formed from the Consultative Peace Jirga's mandate, mainly includes representatives from traditional and religious leadership, former Taliban, and former Northern Alliance members. The few seats allotted to women and civil society representatives do not represent the breadth of interests and concerns of different sectors.[71] It is not clear that these civil society members represent a certain constituency or whether they are included only to present a token face of civil society.[72] The National Peace Council could be the central negotiation table, the place where representatives from other negotiation tables, forums, or channels come to exchange views. By playing such a role, it could relieve pressure on other negotiation tables and make it more likely that a coordinated process could jointly develop solutions to the armed struggle, the crisis in government legitimacy, and the lack of a national public consensus on the future of Afghanistan.

Participation by referendum. In some cases, the public takes part in a referendum on a peace agreement developed by a negotiated agreement. Referendums allow the public to either say "yes" or "no" to a negotiated agreement. Ideally the news media and social marketing campaigns help educate the public about the contents of a peace agreement before the referendum.In Northern Ireland and Macedonia, for example, the public had an opportunity to vote in a referendum to accept or reject the peace agreement developed by the constituent assembly.

One of the benefits of public referendums is that it requires the authors of a peace agreement to have a stake in fully explaining it to the public and urging its support. The public, on the other hand, has the opportunity to oppose the agreement and at the same time the responsibility for supporting it should the referendum pass.

The Afghan government's legitimacy gap requires a variety of strategies. Ensuring that the public has a vote in any peace deal is one way the Afghan government could increase public trust. While other structures for public input into a peace process are necessary, a public referendum on a final high-level agreement could significantly increase the chances that the public understands and supports such a deal.

Participation via media. Afghan journalists and media producers have both the capacity and responsibility to support peace processes. Mass media can play several roles in supporting public participation in a peace process. First, the media has a role in educating the public about the contents of a peace agreement before a national referendum. Media entertainment formats as well as public service announcements, particularly on the widely available and popular Afghan radio stations, could support a peace process by providing educational materials on peacebuilding themes. In Northern Ireland, an international advertising firm developed a marketing campaign to support the Good Friday Peace Proposal. The firm conducted quantitative and qualitative research of key public concerns, developed specific advertisements to target each segment that would vote in the referendum, and monitored media coverage. The marketing campaign included colorful graphic posters, billboards, direct mail brochures, Internet ads, and public service announcements for television and radio to foster awareness and acceptance of the peace agreement among key constituencies.[73] The public eventually approved of the peace agreements in the public referendum, which indicates that the campaign had some level of success.

In Macedonia, a similar multimedia campaign pointed the public to the benefits of the peace agreement several months before a public referendum on the agreement. Audience identification and segmentation led to individualized messages about the peace agreement. The announcements produced in the Macedonian language focused on stability and security as the main benefits to Macedonians. The Albanian announcements emphasized extended civil rights to the Albanian minority as the result of the agreement. Again, the public referendum favored the agreement. It would be an exaggeration to attribute the positive outcomes of the referendum solely to the impact of the campaigns on public opinion. Such causation would be impossible to prove even though the correlation between the campaign's goals and the voters' intentions is apparent.

Second, media outlets can undertake polling of public attitudes on issues related to the peace process. Polls can help all stakeholders understand where there is consensus and where there is great division.

Third, the mass media can foster public discussion to build a national consensus on a vision for a country's future. Media outlets can also use two-way programming where audience members can, for example, call in to a radio show or send a mobile phone SMS (short message service) to discuss or register their opinions on issues relevant to the peace process.[74] Afghan media should use more dialogue-based public programs to build national consensus on the future of the country and to address specific obstacles to peace. If the Afghan public is similar to audiences in other parts of the world, a media-savvy and skeptical public wants to make up its own mind and participate in constructing a vision of its future rather than having it force-fed through a steady diet of redundant advertisements from international security forces, the Afghan government, or the Taliban seeking to manipulate public opinion. In Afghanistan, more participatory media programs could empower local people and prompt reflection. But fostering participatory, media-based dialogue requires new skill sets to handle the inevitable antagonism and diversity when people begin to dialogue. Radio call-in shows, for example, do not communicate nonverbal cues people often use in Afghanistan's rich cultures, thus making dialogue and understanding even more difficult. Afghan media professionals should receive training in how to facilitate media-based dialogue so as to highlight common ground and identify potential solutions developed by audience participation.

Developing Mediation and Technical Support for an Afghan Peace Process

Coordinating a multitiered peace process requires committed teams of internationals, government, and civil society working together. A multidimensional peace process with large numbers of stakeholders by necessity requires a mediation team or technical support group to coordinate efforts. Outsiders often do not coordinate with each other, creating a sense of confusion and redundancy of effort. A peace process is always somewhat chaotic. But it can turn into a cacophony if local and international stakeholders all sing from a different sheet of music. Ideally, the international community develops a comprehensive strategy and regular channels of communication to support a mediation effort, a strategic package of incentives and sanctions, and both the shorter-term support to reach a national peace agreement and the longer-term support to monitor the implementation of an agreement. Coordination helps to ensure that all elements of international assistance and intervention in conflict-affected states are supportive of a peace process. Coordination in developing and applying a shared strategy to prevent certain stakeholders from spoiling the agreement is a common theme among successful processes.[75]

Using Mediation Teams

Mediators assist stakeholders in achieving a principled negotiation process of identifying underlying grievances, developing a joint analysis of key differences and common ground between stakeholders, and brainstorming creative options for addressing the underlying interests of all stakeholders. Mediators assist in this process by bringing cultural insight, authority and/or skills and knowledge to help the stakeholders through a process of negotiation. A mediator can test the reality of each side's perceptions and check for miscommunication and misunderstanding.

Mediation has been an essential component of many comprehensive peace processes, particularly in Africa.[76] In South Africa, a technical support team skilled in mediation helped key negotiators on all sides develop the skills needed to reach a peace agreement. Armed groups are more likely to engage in constructive negotiation efforts if they are familiar with the negotiation process and skilled in negotiation techniques. All stakeholders benefit when all sides have sufficient negotiation skills. The less prepared a group is to negotiate skillfully, the less likely a negotiated outcome is possible. Technical support and capacity building on negotiation and the process of mediation for all key stakeholders makes success more likely.[77] Denying technical support to an armed adversary is counterproductive. The less a group is able to negotiate constructively, the less likely it is that other stakeholders will be able to achieve their own outcomes.[78]

Mediation and technical support teams draw on expertise from a range of contexts and peace processes in other countries to assist stakeholders in the negotiation and dialogue process. Ideally there are two mediation teams, with one including insiders/locals that hold extensive social capital networks with diverse stakeholders and the other including outsiders/internationals with comparative experience with peace processes in other countries.[79] These teams carry out a number of roles that serve a variety of functions, including the following:[80]

- *Process designers and planners.* Develop proposals for how the peace process will work, with various mechanisms for input by diverse stakeholders. Ensure that all stakeholders accept the location of meetings, arrange for security and detail protocols at meetings, maintain a level of confidentiality, and follow other ground rules to foster respectful interactions.
- *Trainers.* Offer stakeholders conflict-coaching training in negotiation, handling and speaking with news media, and other skills necessary to a peace process.
- *Analysis.* Engage in ongoing analysis and assessment of political, social, economic, and security dynamics impacting the peace process.
- *Good offices.* Provide good offices or access to information related to the conflict needed by stakeholders.
- *Envoys.* Help identify, communicate with, transmit messages between, and convene diverse stakeholders.
- *Models.* Demonstrate respect for all stakeholders and constructive communication.
- *Process facilitators.* Ensure each stakeholder has adequate and roughly equal time to share their perspectives, identify shared grievances, highlight common ground, develop creative options, and design next steps together.
- *Reality testers.* Challenge stakeholders to identify their best alternatives to a negotiated agreement and consensus on the way forward for the country. Identify the costs of not reaching an agreement.
- *Catalysts.* Act as catalysts for new forums, programs, and institutions to foster the peace process and ongoing peacebuilding.
- *Sustainers.* Provide continuity and sustainability to a long-term, dynamic process.
- *Monitors.* Follow the implementation of agreements and offer support, sanctions, and incentives where appropriate.

In past peace processes in other countries, mediators succeeded in getting groups to agree to a political settlement but left agreements vague in terms of implementation. Exhaustion has led many mediation teams to let others "work out the details." But this endangers the whole process. Mediation and technical support teams should remain available during the implementation phase of peace agreements, as so many peace agreements fail because stakeholders are unable or unwilling to put agreements into practice.

Given the complexity of stakeholder interests, a comprehensive Afghan peace process is more likely to succeed with the help of internal and external mediation and technical support teams. An internal mediation or technical support team could draw from Afghan civil society expertise and experience in decades of peacebuilding between political, ethnic, and religious groups in Afghanistan. Afghan civil society's peacebuilding capacity could also support the development of internally generated incentives such as face-saving mechanisms for reintegration via grievance-resolution processes. Civil society has a crucial role in helping local governments, tribal leaders, and armed opposition groups identify core grievances and develop local solutions and written agreements. This internal mediation support team should include members from different ethnic groups and those with diverse constituencies. But most important, the Afghans on the internal mediation support team should have technical expertise in peacebuilding, have demonstrated their personal commitment to interacting with all stakeholders, and be people who do not stand to personally gain from the outcome of a negotiated agreement.

Understanding the Structures and Challenges of International Support and Coordination

Most successful peace processes receive substantial and ongoing support from the international community. The role of outsiders in a negotiation process is delicate. Internationals may be perceived as tainted because of their country's role. Personality and personal networks may also be at play. Some diplomats may have more success than others in playing a conciliatory role to move groups toward a negotiation or an agreement. Mediators and technical support teams should have legitimacy in the eyes of key stakeholders.

International support for peace processes comes in a wide variety of models. In rare cases, one international mediator takes the lead and attempts to guide the coordinated effort required for a comprehensive peace process. In most cases a group of states work together in either a "Contact Group" such as the Quartet group working with Israelis and Palestinians or a more informal and mid-level "Group of Friends" made up of four to six countries that support a mediation team effort related to a peace process. Other forms of international support include monitoring implementation of agreements such as the Joint Monitoring Commission in Namibia or the Peace Implementation Council in Bosnia that coordinated international assistance and support for the region after the Dayton Accords.[81]

The benefits of these forms of international coordination and support mechanisms are that outside countries can bring additional leverage, information, resources, and practical help with the coordination. Working together, a group is more likely to be able to put together a strategic package of internal and external incentives and sanctions that complement stakeholders own motivations and interests to move groups toward resolution. Successful peace processes often enjoy support from regional countries such as the roles that Mexico played in the Central American peace processes and Australia and New Zealand's roles in East Timor's peace process. In El Salvador and Guatemala, Mexico's relationship with insurgents made it easier for them to pressure insurgent negotiators while the U.S. pressured governments it had long supported. In the Sudanese peace process, the U.K. liaised with the North, the U.S. related to the South and Norway used conciliation strategies with both North and South.[82]

But there are also challenges to international coordination. A Group of Friends model, for example, has proven most effective when the Group of Friends' interests align. When there are competing interests, conflicts between the Friends can further complicate already delicate negotiations. The Group of Friends supporting the Georgia/Abkhaz conflict, for example, experienced a great deal of conflict among themselves over their fifteen years working together. In situations where the international interests in a peace process diverge, it may be necessary to address the conflict between outside groups wanting to foster a peace process; even a "mediation among potential mediators." Furthermore, external countries often have few diplomats with comparative experience with comprehensive peace process, so they have little technical expertise to share. Furthermore, internal political and budgeting constraints in countries wanting to be involved in a peace process can bring conflicting funding schedules with many pouring an overabundance of funds into short-term projects. But the payoffs of short-term investments in a peace process may be lost without longer-term support for implementation of agreements and consultation mechanisms. The resulting cacophony of conflicting and competing interests and actions may actually prove to pose an even greater challenge or threat to internal groups aiming to foster peace.[83]

International coordination efforts in Afghanistan face a maelstrom of challenges. Afghans perceive that most internationals such as the United States have their own interests in Afghanistan that may not always align with Afghan interests. Afghanistan's regional neighbors more often play a more menacing role than a constructive one. They may even perceive an "unstable" Afghanistan as in their interest and attempt to spoil a peace process. In past peace processes, coordination among different groups proved challenging. First, outsiders in the international community have different and sometimes conflicting or even competing interests. The United Nations and United States have the most investment in the conflict and a desire and responsibility for a role in coordination. Yet both the U.N. and U.S. are seen as a party to the conflict by virtue of their support for the GIROA. A number of commentators note the problems with a U.N. or U.S.-mediated peace agreement and suggest instead that a more neutral, and preferably Muslim, country may have more success.

A United Nations team could provide critical technical support and bring comparative experience from other contexts. However, the United Nations' role might best be to support other outside mediators or technical support teams from Turkey, Saudi Arabia, the United Arab Emirates, or regional organizations like the Organization of the Islamic Conference (OIC) or the Conference on Interaction and Confidence Building in Asia (CICA), as these may be seen as more acceptable alternatives to UN mediators.[84] Canada, Italy, and Germany have also invested resources in a potential peace process and countries such as these may be able to play the role of a Group of Friends.

Conclusion and Recommendations

A comprehensive peace process in Afghanistan requires a much more deliberate design than currently exists. The hope of a quick and tight negotiation process is as illusory as the fantasy that firepower will achieve victory. The road to peace in Afghanistan is not short. Maneuvering through Afghanistan's internal and regional political dynamics is no less challenging than five-dimensional chess.

The Afghan government, Afghan civil society, and the international community should draw on lessons learned from other countries to ensure that an Afghan peace process

- helps all stakeholders recognize the need for an inclusive process and to create mechanisms, or even communication channels to hear the interests and concerns of all groups, even those deemed irrelevant or extremist;
- supports the ability of all stakeholders to use principled negotiation to address the root causes and underlying interests of each group;
- assists each stakeholder in assessing and reality testing their best alternative to a negotiated solution and helps stakeholders develop internally generated incentives—economic, security, political, and identity-based—so that agreements are more likely to be sustainable over the long term;
- develops internal and external mediation and technical support teams.

Recommendations for the Afghan Government

- *Consult with Afghan civil society in the design of a comprehensive peace process.* The Afghan government already asks civil society organizations to help build public support for peace initiatives. But civil society organizations with long-term expertise in local-level mediation and negotiation processes have not been consulted in the development of government reconciliation and peace initiatives.
- *Invest time in training the National Peace Council.* Allow internal and external technical support teams with extensive experience in peace processes and peacebuilding to share skills and conceptual frameworks on principled negotiation and mediation processes.
- *Identify existing incentives and what, if any, negative implications there are to these incentives.* Determine how to create or redesign internal and external incentives in each of the four categories, particularly incentives

that can open up new possibilities for persuading key stakeholders to pursue peace. Sequence incentives for different stages of the peace process, from enticing armed groups to the negotiation table, to staying through difficult issues, and finally to implementing a peace agreement.

Recommendations for Afghan Civil Society

- *Develop a diverse and representative Civil Society Assembly.* Create an ongoing mechanism and forum for identifying key issues and redline interests, such as protection of minority and women's rights.
- *Invest time in training and capacity building.* Give and receive training from technical support teams on principled negotiation and mediation processes.
- *Work with the National Peace Council.* Develop and coordinate public consultation mechanisms.

Recommendations for the International Community

- *Recognize that current international military and financial assistance creates obstacles to a successful peace process.* The greatest leverage available to the international community is less military and financial investment, not more. Current levels of military and financial investments keep the existing dysfunctional system in place, allowing the government to forgo the hard work of earning public legitimacy and consent to govern and providing financial benefits for the continuation of the war and instability.
- *Urge support for a comprehensive Afghan public peace process.* Consult with a broad range of diverse local civil society leaders representative of the various ethnic groups to identify the ideal model of public participation in a peace process and how internationals could support this.
- *Develop strategies for supporting Afghan civil society.* The international community's focus on supporting the legitimacy of the current government overshadow and even undermine efforts to build an Afghan nation with an active, engaged civil society. Internationals could reach out to develop better relationships with diverse civil society leaders in Kabul. Afghan-led civil society peacebuilding efforts such as peace councils and dialogue forums are low cost, yet plant the seeds for longer-term improved relationships.
- *Deploy more diplomatic staff.* Finding a political solution to the conflict in Afghanistan and the region requires more diplomats. For example, they are important for holding town halls to listen to the concerns, ideas, analysis, and points of view of Afghans in all sectors of society. Afghans and Pakistanis both desire a diplomatic surge, noting that they did not

perceive a diplomatic surge to accompany the troop surge. There is a desire to have more U.S. policymakers listen directly to Afghan government ministers, parliamentarians, and civil society leaders.

- *Invite more Afghan government personnel and civil society leaders to Washington or other foreign capitals to talk with policymakers.* Afghans wonder why so few are invited to speak to foreign policymakers about the future of their country. They ask how policymakers, who they perceive as knowing little about their culture and history, can talk about democracy in Afghanistan and then make such big decisions about U.S. policy in Afghanistan without listening to Afghans themselves express their analysis and hopes for the future.

- *Develop a Group of Friends with teams of mediators and peace process technical support capacity.* Small, well-trained teams who have specialist knowledge, experiences, and skills in working on comprehensive peace processes can advise and leverage the support from other sectors of government on behalf of developing a sustainable outcome. Deploy long-term support teams of mediators and diplomats to work on complex regional diplomatic initiatives. Ensure diplomats are trained in principled negotiation and mediation to help support a comprehensive Afghan peace process. Few governments have made supporting peace processes a priority. Technical support teams from a Group of Friends could provide financial support, coaching, negotiation training, and capacity-building measures to all groups in an Afghan peace process, including civil society stakeholders. All parties must understand the process so that they can work together constructively.

Acknowledgments

I worked with a number of Afghan partners during the course of my research, including Mirwais Wardak of Cooperation for Peace and Unity and Peace Training and Research Organization, Aziz Rafiee of Afghan Civil Society Forum Organization, Nilofar Sakhi of Open Society Afghanistan, each of whom also made valuable contributions to this report. I also worked with Suraya Sadeed of Help the Afghan Children, former graduate students from Eastern Mennonite University Ramin Nouroozi, Farishta Sakhi, Hamid Arsalan, and Saeed Murad Rahi, and Ali Gohar of Just Peace International in Pakistan. Special thanks go to Nicole Birtsch and her team at Kabul University's National Center for Policy Research, including Nargis Sadat Asghary and Omar Sadr. I also wish to thank the Ploughshares Fund and Afghanistan: Pathways to Peace, a project of Peacebuild: The Canadian Peacebuilding Network, which provided the funding for the research.

Notes

1. Peace Watch Committee, "Afghan Civil Society Statement on Peace and Reconciliation," April 25, 2011.
2. Catherine Barnes, *Owning the Process: Public Participation in Peacemaking: South Africa, Guatemala, and Mali* (London: Conciliation Resources, 2002).
3. Michael Semple, *Reconciliation in Afghanistan* (Washington, DC: United States Institute of Peace Press, 2009).
4. Peter Dixon, "Civil Society and a Comprehensive Peace Process" (conference paper, "Afghanistan: Pathways to Peace," Kabul, Afghanistan, April 2009).
5. See Lisa Schirch, *The Little Book of Strategic Peacebuilding* (Intercourse, PA: Good Books, 2004).
6. Virginia Page Fortna, *Peace Time: Cease-Fire Agreements and the Durability of Peace* (Princeton, New Jersey: Princeton University Press, 2004).
7. Monica Duffy Toft, "Ending Civil Wars: A Case for Rebel Victory?" *International Security* 34, no. 4 (Spring 2010): 7–36.
8. Catherine Barnes and Aaron Griffiths, "Influencing Resolution: External Roles in Changing the Strategic Calculus of Conflict," in *ACCORD: Incentives and Sanctions in Peace Processes* (London: Conciliation Resources 2008), 14–17.
9. Thomas Ruttig, *The Battle for Afghanistan: Negotiations with the Taliban: History and Prospects for the Future* (Washington, DC: New America Foundation, 2011), 5.
10. Interview with Christian Dennys, UK Defence Academy, June 12, 2011.
11. Barbara Walter, "Bargaining Failures and Civil War," *Annual Review of Political Science* 12 (June 2009): 243–61; *Ending War: The Need for Peace Process Support Strategies, Accord Policy Brief* (London: Conciliation Resources, 2009); and Michael Doyle and Nicholas Sambanis, *Making War and Building Peace* (Princeton, New Jersey: Princeton University Press, 2006), 13.
12. Fortna, *Peace Time*.
13. Summarized from Public Participation in Peace Processes (London: Conciliation Resources, 2009); Barnes, *Owning the Process; and World Development Report 2011* (Washington, DC: World Bank, 2011).
14. A. K. Jarstad and T. D. Sisk, eds., *From War to Democracy: Dilemmas of Peacebuilding* (Cambridge: Cambridge University Press, 2008).
15. Anthony Wanis-St. John and Darren Kew, "Civil Society and Peace Negotiations: Confronting Exclusion," *International Negotiation* 13 (2008): 11–36. See, also, Anthony Wanis-St. John, "Peace Processes, Secret Negotiations and Civil Society: Dynamics of Inclusion and Exclusion," *International Negotiation* 13 (2008): 1–9.
16. "Choosing to Engage: Armed Groups and Peace Processes" Accord 16 (London: Conciliation Resources, 2005).
17. John Paul Lederach, *Building Peace: Sustainable Reconciliation in Divided Societies* (Washington, DC: United States Institute of Peace Press, 1997).
18. See Michael Doyle and Nicholas Sambanis, *Making War and Building Peace* (Princeton, New Jersey: Princeton University Press, 2006).
19. Guy Olivier Faure and I. William Zartman, eds., *Negotiating with Terrorists* (New York: Routledge Press, 2010).
20. Stephen Stedman, "Spoiler Problems in Peace Processes," *International Security* 22, no. 2 (Fall 1997): 5–53.
21. Desiree Nilsson. "Partial Peace: Rebel Groups Inside and Outside of Civil War Settlements," *Journal of Peace Research* (2008): 45.
22. See, for example, Allison M. Coady and Hussein Solomon, "Afghanistan's Arrested Development: Combating Taliban Resurgence with an Eye for Lasting Peace," *South African Journal of International Affairs* 16, no. 1 (April 2009): 103–14.

23. Wanis-St. John, "Peace Processes, Secret Negotiations and Civil Society," 1–9.

24. *Supporting Statebuilding in Situations of Fragility and Conflict* (Paris: Organization for Economic Co-operation and Development [OECD], January 2011).

25. For more on civil society's roles in peacebuilding, see Lisa Schirch, *Civil Society-Military Roadmap on Human Security* (Washington, DC: 3D Security Initiative, May 2011), and Lisa Schirch, "Security from the Ground Up: Civil Society and the Security-Development Nexus," *Journal of International Peace Operation* 4, no. 6 (May 1, 2009).

26. Kanishka Nawabi, Mirwais Wardak, and Idrees Zaman, *The Role and Functions of Religious Civil Society in Afghanistan* (Kabul: Cooperation for Peace and Unity, July 2007).

27. For more on Afghan civil society, see Mary Kaldor and Marika Theros, *Building Afghan Peace from the Ground Up* (Washington, DC: Century Foundation, 2011); Elizabeth Winter, *Civil Society Development in Afghanistan* (London: London School of Economics' Center for Civil Society, June 2010); and Susanne Schmeidl, "Promoting Civil Society in Afghanistan: Deconstructing Some Myths," in *Petersberg Papers on Afghanistan and the Region,* ed. Wolfgang Danspeckgruber (Princeton: Princeton University, Liechtenstein Institute on Self-Determination, 2009).

28. Kaldor and Theros, *Building Afghan Peace from the Ground Up,* 3.

29. Ibid., 14–15.

30. Thomas Kirk, "Afghanistan: Reconciliation Plans, Tribal Leaders and Civil Society," *Small Wars Journal* (January 4, 2011): 5.

31. Kirk, "Afghanistan," 6.

32. David Kilcullen, *The Accidental Guerrilla* (London: Hurst and Co, 2009).

33. Roger Fisher and William Ury, *Getting to Yes: Negotiating Agreement Without Giving In* (New York: Penguin Books, 1981).

34. I. William. Zartman, *Ripe for Resolution* (New York: Oxford Press, 1989).

35. I. William. Zartman, "Ripeness: The Hurting Stalemate and Beyond," in *International Conflict Resolution after the Cold War,* ed. Paul C. Stern and Daniel Druckman (Washington, DC: National Academy Press, September 2000).

36. Matt Waldman, "Navigating Negotiations in Afghanistan," Peace Brief no. 52 (Washington, DC: United States Institute of Peace, September 2010).

37. Conciliation Resources, *Ending War,* 2.

38. See Aaron Griffiths and Catherine Barnes, eds., *Powers of Persuasion: Incentives, Sanctions and Conditionality in Peacemaking* (London: Conciliation Resources, 2009); *Choosing to Engage: Armed Groups and Peace Processes* (London: Conciliation Resources ACCORD, 2009); and Peter Wallensteen and Margareta Sollenberg, "Armed Conflict, Conflict Termination, and Peace Agreements 1989–96," *Journal of Peace Research* 34, no. 3 (January 1, 1997).

39. Sid Noel, ed., *From Power Sharing to Democracy: Post-Conflict Institutions in Ethnically Divided Societies* (Ottawa: McGill-Queen's University Press, 2005).

40. Sarah Ladbury, *Testing Hypotheses of Drivers of Radicalisation in Afghanistan: Why Do Men Join the Taliban and Hizb-i Islami? How Much Do Local Communities Support Them?* (Afghanistan: Cooperation for Peace and Unity, August 2009).

41. Fisher and Ury, *Getting to Yes.*

42. Susanne Koelbl and Holger Stark, "Germany Mediates Secret US-Taliban Talks," *Speigel International Online,* May 24, 2011.

43. Kirk, "Afghanistan: Reconciliation Plans," 5.

44. Ladbury, *Testing Hypotheses of Drivers of Radicalisation in Afghanistan.*

45. Surendrini Wijeyaratne, *Afghanistan: A Study on the Prospects for Peace* (Ottawa: Canada's Council for International Cooperation, March 2008), 31.

46. Washington Post/ABC News/BBC/ARD poll based on in-person interviews with a random national sample of 1,691 Afghan adults, October 29–November 13, 2010. See also Ladbury, *Testing Hypotheses of Drivers of Radicalisation in Afghanistan.*

47. Stanley A. McChrystal, "Commander's Initial Assessment," NATO International Security Assistance Force, Afghanistan, August 30, 2009.

48. Matt Waldman, *Golden Surrender? The Risks, Challenges, and Implications of Reintegration in Afghanistan* (Kabul: Afghanistan Analysts Network, April 2010).

49. *OECD/DAC Handbook on Security System Reform* (Paris: OECD, 2007) 101; Katrin Kinzelbach and Yasmine Sherif, "Security Sector Oversight, Violent Conflict and Peacebuilding," in *Public Oversight of the Security Sector,* ed. Eden Cole, Kerstin Eppert, and Katrin Kinzelbach (Geneva: Geneva Centre for the Democratic Control of Armed Forces, 2008) 341–57.

50. Anna Larson, *Deconstructing Democracy in Afghanistan* (Kabul: Afghanistan Research and Evaluation Unit, May 2011).

51. "Winning 'Hearts and Minds' in Afghanistan: Assessing the Effectiveness of Development Aid in COIN Operations" (report, Wilton Park Conference 1022, Feinstein International Center, Tufts University, March 11–14, 2010).

52. See John Tierney, "Warlord, Inc.: Extortion and Corruption along the U.S. Supply Chain in Afghanistan," in testimony to the United States House of Representatives, Committee on Oversight and Government and Reform, Subcommittee on National Security and Foreign Affairs, June 22, 2010.

53. Mary Kaldor and Marika Theros, *Building Afghan Peace from the Ground Up* (Washington, DC: Century Foundation Report, March 2011), 12.

54. Sven Gunnar Simonsen, "Ethnicising Afghanistan?: Inclusion and Exclusion in post-Bonn Institution Building," Third World Quarterly 25, no. 4 (2004): 707–29.

55. Fighting Corruption From Within: Empowering Citizens to Reduce Corruption in Afghanistan (Kabul: Integrity Watch Afghanistan, June 2011).

56. Farishte Jalalzai. "Mourning Abdul Samad Rohani," Radio Free Europe/Radio Liberty, Radio Free Afghanistan, June 10, 2010.

57. The statement of the one-day conference on justice and reconciliation, Kabul, November 10, 2010.

58. International Center for Transitional Justice (ICTJ) (statement at the conference titled "A Common Voice for Peace and Reconciliation," Kabul, April 10–12, 2010).

59. Aunohita Mojamdar, "Afghanistan Peace Jirga's Unlikely Critics: Victims of War Crimes," *MinnPost.com,* June 2, 2010.

60. Afghan Independent Human Rights Commission (AIHRC), *The Action Plan on Peace, Justice and Reconciliation* (Kabul: AIHRC, 2005).

61. Simonsen, "Ethnicising Afghanistan?"

62. Adapted from a variety of civil society statements, including the one made by ICTJ at the conference, "A Common Voice for Peace and Reconciliation"; Mary Kaldor and Marika Theros, "Building Afghan Peace from the Ground Up" (Washington, DC: Century Foundation, 2011).

63. Hamish Nixon, *Achieving Durable Peace: Afghan Perspectives on a Peace Process* (Oslo: Peace Research Institute Oslo, United States Institute of Peace, and Chr. Michelsen Institute, June 2011).

64. This section draws on *Conciliation Resources, Public Participation in Peace Processes,* and Barnes, *Owning the Process.*

65. Kåre Lode, as quoted in Conciliation Resources, *Public Participation in Peace Processes.*

66. Matt Waldman, *Community Peace-building in Afghanistan* (Kabul: Oxfam International, 2008).

67. *Cooperation for Peace and Unity Annual Report* (Kabul: Cooperation for Peace and Unity, 2008).

68. Peace Training and Research Organization, "Human Security Indicators," 2011.

69. Rachel Sieder, "Reframing Citizenship: Indigenous Rights, Local Power and the Peace Process," in *Negotiating Rights: The Guatemalan Peace Process* (London: Conciliation Resources, 1997), 66.

70. See, for example, the Canadian-funded and led conference in Kabul, April 2010, documented in *Afghanistan: Pathways to Peace Phase One Summary December 2009–June 2010* (Ottawa: Peacebuild, 2010), and an Italian-funded-and-led process held in Rome, Italy, in 2011 called "Promoting Dialogue and Peace in Afghanistan: Strengthening Afghan Civil Society," documented in Fabrizio Foschini, *Towards a More United Voice of Afghan Civil Society: Step Two* (Kabul: Afghan Analysts Network, May 6, 2011).

71. Patricia Gossman, "Afghan High Peace Council Fails to Reflect Afghan Civil Society," Peace Brief no. 74, United States Institute of Peace, January 10, 2011.

72. Ramin Nouroozi, *Afghan Civil Society Perspectives on the National Consultative Peace Jirga* (Washington, DC: 3D Security Initiative, October 2010).

73. Alan Finlayson and Eamon Hughes, "Advertising for Peace: The State and Political Advertising in Northern Ireland, 1988–1998," *Historical Journal of Film, Radio and Television* 20, no. 3 (2000): 397–412.

74. Gordon Adam. "Could the Media Save Afghanistan?" *Prospect Magazine,* July 7, 2010, www.spectmagazine.co.uk/2010/07/could-the-media-save-afghanistan/.

75. *Mediation and Peace Processes* (New York: International Peace Institute, 2009).

76. *Unpacking the Mystery of Mediation in African Peace Processes* (Zurich: Swiss Peace, Center for Security Studies, and Swiss Federal Institute of Technology, 2008).

77. Under current U.S. counterterrorism and material support laws, it is illegal for U.S.-based universities and organizations to provide negotiation training to the Taliban or other groups listed as terrorist organizations.

78. Conciliation Resources, *Ending War.*

79. Simon J. A. Mason, *Insider Mediators: Exploring their Key Role in Informal Peace Processes* (Berlin: SwissPeace and Berghof Foundation for Peace Support, 2009).

80. David Lord and Lisa Schirch, *Mediation Teams and Peace Support Process* (Ottawa: Afghanistan Pathways to Peace, 2009).

81. Teresa Whitfield, "Orchestrating International Action," in *ACCORD: Powers of Persuasion: Incentives, Sanctions and Conditionality in Peacemaking,* ed. Aaron Griffiths with Catherine Barnes (London: Conciliation Resources, 2008.) 21.

82. Ibid., 21.

83. Ibid., 22.

84. Matt Waldman and Thomas Ruttig, *Peace Offerings: Theories of Conflict Resolution and Their Applicability to Afghanistan* (Kabul: Afghanistan Analysts Network, January 2011), 4.

12

Beyond Power Sharing
Institutional Options for an Afghan Peace Process

Hamish Nixon and Caroline Hartzell

I*n this chapter—first published in 2011 in collaboration with PRIO and the
Chr. Michelsen Institute—Nixon and Hartzell cover some of the same ground
as Lisa Schirch in their detailed discussion on how to initiate and structure a
negotiation process, echoing Schirch's emphasis on the importance of inclusiveness to
guaranteeing a sustainable peace. Nixon and Hartzell also reprise the analysis of the
Afghan conflict in chapter 2, but with an eye to better understand how the conflict's
complexity adds challenges to a potential peace process: "This picture of the core players in the conflict is one of complex and potentially incoherent actors who may have
difficulty settling on a single set of negotiating positions and delivering on agreements
as a peace process advances."*

*The point is not to discourage a peace process but to underline that the process
structure should be tailored to "Afghanistan's unique conflict dynamics." "Too often,"
Nixon and Hartzell write, "international actors—whether analysts, policymakers, or
implementers—try to apply lessons that derive from what they know, rather than what
is suited to the context." Their approach is different: "Rather than lifting wholesale the
experience of other peace processes that writ large may have limited applicability to the
complexities of Afghanistan, it examines some specific challenges a peace process in
Afghanistan will face, and then presents theoretical observations and some real world
comparative examples that may be applicable to these challenges."*

*Nixon and Hartzell look further into the future than most existing analyses of po-
tential negotiations with the Taliban. The authors go into significant detail regarding*

Originally published as Hamish Nixon and Caroline Hartzell, "Beyond Power Sharing: Institutional Options for an Afghan Peace Process," Peaceworks 78 (Washington, DC: USIP, 2011).

possible interim arrangements, then address what they describe as "institutional arrangements for the long term." This is based on a description of the "dimensions of state power"—political, military, economic, and territorial—and how power overall can be allocated among them: through mechanisms of power sharing, power dividing, power creating, and power diffusing. The resulting matrix offers a menu for designing long-term institutional arrangements that satisfy a variety of stakeholders in a peace process.

Lurking behind the analysis is the structure of a state that failed to appear during the Bonn process. The rush between the fall of the Taliban and the conclusion of the Bonn Agreement—a matter of months—did not allow for the systematic analysis that has been brought to bear in Afghanistan since. The Bonn negotiation was concluded in ten days, and those sitting around the table were hardly representative of Afghanistan's political environment. This concluding chapter could guide negotiators if a representative group of Afghans were to gather around the table again.

Introduction: Peace Is Possible

The need for a peace process to end the conflict in Afghanistan becomes clearer with each passing month, just as quickly as hopes for one often seem to recede. Despite many positive changes, ten years of deepening international involvement, both military and civilian, have been accompanied by a pattern of mounting violence. Since 2009 a dramatic escalation by NATO of both conventional counterinsurgency and special operations has certainly cost the insurgency lives and territory, and the prospects of an outright Taliban victory seem negligible. At the same time, the Taliban movement and its allies have shown resilience and flexibility, presenting a consistent tactical challenge in narrowing areas of the south and broad areas in the southeast and east, while extending their reach in the north.[1] A string of high-profile attacks and assassinations has undermined government and NATO claims of increasing security and eliminated key government allies, while deepening tensions among political factions with distinct ethnic overtones, raising the specter of a widening civil conflict.[2]

The United States and its partners seek to transfer the bulk of security responsibilities to the Afghan government by 2014, and there are concerns about the quality, unity, and sustainment costs of regular Afghan security forces and the effect of proliferating irregular units on government legitimacy.[3] A succession of governance crises has undermined the last two national elections, threatens the continued delivery of international development assistance, and has paralyzed executive-legislative relations, bringing most avenues of institutionalized politics to a standstill. The security transition to 2014 will thus be accompanied by a challenging political succession and destabilizing economic conditions as output shrinks by upward of one third on the back of declining security and aid inflows.[4]

Such circumstances heighten the conclusion, already acknowledged by the United States, its international partners, and the Afghan government, that a diplomatic solution offers the best chance to avoid a deepening conflict. The Afghan government has pursued both private and public outreach to neighboring countries and insurgent groups centered on a seventy-member High Peace Council appointed in late 2010—an approach that encountered a serious setback with the September 20, 2011, assassination of council Chairman Burhanuddin Rabbani. Nevertheless, the United States, the Taliban, and more recently the Haqqani network have all claimed participation in preliminary talks, while contact between Gulbuddin Hekmatyar's Hezb-e Islami and Kabul has long been quite open.[5]

Yet, while the desirability of a negotiated outcome is increasingly clear, there are deep doubts about the chances of achieving a settlement. There are two important strands to such objections: (1) that the Taliban themselves are uninterested in negotiating and (2) that Pakistan will prevent an effective negotiation in order to preserve its influence over the outcome in Afghanistan. The claim that the Taliban leadership will never negotiate, either due to absolutist ideology or the perception that the war can be won through waiting out the U.S. drawdown, bears little scrutiny. The existence of a current of "pragmatic, politically thinking, pro-talks Taliban" has been demonstrated through contacts dating from 2007–08, their more recent participation in preliminary talks, and statements including but not limited to Mullah Omar's 2011 Eid message that claim the Taliban are focused on Afghan-specific goals and not international jihad. This evidence suggests recognition of the need to share political power with other groups, and potential moderation of some views on social issues. Evidence from field commanders also suggests some see talks with the leadership as acceptable.[6]

Admittedly, the relative influence of this current within the movement at present is unclear. However, this question and the spectacular assassination of Chairman Rabbani do not indicate the impossibility of negotiation as has been asserted.[7] Continued or intensified hostilities by branches of the insurgency do not in themselves demonstrate an unshakeable rejection of talks, just as intensified action by NATO or the Afghan government also does not. In fact, the current escalation reflects similar patterns in other conflicts as parties seek to leverage their position in advance of a potential negotiation. A study of relationships between escalation and negotiation in ten conflicts published in 2005 finds "that decisions to negotiate follow a party's escalation of the conflict" and "that these correlations do, indeed, have a causal effect."[8] Consistent with this reading, for example, the head of the madrassa that trained Mullah Omar has called for continued armed struggle against U.S. forces in Afghanistan while offering to mediate between them and the Taliban.[9] A key challenge of any peace process will be to enhance the appeal of negotiation among reluctant insurgents.

The second view—that without the acquiescence of the Pakistani security establishment no settlement is possible, and that that condition is unlikely to be fulfilled—is widely held in Afghanistan and among parts of the U.S. policy community. Much has been made of Pakistani efforts to maintain control over nascent negotiations through the arrest of "pro-talks" individuals during 2010, and the public reaction by the Karzai government to the Rabbani assassination reflects this line of thinking.[10] A 2011 study suggests that Pakistan's policy elites perceive that their interests increasingly lie with a stable and inclusive Afghan government—potentially including Taliban representation—that can protect Pakistan's interests, chiefly by preventing excessive Indian influence. In this light, Pakistan's interference in the peace process can be seen as hedging that results from skepticism over the chances of a successful negotiation, which in turn stems from the ambiguity of U.S. policy toward such talks.[11]

Pakistani hostility, rather than being absolute, is in this sense part of a vicious circle driven by uncertain progress or prospects for an intra-Afghan process that would accommodate Pakistan's concerns. It is possible that such progress might motivate gradual adjustments within Pakistan, converting a vicious circle of hedging to a more virtuous one of increasing prospects for peace.[12] Certainly, establishing the general parameters of a peace process and future institutional options as described in this paper, incorporating Pakistani input and broader regional agreement, could make a contribution to Pakistan's confidence that a peace process could meet its concerns. Furthermore, even if one argues such a change in Pakistani security policy is *necessary* to achieve a settlement in Afghanistan, it is certainly not *sufficient* to make such a settlement stick. Therefore, an intra-Afghan settlement needs to be hammered out, as prominent advocates, including U.S. secretary of state Hillary Clinton, have noted.[13] While this report focuses on the intra-Afghan terms of such a settlement, by no means do we consider that Pakistan's engagement with those terms is not an important key to a lasting settlement.

The idea that the core of this intra-Afghan settlement will involve the sharing of political power and positions with Taliban representatives either at the central or provincial level is both widespread in public discourse, and the cause of considerable opposition.[14] This opposition has two main strands. On the one hand, leaders of Afghan political or military factions that have a history of opposing the Taliban, or who represent minority communities that particularly suffered under their rule, warn that inclusion of the Taliban in a power-sharing agreement would ignite renewed factional struggle.[15] On the other, a range of forces that can be broadly defined as civil society, including traditionally oriented tribal leaders, modernizing political parties, human rights and women's groups, fear the consequences of accommodation with the Taliban for newfound democratic institutions and individual rights.[16] The worst outcome from the point of view of any of these groups is a closed deal dividing influence between the current regime and the Taliban—in the eyes of many precisely the route pursued by Kabul prior to the Rabbani killing.

While these issues are formidable, they are also potentially surmountable by the right kind of process and settlement. This report attempts to contribute to the evolution of a peace process that may be able to confront such objections about an agreement with the Taliban. A peace process requires both *ideas* and *will*. Of these, will is clearly most important: without the desire and efforts of leaders and their followers to exit conflict and seek peace, no quantity of well-meaning mediators, policy reports, or peacebuilding programs can lead to a durable settlement. However, ideas are needed to convert that will into a path toward a settlement, and to increase the chance of that settlement enduring:

> Factors important in creating "ripe opportunities" for conflict resolution are . . . the availability and increasing acceptability of new sets of basic ideas, principles and concepts for addressing the conflict and, eventually, craft[ing] viable formulas and resources [for] peace agreements.[17]

Indeed, rich experience exists internationally to provide suggestions, lessons, and models, as a recent call from the Brookings Institution for a more robust political strategy in Afghanistan observes:

> The international community can offer ideas here, based on previous experiences ranging from the termination of civil wars in Central America and Angola and Rwanda to the war crimes processes in the Balkans and Liberia to the Truth and Reconciliation process in South Africa to the mixed indigenous-international arrangements employed in Cambodia.[18]

However, to have any chance of success, such ideas must respond to Afghanistan's unique conflict dynamics. Too often international actors—whether analysts, policymakers, or implementers—try to apply lessons that derive from what they know, rather than what is suited to the context. Military planners may tend to draw on recent experiences in Iraq, UN officials from major peacebuilding efforts such as those in Bosnia-Herzegovina or East Timor, and diplomats from their own country's experience, such as that of the United Kingdom in Northern Ireland.

This report takes a different approach. Rather than lifting wholesale the experience of other peace processes that writ large may have limited applicability to the complexities of Afghanistan, it examines some specific challenges a peace process in Afghanistan will face, and then presents theoretical observations and some real world comparative examples that may be applicable to these challenges. The report does not aim to recommend a complete or a single set of institutions for an Afghan peace process, but rather to stimulate discussion on how to connect the particular challenges an Afghan peace process faces with the possibilities for peace that careful and innovative arrangements can and have produced even in complex and seemingly intractable conflicts.

To do this, the report develops in its next section a conflict analysis to clarify some of the particular challenges that the Afghan conflict presents. Following that, the paper discusses the challenges of initiating and structuring intra-Afghan negotiations to reach a settlement, focusing on the need for effective engagement by third parties, a support structure, and a negotiating framework with provisions for careful inclusion. Next, it discusses the key challenges and functions of transitional arrangements that will be needed in a settlement during the implementation of key provisions. Finally, it details longer-term institutions that can dampen fears about sharing power with the Taliban while addressing root causes of the conflict. In particular, the report outlines a range of examples of power-sharing, power-dividing, power-creating, and power-diffusing models that go beyond the current focus on sharing power with insurgents to integrate elements of much-needed reform.

Challenges for a Peace Process: Analyzing the Afghan Conflict

It is beyond the scope of this report, and indeed the abilities of its authors, to comprehensively analyze or summarize the conflict in Afghanistan. Nevertheless, there are patterns that present challenges to any potential peace process discernible in the available literature on the conflict, and in the primary research conducted under the study of which this report forms a part. If used carefully and flexibly, formal conflict analysis frameworks can help focus attention on some of the challenges that a peace process must face.

Conflict resolution specialists have developed detailed conflict-mapping frameworks that emphasize history, context, and variations in the kinds of actors, the nature of the issues, and the contrasting beliefs and orientations that drive a given conflict.[19] Most frameworks developed for practitioners—inevitably a little reductive—tend to stress three main elements:

- *structures* (sometimes referred to as root causes or conflict issues: "what is the conflict about?"—including international, regional, historical, and contextual factors);
- *actors* ("who are the parties to the conflict?"—including whether these are "primary," "secondary," or "third parties," their interests and motivations, their relationships, resources, and capacities, and therefore their likely responses to different incentives); and
- *dynamics* (triggering or proximate causes of conflict, escalating factors, and changes in structures or issues as conflicts become longer and deeper rooted, or local capacities for management or resolution).[20]

The Afghanistan conflict exhibits complications in each of these areas: it has many overlapping structures and causes, a large number of incoherent actors, and rapidly changing causal and escalating dynamics.

Structure: Dimensions of the Conflict

It goes without saying that the Afghan conflict actually comprises a number of interacting disputes at international, regional, national, and local levels. One attempt to outline this "conflict net" describes the international "war on terror" intertwined with regional disputes between India and Pakistan, between Pakistan and Afghanistan over the border and with Taliban groups active in both countries, between Saudi Arabia and Iran, and between the United States and Iran.[21] Within Afghanistan, the struggle of International Security Assistance Force (ISAF) troops and increasingly Afghan security forces against a complex and cross-border insurgency is the dominant "lens" through which Western actors view the conflict. A well-publicized September 2011 discrepancy in the interpretation of security trends is a telling example of the difference of perspective between those who measure progress as a decline in insurgent attacks and those observing overall violence.[22]

However, this counterinsurgency conflict is one layer over a more complex struggle for influence among political-military factions with roots in previous decades of conflict, that is in turn being shaped by ethnic, tribal, regional, and economic factors operating both nationally and locally. There is consequently a fragmentation of understandings of what the Afghanistan conflict is "about" among different actors, for different audiences, and in different locales. Many national-level Afghan leaders emphasize Afghanistan's victimization in these wider regional struggles, while internally some focus more on U.S. and government actions driving the insurgency, poor governance and the benefits corrupt elites derive from conflict, or historical ethnic rivalries and patterns of rule.[23]

The insurgency does not tend to see or present itself as an ethnic Pashtun movement and has achieved modest expansion among other ethnicities primarily through clerical networks and in remote areas, yet some outside the insurgency view it in ethnic terms.[24] Within the Pashtun sphere, the tribe has a fluid, relative, and localized role in the conflict, just as it does in Afghan society more generally.[25] While the conflict cannot be understood without reference to tribal dynamics, these are but one factor or "arena" among others such as religious and commander networks dating to earlier conflicts, competition over opium production and trafficking, and a lack of articulated Pashtun political alternatives.[26]

In addition to insurgency, regional, and factional dimensions, the Afghan conflict increasingly turns on a broad-based legitimacy crisis. The Taliban grew out of and benefited from widespread disillusionment with the outcome of short-lived power-sharing agreements among the mujahedin factions after

1992 and the resulting civil war and disorder.[27] Similarly now, the conflict is "for a broad cross-section of stakeholders, a legitimacy crisis stemming from a system of power and patronage distribution" that has resulted in the capture of the government by narrow elite interests who enjoy declining legitimacy and seek to mobilize societal tensions such as ethnic divisions to maintain their influence.[28] An important structural cause of the conflict therefore remains weak governance, and any peace process will need to address this issue through reform as well as power sharing if it is to lead to a durable peace.

Actors: A Cast of Complex and Incoherent Players

This multiplicity of conflict structures or "lenses" in turn complicates analysis of the conflict actors. Underlying much conflict analysis is an explicit or implicit assumption that actors—in the sense of discrete decision-making units—can be identified, and their motivations and resources catalogued.[29] For Afghanistan, the number, identity, and nature of the most relevant actors are matters of interpretation and are contested. As noted earlier, a counter-insurgency reading of the conflict suggests a government and its NATO allies with generally congruent interests confronted by an insurgency with several components, surrounded by concentric "rings" of regional and global players with their own interests.[30] An interpretation that focuses on the struggle among political-military factions emphasizes a larger range of actors engaged in armed and unarmed competition with each other in a "violent political marketplace" characterized by neo-patrimonial deal making.[31] In turn, analyses of the war economy emphasize the importance of numerous war profiteers—so-called malign actor networks—in driving the conflict, whether their resources derive from drugs, or international transport and security contracts.[32]

The result is a shifting cast of conflict actors depending on what aspects of the conflict are seen as most salient. Furthermore, those actors that can be identified exhibit great internal complexity and incoherence. Much attention in this regard has been paid to the insurgency. At the highest level of aggregation, division of the insurgency among three broad networks—the Quetta Shura Taliban, the Haqqanis, and Gulbuddin Hekmatyar's Hezb-e Islami—is largely uncontroversial, though some prefer to distinguish between a Kandahari and Paktiawal/Waziristan network of Taliban.[33] It is fairly widely understood that these organizations have some shared and some distinct objectives and positions, and that a peace process may need to deal with them separately, exclude one or more of them, and may find them acting as spoilers.[34]

Within this macrostructure, there is vibrant debate about the continuity of the Taliban organization, the coherence of its command and control and the impact of accelerated capture and kill operations, and the likelihood it can be split constructively, or will fragment destructively, during a peace process.[35]

The Taliban form a network of networks that each draw on different group-based motivations. Depending on local dynamics, these groups can be tribal or subtribal, have roots in jihadi party divisions, or in closer ties of "andiwal" (allegiance based on past history of common struggle). They may be motivated by grievances against government policies or officials, revenge for abuses, ideological affinity, the need for support in local disputes, or desire to commit crimes or extract rents.

However, these disparate building blocks are also mobilized by a central Taliban leadership, and bound together through radicalization into an Islamist and increasingly nationalist ideological frame of reference.[36] Thus,

> the system of reference individual Taleban or their leaders allude to—tribal, nationalist, or Islamist—depends on the circumstances under which a particular decision is taken and on the particular tactical or strategic aim at stake.[37]

The Taliban as an organization also features a considerable degree of decentralization, despite the totalizing ideological views of the Taliban "emirate." For example, in general its much-discussed "justice" system has not been imposed from the top down, but rather by establishing Taliban courts as available alternatives that adapt to the varying local roles and status of existing clerical networks.[38] While the Taliban code of conduct, the *layha*, establishes a loose set of centralized policies in military organization and behavior, significant decision-making powers—for example, over appointment of deputies, dress, non-governmental organization (NGO) activities, and celebrations—have been decentralized to the provincial level or below.[39] In the words of one Taliban cleric, "Commanders are responsible to Mullah Omar, but have to respond to the public."[40] This structure allows a considerable degree of coordination and an ideological and material infrastructure, while enabling autonomy and resilience.[41] However, it also makes it very difficult to judge the coherence of policy toward a negotiated political settlement, and creates a high probability of splits and independent action by segments whose local concerns are not met by a peace process: in short, spoilers.

It is not only the insurgency that features a complex and potentially incoherent structure. In fact, the Afghan government, the other political factions within the national scene, and even the international coalition exhibit divisions that prevent effective concerted action in relation to a peace process. Despite a presidential policy emphasizing "reconciliation" with the Taliban and a High Peace Council charged with the public pursuit of this policy, interviews with senior members of both the government and the council suggest both include individuals actively opposed to negotiations.[42] What is sometimes known as the political or legal opposition has been struggling to cohere around a unified position or to agree to a leadership configuration; describing these actors based on pre-2001 labels such as the "Northern Alliance" or the Jamiat-e Islami is increasingly difficult as these are split into camps opposed to or allied to President Karzai.[43]

Despite outwardly parallel mandates to support Afghanistan, the international community represented by the United States, NATO and its other members, and the United Nations may be among the least coherent of the groups of actors involved in this conflict. One need look no further than the diversity of views during development and implementation of the Afghanistan Peace and Reintegration Program to uncover significant differences of analysis and approach between ISAF, the Afghan government, and the United Nations.[44] Even within the United States government, there is a pattern of divergence between departments such as State and Defense on Afghan policy as a whole, and a negotiated settlement in particular.[45]

This picture of the core players in the conflict is one of complex and potentially incoherent actors who may have difficulty settling on a single set of negotiating positions and delivering on agreements as a peace process advances. As one comprehensive review of the actors notes,

> Low coherence is not good news for the prospects of an accord. Incoherent actors are difficult and unreliable counterparties in any negotiation. The actors may change course in midstream, their terms are likely to shift and be retraded, and their commitment to implementation is always suspect. For these reasons, an Afghan peace process will probably bear little resemblance to the Congress of Vienna, the Treaty of Versailles, or the Six Party Talks on Korea, all cases in which the participants had pretty clear ideas about their interests, objectives, and limitations.[46]

A key quality of any viable peace process for Afghanistan will therefore be the ability to encourage pro-dialogue opinion within actors on all sides, generate increased coherence within conflict actor networks, and protect the peace process against the splits and violent setbacks that will inevitably arise.

Dynamics: Impact of a Changing Conflict

Finally, an examination of the conflict dynamics in Afghanistan illustrates additional challenges. As described earlier, the conflict in Afghanistan is a confluence of intersecting regional and internal conflict structures linking the post-2001 U.S. "war on terror" with regional tensions, internal historical rivalries, and legacies of past conflicts, governance weakness, and war, aid, and drugs economies. However, the balance of these factors is changing over time, altering the complexion of the conflict as quickly as efforts to resolve it are introduced.

A brief review of the development of the conflict after 2001 illustrates this dynamism. The trajectory of Taliban resurgence across the country has been examined in some detail.[47] While the top leadership fled to Pakistan, in the south and southeast many mid-level Taliban commanders attempted to melt back to their communities or negotiate a secure exit. In case after case, the installation of new local officials and the elevation of certain patronage networks fed rivalries that drove such men back into the Taliban organization.[48] In the south, this exploitation of local rivalries and events led to "widespread disillusionment with the government and foreign forces, giving the Taliban a rank-and-file force."[49] While combinations of factors were at play everywhere, in some places this process ran more along tribal lines (Kandahar) or between confederacies of tribes (Uruzgan); in other places ethnicity (Ghazni), political factionalism (Loya Paktia), or competition over narcotics networks (Helmand) infused the process. This reliance on interested power brokers was combined with a "light-footprint" policy that saw foreign troops restricted to Kabul or engaged in special operations, often against targets suggested by the same brokers. The devastating impact of this lack of a political solution for the Taliban and the inadequate provision of security on the conflict has been outlined in considerable detail.[50]

When NATO troops were deployed to the south in numbers during 2006, they were unable to prevent this political process, and some actions of the intensified international engagement, such as the removal of certain regional power brokers or counternarcotics activity, also exacerbated tensions.[51] The resultant pattern of direct confrontation between a growing international military force and the insurgency generated new insurgent strategy and tactics influenced by Iraq, as larger scale engagements were supplanted by increased use of suicide attacks and improvised explosive devices.[52] Thus, the post-2006 phase of the conflict has been characterized by escalation on both sides, with ISAF forces approximately quadrupling in number and insurgent attacks per week increasing by about ten times between early 2008 and 2010.[53] These quantitative changes have enabled an insurgent discourse increasingly referring to national liberation from foreign occupation, such that the presence and behavior of foreign forces has become the most prominent grievance of both local fighters and insurgent leaders.[54] This ideological change has assisted the insurgency's ability to extend beyond the south and east into northern regions, often via clerical opposition to international military forces.[55] In this sense, the conflict became increasingly "about" something new in the post-2006 period.

As the conflict proceeds into a new phase characterized by what is now called "transition," changes in its structure can also be expected.[56] A shift away from direct ISAF military involvement toward the expanded Afghan National Security Forces or local counterinsurgent irregulars and decreasing financial flows will reemphasize the kind of local disputes and rivalries that were prominent in the insurgency's early spread. It will also allow regional dimensions of the conflict with Pakistan, Iran, and India to gain even greater salience. The reorientation of political allegiances promised by elections scheduled for 2014 and possible agreements with segments of the insurgency will deepen already apparent tendencies to ethnic mobilization. It is likely there will be hard-core ideological opponents to any agreement no matter its terms, though the influence of these over their rank and file will vary as a process develops. If progress toward settlement is made, networks within and outside the principal political actors will be marginalized and will seek—indeed, probably have already sought—to derail the process through violence. Furthermore, progress may, perversely, enhance the destabilizing economic patterns caused by "transition" as cash-strapped foreign backers see less need to fund government security and potentially development expenditures. Shrinking flows will prompt existing networks, possibly on both sides of the Durand Line, to intensify criminal activities, or fragment as they become unable to maintain the patronage that binds them together.

In short, if after 2006 the conflict became increasingly structured as a counterinsurgency, after 2011 it will increasingly revert to a multipolar struggle among a combination of political factions with economic dimensions. In effect, the peace process will have to address a conflict that is again changing in character. This dynamism provides some information about the likely contours of the spoiler problem. Rather than dealing with a narrow range of splits between political "hard" and "soft" liners, the peace process in Afghanistan will need to be resilient in managing violence from a range of political, economic, and regional spoilers.[57] Structuring a settlement simply as an agreement between a "government" and "insurgents" will ignore the changing nature of many of the conflict actors. Instead, the process will have to involve institutional changes to help incorporate some of these spoilers into the new dispensation, or generate enough legitimacy to marginalize them despite ongoing violence.

These problems—the need to address multiple interrelated conflict structures, numerous and incoherent actors, and changing dynamics that multiply spoilers—are not unique to the Afghan conflict, but they complicate the challenges that a peace process will face. The following sections of the report examine the kinds of provisions that have been applied in other cases to constructively tackle these challenges at the different stages of a peace process, beginning with the challenges of arriving at and carrying out negotiations.

Initiating and Structuring a Negotiation

As the introduction to this report outlines, in Afghanistan, the government and its international backers already accept the desirability of a negotiated settlement, and there are real indications that elements of the insurgency would explore this avenue under certain circumstances. However, confidence on all sides in the possibilities of a negotiated outcome to deliver core aims or result in sustainable peace is very low, and this is itself a major barrier to initiation of a process. As far as can be discerned publicly, current diplomatic efforts to initiate negotiations are largely passive, meaning they rely on a presumed continued military stalemate and efforts to prompt an improved regional situation to alter insurgent willingness to negotiate. Without a doubt, efforts to feel out the conditions under which Pakistan can be more supportive are important, and should continue. However, as noted in the introduction, these may also be aided if they are coupled with concrete possibilities for a negotiation and settlement that reassures the Pakistani security establishment.

It is often observed that the willingness to enter into a peace process is related to the emergence of a "mutually hurting stalemate."[58] However, for this negative structural condition to lead to a viable peace process, it should contribute to a broader reevaluation of the armed group's (and its supporters) chances of achieving key goals through negotiation:

> What is more important than external pressures is the armed group's subjective appreciation of a negotiated settlement as the first prize—as something that can actually deliver on their bottom line demands.[59]

The insurgent organization shifts from a militant position, in which armed conflict is the only option, to a "dual strategy" open to the opportunities of both military action and negotiations, and eventually to an outright preference for a negotiated solution. Such a shift typically has less to do with individual attitudes or splits between "hawks" and "doves" than with the balance of arguments for each approach under the circumstances of the moment.[60] In fact, the most effective insurgent interlocutors in such a negotiation are not soft-liners, but rather militants who have come to view negotiations as a possible route to achieving group aims.[61]

Beyond the military situation, two important influences can alter that balance for a nonstate armed group. The first is increased confidence that entering into a negotiation process per se will not fatally undermine its interests. The second is the availability of possible outcomes that can meet enough core goals to be worth exploring. In short, to make the decision to negotiate seriously, the conflict actors may need reassurance both in terms of process and potential outcomes. A key task of the peace process at the prenegotiation stage will thus be to overcome this lack of confidence among the armed conflict parties about a negotiation process. A well-considered peace process can help generate these reassurances through effective third-party engagement, support for parties to be more effective negotiators, and development of a negotiating framework or "road map" with both procedural and substantive elements. However, equally important will be using such a framework for reassuring other stakeholders that the resulting process will not be so dominated by armed actors that its outcome will generate renewed conflict or enjoy no legitimacy.

Effective Engagement and Support for an "International Facilitator"

Why are the exploratory contacts and increased clarity in the U.S. position in favor of a settlement not producing the required change of orientation on the part of the armed nonstate actors? As two highly experienced diplomats observe, this lack of progress is caused by

> mistrust among all those so engaged, the low level of coherence in the objectives of most of the players, and the limited capacity to put together such a complex, multitiered diplomatic process. The United States has that capacity, but . . . as one of the major combatants, the United States is not well placed to mediate even a procedural accord.[62]

Effective prenegotiation must help address this lack of confidence, coherence, and capacity. What kind of engagement is likely to be constructive in the Afghan conflict? First of all it is important that it be proactive, not based on waiting for insurgents to come to the table:

> Successful engagement tends to strengthen the pro-dialogue elements within armed groups, while political isolation tends to strengthen hardliners. This suggests that minimal levels of engagement need to be the norm, not a concession.[63]

Knowledgeable analysts of the insurgency describe just such currents of "pragmatic pro-talks" and militant Taliban, rather than ideological divisions:

> There is no organised or recognisable "moderate" (or any other "political") "faction" in the Taleban—to counterbalance the "religious" hardliners. . . . It appears to be more useful to differentiate between currents. . . . On one side, there are pragmatic, politically thinking, pro-talks Taleban who understand that a political solution is desirable but who still are conservative Islamists. On the other side are those who favour a purely military approach, often combined with a hypertrophic recourse to terrorist means.[64]

One factor that works against pro-talks opinion within nonstate armed groups is the likelihood that negotiating with state (especially great power) counterparts will leave them at a disadvantage. There are also well-founded concerns about recognizing violent nonstate groups as equal negotiating partners, and negotiation structures can vary to reflect these concerns. Inevitably the distribution of power during negotiations is important in generating a decision to negotiate in the first place:

> parties to a conflict—especially armed groups—are less likely to choose to negotiate if they consider the process strongly biased against their interests. They are likely to reject pre-conditions that require them to give up core goals [in] advance or their existing strategic advantages gained during conflict. . . . Instead they are likely to demand to enter

talks on the basis of "parity of esteem" within the process and demand equal power in decision-making.[65]

This is why considered engagement by a third party can be effective if it provides some legitimacy and recognition to the nonstate actors, while politically buffering state actors from the implications of full recognition of their enemies and their means:

> Respect is the basic condition of any negotiation. The opponent must be recognized as a party with standing—a negotiating partner because of its ability to veto any agreement and an actor with identifiable reasons behind its actions. However, respect does not mean sympathizing with the terrorists' aims and goals or even recognizing their legitimacy.[66]

Increasingly, there have been high-profile calls for an international facilitator—via a range of possible institutional avenues including the United Nations, the Organization of the Islamic Conference (OIC), states, private organizations, or high-profile individuals—to lead exploratory discussions.[67] Such third-party engagement is needed not only to coordinate disparate initiatives toward a coherent track, but also to rebalance the internal relationships of the actors toward dialogue by reinforcing the sense that they can achieve their aims through negotiation. This will place complex demands on facilitation, including sustaining contact with nonstate actors that remain proscribed and potentially incoherent, supporting the credibility of the process despite limited international acceptance of the nonstate actors' goals, supporting the negotiating capacity of the actors, and determining tricky logistics and security arrangements. Considerable and carefully considered support will be needed to carry out this challenging set of tasks and thus generate confidence.

It is likely no one facilitator or organization alone can bring all that is required to the table(s). Instead of focusing on the choice of a single mediation arrangement, some combination of a mediator or facilitator with a "group of friends" or contact group that brings diverse resources to the task may be useful, though there are potential pros and cons:

> Potential benefits of grouping the external actors in some way include enhancing the leverage of the mediator, raising the visibility of the peace process, preempting rival mediation initiatives, and preparing for sustained support in implementation. However, groups also have disadvantages. The question of composition is delicate, as small groups, although undoubtedly more effective, risk excluding—and thus offending—significant potential partners. . . . In regionally intertwined conflicts, or conflicts that take place in the shadow of a regional power, what to do about the neighbors will be a constant concern.[68]

Such a group might consist of states, as with early examples of such mechanisms in the Central American peace processes or in the "standing

Box 1. The Contadora Group—Framing the Principles of Central American Peace

The Contadora group, comprising interested but not directly involved states of Mexico, Venezuela, Panama, and Colombia, was formed in January 1983 to support a peace process in Central America, where several insurgencies were tied in with regional conflicts and Cold War dynamics. The groups' foreign ministers met with the Central American governments to try to develop a peace plan focusing on regional and internal causes of the conflicts. Three core elements of the plan, known as the "21 Objectives," were the termination of foreign interference and the nonuse of neighboring territories to support insurgencies; respect for human, political, civil, economic, and social rights and measures to democratize; and the establishment of an appropriate verification and monitoring system—later requested from the United Nations.[1]

While the Contadora plan in itself could not bring about an end to the conflicts, as conditions did not allow internal peace talks with insurgents in Nicaragua and El Salvador until later in the decade, these principles formed the backbone of all subsequent efforts, including those that formed the Salvadoran accords. Individual states from the group also continued to provide important assistance, with Spain providing the idea for a joint multiparty monitoring mechanism in El Salvador (COPAZ, discussed later in this report).

1. Dario Moreno, *The Struggle for Peace in Latin America* (Gainesville, FL: University Press of Florida, 1994), 55–60; "21 Objectives Document" (September 9, 1983), reproduced in Jack Child, *The Central American Peace Process, 1983–1991: Sheathing Swords, Building Confidence* (Boulder, CO: Lynne Rienner Publishers, 1992), 174–177.

international conference" suggested in the Century Foundation report for Afghanistan (see box 1).[69] Groups under United Nations auspices "have generally been a mix of permanent members of the Security Council, interested regional actors, and midsize donor states or 'helpful fixers' with experience of the conflict" that can bring a range of resources to bear.[70] The mechanism must be able to build the credibility of the process and increase confidence in its lack of bias among all the parties. This requirement is one motivation for the frequent mention of the OIC, Saudi Arabia, or other Gulf states as potential mediators for the Islamic context of Afghanistan. In Afghanistan, as was the case in Central America, it is likely that neighboring countries will need to act as parties to a regional peace process, rather than members of a third-party support group. With these considerations in mind, one can picture a range of possible groups of friends from among one or more interested midsized Western states, sizeable distant Muslim states, along with Islamic partners who can reassure the insurgent parties, such as Saudi Arabia, or interested but removed regional powers, such as Turkey or the OIC.

However, such support mechanisms need not be comprised only of states or multilateral organizations, though these may certainly be important for the "heavy lifting" of logistics, security, and implementation guarantees. Recently

Box 2. The Philippines International Contact Group—Mixed Composition Support

The 2008 breakdown of peace negotiations between the government of the Philippines and the MILF over provisions for the Autonomous Region of Muslim Mindanao (ARMM) later produced an agreement to create an international contact group empowered to "attend and observe the negotiations, visit and advise the parties to conflict . . . and meet with the parties upon request to resolve outstanding issues," under the coordination of the Malaysian facilitator of the negotiations. The agreement specified a preference for the inclusion of countries from the OIC and the European Union and allowed for the inclusion and support of international NGOs.[1]

In addition to the United Kingdom, Turkey, Japan, and Saudi Arabia, the group includes the Asia Foundation (a regional INGO with broad activities), Conciliation Resources (a peacebuilding resource and training organization), the Centre for Humanitarian Dialogue (a mediation and mediation support organization), and Muhammadiyah (an international Islamic NGO). Before and after the formation of the group, these organizations have provided numerous forms of active support and expertise to the peace process locally and nationally. Their inclusion leverages these experiences and resources but also enables, through their local partners, an organic connection between the peace process and the broad scope of civil society in the Philippines involved in peacebuilding.

1. Claudia Hoffman, "Peace Negotiations in the Philippines: The Government, the MILF and International NGOs," Peace Brief, United States Institute of Peace, 2011.

restored negotiations between the government of the Philippines and the Moro Islamic Liberation Front (MILF) feature a novel form of international contact group that brings together four third-party governments with four interested international nongovernmental organizations (INGOs) with wide expertise in peacemaking and peacebuilding generally, and in the Philippines specifically (see box 2).

While this example corresponds to an ongoing negotiation, the introduction of NGOs suggests possibilities for new kinds of support for mediation even in exploratory stages. In Afghanistan, there might be potential to increase the credibility of the process among the nonstate actors by including nongovernmental or educational institutions with particular Islamic credentials, as well as organizations specializing in mediation or peacebuilding. Such engagement will need to come through an active third party, and may require a mechanism for diverse support that can provide legitimacy and credibility to the process, flexible negotiation support, and some heavy lifting as well.

Supporting the Parties' Negotiating Capacity

Effective third-party engagement can help reassure parties and thus help induce and support a negotiation. However, governments, armed groups, political parties, and civil-society actors who have been immersed in a conflict environment for an extended period may be fragmented, lack negotiating skills or clearly developed positions, and be unaccustomed to the give and take of negotiations. Some groups may "need technical support to articulate their negotiation strategy and to develop skills and confidence in their ability to negotiate" an agreement.[71] Accordingly, third parties should attempt to determine whether divided groups need help reconciling their positions and developing a common bargaining position before attempting to negotiate with other groups. Such support may increase their confidence to pursue a negotiated outcome:

> When leaders are more confident in the prospects of attaining their interests through political—rather than military—means and feel themselves able to skillfully negotiate to achieve their objectives, then a negotiated process become a more attractive option.[72]

Training and capacity building that enables actors to analyze the sources of conflict and identify potential solutions, engage in policy formulation, and negotiate effectively can increase the probability that the negotiation process will be successful. However, groups may react if they see rival groups receiving support to enable them to play a more effective role, and thus support needs to be approached with sensitivity by third parties, perhaps by using one of the models of support groups described earlier. But properly preparing groups for the possibility that their rivals may also receive support can help to alert them to the role reciprocity plays in the negotiation process. Third parties should consider these types of support an investment in the peace process, in later policy processes, and in "good politics" after the settlement.[73]

One example of multipronged third-party support to build the capacity and coherence of actors for a negotiation process took place in Mozambique. Although the years since the signing of the country's peace accord have not seen the Mozambican National Resistance (RENAMO) become a particularly effective opposition party, the support the group received in the run-up to and during the peace negotiations helped to secure its commitment to the peace process (see box 3).

Another example of a more structured technical support program was the Palestine Negotiation Support Unit (NSU), established in 1999 with mixed results (see box 4).

Establishing a Negotiating Framework

To further enhance the chances that the parties will accept a negotiation as a viable route to important preferred outcomes, the goal of third-party engagement and early negotiation support should be to achieve as comprehensive and explicit a framework for negotiation as possible. Ideally, such a framework will have two broad elements, each contributing to reassuring the parties that negotiation is the way forward:

Box 3. Mozambique—Capacity Support for Negotiations and Transformation

Mozambique's ten-year civil war ended with a settlement signed by the governing party, the Liberation Front of Mozambique (FRELIMO), and RENAMO, in 1992. At the start of the negotiation process, FRELIMO had significant advantages, including a well-established party structure, a tradition of unity, and experience as the government in power. RENAMO, on the other hand, lacked ideological coherence, knowledge of constitutional and electoral processes, and experience carrying out basic administrative and political tasks. It remained wary during early diplomatic activity prior to formal talks beginning in Rome in 1990.

South Africa, a RENAMO ally in the conflict, began to consider the group's future in light of unfolding political changes in southern Africa, and shifted its support away from military means toward encouraging and assisting the group to formulate and consolidate its political demands. During the negotiations, logistical and financial assistance provided by the international community enabled RENAMO leaders to participate on an equal footing.

The United Nations fostered a plan to hold democratic elections in 1994, giving RENAMO two years to develop into an opposition party. After the signing of Protocol 111 of the General Peace Accords that dealt with the electoral laws and guarantees of logistical support for RENAMO in the cities, the United Nations set up a trust fund to support the rebel group's transformation. Resources in the amount of US$17 million gave RENAMO's leadership a realistic chance of competing in the multiparty elections and provided its former military commanders with salaries, houses, offices, and vehicles.

Funds from the international community bolstered Afonso Dhlakama's leadership position, allowing RENAMO to pay off military leaders and other officials it could no longer use; maintain the loyalty and services of selected party leaders; and attract new leaders and activists. Initially, financial support was disbursed directly to the party leadership for discretionary use. After the elections, party funding was to become contingent upon the party's ability to win office.[1]

---

1. Giovanni M. Carbone, "Emerging Pluralist Politics in Mozambique: The FRELIMO-RENAMO Party System," Working Paper no. 23 (LSE Crisis States Programme, 2003), http://eprints.lse.ac.uk/28268/1/WP23GC.pdf; Carrie Manning, *The Politics of Peace in Mozambique: Post-Conflict Democratization, 1992–2000* (Westport, CT: Praeger, 2002); Severine Rugumamu and Osman Glba, "Studies in Reconstruction and Capacity Building in Post-Conflict Countries in Africa: Some Lessons of Experience from Mozambique" (African Capacity Building Foundation, 2003); Jeremy Weinstein, "Mozambique: A Fading U.N. Success Story," *Journal of Democracy* 13, 1 (2002): 141–156.

- a *procedural* agreement that outlines how negotiations will proceed in terms of mediation, representation, sequencing, and decision making, as well as practical but difficult issues of logistics and security;
- a statement of *fundamental principles* that outlines core substantive elements and limits, reassuring the parties that primary or existential interests will not be sacrificed and specifying agenda items that need to be negotiated.

A procedural agreement should determine how parties are represented and how many are included, thus suggesting how power will be structured during

Box 4. The Palestine Negotiations Support Unit

The Palestine Negotiations Support Unit was established in 1999 through a request from the Palestine Liberation Organization (PLO) to the British government for technical and financial support in the run-up to the (eventually failed) final-status negotiations in 2000–2001. The unit was partially funded by the United Kingdom and later several other European nations with a mandate to provide legal, communications, and policy advice to Palestinian negotiators. The unit was integrated into the PLO's Negotiations Affairs Department in Ramallah and drew on the expertise of Palestinian-American and other Western-trained lawyers and officials.

The unit has a legal and policy department that aimed to strengthen and refine existing Palestinian negotiation positions, develop new positions, and contribute to resumption of permanent status negotiations. It provides advice on the permanent-status issues (security, settlements, Jerusalem, refugees, borders, and water), as well as other issues (economic relations, compensation, agriculture, tourism, health, transport, energy, telecommunications, and archaeology). The Communications Department publicizes and explains Palestinian negotiation positions.[1]

The unit was embroiled in controversy in early 2011 after it was determined three employees were behind a leak to Al Jazeera of 1,600 key internal documents on Palestinian negotiation strategy over a ten-year period, prompting the resignation of the Palestinian Authority's chief negotiator.[2]

1. The authors are grateful for a suggestion by Michael Keating of the United Nations Mission in Afghanistan (UNAMA) regarding the NSU, personal communication, July 15, 2011. PLO Negotiations Affairs Department Web site, "About Us," www.nad-plo.org/etemplate.php?id=182.
2. Seamus Milne and Ian Black, "The Story Behind the Palestine Papers," *Guardian*, January 24, 2011.

negotiations. Decision-making formulae, the makeup of delegations, logistical questions, the role and powers of the third party suggested time frames and pacing, and communications, recording, and confidentiality procedures can all contribute to clarity regarding the direction of the peace process. Two of the most important procedural issues that will need to be considered are the role of the third party and the structure of the negotiation. A mediator can play a stronger or weaker, a more or less active, role in a negotiating process. A strong mediator with solid international backing may be able to commit these resources to pushing a high-profile plan with top leaders, and to mobilize significant rewards or coercive provisions. A lower-profile mediator from a nongovernmental institution may have more flexibility in methods and formality, perhaps more easily gaining confidence and thus influence from knowledge or informational power.[74]

The mediator may play a very active role, suggesting solutions and formulae and proposing texts based on consultation with the parties, or a more passive one that focuses on bringing the parties together and letting them resolve key questions. A fairly active mandate to integrate positions and suggest formulae can be an important way to support the balance between nonstate parties and states by elevating the position of the less legitimate actor while providing a buffer for the governments involved. For example, in El Salvador, Salvadoran government negotiators tried to push a minimal role for the United Nations mediator and continuous negotiations to capitalize on the weaknesses of a nonstate insurgent actor that had several component organizations and lacked coherence, while guerrilla groups sought an active mediation that could suggest settlement formulae to rebalance the relationship (see box 5). What kind of role is appropriate will depend on the nature of the mediator and the kind of support system available.

The structure of substantive talks might consist of direct or shuttle diplomacy, be conducted in parallel according to theme or sequenced over time, and held in continuous or punctuated sessions. In Afghanistan one might imagine a military-security negotiation focused on cease-fires or cantonment, future security arrangements, and verification measures such as military observation. This will primarily involve the United States, the Afghan government and insurgents, and perhaps the United Nations. A parallel political and social negotiation might involve wider inclusion of Afghan groups, perhaps with additional mediation from respected figures from within or outside Afghanistan, particularly with legitimate Islamic credentials and reputation.

However, such an approach may founder on the inability to separate these issues—a lasting cease-fire is unlikely to be agreed in the absence of political and social agreements. An alternative approach would be a series of consecutive negotiations, building upon each other and perhaps with varying participation, aiming to build momentum by generating a track record of mutual accommodation. For example, an agreement on allowing humanitarian access and limited cease-fires might come first to initiate the process. Talks on the future electoral system or power-sharing institutions and governance of the security forces might lead to a broader but "armed" cease-fire. This progress may be followed by final negotiations over demobilization, the withdrawal of international forces, and the means for verification of counterterrorism provisions including a clear break between insurgents and Al Qaida militants, as these are likely to be among the last cards "played" in a peace process.

A key advantage of such a process is that it can be paced in such a way that there is an opportunity for shuttling and consensus building not just between but also within incoherent parties. In South Africa, where the groups' goals and command structures were quite clear, the African National Congress still required several months to bring lower-level cadres around to some aspects of the agreements. In addition, when difficulties or setbacks arise, attention can be shifted to different agenda items or onto new tracks, as occurred in

Box 5. El Salvador—Sequential Negotiations, Resilience, and Consensus Building

The Salvadoran peace agreements were reached sequentially, with consecutive agreements building on earlier pacts. After transformations within both the regime and the insurgent Farabundo Martí National Liberation Front (FMLN, itself comprised of five separate insurgent parties) that enabled both to envision negotiating their core objectives, talks began in 1989.[1] Violent escalation on both sides followed, but served to weaken militant elements and heighten momentum for a settlement. The government wanted minimal UN involvement and continuous negotiations, while the FMLN needed active UN mediation and long breaks to consult its field commanders to balance the playing field.[2] The resulting "road map" signed in Geneva in 1990 specified alternating continuous and shuttle diplomacy, and set an agenda of future agreements on the armed forces, human rights, the judicial system, the electoral system, constitutional reform, economic and social issues, and UN verification. How to time the beginning of the cease-fire was a key question: it was agreed that each of these substantive issues would be negotiated prior to an "armed cease-fire," which would then last until provisions for demobilization and reintegration of combatants were agreed.

However, the future of the Salvadoran Armed Forces was a major point of disagreement, and could not be settled first. Alvaro de Soto, the secretary-general's appointed mediator, passed over this agenda item and provided text for an accord on human rights that was agreed easily, rebuilding some momentum. Subsequent active UN promotion of solutions for the security forces achieved several interrelated agreements, including purging the military with an ad hoc commission, dissolving certain special forces battalions and the police, and creating a new National Civilian Police. In a parallel process, constitutional reforms agreed to by the government, insurgents, and civilian political parties included a powerful human rights ombudsperson, a requirement that Supreme Court justices be approved by two thirds of the National Assembly, and a new Supreme Electoral Tribunal with multiparty representation in its leadership.

In order to achieve agreement on sequencing its demobilization with these other steps, the FMLN needed time and opportunity to intensively lobby its own commanders, even bringing them to Mexico to observe negotiations.[3] Following the resolution of these key issues, a "compressed agenda" allowed settlement of outstanding points and details quite quickly, and an ad hoc temporary cease-fire became permanent when a comprehensive accord was signed in January 1992.

1. United Nations Department of Public Information, "The United Nations and El Salvador, 1990–1995," 11.
2. Alvaro de Soto, "Ending Violent Conflict in El Salvador," in *Herding Cats: Multiparty Mediation in a Complex World*, ed. Chester Crocker, Fen Osler Hampson, and Pamela Aall (Washington, DC: United States Institute for Peace Press, 1999).
3. Sir Marrack Goulding, *Peacemonger* (London: John Murray, 2002), 229–230.

El Salvador during the sequential negotiation of six separate accords (see box 5). These features enhance the resilience of the peace process compared to a "big bang" peace conference to produce a comprehensive settlement. As also occurred in El Salvador, as momentum builds the configuration of talks can be adjusted to cover ground more quickly.

A procedural framework for Afghan negotiations might take a number of forms, but the need to generate confidence among the parties, especially insurgents, suggests a few features that might be helpful. A mediation mechanism will be needed that can be flexible, that can draw upon wide-ranging resources, including some that confer Islamic legitimacy, and that can actively promote solutions around sensitive issues like representation of the parties. A negotiation structure that can gradually generate momentum and provides space to build coherence within and between the multiple incoherent actors is also needed, suggesting that at least initially a procedural accord might seek to set a sequential and punctuated agenda. Of course, practical logistics and security issues will also be crucial, but they will depend on the mediation and support arrangements discussed in the previous section and lie beyond the scope of this report.

Once a procedure is established, one might assume the natural sequence is that parties decide to negotiate, and then through negotiations determine the nature of a settlement. In fact, it is more likely that further elaboration of the terms of a settlement will help initiate the process:

> experience suggests that parties can only enter into negotiations when they have some idea of the parameters of a settlement. A framework document outlining these parameters has often been an effective element in bringing about a ceasefire and peace process.[75]

A negotiating framework may benefit from an agreement or declaration that establishes some fundamental principles of the peace process, lays out key issues for negotiation, and may even suggest the overarching structure of a peace agreement. This process does not need to go into great detail, but a broad outline can help clarify areas of common interest and key issues for negotiation, and help reassure stakeholders on some fundamental issues. In South Africa a road map between the government and the African National Congress (ANC) developed in a series of "minutes" addressing issues such as defining political offenses, releasing prisoners, suspending armed action by the ANC, leveraging national, regional, and local structures to address situations of conflict, and reaching agreement for the commencement of constitutional exploratory talks.[76]

In Afghanistan such principles might try to incorporate core concerns of different stakeholders to the conflict. For example, goals of the peace process might be stated along the following lines:

- establishing the conditions for Afghanistan's independence from any foreign interference and the removal of foreign forces of any origin from its soil;
- preventing the use of Afghanistan's territory for attacks outside the country or against the interests of other states;

- ending the suffering of the Afghan people by achieving a cease-fire, protecting civilians, and establishing means for resolving conflicts through peaceful means;
- promoting the development and well-being of Afghanistan's people through the strengthening of national unity and participation of all members of society in national life, governance in accordance with Islamic principles, and respect for the rights of men, women, and children, including access to education, economic development, justice, and protection from crime and corruption;
- providing for adequate verification acceptable to all signatories.

Without doubt, even principles such as these may prove difficult, but any agreement, even if purposely vague, may be of use in generating momentum. Additionally, it may be possible to establish key structural elements of the agreement by linking these goals together with specific means or elements of a procedural framework in some form of *x will do this when y has done that.* For example, the removal of all foreign troops may be linked to the establishment of an agreed mechanism for international verification that terrorist groups cannot operate from Afghanistan and that all Afghan groups have broken ties with Al Qaida militants.

The development of such a negotiating framework may occur through engagement by a mediator or members of a support group with leaders of the conflict parties and other stakeholders through informal channels or shuttle diplomacy. However, the process can also be prompted by unilateral proposals or declarations of basic principles by third parties or even the primary conflict actors. For example, in the Mozambique conflict, a negotiating framework grew out of unilateral declarations by the FRELIMO of "twelve principles" for direct dialogue, answered by an alternative "sixteen-point declaration" by the opposition RENAMO. These clarified both the considerable gaps that needed to be overcome procedurally, while establishing agreement on seeking a peaceful settlement.[77]

Alternatively, ideas to fill out a negotiating framework can emerge through track II or track "1.5" efforts that focus on dialogue among unofficial representatives or mid-level players before an official mediation begins, as occurred through the inter-Tajik dialogue (see box 6). A track II process can also contribute to solving a problem that has been prominent in engagement efforts in Afghanistan, namely identifying who to talk to.

It is a kind of catch-22 that a conflict actor may not have enough confidence to enter into negotiations without some assurances about the process and outcomes, yet these will not be certain until a negotiation takes place. Developing a negotiating framework provides a bridge between phases of the peace process, and developing such frameworks can help transform a passive strategy for initiating negotiations into a more active one. However, beyond the conflicting

Box 6. The Inter-Tajik Dialogue—Helping to Frame the Peace Process

The inter-Tajik dialogue was initiated in 1993 via the Dartmouth Conference, a long-standing bilateral U.S.-Russian informal negotiating mechanism, to see if "a group can be formed from within the civil conflict to design a peace process for their own country." The participants were chosen from among the second or third layer of decision makers in the conflict factions. A conflict-mapping exercise was carried out, identifying key problems for a peace process, such as allowing displaced people to return home or developing a platform to represent the dispersed opposition—later resembled by the United Tajik Opposition. The dialogue group recorded its deliberations and contributed to the perception that negotiations were viable, meeting six times before track I negotiations began.

As official UN-mediated negotiations began in April 1994, the dialogue prepared the first of eighteen memoranda that conveyed ideas and suggestions about the peace process, and members served on the official delegations. The dialogue had an impact on the measures to monitor implementation of the eventual General Agreement through a multiparty commission. While the dialogue was very focused on the conflict parties, it continued to meet after the agreement and implementation concluded, turning its attention to civil society and other issues.[1]

1. Randa M. Slim and Harold H. Saunders, "The Inter-Tajik Dialogue: From Civil War toward Civil Society," in *Politics of Compromise: The Tajikistan Peace Process*, ed. Kamoludin Abdulaev and Catherine Barnes (London: Conciliation Resources, Accord, 2001), 44–47.

parties, mechanisms in the negotiating framework for the inclusion and influence of other interests are also very important for the viability and durability of the peace process as it progresses.

The Importance of Broadening Inclusion in the Peace Process

The preceding discussion has focused on gaining the consent of the conflicting parties to negotiate. Often this process is delicate and undertaken through confidential channels focusing on the leaders or representatives of conflict parties before a formal process can begin. Experienced diplomats or conflict resolution theorists often stress the need for confidentiality during this phase, though some emphasize that a separate "public arena" still has a contribution to make by providing ideas and honing understandings of the conflict during "prenegotiations."[78]

However, there are a number of arguments for peace processes to include other actors and interests, with interrelated normative and pragmatic dimensions. The normative argument is that civilians and vulnerable groups are often the biggest victims of armed conflict, and therefore deserve to have a voice in efforts to resolve it. Leaders and groups that have pursued their aims through force should not be rewarded with the only seats at the table. Instead the peace process should try to redress the imbalance between the powerful and the powerless in conflict situations to prevent widespread "alienation" from the outcome and bolster the protection of vulnerable groups such as religious minorities and women, a particular concern in Afghanistan.[79]

However, this inclusion should not be considered simply desirable yet optional. Case studies by practitioners and increasingly systematic studies by researchers are showing that peace is more durable when peacemaking goes beyond the inclusion of conflict elites to provide structures for civil society and mass inclusion, representation, or consultation.[80] The causes of this positive impact may include wider acceptance of a settlement because groups feel they were consulted, a settlement that deals better with root causes of the conflict because it addressed a wider cross section of interests, or better preparation for peaceful politics in the future by not only privileging armed groups.[81]

In short, the way that the negotiations take place is important for the quality and durability of the outcome they are likely to produce:

> The complexity of a conflict situation may require a comprehensive response. It may require a negotiation structure capable of addressing a number of interconnected conflicts within the state or region. . . . Substantively, a comprehensive negotiation agenda deals with the multiple causes of conflict and addresses the needs and rights of the wider society as well as those of the belligerents.[82]

The impact of lack of inclusion on the resilience of a peace settlement is "a particular concern in situations where the government and the armed groups lack a strong social support base and thus neither are seen as legitimate representatives of public interests."[83] As described earlier in this report, the Afghan conflict consists of several overlapping structures, and the legitimacy of the conflict parties is a particular issue. Afghan politics over the last decade has been largely rebuilt around the leaders and networks of jihadi parties with ethnic bases, privileging them over other forces that may be legitimate. The Afghan government is widely seen as corrupt and captured by narrow interests, the insurgency is considered a tool of foreign influences, and historical jihadi ethnic leaders are losing credibility even as they stoke ethnic fears to bolster their positions.[84] Just as the Taliban do not represent majority Pashtun opinion, a wider range of social forces exists in mainstream Afghan society, and their exclusion has weakened the center ground of politics.

If the multilayered structure of the Afghan conflict is to be adequately addressed, it is imperative that a negotiation process broaden beyond combatant groups or leaders to encompass diverse representatives of other social groups and forces. Contrast this need with the approach taken in formulating the Bonn Process in 2001, since acknowledged by Lakhdar Brahimi himself as incomplete:

> The group assembled in Bonn did not represent the people of Afghanistan, either directly or indirectly. The UN veteran and former Algerian foreign minister Lakhdar Brahimi . . . repeatedly stressed that

no one would remember how unrepresentative the meeting had been
if the participants managed to fashion a process that would lead to a
legitimate and representative government.[85]

In addition, such inclusion can have the advantage of diluting the impact
of allowing the insurgency representation, and increase the palatability of negotiating with the Taliban for both internal opponents and skeptical international actors. For these reasons, any negotiating framework should include as
a fundamental principle the incorporation of a range of unarmed actors and
representatives throughout the peace process.

What should be the specific means for ensuring this kind of inclusion takes
place in Afghanistan's peace process? There is a range of experience for including noncombatants in peace processes, and the best combination should be
determined by Afghan stakeholders. However, three broad approaches are
sometimes described:

- *representative* participation through political parties or other organizations;
- *consultation*, in which parallel public processes influence and contribute
  to *negotiations*;
- *direct participation,* where civil society is able to participate in negotiations
  directly, either at local or national levels.[86]

To this list can be added debate facilitated by the media, and ratification or
legitimation of negotiated agreements through election or referendum—a more
ex post form of consultation. Each of these modes of participation may have
a role to play in Afghanistan, and Lisa Schirch has developed in some detail
examples for consideration in Afghanistan, such as a civil-society assembly as
was created in Guatemala, or local-level direct conflict resolution as in Mali and
already found in Afghanistan through diverse initiatives.[87] Whatever means
are chosen, a few key issues specific to Afghanistan need to be considered.

First, Afghan civil society must be viewed broadly, going beyond Western-
style nongovernmental, women's, or professional organizations to encompass a wide range of customary, tribal, and religious networks.[88] It should
not be expected that this "sector" can or will speak with one voice, especially on issues as controversial as an acceptable peace settlement and
the political future of the country. However, consultation with these social
forces in recent years has repeated a quite superficial and narrow pattern.
It has typically involved the convening of large assemblies under the Loya
Jirga (Grand Assembly) label to ratify policies already determined among
key domestic and international actors, and/or the opportunity to present a
list of recommendations by a nominal number of "civil-society representatives." This pattern has been repeated in both domestic fora such as the National Consultative Peace Jirga in June 2010, and international conferences

like the London conference of 2010 and the Bonn international conference in December 2011. Future arrangements need to go beyond imagining civil society as a coherent sector and structure mechanisms to represent the diversity of interests beyond the conflict parties and major political factions.

A second issue is how actively civil society should relate to the peace process. The described pattern of consultation has meant that civil society in Afghanistan is cast in a passive or reactive role, having to respond to political steps and developments that are determined without its input. Given the fitful progress of engagement with the insurgency, and doubts about the rapid development of a regional atmosphere more conducive to progress, is there scope for civil-society actors to take a more active role in framing a potential peace process, as women's networks did in Liberia in 2003 (see box 7)?

This approach implies a considerably more active role for civil society than the current one of hoping to be recipients of commitments that the conflict parties will widen a future negotiation to noncombatant representatives:

> If civil society organizations and a broader proportion of the overall public are sufficiently prepared to engage in peacemaking, it can both create a climate conducive to negotiations and help to ensure that the social infrastructure is developed for their voices to be heard at formal peace talks.[89]

What structures should be adopted to advocate for representation? Should civil society seek to create broad alliances of noncombatants to advocate for civilian representation in a peace process, or pursue specific issue-based agendas, for example, in focusing on issues related to women specifically or victims of violence?

Finally, how can these efforts be supported? Just as initiation of a peace process may be encouraged by support to conflict parties, it should be asked what can be done for noncombatants and civil society in their efforts to overcome the disadvantages of their nongovernmental and pacific status to play meaningful roles. Such support may be material, but it can also be moral through consistent assertion of the need for broad participation beyond the conflict parties, and institutional through promotion and support of new mechanisms and reforms that foster ongoing participation.

Progress toward mechanisms for deliberation, debate, and the emergence of an active peace agenda among civil society should also translate to a broader conception of power sharing than the division of spoils or influence among the current government and the insurgents. In this sense, the shape of the negotiation process is in fact intimately connected to the forms of power sharing that emerge from it:

> The negotiations at the center of most war-to-peace transitions have profound implications for the political settlement and even the state itself. . . . A process that includes formerly excluded groups can lead to a more inclusive and therefore resilient settlement in the future.[90]

Box 7. Liberia—Women Take the Lead in the Peace Process

In Liberia, women's organizations and individual women, supported by the Women in Peacebuilding Network (WIPNET) and the Mano River Women's Peace Network (MARWOPNET), played an active role in pushing for peace at various points in the conflict. A defining moment for WIPNET's inclusion occurred when President Charles Taylor challenged its members to find the rebel leaders. The women funded a small delegation to Sierra Leone and arranged meetings between Taylor and the rebel leaders, earning them a reputation as objective intermediaries. In 2003, the Women of Liberia Mass Action for Peace Campaign engaged rebels by traveling all over the country.

MARWOPNET mediated a cease-fire between President Taylor and Liberia's rebels, the Liberians United for Democracy (LURD) and the Movement for Democracy in Liberia (MODEL). As a result, the Economic Community of West African States (ECOWAS), which sponsored subsequent peace negotiations, officially invited MARWOPNET to participate. It was the only women's group that received accreditation for the talks, and with the Liberian Bar Association and the Inter-Religious Council for Liberia was among the civil-society groups and political parties that signed the agreement. 2011 Nobel Laureate Leymah Gbowee also led a delegation of Liberian women to Ghana to continue to apply pressure on the warring factions during the peace process. They monitored the talks and staged a silent protest outside the presidential palace in Accra. When the talks stalled, the women closed the exits, refusing to let the negotiators out until progress was made.

After the Accra 2003 Comprehensive Peace Agreement (CPA) was signed, WIPNET shifted its focus from mediation to implementation. WIPNET demystified the peace agreement and empowered civil society to monitor its implementation by disseminating clear information to the Liberian public and women in particular.[1]

---

1. UN Women, "Case Study: Liberia," http://progress.unwomen.org/2011/07/case-study-liberia/; Desirée Nilsson, *Crafting a Secure Peace: Evaluating Liberia's Comprehensive Peace Agreement 2003* (Uppsala: Uppsala University, Department of Peace and Conflict Research, 2009), 22.

Transitional Arrangements and Implementation Challenges

A key dimension of any negotiated settlement to the Afghan conflict will be a set of transitional arrangements to govern the period between the signing of a peace settlement, a cease-fire, and the entry into force of more permanent institutions for the management of conflict. These interim arrangements are important because they can influence actors' commitment to the peace. They may take many forms, make limited or more dramatic alterations to the current institutional order, and involve different actors during the implementation period. This includes civil-society organizations, which may be able to exercise considerable influence, as well as third parties called upon to play a role in implementing these transitional arrangements. Finally, actors must keep in mind that the transitional arrangements they select create a political order that shapes long-term institutional choices and the nature of the peace that will be consolidated.

When deciding on transitional arrangements, it is important to consider the functions of the arrangements and the particular transition issues they must address. Typically, it is during this period that "war-torn societies initiate the lengthy struggle to construct legitimate political institutions, demobilize soldiers and resettle displaced populations, come to terms with past human-rights abuses and institutionalize rule of law, and begin moving their economies from relief to development."[91] The transition period in Afghanistan will be particularly sensitive given the failure to complete these tasks in the preceding decade despite progress in many areas. Based in part on the conflict analysis earlier in this report, four functions in particular may stand out for transitional arrangements in an Afghan peace process:

- overcoming mistrust and insecurity among the parties;
- addressing governance drivers of the conflict;
- defining the political order, including balancing the relationships among the conflict parties and other stakeholders during the transition;
- setting the role of third parties in verification and providing resilience against challenges and setbacks.[92]

Overcoming Security Dilemmas

Before a sustainable peace can be constructed, the parties to the conflict and the Afghan population must feel more secure. In the absence of such a sense of security, actors' commitment to the peace process will rapidly erode. However, the range of potential spoilers and the transition away from the security umbrella provided by ISAF will present acute challenges during the interim period of any Afghan peace process. In the words of one thorough assessment,

> The most difficult challenge confronting any peace process in Afghanistan will be establishing and sustaining, despite the many potential spoilers, a minimum of law and order going into and lasting throughout the resultant political transition. It will be important— and difficult—both for the parties to an accord and for international peacekeepers to identify deliberate violations of cease-fires that occur against the country's high level of background violence.[93]

This makes it imperative to achieve real security gains during the transitional period. Although minimizing the role that violence plays in society will take time, requiring as it does the building of the rule of law, reform of the security sector, and changes in political culture, significant steps toward providing for the security of conflict actors and the population can be taken during the transitional period.

In light of the security dilemma, one of the most difficult steps for adversaries to take during the transition period is to demobilize their forces.[94] This step is a critical one, though, in the process of establishing an increased sense of security for the population and for the demilitarization of politics. As Afghans well know, having already experienced an internationally led disarmament, demobilization, and reintegration (DDR) program (the Afghan New Beginnings Program), long-term peace is not possible in the absence of a commitment to demobilization by powerful actors who benefit from armed conflict. It is also not possible with politicians who are determined to use the demobilization process to fulfill their own goals and distracted international actors who are not, for whatever reasons, fully committed to demobilization.[95] Fortunately, there is a range of transitional arrangements that can lay the groundwork for a successful DDR program and help foster security in the post-conflict environment.

Interim security arrangements can be conceptualized along a continuum, with the most basic and (supposedly) easiest-to-agree-upon options appearing at one end and the more politically and logistically difficult measures at the other. Among the first tasks that occur once a cease-fire has been agreed are a disengagement of forces and the disclosure by contending factions of their military dispositions. Because these processes will require some form of verification, decisions regarding the interim institution that is to be charged with that responsibility should already have been made. Formerly warring groups can work together to jointly monitor a cease-fire, as was done in Mozambique, combine with civil-society actors to monitor a cease-fire, as in the Local Monitoring Teams used in the Philippines, or rely on a third party to perform that function, as in the many examples of UN peacekeeping or military observation.[96] Some combination may be needed in Afghanistan, as well as the ability eventually to confirm a break with Al Qaida and other outside terrorist organizations.

A number of arrangements can help provide for the security of contending factions during the period following a cease-fire and before demobilization and disarmament take place. One of these is buffer or confidence zones, areas patrolled by a neutral force designed to keep rivals apart. This mechanism was employed in Côte d'Ivoire, where 11,000 French troops and UN peacekeepers separated rebel and government forces across a 600-kilometer-long buffer zone. Alternately, fighting forces can be assigned to cantonment areas agreed among the parties, with arrangements for the storing and management of arms. The 2006 peace agreement in Nepal, for example, agreed to United Nations assistance to monitor "the confinement of Maoist army combatants and their weapons within designated cantonment areas and monitor the Nepal Army (NA) to ensure that it remains in its barracks and its weapons are not used against any side."[97] Similar arrangements were used

Box 8. Selected Interim Security Institutions and Cases

Cease-fire: including cessation of hostilities and disengagement of forces; disclosure of military disposition; verification
Buffer zones (Côte d'Ivoire)
Cantonment of troops (El Salvador; Burundi; Nepal)
Storage and management of arms (Nepal; Northern Ireland)
DDR (Mozambique; Sierra Leone)
CIVPOL (East Timor; Kosovo)
Military observers (Guatemala; Cyprus; Macedonia)
Peacekeeping forces (Liberia; Democratic Republic of Congo; Timor-Leste)

to contain insurgents and military forces in El Salvador while confidence was built in the political process.

Not all of the arrangements will be suitable for use in every conflict environment (see box 8). If successfully implemented, cantonment arrangements in particular can serve to provide not only for the security of the rival fighting groups but also for populations that have borne much of the brunt of armed violence, and may cope better with the intermixing of rival forces implied by asymmetric warfare in Afghanistan. It may also be particularly useful to consider monitoring models that put weapons "beyond the use" of demobilizing factions in order to avoid the cultural and security implications inherent in "laying down" or "surrendering" arms to the government. In addition, some arrangements are more complex and costly and require considerable commitment of third parties, including military observers (as in Guatemala, Cyprus, and Macedonia) or UN or other peacekeeping forces. United Nations Civilian Police (CIVPOL) have also been used widely, but typically in smaller peacebuilding cases such as Kosovo.

The availability and capacity of third-party options to implement or monitor the security provisions of an Afghan peace agreement will have to be considered carefully given the current trend to reduce international involvement in Afghanistan, the inherent risks due to spoilers, and the demands presented by the terrain. It may be that joint monitoring of security provisions by the Afghan parties themselves, preferably with civilian participation via civil society or institutions such as the Afghanistan Independent Human Rights Commission (AIHRC), will be needed, and international monitoring might be focused on areas of particular concern, such as borders.

More generally, civil-society representatives should have an important role in the design and implementation of security-related measures. As actors who have been affected by the conflict, they wield influence within communities that can shape local commitment to security initiatives, including the reintegration of ex-combatants into society.[98]

Addressing State Weakness and Governance

Second, the transitional arrangements should confront sources of state weakness and governance issues that have been identified as key drivers of the conflict. In Afghanistan these issues include a perception that the state has been captured or divided among a small elite, high levels of corruption, and the inability of the state to provide security to the general population.[99] Although it is unlikely that these problems can be wholly resolved during the transition period, some progress on such issues must be achieved in order to shore up commitment to the peace process. In addition, unless the state becomes effective enough to perform key functions once third-party actors have departed the scene, long-run peace is unlikely to prevail. These arrangements may also need to provide for some alterations to the political order and the distribution of decision-making power.

Specialized arrangements can be designed to deal with governance during the transitional period. In Liberia, several innovative interim institutions were established to address serious government shortcomings in terms of capacity, corruption, and accountability that had contributed to the conflict. These institutions included an independent Governance Reform Commission to recommend public administration, decentralization, and anticorruption reforms, and an intrusive joint international-Liberian management and monitoring system for key economic governance tasks (see box 9).

Similar institutions in Afghanistan have been created to address some key governance challenges. However, unlike the Liberian Governance Reform Commission, the leadership of Afghanistan's nominally independent Independent Administrative Reform and Civil Service Commission (IARCSC) and its Independent Directorate of Local Governance (IDLG) are appointed by the president alone, and do not enjoy financial or operational autonomy or a clear mandate. The Afghanistan Reconstruction Trust Fund (ARTF) and related public financial management reforms also involve joint oversight by international institutions and the host government. They have been remarkably successful in putting in place a sound core public financial management system for resources channeled to the national budget or national programs, but this system is not comprehensive as huge flows of development assistance remain outside it.[100] Consideration might be given to measures with greater independence or more comprehensive buy-in by partners to address governance challenges more effectively.

In contrast to technocratic arrangements that rely on third-party actors or independent commissions, interim institutions can also place an emphasis on process and encourage joint decision making to create resilience during implementation. Institutions constructed on the basis of "collaborative decision-making, transparency, and confidence-building" have proved

Box 9. Liberia—Interim Arrangements for Addressing Governance Problems

The site of brutal civil wars in 1989–1996 and 2000–2003, Liberia has suffered decades of corrupt, inefficient, weak, and unaccountable government. A Governance Reform Commission (GRC) was created by the August 2003 Accra Comprehensive Peace Agreement to "promote the principles of good governance" by developing public sector reforms, improving decentralization and participation, supporting regional balance, quality, and integrity in appointments, and ensuring transparency and accountability by acting as a public ombudsperson.[1] The GRC wrote anticorruption legislation and a code of conduct for government employees, and designed decentralization reforms. The commissioners were appointed by the transitional government after confirmation by the transitional legislature: prior to her 2005 election to the presidency, Nobel Laureate Ellen Johnson-Sirleaf served as chair. In 2007, the Liberian government transformed the GRC into a permanent, financially and operationally autonomous Governance Commission to "promote good governance by advising, designing, and formulating appropriate policies and institutional arrangements and frameworks . . . and promoting integrity at all levels of society and within every public and private institution."[2]

Concerned about the effects of corruption and mismanagement of public finances on the prospects for stable peace in Liberia, the country's international partners—the United Nations, the World Bank, the International Monetary Fund, the European Community/European Union, Ghana, Nigeria, the United States, ECOWAS, and the African Union—initiated the Governance and Economic Management Assistance Program (GEMAP). GEMAP, signed by the National Transitional Government of Liberia (NTGL) in 2005, targeted management and accountability of public finance in revenue collection, expenditure controls, and government procurement and concession practices. It included a set of international controls, including placing international experts with co-signature authority in selected government ministries, agencies, and state-owned enterprises; international management contracts for selected institutions; and an international administrator in the Central Bank. GEMAP provided for the establishment of an Anti-Corruption Commission to enforce the law and a steering committee, chaired by the head of state with a representative of Liberia's international partners as deputy, to oversee implementation.[3]

---

1. Republic of Liberia Governance Reform Commission, "First Quarterly Report," June 30, 2004, http://codexijoma.ws/gvn/First_Progress_Report_of_GRC.html.
2. Government of the Republic of Liberia, "An Act of the Legislature to Establish the Governance Comission," Section 3.1, August 2007.
3. Renata Dwan and Laura Bailey, "Liberia's Governance and Economic Management Assistance Program (GEMAP)" (joint review by the Department of Peacekeeping Operations' Peacekeeping Best Practices Section and the World Bank's Fragile States Group, May 2006), www.peacekeepingbestpractices.unlb.org/PBPS/Library/DPKO-WB%20joint%20review%20of%20GEMAP%20FINAL.pdf.

effective in countries ranging from El Salvador to Mozambique.[101] Widening participation in governance institutions by structuring them to include representatives of various groups, including civil society, might also help to address "negative-sum" perceptions regarding state capture and introduce more checks and balances.[102]

Civil-society organizations and third-party actors have been involved in post-conflict transition settings in a variety of ways. They may do this through actual participation in interim arrangements or by acting as "a pressure group and a monitor of the implementation of agreement provisions."[103] The extent of the impact that civil-society groups are able to have during the transition period ultimately will depend on how well organized they are, their ability to propose and assess policy options, the resources they command, and the extent to which opportunities are structured for them to participate in the transition process.[104] Such structures for inclusion will form an important part of defining the interim political order.

Establishing the Nature of the Interim Political Order

The transitional arrangements established during the unsettled period following the end of a civil war act as a bridge between an environment in which violence is used as a means of settling conflicts and one in which legitimate and established institutions become the basis for managing conflict. By creating "precedents, expectations, and patterns of behavior," the interim institutions that are put into place during this period can shape the manner in which politics will function in the longer term.[105] These interim arrangements thus constitute an important first step in the process of establishing a post-conflict political order. The types of interim arrangements that may be put in place during this period can vary in two broad respects:

- the extent to which they preserve the government in power or confer some degree of power on previously excluded groups through power sharing;
- the extent to which they retain the institutions of the state or reform them or create new institutions designed to constrain the government's power.

Based on these factors, it is possible to distinguish among three general types of transitional political orders—those that are *status quo*—oriented, those that are *hybrid* in nature, and those that are *power sharing*.

Generally speaking, interim political orders that are *status quo*–oriented resemble the political order that was in place prior to the settlement that ended the fighting. In these instances, settlements do not call for a transitional government. Rather, the government in power at the time of the settlement remains in office. Status quo interim political orders also tend to be ones where few or no reforms take place to constrain the government's power. Finally, although this type of political order may allocate some type of influence to previously excluded groups or allow for their future participation in politics, the power(s) granted are not likely to give those groups any real ability to hold the government to the commitments it made as part of the settlement. Status quo interim political orders tend to be the product of negotiated truces rather than fully negotiated settlements of intrastate conflict.[106] Moldova and Morocco serve as examples of this type of interim political order. In the case of Moldova, although the 1992 cease-fire agreement did create a tripartite Joint Control Commission to work on an agreement to prevent future violence, it also deferred issues regarding the Transdniestrian region's status to a future political settlement. Morocco's 1991 Settlement Plan put off any real type of political change by calling for a referendum on Saharawi self-determination that has yet to be held.

At the opposite end of the spectrum, purely *power-sharing* peace settlements call for a transitional government to be established that includes opposition groups at the political center. In the case of these interim political orders, governments of national unity see contending groups share—or divide—power. Power can be distributed among groups politically, with cabinet seats being allocated to different factions, militarily (groups integrate their military forces during the transition period), or based on the division of economic or territorial spoils. During the Cambodian transitional period, state sovereignty was vested in a twelve-member Supreme National Council whose seats were divided between the incumbent governing party, the political opposition, and the insurgents. However, the incumbents' retention of the public administration and military apparatus allowed them to leverage a dominant position after the elections at the transition's end.

In between these extremes, a wide range of *hybrid* interim political orders are possible that combine some degree of continuity with power sharing and reform of institutions. Such combinations may be able to balance a need for stability with the demands of a negotiation for change in sensitive situations such as the multipolar Afghan context. Whether or not a transitional government is put into place, the settlements associated with this type of interim political order generally call for reforms that create institutions or rules that can constrain the government. Liberia and El Salvador offer two contrasting examples of hybrid political orders. The Liberian settlement established power sharing within the framework of an interim government with the added participation of civilian political parties and civil society (see box 10).

In contrast, the Salvadoran settlement maintained the constitutional framework and incumbent government during the transition, retaining considerable continuity and forcing the insurgents to gain access through competing within a democratic framework. However, it also introduced significant reforms that constrained the regime and gave both the insurgents and members of political and civil society a role in determining the nature of key institutions, such as the security organs and the electoral system (see box 11).

Given the concern over the protection of elements of the constitutional framework and international acceptance of the current government, the right combination of continuity, power sharing, and reform will be key to including

Box 10. Liberia—Hybrid Political Order with an Interim Government

Liberia's 2003 CPA established an interim government that combined power sharing by the warring parties with the inclusion of political parties and civil-society representatives at the political center through two transitional institutions. The CPA established the NTGL and the NTLA. The transitional government was headed by a chairman and a vice-chairman from political parties or civil society, and the twenty-one ministries were divided among the government and two armed factions (LURD and MODEL), political parties, and civil society. The warring factions each received five ministries, with the remaining six going to the political parties and civil society.

Seats in the Transitional National Assembly were also distributed in an inclusive manner with the three warring parties—the government of Liberia, LURD, and MODEL—each receiving twelve seats, political parties getting eighteen seats, civil society and interest groups taking seven seats, and each of Liberia's fifteen counties being assigned one seat. Other institutional reforms supported the more consensual politics based on these inclusive power-sharing bodies.[1]

1. Nilsson, *Crafting a Secure Peace.*

but also constraining armed groups in general, and the Taliban in particular, in an Afghan peace settlement. A judicious combination of retaining the broad features of the constitution and government, but addressing significant reforms that provide both insurgent leaders and unarmed political and civil actors real influence and control over important decisions, such as security forces and the electoral system, may hold the best chance of managing a delicate transition.

Third-Party Roles in Verification and Creating Resilience

The signing of an agreement marks the beginning of new challenges, and the line between settlement and implementation may become blurred as unexpected events, new issues, questions, and disagreements arise. In Afghanistan the complexity of the conflict drivers, the multiplicity of actors and interests, and the prevalence of spoilers mean that setbacks and unforeseen challenges will be inevitable. Transitional arrangements will be needed that provide means for actors to consult with one another regarding issues that were not addressed during the process of negotiating the settlement and to contend with problems or setbacks that arise during the settlement implementation process. Provisions for inclusion and consultation among the conflict parties are key to providing this resilience, but they will also need to be supported by outsiders.

Third-party actors—states, coalitions of states, regional and international organizations, and NGOs—may play a relatively limited or an extensive and even intrusive role during the post-conflict transition process. Third parties have in some instances limited themselves to providing oversight during the transitional period, while in others they have committed

Box 11. El Salvador—Hybrid Political Order with Continuity and Reform

El Salvador's peace settlement produced a hybrid interim political order. The country's 1992 settlement retained the constitutional framework and did not call for an interim government before the national elections in 1994, instead allowing the incumbent government to remain. However, it did mandate a number of reforms that constrained the power of the government and began to address key causes of the conflict.

These reforms included establishing a civilian commission to purge the officer corps of human rights violators, reducing the size of the army and disbanding the national police, treasury police, and national guard. In addition, it set up a National Commission for the Consolidation of the Peace (COPAZ)—including two government representatives, two representatives of the insurgent FMLN, and two representatives of other political parties in the legislative assembly—to monitor the implementation of the peace settlement. COPAZ, with its multi-party membership, was given key responsibilities that affected all the parties during the transitional period, such as drafting a revised electoral law, appointing the Supreme Electoral Tribunal, and recommending leadership of a new military academy.[1]

---

1. "The New York Agreement," Section I. Text available in United Nations Department of Public Information, *The United Nations and El Salvador, 1990–1995* (United Nations, 1995), 159.

personnel to perform active roles in the political, security, and economic realms. For example, the OIC performed a narrow oversight function for the 1996 peace agreement signed by the government of the Philippines and the Moro National Liberation Front, while by far the most intrusive type of third-party involvement—and thus one of the least frequently employed—is the international trusteeship model seen in Bosnia and Herzegovina.

The impact that third-party involvement in transitional arrangements has on the duration and shape of the peace is likely to depend on a number of factors, including the nature of the conflict, the number and identity of the third parties that play a role, and the level of resources these parties commit. Evidence indicates that the weaker the capacity of the post-conflict state, the more important international assistance during the transition stage is likely to be in helping to build the basis for a durable peace.[107] Third-party commitments in relatively limited conflicts and small states such as Sierra Leone and Timor Leste have been dramatic indeed.

However, there are limits to international involvement based on third-party interests and commitment and the complexity of the recipient post-conflict milieu. The risks of very intrusive approaches are considerable, particularly in large and complex environments such as Afghanistan. Intensive international involvement can crowd out domestic capacity and create a form of unsustainable rentier state, with external resources contributing to corruption and conflict through the distortion of heavy aid economies.[108] Deep involvement in implementation can reduce the ability of third parties to retain a neutral role in mediating disputes as they arise. This problem has arguably occurred with the United Nations Assistance Mission in Afghanistan (UNAMA) as its mandate to support the Afghan government has increasingly conflicted with the need for good offices in the country. The United Nations Mission in El Salvador (ONUSAL) was a small, limited verification mission, but this hands-off orientation meant the United Nations was able to retain sufficient credibility with all parties to mediate several serious disputes during settlement implementation regarding cantonment, demobilization and disarmament, and land transfers that could have derailed the peace process.[109]

Of course, the final function of transitional arrangements in a peace settlement must be an agreed manner to transition to a longer-term set of institutions. This process often centers on elections, the ratification of a new constitution, or some other legitimating exercise such as a referendum. Indeed, the Bonn Process in Afghanistan was structured in such a way. Research suggests that most Afghans, and surprisingly even some active Taliban commanders, continue to support using elections to choose who governs Afghanistan, though concerns about foreign imposition of these mechanisms or the corruption of the process are also widespread. Some Afghan stakeholders still point to the Emergency and Constitutional Loya Jirgas held during the Bonn Process as legitimate forms of representation due to their inclusion of representatives from throughout the country, but they also view their outcomes as having been manipulated and hijacked by foreigners and leaders of armed factions.[110] A key question for an Afghan peace process, given the political orientation of some parties and recent negative experience with elections, will be the acceptance across parties of elections, and if so, under what reform circumstances.

Beyond Power Sharing: Institutional Arrangements for the Long Term

Transitional and implementation arrangements can be considered successful if they solidify actors' commitment to the peace during the uncertain period following the end of armed conflict. These arrangements do not provide a means for consolidating the peace, however:

> If negotiations are conceived only as a means to reach agreement on ending a war, too often the results are a recycling of power within the same basic structures leaving the underlying causes largely untouched. . . . A peace process can present an opportunity that can be seized to develop a more peaceful future by addressing the issues generating conflict, reforming state institutions and key policies, as well as forging a sound basis for future relationships between those involved in the conflict.[111]

Divided societies that have experienced armed conflict face critical choices regarding the institutions they will rely upon in order to peacefully manage conflict. Rules or institutions regarding the nature and distribution of decision-making rights within the state must be agreed if a functioning state is to re-emerge. Those rules must provide the state with sufficient power to establish and maintain domestic order, enforce rules for the management of conflict, and make decisions regarding the distribution of resources.

Yet it is precisely this power that concerns groups in conflict. What if a rival faction comes to rule the state? How can a group ensure that its rival will not use its control of political power, coercive force, and economic resources to benefit some and against others?[112] These concerns are particularly pronounced in Afghanistan, where a history of contests over central power and widespread perceptions that the state is captured are drivers of conflict. While enabling governance, institutions must not threaten the survival of any of the key parties to the conflict. One type of institutional arrangement that has been used to bridge these contending interests is political power sharing among contending factions. Sometimes power sharing is used to describe measures such as the division of cabinet posts or the ceding of territory among rival groups. As noted in the introduction, the prospect of this kind of division of spoils among conflict leaders is the source of considerable opposition to a peace process among Afghan political and social forces. Indeed, such a crude form of power sharing may present serious problems.

First, to the extent that peace agreements distribute state power among contending groups based on their military strength, power-sharing arrangements prevent weak or noncombatant parties from participating in government. Excluding weak armed groups can produce spoilers, and excluding nonarmed actors such as civil society or nonmilitarized political parties neglects the interests of stakeholders not represented by armed groups. Power sharing may thus limit representation in government to extremists at the expense of moderates, and leave the elites least likely to uphold norms of nonviolent bargaining and conflict resolution in control of the state.[113] The continued influence of the leaders of Afghan mujahedin factions in central or provincial government provides a salient example of this form of politics. A final concern is that the patronage networks connected to such leaders will have to share a potentially decreasing resource pool as transition proceeds, worsening the destabilizing implications of simply expanding inclusion in the current patronage setup to new armed parties.

However, power sharing can be seen more broadly than as the inclusion of war leaders in executive power. While definitions vary in the academic literature, power sharing is fundamentally about the distribution of decision-making rights among different political actors, especially when "designed to marry principles of democracy with the need for conflict management in deeply divided societies."[114] The concept often encompasses constitutional forms that give conflicting groups a stake in government through means such as coalition government, territorial autonomy, and minority rights. Some widen the idea to include procedures (such as electoral systems that encourage candidates to appeal across group lines) that aim to integrate conflicting groups.[115]

Many current conceptions of power sharing, particularly as it relates to peace processes, emphasize any of a wide range of institutions that distribute decision-making powers among groups in the society rather than concentrating powers in a narrow elite or single party.[116] Rigorous studies of a large number of conflicts have correlated such institutions with successful conflict settlement and more durable post-conflict peace.[117] Recently two important findings in research on power sharing and conflict have been emerging. One is that the diversity of power-sharing configurations allows that combinations of more than one power-sharing institution can be used to reinforce each other and in turn greatly prolong peace.[118] A second trend—discussed earlier—is the finding that peace is more durable when peacemaking and the resultant power-sharing institutions foster civil society inclusion, representation, or consultation.

Many analyses already recognize that an Afghan peace process must go beyond a narrow deal between the government and Taliban to encourage an "enlarged coalition government" on the one hand, or more "comprehensive" arrangements for social groups outside the main combatant factions.[119] This also means going beyond the narrow and misplaced application of the term "reconciliation" to describe such a narrow negotiation between the Afghan government, the Taliban, and potentially Pakistan.[120] In addition, any arrangements in an Afghan peace process should aim to reduce the current great distance between the formal institutions that are found in the constitution and political sphere, and the informal practices that currently shape decision-making through negotiations among a range of patronage networks, outside or alongside the channels of institutionalized politics. The concentration of formal powers in the presidency is a key facilitating condition creating this distance.

But specifically what means can be used to distribute decision-making powers beyond sharing power in the executive? This section describes how a combination of *power-sharing, power-dividing, power-creating,* and *power-diffusing* mechanisms can provide groups within divided societies with assurances that they will not be permanently excluded from state power and resources, or shut out of the policymaking process. In addition, such mechanisms can distribute decision-making powers and rights across a number of different dimensions of state power—that is, *political, military, territorial,* and *economic.* Building on this diversity, it is possible to get beyond the idea (and fears) of a political power-sharing arrangement among a narrow elite of war leaders to more varied and multidimensional solutions.[121] Not all of these will be equally well suited to the

Afghan context. Nevertheless, knowledge of the array of institutional options that exists as well as the different types of conflicts in which these institutions have been employed can help actors to design those arrangements that are most suitable given the parameters of the Afghan conflict.

Dimensions of State Power

State power may be viewed as having political, military, territorial, and economic dimensions. As any one of these can add to a conflict party's power, potentially to the detriment of other groups, rules (that is to say, institutions) regulating the exercise of power across each of these dimensions are of interest to groups in divided societies. However, each of these dimensions of state power is also divisible in ways that are different from the others, meaning it is possible to create institutions that impede any single group from exercising overall control over too many dimensions of state power.

The political dimension. The political dimension encompasses the exercise of power by actors at the political center via their control of decision-making and/ or agenda-setting processes. Groups in divided societies are concerned that politics could become a zero-sum game in which one group seizes control of the government and uses it to dominate or marginalize other groups. Power at the political center is generally allocated via one of three means—*elections, executive appointments,* and *administrative appointments.*

The military dimension. Military power, particularly the extent of the state monopoly on the legitimate means of violence, is a central dimension of state power. Who controls the military and other state security forces in the aftermath of armed conflict is of particular concern to groups in a divided society. Leaders and followers fear that, once they disarm, those who control the state's coercive forces may use them to eliminate rival groups or damage their interests in some other way. Citizens and civil-society actors not represented by armed groups also have reason to fear this dimension of state power in the absence of checks on those who control the military levers of the state.

The economic dimension. The economic dimension of state power centers on the control and use of economic assets under the jurisdiction of the state. One form this may take is state ownership or control of subsoil resources. States may have the power to distort or limit market competition or define and alter property rights to direct resources and economic opportunities to favored groups. Although fostering distributive justice among groups may be necessary for long-term peace and development, groups in divided societies are likely to have a more immediate concern—ensuring that control of the state's economic power does not provide some group with the means to exclude or threaten rivals—for example, by financing a return to armed conflict.

The territorial dimension. This dimension of state power focuses on the exercise of political and administrative control over subnational units of the national territory. Political influence can be divided among different levels of government through territorially based decentralization (i.e., federalism, regional autonomy, or more modest forms of political decentralization) that provides groups with some degree of power and autonomy vis-à-vis the central government through locating certain kinds of decision making at subnational levels.

One may distinguish between power-sharing, power-dividing, power-creating, and power-diffusing mechanisms for distributing decision-making powers within the state. When combined with the four different dimensions of state power, this yields a wide variety of potential institutional arrangements. The most significant combinations are discussed next.

Power Sharing

Power-sharing mechanisms balance state power among former adversaries by including multiple elites in decision making. Power sharing can occur along political, military, and economic dimensions of state power.

Political power sharing.[122] When groups feel threatened by majority rule, political power sharing can be designed to provide them with some guarantee of access to political power. Political power-sharing institutions rely on proportional strategies that share political power on the basis of some demographic (e.g., ethnicity or race) or political (e.g., party affiliation) principle. Groups are guaranteed representation within governing institutions by virtue of their group affiliation. The institutions at the heart of a proportional strategy for distributing political power are electoral proportional representation, administrative proportional representation, and proportional representation in the executive branch.

Electoral proportional representation uses systems that tend to lower the level of voter support a candidate or party must achieve to gain political office, decreasing the intensity of political competition and minimizing the disparity between a party's share of votes and the number of parliamentary seats it occupies. Administrative proportional representation guarantees groups' access to influence through positions on courts, commissions, the civil or foreign services, and other offices. Finally, proportional representation in the executive branch ensures groups a voice in the innermost circle of political power by appointing representatives to cabinet positions.

Political power sharing may utilize just one of these types of institutions or some combination of two or three of them. *Consociationalism* is a form of political power sharing using several proportional measures to guarantee ethnic, religious, or cultural groups representation at the political center. These

Box 12. Burundi—Consociational Power Sharing in an Ethnically Divided Society

Burundi has experienced several ethnically based civil wars between the dominant Tutsi minority and the Hutu majority since the country became independent in 1961. The country's most recent conflict, which began in 1993, ended with agreements signed in 2000, 2003, and 2006 calling for Tutsis and Hutus to share power at the political center. This is done within the executive branch by having the president assisted by two vice presidents who must be a Hutu and a Tutsi. In addition, the government is to include 60 percent Hutu and 40 percent Tutsi in its cabinet.

Within the legislative branch, Hutu and Tutsi representation is to hold at the same proportion. The Senate is to consist of an equal number of Hutu and Tutsi representatives. Should elections fail to produce the required quota, the constitution allows "the rectification of the imbalances through the co-optation mechanism provided by the electoral code" (Article 164). Finally, Burundi's postwar constitution also calls for political power sharing at the communal level, with no more than 67 percent of the country's mayors to belong to either the Tutsi or the Hutu group.[1]

1. René Lemarchand, "Consociationalism and Power-Sharing in Africa: Rwanda, Burundi, and the Democratic Republic of the Congo," *African Affairs* 106, no. 422 (2006): 8.

measures include coalition cabinets in which executive power is shared among the parties, equality of power among ministers, and electoral proportional representation.[123] These features aim to produce a mutual veto among groups over issues of mutual concern such as economic policy, and control by a single group over issues of concern to the group, such as cultural affairs. Consociationalism also calls for other measures such as balance of power between the executive and the legislature that might be classified as power dividing rather than power sharing.

While consociationalism can be an effective way of enabling deeply divided societies to manage ethnic or other group differences, it also broadly defines politics according to those differences, and may introduce rigidity over the long term, as shown by the provisions in Burundi or Lebanon's consociational pacts (see boxes 12 and 13).

Military power sharing. To allay adversaries' concerns about a rival group's ability to use the state's security forces to threaten their interests, the state's coercive forces must somehow be neutralized or balanced. One way to achieve this is through military power sharing. Military power sharing calls for integrating rival factions' armed forces and reconstituting them as the state's security forces. This can be done either on the basis of some proportional formula representative of the size of the armed factions or on the basis of a strict balance in troop numbers among the contending parties. A military

Box 13. Lebanon—Religious Consociationalism

Lebanon's Ta'if Accord, signed in 1989 as a means of ending the country's fifteen-year civil war, is a reformulation of a previous conflict management agreement, the National Pact of 1943. Both agreements are organized along religious confessional lines. Sectarian proportionality is still a characteristic of the agreement, but the proportion of Muslim to Christian legislators and officials has been increased to 50/50. The president of the republic remains a Maronite Christian, but his powers have been substantially reduced. The prime minister remains a Sunni Muslim, but the powers of the Council of Ministers, which he chairs, have been increased. The office of president of the Chamber of Deputies still goes to a Shiite, but his term is increased from one year to four, as is his influence. The power of the chamber has been increased by the elimination of the old provision allowing the executive to pass "urgent" legislation without parliamentary involvement. Finally, the Ta'if Accord calls for a gradual phasing out of political sectarianism.[1]

1. Michael C. Hudson, "Lebanon after Ta'if: Another Reform Opportunity Lost?" *Arab Studies Quarterly* (1999).

power-sharing arrangement has been put into effect in Burundi, where the state's security forces are to include equal numbers of Hutus and Tutsis.

Economic power sharing. Economic power sharing attempts to mitigate contending groups' concerns regarding state control of resources. Rules distribute wealth and income on some group basis, or at least prevent any one group from dominating economic resources. Economic power-sharing institutions may call for the state to allocate some specific pattern of resources to disadvantaged groups or to direct economic assets toward groups on the basis of geographic location. Sudan's 2005 Comprehensive Peace Agreement roughly divides net revenue from oil between North and South Sudan.[124]

Power-sharing institutions in general are based on the logic that an assigned part of the influence available in a given domain should be allocated to contending factions on some group basis. This allocation is assumed to encourage a sense of mutual security. However, there are other ways to distribute such influence that may also be able to secure the assent of competing groups.

Power Dividing

Power-dividing institutions distribute decision-making powers by providing checks and balances that avoid the concentration of power within any single part of the government, thereby preventing one actor from dominating decision making within a particular dimension of power.

Political power dividing. Political power-dividing institutions allocate decision-making powers horizontally among the different branches of the government.

Box 14. Rwanda—Decentralization as a Power-Dividing Process

The Rwandan decentralization policy notes that decentralization is part of the "principle of power-sharing as expressed in the Arusha Peace Accord between the Government of the Rwandan Republic and Rwandan Patriotic Front. Up to now power-sharing has only been seen among the political elite at Parliament and Executive levels. The decentralization policy will reinforce power-sharing by ensuring that the Rwandese people themselves are empowered to shape their political, economic, and social destiny."[1] Decentralization has enabled districts and communities to determine their leadership through democratic elections, institutionalized participatory development planning, and involved groups such as women, youth, and the disabled in decision making. However, the process began as a top-down initiative after the peace agreement, and generating the necessary political, civic, and bureaucratic buy-in to effectively decentralize real authority over decision making and resources has taken over a decade, and must be considered an ongoing process rather than a single reform.[2]

1. Government of Rwanda, "Decentralization Policy," Ministry of Local Government, Good Governance, Community Development and Social Affairs, May 2000.
2. John-Mary Kauzya, "Political Decentralization in Africa: Experiences of Rwanda, Uganda and South Africa" (discussion paper, Governance and Public Administration Branch, United Nations Department for Economic and Social Affairs, December 2007).

A typical division of power is among the executive, legislative, and judicial branches of the state. Each of these branches is endowed with separate and independent powers and responsibilities, with no single branch to have more power than the others. Following Costa Rica's civil war in 1948, a new constitution established the three supreme powers as the executive, legislative, and judicial branches, with the Congress and judiciary seeing an increase in their powers, thus ensuring a balance of power among all three branches of the government. Lack of clarity and poor implementation in the constitutional relationships between branches of the Afghan government have bedevilled politics since the election of the National Assembly in 2005, with the executive branch using a range of methods to subvert and minimize the role of the Assembly.

Military power dividing. Military power-dividing mechanisms attempt to provide a means of checking the ability of a majority group to use the coercive apparatus of the state to damage the interests of weaker groups. A principal means by which this has been done is to mandate the appointment of members of a subordinate group to key leadership positions including general, commander, director, or defense minister in the state's security forces, thereby ensuring that the chain of command is shared among groups. An example of this type of institution is the commissioning of Southern Sudan Liberation Movement leader and Anya-Nya commander-in-chief Major General Joseph

Box 15. Macedonia—Power Dividing through Decentralization to Municipalities

The 2001 Ohrid Framework Agreement aimed to provide a political settlement to conflict among Macedonia's majority Macedonians and the Albanian minority. Among its basic principles, the framework agreement declared, "The development of local self-government is essential for encouraging the participation of citizens in democratic life, and for promoting respect for the identity of communities" but also that "there are no territorial solutions to ethnic issues," rejecting federalism and autonomy, perceived as possible stepping-stones for secession. Instead, symmetric decentralization to an adjusted number of municipalities was pursued to offer limited autonomy to Macedonia's ethnic communities by increasing the number of competencies administered at the municipal level, including greater use of national languages and symbols, equitable representation of municipal employees, the use of "double-majority" voting in municipal councils, and municipal Committees for Inter-Community Relations.

The decentralization process in Macedonia has widely been regarded as a success story and is frequently considered a suitable model of ethnic conflict management that can be replicated in other regional contexts. However, the lack of transparency with which the boundaries of the eighty-three municipalities were redrawn gave rise to accusations that decentralization was becoming a "zero-sum" negotiation over control and access to resources between the two largest ethnic groups, and many smaller ethnic communities living scattered throughout the country fail to reach the thresholds required to benefit from the protection mechanisms.[1]

---

1. A. Lyon, "Municipal Decentralisation in the Republic of Macedonia: Preserving a Multi-Ethnic State?" *Federal Governance* 8, no. 3 (2011): 28–49.

Lagu as major general in the unified Sudanese army at the end of Sudan's civil war in 1972. Concerns about the ethnic composition of the leadership of the security forces in Afghanistan are frequently cited by leaders of various political factions.

Territorial power dividing. Power may also be divided vertically among levels of government, and may involve the allocation of territorial power among groups. By strengthening territorial units, territorial power-dividing institutions provide groups at the subnational level with some degree of autonomy vis-à-vis the central government. Examples of territorial power-dividing institutions include decentralization (also called devolution; see box 14), regional autonomy, and federalism.

Territorial power-dividing institutions can also be shaped to address specific groups or conflict drivers more directly. In Macedonia, following a brief ethnic conflict, decentralization to municipalities aimed to pass ethnically based cultural protections down to local levels (see box 15).

Economic power dividing. Generally used in conjunction with territorial power-dividing institutions, economic power-dividing measures are ones that transfer responsibilities over certain areas of activity and corresponding fiscal powers—that is, taxing and spending rights—to political subunits. Examples can be the use of community development funds (CDFs) in which communities or other subnational units choose their own priorities for the use of development spending, as in the National Solidarity Program in Afghanistan or the Indonesian Kecamatan Development Program.

Power Creating

Institutions that create new centers of power can act as a counterweight to existing centers of decision making. New centers of power or decision-making rights can be created from scratch. They can also be developed by giving formal recognition and legal structure to powers heretofore exercised informally by customary institutions or actors, or indeed by creating new functions for customary institutions. Numerous examples of power-creating institutions exist for the political dimension of state power, with some countries devising new institutions of government as a means of checking the power of the executive, for example. An example of an economic power-creating institution is an independent central bank which is empowered to set monetary policy. Costa Rica, after its 1948 civil war, created new centers of power and diminished executive dominance by moving key functions such as elections and oversight of public finance to newly created autonomous institutions (see box 16).

In Afghanistan, new institutions such as the Afghanistan Independent Human Rights Commission, the Independent Administrative and Civil Service Reform Commission, and the Independent Electoral Commission have been created. However, these notably lack independence or a clearly mandated set of roles that would enable them to act as power-creating institutions.

Power Diffusing

Power-diffusing mechanisms spread decision-making rights and powers that had previously rested with one actor to multiple actors, thereby involving multiple influences in a consensual process. This type of institution has typically been used within the political dimension as a means of reducing the power of the executive, and often relates to appointment processes.[125] One illustration of the diversity of power-diffusing arrangements is the power to appoint ministers, particularly where legislators are able to use proportionality or other rules to introduce balance vis-à-vis partisan, identity, or regionally based appointments made by the executive. In some countries, such as Mongolia, the legislature appoints ministers outright.

Box 16. Costa Rica—Political Power-Creating Institutions

Following the country's civil war in 1948, Costa Rica created two autonomous state organs that are equivalent in power to the legislative, executive, and judicial branches, although they are not equivalent in rank. The first is the Supreme Electoral Tribunal (TSE), an independent constitutional agency with full power to administer elections. The judges that make up the TSE are appointed by two thirds of the members of the Supreme Court of Justice for a period of six years with the possibility of a renewed appointment. The TSE has the power to organize, implement, and supervise all elections, including presidential, legislative, and local elections. Its decisions on the outcome of these elections are not subject to appeal.[1]

The second institution to be created in Costa Rica at this time was the Office of the Comptroller General, an autonomous and independent state organ nominally subordinate to the Legislative Assembly. The Comptroller General's powers lie in the area of the vigilance of public finance. It is responsible for approving all budgets and can initiate actions leading to the removal of actors who have misappropriated public funds.[2]

---

1. Rubén Hernández Valle, "Costa Rica: A Powerful Constitutional Body," in *Electoral Management Bodies* (Stockholm: International IDEA), www.Idea.int/publications/emd/upload/EMD_CS_Costa_Rica.pdf.
2. Costa Rica, Office of the Comptroller General of the Republic, "Political Constitution," www.intosaiitaudit.org/mandates/mandates/Mandates/Costa%20Rica.html#Costa_Rica.

In others, the legislature exercises appointment powers on the recommendation of the executive, as in Bulgaria and Ireland, or the executive may be required to appoint ministers in proportion to the representation of parties in the legislature, as in Fiji. Another form of this power diffusion is the right to approve the government as a whole, though not individual ministers, as is found in Romania.

In Afghanistan the constitution requires appointed ministers to receive approval from the legislature, as is also the case in China, but this requirement has been flouted in practice. In the absence of a developed party system or a proportional electoral framework, such power diffusion can also act as an opportunity for corruption. Furthermore, diffusing power over the composition of the government may be limited as a source of influence if policy making largely lies outside the cabinet in informal political arrangements with power brokers, as is often currently the case in Afghanistan.

However, power can be diffused over other kinds of appointments. The president of Afghanistan enjoys an extraordinarily high degree of autonomy in the power of appointment to judicial, administrative, and subnational posts, a problem that has also been known to contribute to governance problems in divided societies such as the Philippines. Such concentration of appointment power is not an inherent feature of presidential systems, and when it is present it tends to encourage a personalistic, zero-sum, and transactional form of

Box 17. Inadequate Diffusion of Appointment Powers in the Philippines

The president of the Philippines appoints the following officials with only nominal and ineffective checks by the legislature:

- secretaries (ministers) and undersecretaries of departments
- chairpersons or heads of bureaus or offices
- members of Constitutional Commissions (including on human rights), and the Office of the Ombudsman
- ambassadors and consuls
- officers of the armed forces, from the rank of colonel or naval captain
- heads of government-owned or -controlled corporations and their subsidiaries
- all other officers of government whose appointments are not otherwise provided by law.

These broad powers of appointment encourage patronage politics and corruption, and result in an "imperial presidency" that overwhelms the other branches and politicizes the judiciary. This undermines the creation of professional institutions that could render the presidency accountable, and has threatened government legitimacy, prompting calls for more effective checks.[1]

1. Aquilino Q. Pimentel, "The Presidential Form of Government in the Philippines: A Critique," in Comó Hacer Que Funciona el Sistema Presidencial, ed. Andrew Ellis, J. Jesús Orozco Henríquez, and Daniel Zovatto (Mexico City: UNAM/International IDEA 2009), 151–156.

politics, rather than the institutionalization of processes, checks, and balances (see box 17).

Legislatures might play a role in appointing or approving members of the judiciary or the civil service, perhaps making use of proportionality or other types of rules (the nature of these rules should be made as transparent as possible) to ensure that power is diffused in conflict-sensitive ways. Other actors could also play a role in appointment processes. Members of civil society or the Afghanistan Independent Human Rights Commission might serve on commissions charged with vetting candidates for public administrative or military positions, for example. It is important to note that the enforcement of these rules must be strongly incentivized—half-hearted attempts to give a relatively neutral Senior Appointments Panel or the Independent Directorate of Local Governance roles in choosing key administrative appointees have both foundered in Afghanistan. Given the role of the international community in funding the expenses and salaries of many officials, more could be done to encourage such diffusion of power.

Distributing Decision-Making Power

Table 1 illustrates some examples of the different categories of institutions discussed, and thus illustrates the breadth of the menu of options available to

Table 1. Distributing Decision-Making Powers in Divided Societies
Types of Mechanisms

DIMENSION OF STATE POWER	POWER-SHARING	POWER-DIVIDING	POWER-CREATING	POWER-DIFFUSING
Political	Political assignment of vice presidencies or cabinet positions; electoral proportional representation; rotating presidency	Improve balance of power among branches of government	Genuinely independent electoral commission; independent public finance authority	Effective legislative role in cabinet selection; approval of judicial and administrative appointments shared among political and civil society actors
Territorial	Assignment of provincial governorates	Political and administrative decentralization; territorial autonomy; federalism	Formation of new levels of government	Elected provincial governors
Military	Integration of rival militaries	Appointment of member of rival military as head of military forces	Disbandment and recreation of civilian military forces	Party-based, civil, or human rights vetting of military appointments; allow rival groups to retain security forces
Economic	Revenues shared on group basis	Fiscal decentralization	Independent central bank	

describe the allocation of decision-making powers in a political settlement. Some mechanisms that may have particular potential for addressing aspects of the Afghan conflict appear in bold font. These are but some examples of the range of institutions beyond executive power sharing that can distribute decision-making powers, contribute to actors' security in the long term, and involve new players such as civil society. They are offered in order to prompt discussion, and not as a definitive or exhaustive list.

Much of the debate about a peace settlement with insurgents in Afghanistan focuses only on two of the sixteen available cells in this matrix: political or territorial power sharing through assignment of central or provincial executive positions. However, a wide range of potential measures could create opportunities among the conflicting parties in Afghanistan to share influence, as well as balance that influence among conflict parties with more roles for noncombatants, civilian political actors, and vulnerable groups.

Decisions regarding how state decision-making rights and powers are to be distributed are not the only challenging issues facing Afghanistan. Nevertheless, an awareness of the different types of institutions that have been used to manage conflict in countries emerging from violence, coupled with an assessment of those most appropriate for the Afghan context, can serve as a basis for structuring a peace that addresses the sensitivities and mistrust, legitimacy crisis, and sense of lose-lose politics that are currently rife in the country.

These power-sharing, power-dividing, power-creating, and power-diffusing institutions are not without their limitations. For one, they reflect the formal institutional channels of politics, which as noted earlier are often supplanted in Afghanistan by a government of relationships. However, the creation of mechanisms that include more stakeholders in formal decision making can over time lessen the distance between state institutions and the informal practices of power by increasing the need to negotiate and build consensus and improving transparency. These types of institutions tend to be elite-centric and, focused as they are on balancing power among various groups, may be limited in their potential to generate new interests that cut across group lines. While it is important to be mindful of these limitations, these institutional arrangements may also reflect the art of the possible given current conditions, and could play a role in laying the ground for a future defined not by violent competition but by political interaction.

Conclusions

This report has addressed broadly the impacts that the complexity of the Afghan conflict may have on the various phases of a peace process to bring the country to a durable negotiated political settlement, and introduced a selection of theoretical and practical institutional options that might help address these impacts. Some general conclusions about those options at each phase are presented here, building on the more detailed discussion in the body of the report.

A peace process requires still more active engagement. Outright military victory for any side appears unlikely, but the military situation is not sufficiently stable or acute to bring the parties to the table. While there is an increasing awareness of the need for a negotiated solution, the emergence of a peace process is also blocked by deep mistrust, incoherence, and insecurity on the part of the primary actors, whether domestic, regional, or international. Active engagement is needed to encourage the initiation of a process.

- A framework of interested (but not overly implicated) and resourceful supporters from other states and potentially NGOs, Islamic institutions, or multilateral associations, coupled with an impartial mediator, could introduce confidence. The involvement of third-party actors who have an unambiguous pro-peace process agenda can add credibility to the process by bringing proposals and resources to the problems of initiating negotiations.
- Despite concerns about full recognition of insurgent actors, support structures will need to increase the confidence of insurgents that negotiations represent a viable path to achieving security and some core aims in order to strengthen pro-dialogue arguments among hard-line conflict actors. At the same time, these structures need to reassure other actors and potential political and regional spoilers.

A negotiation may be preceded by efforts to agree on a negotiating framework. Part of the decision to enter negotiations with serious intent will rest on the negotiating framework for such talks and some parameters for the goals of the talks being agreed to by key parties. Even a set of minimally acceptable principles and basic procedures will help generate confidence. These are not the same as unilateral preconditions, though constructive unilateral declarations can play a role in developing them.

- More detailed proposals are needed for a negotiating framework that reflects procedural and substantive concerns of the parties in formulae for participation, agenda, sequencing, and verification; these could emerge through unilateral declarations, active mediation, exchanges between the parties, track II engagement, or combinations of these means.
- It should not be expected that such a negotiating framework can be agreed to quickly. Time and effort will be needed to establish some degree of consensus among and within the relevant parties and establish necessary practical confidence measures to facilitate negotiations, and in doing so generate some momentum toward talks.

Beyond gaining the assent of the primary conflict parties to initiate a peace negotiation, it is vital that the process be framed to include other political and social interests. It is not only desirable but essential for the quality and the durability of the outcome that diverse political actors and civil-society opinions have avenues for expression and inclusion in the peace process.

- The conflict in Afghanistan consists of a number of overlapping structures, and the dynamics of these conflict structures will change as transition proceeds. It is important that stakeholders beyond the government and the insurgents be represented in order to support a process that addresses a wider range of root causes or risk factors, such as governance, ethnicity, and gender.

- Broadening inclusion beyond the government and insurgents can move negotiation of political elements of a peace settlement beyond the extremes normally represented by armed actors in a conflict to reflect the range of—possibly more moderate—opinions represented by civilian social forces.
- There is a range of ways to facilitate expanded inclusion, such as through representation by civilian politicians, consultation with civil-society assemblies, or direct representation of civil society in negotiations locally or nationally. Civil-society actors should also consider how active to be in leading discussion or pressuring for certain processes, and around what issues or interests organization and action will be most effective.

Transitional arrangements will need to be designed and agreed on that can help address difficult security, governance, and verification concerns in order to generate confidence in a peace process. Reaching a settlement will require considerable detail on certain key challenges for the transitional period.

- Security is and will continue to be a paramount risk to any process, given the incoherent conflict actors and likely spoilers and the difficulties inherent in providing security support in Afghanistan. Creative use of armed cease-fires, cantonment, joint monitoring, and third-party support will likely be needed.
- The outlines of a hybrid interim political arrangement that combines aspects of the current regime and assurances for stakeholders invested in it with necessary checks and reforms for new actors will be needed. Transitioning from this interim order to a longer-term settlement may require careful consideration of means such as elections or representative assemblies, given the challenges these means have faced already.
- Given the mistrust and the incoherence of the parties, robust monitoring, verification, and problem-solving institutions will be needed and will be difficult to establish. These mechanisms may be a good avenue for including civilian actors along with conflict parties in joint monitoring and implementation support mechanisms. The balance between intrusive and more neutral third-party support will also be an important consideration: while robust international support may be warranted, this must also be weighed against appetite and the risks for third-party neutrality and flexibility in assisting with problems during implementation.

Power sharing and reform are not mutually exclusive approaches to addressing the political dimensions of the conflict in Afghanistan. A false dichotomy has at times been drawn between negotiating peace with insurgents and pursuing necessary governance reforms. Power sharing will be part of any long-term agreement, but this should not be conceived of as simply sharing posts between government and insurgent, but as a range of mechanisms to include many stakeholders in generating more effective and accountable governance and in establishing the foundations for a more capable, accountable, and resilient state.

- Discussions among political, social, and civil-society elements in Afghanistan can consider the range of institutional options available that help share, divide, diffuse, or even create decision-making power across different dimensions of state power.
- Broadening the agenda to include a range of potential reforms across many institutions may be a good way to make space for the concerns of a larger range of stakeholders, and protect the interests of more groups, whether conflict parties or unarmed civilian actors, against the consequences of actual or perceived domination of decision making by others.

An important theme running through this report is the interdependence of the phases of the peace process. To prepare and then begin a negotiation process requires not just a conducive military situation, but also the development of options for future phases that can induce interest from all parties and generate the confidence needed to take the initial steps. Establishing a negotiating framework in turn requires some determination of key issues and parameters for the peace settlement even in advance of that negotiation, as well as preparing for the challenges of maintaining coherence and addressing setbacks and spoilers.

Conversely, the kind of process established to handle negotiations will influence the comprehensiveness, quality, and therefore sustainability of the outcomes both in the transitional period and over the longer term. In this sense, all the phases of a peace process are linked. That is why, precisely when doubts about the likelihood of a negotiated settlement may weigh heaviest on the parties to the Afghan conflict, it is so important to work hard to imagine options that might overcome those barriers.

Notes

1. International Security Assistance Force, "ISAF Violence Trends," Unclassified Monthly Release (presentation, Kabul, September 30, 2011), 4.
2. Prominent assassinations in 2011 include General Seyyedkheil (Kunduz police chief, March 10), Khan Mohammad (Kandahar police chief, April 15), General Daud Daud (police commander for Northern Zone, May 28), Ahmad Wali Karzai (head of Kandahar Provincial Council, July 12), Hikmatullah Hikmat (head of Kandahar *ulema shura*, July 14), Jan Mohammad Khan (senior presidential adviser, July 17), Ghulam Haydar Hamidi (mayor of Kandahar city, July 27), and Burhanuddin Rabbani (chairman of the High Peace Council, leader of Jamiat-e Islami, September 20). While attribution of all the killings to the Taliban is questionable, along with numerous attacks on less prominent figures, they demonstrate a dramatic escalation and a chilling effect on state functioning. See Kate

Clark, Killings Keep Leaders at Home, blog post, *Afghanistan Analysts Network*, August 4, 2011, www.aan-afghanistan.org/index.asp?id=1983.

3. For concerns with Afghan National Security Forces (ANSF) attrition rates, leadership, and sustainment costs, see Anthony H. Cordesman, "Afghanistan Win or Lose: Transition and the Coming Resource Crisis" (presentation, Center for Strategic and International Studies, September 22, 2011), http://csis.org/publication/afghanistan-win-or-lose-transition-and-resource-crisis. On concerns with irregular forces, see Human Rights Watch, " 'Just Don't Call It a Militia': Impunity, Militias, and the 'Afghan Local Police,' " September 2011.

4. The U.S. Treasury estimates of the economic contraction due to decreasing security and aid expenditures range from 12 to 40 percent, while the World Bank assesses that some 54 percent of GDP is related to services primarily linked to international military and aid spending. Cordesman, "Afghanistan Win or Lose," 2.

5. Kathy Gannon and Anne Gearon, "US-Taliban Talks Were Making Headway," *Associated Press*, August 29, 2011); "Haqqani Network Denies Killing Afghan Envoy Rabbani," *BBC Online*, October 3, 2011, www.bbc.co.uk/news/world-south-asia-15143513; Carlotta Gall, "Insurgent Faction Presents Afghan Peace Plan," *New York Times*, March 23, 2010.

6. Thomas Ruttig, "Negotiations with the Taliban: History and Prospects for the Future," New America Foundation, May 23, 2011, 7, 22; Ahmed Rashid, "What the Taliban Wants," blog post, *New York Review of Books*, August 29, 2011, www.nybooks.com/blogs/nyrblog/2011/aug/29/what-taliban-wants/. For a rebuttal of Rashid's analysis, see S. Iftikhar Murshed, "Mullah Omar's Eid Message," *International News*, September 25, 2011. For evidence from former Taliban officials and insurgent commanders, see Hamish Nixon, "Achieving Durable Peace: Afghan Perspectives on a Peace Process," PRIO Paper (Oslo: Chr. Michelsen Institute/Peace Research Institute Oslo/United States Institute of Peace, May 2011), 16–17.

7. Susan Sachs, "Failed Peace Council Dashes Hopes Afghans Can Achieve Reconciliation," *Globe and Mail*, October 16, 2011.

8. I. William Zartman, "Structures of Escalation and Negotiation," in *Escalation and Negotiation in International Conflict*, ed. I. William Zartman and Guy Faure (Cambridge: Cambridge University Press, 2005), 177. For example, in El Salvador in 1989, insurgents pursued "spectacular" attacks in the capital, San Salvador, successfully demonstrating that security could not be preserved in the most guarded precincts of the country. The Bosnian conflict was marked with large territorial gains, severe massacres, and the widest NATO escalation of air strikes in the year before the Dayton agreement was signed.

9. Associated Press, "Head of Islamic School that Spawned Taliban Insurgents Offers to Help Afghan Talks," November 1, 2011.

10. Ruttig, "Negotiations with the Taliban," 10; CNN Wire Staff, "Karzai Seeks Peace Talks with Pakistan, not Taliban," *CNN Online*, October 1, 2011.

11. Moeed Yusuf, Huma Yusuf, and Salman Zaidi, "Pakistan, the United States and the End Game in Afghanistan: Perceptions of Pakistan's Foreign Policy Elite," Policy Brief/Peace Brief, Jinnah Institute/United States Institute of Peace, July 25, 2011, 3.

12. See, for example, Omar Samad, "Afghanistan at a Critical Juncture," AfPak Channel blog post, *Foreign Policy*, October 6, 2011, http://afpak.foreignpolicy.com/posts/2011/10/06/afghanistan_at_a_critical_juncture.

13. Century Foundation, "Afghanistan: Negotiating Peace, the Report of The Century Foundation International Task Force on Afghanistan in Its Regional and Multilateral Dimensions" (New York: Century Foundation, 2011), 27; U.S. Department of State, "Secretary of State Hillary Rodham Clinton, Launch of the Asia Society's Series of Richard C. Holbrooke Memorial Addresses," transcript of remarks, February 18, 2011.

14. For examples, see "Could a Deal with the Taliban End the war in Afghanistan?" editorial, *Washington Post*, October 7, 2010; Astri Suhrke et al., "Conciliatory Approaches to the

Insurgency in Afghanistan: An Overview," in *CMI Report* (Bergen/Oslo: Chr. Michelsen Institute/PRIO, 2009), 4. The Century Foundation report notes that a sharing of ministries is likely and also considers the broader political order over the longer term. See Century Foundation, "Afghanistan," 28. In July 2011, civil-society activists in Kabul speculated that certain ministries (Foreign Affairs, Education, Defense) were being kept filled with "acting" ministers to ease such a process. Afghan civil society leader, interview, Kabul, July 2011.

15. Nixon, "Achieving Durable Peace," 13–14; Alissa J. Rubin, "Thousands of Afghans Rally in Kabul to Reject Any Peace with Taliban," *New York Times,* May 5, 2011.

16. Ruttig, "Negotiations with the Taliban," 22.

17. Catherine Barnes, "Renegotiating the Political Settlement in War-to-Peace Transitions," paper commissioned by DFID (London: Conciliation Resources, 2009), 20. The concept of "mutually enticing opportunities" (MEOs) as necessary supplements to stalemate is discussed in Thomas Ohlson, "Understanding Causes of War and Peace," *European Journal of International Relations* 14, no. 1 (2008): 147; I. William Zartman, "MEOs and Durable Settlements: A Theoretical and Empirical Evaluation of the Reasons for Durability of Peaceful Settlements in Civil Wars" (paper presented at the Annual Meeting of the American Political Science Association, September 2–5, 2004, http://citation.allacademic.com/meta/p_mla_apa_research_citation/0/6/0/1/7/pages60174/p60174-1.php.

18. Gretchen Birkle, Michael O'Hanlon, and Hasina Sherjan, "Toward a Political Strategy for Afghanistan," Policy Paper 27 (Washington, DC: Brookings Institution, May 2011), 10.

19. A seminal conflict-mapping framework is presented in Paul Wehr, *Conflict Regulation* (Boulder, CO: Westview Press, 1979); see also Dennis Sandole, "A Comprehensive Mapping of Conflict and Conflict Resolution: A Three Pillar Approach," *Peace and Conflict Studies* 5, no. 2 (December 1998): 1–30. For other references, see Paul Wehr, "Conflict Mapping," in *Beyond Intractability,* ed. Guy Burgess and Heidi Burgess (September 2006), www.beyondintractability.org/essay/conflict_mapping/.

20. For examples, see Swedish International Development Agency, Manual for Conflict Analysis (Stockholm: SIDA, 2006), 9–15; Jonathan Goodhand, Tony Vaux, and Robert Walker, Conducting Conflict Assessments: Guidance Notes (London: Department for International Development, 2002), 10–17.

21. Corinna Vigier, Conflict Assessment Afghanistan (American Friends Service Committee, 2009), 34–57.

22. The United Nations reported a 39 percent rise in security incidents in the first eight months of 2011 over the same period in 2010. United Nations, "The Situation in Afghanistan and Its Implications for International Peace and Security," Report of the Secretary-General, UN Doc A/66/369-S/2011/590, September 21, 2011. In contrast, ISAF claimed improved security, noting declines in "enemy-initiated attacks" during July–August 2011 as compared to 2010, a discrepancy explained by the exclusion of coalition actions as well as several categories of events including assassinations (of which the United Nations recorded 126 in July and August). ISAF, "Violence Statistics and Analysis Media Brief," September 29, 2011, www.isaf.nato.int/article/isaf-releases/isaf-violence-statistics-and-analysis-media-brief-sept.-29-2011.html.

23. Nixon, "Achieving Durable Peace," 7–14.

24. Sippi Azarbaijani-Moghaddam, "Northern Exposure for the Taliban," in *Decoding the New Taliban: Insights from the Afghan Field,* ed. Antonio Giustozzi (New York: Columbia University Press, 2009), 264; Antonio Giustozzi, *Koran, Kalashnikov and Laptop: The Neo-Taliban Insurgency in Afghanistan* (London: Hurst & Company, 2008), 48; Antonio Giustozzi, "The Taliban Beyond the Pashtuns," *The Afghanistan Papers* (Waterloo, ON: Centre for International Governance Innovation, 2010), 12.

25. Bernt Glatzer, "Is Afghanistan on the Brink of Ethnic and Tribal Disintegration?" in *Fundamentalism Reborn? Afghanistan and the Taliban,* ed. William Maley (London: Hurst

and Co., 1998); Bernt Glatzer, "The Pashtun Tribal System," in *Concept of Tribal Society,* ed. G. Pfeffer and D. K. Behera (New Delhi: Concept Publishers, 2002).

26. Martine van Bijlert, *The Battle for Afghanistan: Militancy and Conflict in Zabul and Uruzgan* (Washington, DC: New America Foundation, 2010), 3; Thomas Ruttig, "How Tribal Are the Taliban? Thematic Report" (Afghanistan Analysts Network, 2010), 3, 24. For the view that tribe is overemphasized, see Giles Dorronsoro, "Focus and Exit: An Alternative Strategy for the Afghan War" (Washington, DC: Carnegie Endowment for International Peace, 2009), 4. On the role of drugs in fueling both order and disorder, see Tom Coghlan, "The Taliban in Helmand: An Oral History," in *Decoding the New Taliban: Insights from the Afghan Field,* ed. Antonio Giustozzi (New York: Columbia University Press, 2009), 122–124, and Jonathan Goodhand, "Corrupting or Consolidating the Peace? The Drugs Economy and Post-Conflict Peacebuilding in Afghanistan," *International Peacekeeping* 15, no. 3 (June 2008).

27. The seminal account being Ahmed Rashid, *Taliban: The Story of the Afghan Warlords,* 2nd ed. (London: Pan, 2001), ch. 1.

28. Nixon, "Achieving Durable Peace," 10–12.

29. See for example, Swedish International Development Agency, "Manual for Conflict Analysis," 11.

30. James Shinn and James Dobbins, "Afghan Peace Talks: A Primer" (Santa Monica, CA: RAND Corporation, 2011), 17–69. The authors do take care to enumerate divisions and divergences of interests within the dozen actors they identify, a task requiring more than fifty pages of description.

31. For a recent example of such an analysis, see Citha Maas and Thomas Ruttig, *Is Afghanistan on the Brink of a New Civil War? Possible Scenarios and Influencing Factors in the Transition Process,* SWP Comments (Berlin: German Institute for International and Security Affairs, 2011). For the model of the "violent political marketplace," see Alex de Waal, "Mission without End? Peacekeeping in the African Political Marketplace," *International Affairs* 85, no. 1 (2009): 106.

32. Council on Foreign Relations, "Combating Afghanistan's 'Malign Governance,' " interview with Stephen Biddle, October 1, 2010, www.cfr.org/afghanistan/combating-afghanistans-malign-governance/p23071.

33. On the Kandahari/Paktiawal fissure, see Ruttig, "How Tribal Are the Taliban?" 13; on the "Waziristan militant complex," see Michael Semple, "How the Haqqani Network Is Expanding from Waziristan," Snapshots, *Foreign Affairs,* September 23, 2011, www.foreignaffairs.com/articles/68292/michael-semple/how-the-haqqani-network-is-expanding-from-waziristan.

34. For example, on the question of linkage to Al-Qaida, compare Jeffrey Dressler, "The Irreconcilables: The Haqqani Network," Backgrounder (Institute for the Study of War, 2010) with Alex Strick von Linschoten and Felix Kuehn, "Separating the Taliban from Al Qaeda: The Core of Success in Afghanistan" (New York: University Center on International Cooperation, February 2011).

35. On continuity, emphasis varies between preservation of the leadership structures on the one hand, and adoption of new techniques and policies on the other. See Ruttig, "How Tribal Are the Taliban?" 3, and Giustozzi, *Koran, Kalashnikov and Laptop.* On command and control, Kilcullen notes higher cohesion in the south than the southeast and east, and Mackenzie observes centralized disciplinary action and revenue channels in Helmand. David Kilcullen, "Taliban and Counter-Insurgency in Kunar," in *Decoding the New Taliban: Insights from the Afghan Field,* ed. Antonio Giustozzi (New York: Columbia University Press, 2009), 211; Jean McKenzie, *"The Battle for Afghanistan: Militancy and Conflict in Helmand"* (Washington, DC: New America Foundation, 2010), 14. By contrast there are examples of inability to maintain discipline in Ghazni, Helmand, and Badghis. See Christoph Reuter and Borhan Younus, "The Return of the Taliban in Andar District," in *Decoding the New Taliban: Insights from the Afghan Field,* ed. Antonio Giustozzi (New

York: Columbia University Press, 2009); Coghlan, "The Taliban in Helmand," 150; Stephen Carter and Kate Clark, "No Shortcut to Stability: Justice, Politics and Insurgency in Afghanistan," (London: Royal Institute of International Affairs, 2010), 19. On regenerative capacity, see Graeme Smith, "What Kandahar's Taliban Say," in *Decoding the New Taliban: Insights from the Afghan Field*, ed. Antonio Giustozzi (New York: Columbia University Press, 2009), 193–194, and van Bijlert, "Militancy and Conflict in Zabul and Uruzgan," 15. For analysis that more could be done to encourage splits via negotiation, see Michael Semple, *Reconciliation in Afghanistan* (Washington, DC: United States Institute of Peace, 2009). For evidence from local commanders of cohesion over negotiations, see Deedee Derksen, "Peace from the Bottom-Up? The Afghanistan Peace and Reintegration Program," PRIO Paper (Oslo: Chr. Michelsen Institute/Peace Research Institute Oslo/United States Institute of Peace, September 2011), 19–20.

36. On the sequence of mobilization and radicalization, see Sarah Ladbury and Center for Peace and Unity (CPAU), *Testing Hypotheses on Radicalisation in Afghanistan* (Kabul: CPAU, 2009).

37. Ruttig, "How Tribal Are the Taliban?," 2. See also Thomas Ruttig, "The Other Side: Dimensions of the Afghan Insurgency: Causes, Actors and Approaches to 'Talks,'" Afghanistan Analysts Network, 2009.

38. Abdul Awwal Zabulwal, "Taliban in Zabul: A Witness' Account," in *Decoding the New Taliban: Insights from the Afghan Field*, ed. Antonio Giustozzi (New York: Columbia University Press, 2009), 187; The Liaison Office, "Khost's Tribes: Between a Rock and a Hard Place," Policy Brief (Kabul: TLO, 2010), 10–11, and Mohammad Osman Tariq Elias, "The Resurgance of the Taliban in Kabul: Logar and Wardak," in *Decoding the New Taliban: Insights from the Afghan Field*, ed. Antonio Giustozzi (New York: Columbia University Press, 2009), 50.

39. On the *layha*, see Kate Clark, "The Layha: Calling the Taliban to Account," Afghanistan Analysts Network Thematic Report, July 2011, 7–15. On cases of decentralization, see Coghlan, "The Taliban in Helmand," 140–48, and van Bijlert, "Militancy and Conflict in Zabul and Uruzgan," 12.

40. Coghlan, "The Taliban in Helmand," 148.

41. Dorronsoro, "Focus and Exit: An Alternative Strategy for the Afghan War," 5, and Giustozzi, *Koran, Kalashnikov and Laptop*, 81–146.

42. Nixon, "Achieving Durable Peace," 12, 23.

43. Pamela Constable, "Rivals to Afghanistan's President in Disarray," *Washington Post*, June 13, 2011; Afghan NGO director, personal communication, July 18, 2011.

44. Derksen, "Peace from the Bottom-Up?" 4–5.

45. Birkle, O'Hanlon, and Sherjan, "Toward a Political Strategy for Afghanistan," 1–2.

46. Shinn and Dobbins, "Afghan Peace Talks," 18.

47. In particular, see the volume of essays edited by Antonio Giustozzi, *Decoding the New Taliban: Insights from the Afghan Field* (New York: Columbia University Press, 2009) and the "Battle for Afghanistan" reports published by the New America Foundation; Anand Gopal, *"The Battle for Afghanistan: Militancy and Conflict in Kandahar"* (Washington: New America Foundation, 2010); McKenzie, "Militancy and Conflict in Helmand"; and van Bijlert, "Militancy and Conflict in Zabul and Uruzgan."

48. For detailed accounts of attempts by Taliban leaders to retire in return only for security guarantees after 2001 and the ensuing difficulties they faced in Uruzgan, Zabul, Kandahar, Helmand, Ghazni, and beyond, see Martine van Bijlert, "Unruly Commanders and Violent Power Struggles: Taliban Networks in Uruzgan," in *Decoding the New Taliban: Insights from the Afghan Field*, ed. Antonio Giustozzi (New York: Columbia University Press, 2009), 157–158; Gopal, "Militancy and Conflict in Kandahar"; Giustozzi, *Koran, Kalashnikov and Laptop*, 37–38; Reuter and Younus, "The Return of the Taliban in Andar."

49. Gopal, "Militancy and Conflict in Kandahar," 11.

50. Ahmed Rashid, *Descent into Chaos: How the War against Islamic Extremism Is Being Lost in Pakistan, Afghanistan and Central Asia* (London: Allen Lane/Penguin, 2008).

51. There were warnings of failure when international military forces still numbered 30,000 and there had been a mere "handful" of suicide attacks. See Seth G. Jones, "Averting Failure in Afghanistan," *Survival* 48, no. 1 (2006).

52. A brief account of the influence of Mullah Dadullah (and behind him al Zarqawi) on Taliban tactics is given in Ruttig, "How Tribal Are the Taliban?" 17.

53. Ian S. Livingstone and Michael O'Hanlon, "Afghanistan Index: Tracking Variables of Reconstruction and Security in Post-9/11 Afghanistan" (Washington, DC: Brookings Institution, September 29, 2011).

54. Analysts note that two fast-growing categories of fighters have been those motivated by revenge for ISAF or government attacks and those who are released or related to U.S. or government captives. See Smith, "What Kandahar's Taliban Say," 199–200; McKenzie, "Militancy and Conflict in Helmand," 7–8; van Bijlert, "Unruly Commanders and Violent Power Struggles: Taliban Networks in Uruzgan," 159. See also Matt Waldman, "Dangerous Liaisons? An Assessment of the Feasibility and Risks of Negotiations with the Afghan Taliban," Special Report (Washington, DC: United States Institute of Peace Press, 2010), 3–4.

55. Antonio Giustozzi and Christoph Reuter, "The Insurgents of the Afghan North: The Rise of the Taleban, the Self-Abandonment of the Afghan Government and the Effects of ISAF's 'Capture-and-Kill' Campaign," Thematic Report 4 (Afghanistan Analysts Network, 2011), 9 10.

56. "Transition" has been adopted by U.S. and international forces and the Afghan government to refer to the process of handover of security responsibilities to the Afghan government, as well as accompanying shifts in support.

57. For detail on potential internal and regional interests opposed to a settlement, see Shinn and Dobbins, "Afghan Peace Talks," 14, 33, 55–56.

58. The concept of mutually hurting stalemate is laid out in, among others, I. William Zartman, "Ripeness: The Hurting Stalemate and Beyond," in *International Conflict Resolution after the Cold War*, ed. Paul C. Stern and Daniel Druckman (Washington, DC: National Academy Press, 2000).

59. Nicholas Haysom, "Engaging Armed Groups in Peace Processes: Lessons for Effective Third-Party Practice," in *Choosing to Engage: Armed Groups and Peace Processes*, ed. Robert Ricigliano (London: Conciliation Resources, Accord 16, 2005), 86.

60. Clem McCartney, "From Armed Struggle to Political Negotiations: Why? When? How?" in *Choosing to Engage: Armed Groups and Peace Processes*, ed. Robert Ricigliano (London: Conciliation Resources, Accord 16, 2005).

61. Nigel Quinney and A. Heather Coyne, eds., *Talking to Groups that Use Terror*, Peacemaker's Toolkit (Washington, DC: United States Institute of Peace Press, 2011), 36.

62. Shinn and Dobbins, "Afghan Peace Talks," 77.

63. Barnes, "Renegotiating the Political Settlement in War-to-Peace Transitions," 21.

64. Ruttig, "How Tribal Are the Taliban?" 24.

65. Barnes, "Renegotiating the Political Settlement in War-to-Peace Transitions," 22.

66. Quinney and Coyne, eds., *Talking to Groups that Use Terror*, 55–56.

67. Century Foundation, "Afghanistan: Negotiating Peace," 50–53.

68. For a discussion of different groups of friends and their pros and cons, see Teresa Whitfield, *Paying the Price: Ignacio Ellacuría and the Murdered Jesuits of El Salvador* (Philadelphia: Temple University Press, 1994), 24; for an Afghanistan-specific discussion of key questions, see Lisa Schirch, "Designing a Comprehensive Peace Process for Afghanistan," Peaceworks (Washington, DC: United States Institute of Peace Press, 2011), 31–32.

69. Century Foundation, "Afghanistan: Negotiating Peace," 53–54.

70. Whitfield, *Paying the Price: Ignacio Ellacuría and the Murdered Jesuits of El Salvador*, 16.

71. Conciliation Resources, "Ending War: The Need for Peace Process Support Strategies," Policy Brief, *Accord: An International Review of Peace Initiatives* (2009), www.c-r.org/our-work/accord/pdfs/cr_support_strategies_brief.pdf. For detailed discussion of support to prepare parties in Afghanistan, see Schirch, "Designing a Comprehensive Peace Process for Afghanistan," 28–29.

72. Barnes, "Renegotiating the Political Settlement in War-to-Peace Transitions," 5, 28.

73. Conciliation Resources, "Ending War," 4.

74. Amy L. Smith and David R. Smock, *Managing a Mediation Process*, Peacemaker's Toolkit (Washington, DC: United States Institute for Peace Press, 2008), 21–22, 46–47.

75. McCartney, "From Armed Struggle to Political Negotiations," 33.

76. "Pretoria Minute" and "National Peace Accord," ANC Web archive, www.anc.org.za/ancdocs/history/transition/npaccord.html.

77. Dínis S. Singulane and Jaime Pedro Gonçalves, "A Calling for Peace: Christian Leaders and the Quest for Reconciliation in Mozambique," in *The Mozambican Peace Process in Perspective*, ed. Alex Vines and Dylan Hendrickson (London: Conciliation Resources, Accord, 1998), 30.

78. Sir Marrack Goulding, "Public Participation and International Peacemaking," in *Owning the Process: Public Participation in Peacemaking*, ed. Catherine Barnes (London: Conciliation Resources, Accord 13, 2002), 86–89; Harold Saunders, "Prenegotiation and Circumnegotiation: Arenas of the Peace Process," in *Managing Global Chaos*, ed. Chester Crocker, Fen Osler Hampson, and Pamela Aall (Washington, DC: United States Institute of Peace Press, 1996), 419–432.

79. Catherine Barnes, "Democratizing Peacemaking Processes: Strategies and Dilemmas for Public Participation," in *Owning the Process: Public Participation in Peacemaking*, ed. Catherine Barnes (London: Conciliation Resources, Accord 13, 2002), 6.

80. For case studies of public participation increasing settlement legitimacy, see Catherine Barnes, ed., *Owning the Process: Public Participation in Peacemaking* (London: Conciliation Resources, Accord 13, 2002); a broader comparative analysis of civil society inclusion is Anthony Wanis-St. John and Darren Key, "Civil Society and Peace Negotiations: Confronting Exclusion," *International Negotiation* 13 (2008); a quantitative analysis of post-conflict "mass" power sharing is in Helga Malmin Binningsbø, "A Piece of the Pie: Power Sharing and Postconflict Peace," doctoral dissertation (Norwegian University of Science and Technology, 2011), 64.

81. Barnes, "Renegotiating the Political Settlement in War-to-Peace Transitions," 24; Schirch, "Designing a Comprehensive Peace Process for Afghanistan," 7–8.

82. Conciliation Resources, "Ending War," 3.

83. Barnes, "Democratizing Peacemaking," 6.

84. Nixon, "Achieving Durable Peace," 7–14.

85. Barnett Rubin, "Crafting a Constitution for Afghanistan," *Journal of Democracy* 15, no. 3 (2004): 7.

86. Barnes, "Democratizing Peacemaking," 8.

87. Schirch, "Designing a Comprehensive Peace Process for Afghanistan," 23–28; on local peacebuilding initiatives, see Matt Waldman, "Community Peacebuilding in Afghanistan: The Case for a National Strategy" (Oxford: Oxfam International, 2008).

88. Schirch, "Designing a Comprehensive Peace Process for Afghanistan," 11. See also Mary Kaldor and Marika Theros, "Building Afghan Peace from the Ground Up" (working paper, Century Foundation, 2011); Elizabeth Winter, "Civil Society Development in Afghanistan" (working paper, London School of Economics Center for Civil Society, June 2010).

89. Quentin Oliver, "Developing Public Capacities for Participation in Peacemaking," in *Owning the Process: Public Participation in Peacemaking*, ed. Catherine Barnes (London: Conciliation Resources, Accord 13, 2002), 91.

90. Barnes, "Renegotiating the Political Settlement in War-to-Peace Transitions," 3.

91. Terrence Lyons, "Postconflict Elections: War Termination, Democratization, and Demilitarizing Politics" (working paper no. 20, Institute for Conflict Analysis and Resolution, George Mason University, 2002), http://icar.gmu.edu/Work_Paper 20.pdf.

92. Terrence Lyons, "Soft Intervention and the Transformation of Militias into Political Parties," in *Strengthening Peace in Post-Civil War States: Transforming Spoilers into Stakeholders*, ed. Matthew Hoddie and Caroline A. Hartzell (Chicago: Chicago University Press, 2010), 147.

93. Shinn and Dobbins, "Afghan Peace Talks," 83.

94. For a discussion of the security dilemma and its application to internal conflict, see Jack Snyder and Robert Jervis, "Civil War and the Security Dilemma," in *Civil Wars, Insecurity, and Intervention*, eds. Barbara F. Walter and Jack Snyder (New York: Columbia University Press, 1999), 15–37.

95. Caroline A. Hartzell, "Missed Opportunities: The Impact of DDR on SSR in Afghanistan," Special Report 270 (Washington, DC: United States Institute of Peace Press, April 2011).

96. The Local Monitoring Teams include representatives of the local government unit, the local Moro Islamic Liberation Front command, two NGO representatives appointed by the parties, and a local religious leader. See Hoffman, "Peace Negotiations in the Philippines: The Government, the MILF and International NGOs," 3.

97. Nepal, "Agreement on Monitoring of the Management of Arms and Armies, 28 November 2006," www.satp.org/satporgtp/countries/nepal/document/papers/28nov2006.htm.

98. Comfort Lamptey, "Engaging Civil Society in Peacekeeping: Strengthening Strategic Partnerships between United Nations Peacekeeping Missions and Local Civil Society Organisations during Post-Conflict Transitions," August 2007, http://pbpu.unlb.org/pbps/Library/Engaging%20Civil%20Society%20in%20Peacekeeping.pdf.

99. Nixon, "Achieving Durable Peace," 10–11, 17–20.

100. World Bank/DFID, *Afghanistan: Public Financial Management Performance Assessment* (World Bank/DFID, June 2008).

101. Lyons, "Soft Intervention and the Transformation of Militias into Political Parties," 150.

102. Nixon, "Achieving Durable Peace," 12.

103. Peter Wallensteen and Mikael Eriksson, *Negotiating Peace: Lessons from Three Comprehensive Peace Agreements* (Uppsala and New York: Uppsala University and the Mediation Support Unit, Department of Political Affairs, United Nations, 2009), 27.

104. On the latter point, see Lisa Schirch, "Afghan Civil Society and a Comprehensive Peace Process," Peace Brief 99 (Washington, DC: United States Institute of Peace, July 21, 2011).

105. Lyons, "Soft Intervention and the Transformation of Militias into Political Parties," 150.

106. See Caroline A. Hartzell and Matthew Hoddie, *Crafting Peace: Power-Sharing Institutions and the Negotiated Settlement of Civil Wars* (University Park, PA: Pennsylvania State University Press, 2007) for details regarding the distinction between negotiated truces and negotiated settlements.

107. Karl DeRouen Jr., Mark J. Ferguson, Samuel Norton, Young Hwan Park, Jenna Lea, and Ashley Streat-Bartlett, "Civil War Peace Agreement Implementation and State Capacity," *Journal of Peace Research* 47, no. 3 (2010): 333–46.

108. Astri Suhrke, "When More Is Less: Aiding Statebuilding in Afghanistan" (Madrid: Fundación para las Relaciones Internacionales y el Diálogo Exterior, 2006).

109. Report of the Secretary-General on the Activities of ONUSAL Since the Cease-fire between the Government of El Salvador and the FMLN, UN Document S/23999, Section III, May 26, 1992; Graciano del Castillo, "The Arms-for-Land Deal in El Salvador," in

Keeping the Peace: Multidimensional UN Operations in Cambodia and El Salvador, ed. Michael W. Doyle, Ian Johnstone, and Robert C. Orr (Cambridge: Cambridge University Press, 1997), 347–48.

110. Anna Larson, "Deconstructing 'Democracy' in Afghanistan," Synthesis Paper Series (Kabul: Afghanistan Research and Evaluation Unit, May 2011), 28–30; Nixon, "Achieving Durable Peace," 33.

111. Conciliation Resources, "Ending War: The Need for Peace Process Support Strategies," 2.

112. Caroline A. Hartzell, "Explaining the Stability of Negotiated Settlements to Intrastate Wars," *Journal of Conflict Resolution* 43, no. 1 (February 1999): 3–22.

113. Anna K. Jarstad, "Power-Sharing: Former Enemies in Joint Government," in *From War to Democracy: Dilemmas of Peacebuilding*, ed. Anna K. Jarstad and Timothy D. Sisk (Cambridge: Cambridge University Press, 2008); Andreas Mehler, "Peace and Power-Sharing in Africa: A Not So Obvious Relationship," *African Affairs* 108, no. 432 (2009): 453–473.

114. Timothy Sisk, "Power-Sharing" (Beyond Intractability, September 2003), www.beyondintractability.org/essay/power_sharing/?nid=1382.

115. The seminal discussion of this "integrative" approach is found in Donald Horowitz, *Ethnic Groups in Conflict* (Los Angeles and Berkeley: University of California Press, 1985).

116. Pippa Norris, *Driving Democracy: Do Power-Sharing Institutions Work?* (New York: Cambridge University Press, 2008), 4–5.

117. Key examples include Barbara F. Walter, *Committing to Peace: The Successful Settlement of Civil Wars* (Princeton, NJ: Princeton University Press, 2002); Bumba Mukherjee, "Does Third-Party Enforcement or Domestic Institutions Promote Enduring Peace after Civil Wars: Policy Lessons from an Empirical Test," *Foreign Policy Analysis* 2, no. 4 (2006): 405–30; Michaela Mattes and Burcu Savun, "Fostering Peace after Civil War: Commitment Problems and Agreement Design," *International Studies* Quarterly 53, no. 3 (2009): 737–59; and Hartzell and Hoddie, *Crafting Peace*.

118. Hartzell and Hoddie, *Crafting Peace*; and Malmin Binningsbø, "A Piece of the Pie," 110.

119. Shinn and Dobbins, "Afghan Peace Talks," 72, 101; Schirch, "Designing a Comprehensive Peace Process for Afghanistan," 5–8. See also for examples, Waldman, "Dangerous Liaisons?" 13–14; Martine van Bijlert, "The Government's New Peace Strategy: Who to Talk To?" blog post, Afghanistan Analysts Network, October 4, 2011, www.aan-afghanistan.org/index.asp?id=2109.

120. Schirch, "Designing a Comprehensive Peace Process for Afghanistan," 5; Tazreena Sajjad, "Peace at All Costs? Reintegration and Reconciliation in Afghanistan," Issues Paper (Kabul: Afghanistan Research and Evaluation Unit, 2010), 3–5, 26–7.

121. Our thoughts on this issue and throughout the section benefitted from discussion with Scott Gates, personal communication, June 17, 2011.

122. The discussion of political power sharing draws on Hartzell and Hoddie, *Crafting Peace*.

123. The development of the theory of consociational power sharing has been most associated with the work of Arend Lijphart. See Arend Lijphart, *Democracy in Plural Societies: A Comparative Exploration* (New Haven: Yale University Press, 1977); Arend Lijphart, *Patterns of Democracy: Government Forms and Performance in 36 Countries* (New Haven: Yale University Press, 1999).

124. Nicholas Haysom and Sean Kane, "Negotiating Natural Resources for Peace: Ownership, Control and Wealth-Sharing," Briefing Paper, Centre for Humanitarian Dialogue, October 2009, 22, 30.

125. Alexander Mayer-Rieckh and Pablo de Greiff, ed., *Justice as Prevention: Vetting Public Employees in Transitional Societies* (New York: Social Science Research Council, 2007).

Contributors

Editors

Scott Smith is the deputy director of Afghanistan programs at the U.S. Institute of Peace. Previously, he spent thirteen years at the United Nations, focusing on Afghanistan and democratization issues. He was the senior special assistant to the special representative of the secretary-general in Kabul from January 2009 to August 2010. He is the author of *Afghanistan's Troubled Transition: Politics, Peacekeeping, and the 2004 Presidential Election* and an adjunct professor at Columbia University's School of International and Public Affairs (SIPA). Smith holds a bachelor of science in foreign service from Georgetown University and a master's degree in international affairs from SIPA.

Moeed Yusuf is the South Asia adviser for the Center for Conflict Management at the U.S. Institute of Peace and is also responsible for managing the Institute's Pakistan program. Before joining USIP, Yusuf was a research fellow concurrently at Boston University's Frederick S. Pardee Center for the Study of the Longer Range Future and at Harvard University's Mossavar-Rahmani Center. In 2007, he cofounded Strategic and Economic Policy Research, a private sector consultancy firm in Pakistan. From 2004 to 2007, he was a full-time consultant with the Sustainable Development Policy Institute (SDPI), Pakistan's premier development-sector think tank. Yusuf has consulted for a number of international organizations and has also taught at Boston University and at Quaid-e-Azam University, Pakistan. His most recent book, *South Asia 2060: Envisioning Regional Futures* (coedited with Adil Najam), was published by Anthem Press in 2013.

Colin Cookman is a researcher for the U.S. Institute of Peace and a master's degree candidate at Johns Hopkins University's School of Advanced International Studies. He previously served as a research analyst at the Center for American Progress from 2008 to 2013, where his work focused on the internal politics of and American policy toward Afghanistan and Pakistan. He has contributed to Economist Intelligence Unit publications on the region and was a member of Democracy International's election observation team during the 2010 parliamentary elections in Afghanistan. He is a 2005 graduate of Boston University with a bachelor's in international relations.

Contributors

Noah Coburn is a sociocultural anthropologist who has conducted research in Afghanistan since 2005. He joined the faculty at Bennington College in 2012; he previously taught at the American University of Afghanistan, Boston University, the University of Michigan, and Skidmore College. His doctoral research at Boston University focused on conflict and political structures in the Shomali Plain north of Kabul. In 2009 and 2010, Coburn led the U.S. Institute of Peace's informal justice work in Afghanistan. He also contributed to publications for the Afghan Research and Evaluation Unit and the Aga Khan Trust for Culture. He is the author of *Bazaar Politics: Power and Pottery in an Afghan Market Town*.

Sunil Dasgupta is director of the University of Maryland Baltimore County's political science program at the Universities at Shady Grove and a nonresident senior fellow at the Brookings Institution in Washington, DC. He teaches political science, international affairs, and security studies and writes on military strategy, organization, and operations. He is coauthor of *Arming without Aiming: India's Military Modernization* and is presently working on a project investigating Chinese and Indian grand strategic approaches.

Deedee Derksen is author of *Tea with the Taliban,* a Dutch book nominated for a nonfiction award. From 2001 to 2009, she served as a Kabul correspondent for the Dutch newspaper *de Volkskrant* and the current affairs television program *NOVA*. She received a master's in international relations from the University of Amsterdam and completed a postdoctorate course in journalism from Erasmus University in Rotterdam. She is currently a candidate for a PhD at the War Studies Department of King's College in London. Her contribution to this volume was part of a joint project by the Chr. Michelsen Institute, Peace Research Institute Oslo, and the U.S. Institute of Peace to identify issues and options to help Afghanistan move toward sustainable peace.

Caroline Hartzell is a professor of political science at Gettysburg College and was founding director of the college's Globalization Studies program. Hartzell was a Jennings Randolph Senior Fellow at the U.S. Institute of Peace in 2010 and 2011. Her research focused on the effects of civil war settlements on postconflict economic growth. In Colombia, Hartzell evaluated a U.S. Agency for International Development–funded project seeking to establish the presence of the Colombian government in postconflict zones and conducted research as a Fulbright scholar on the effects of the civil war on subsequent economic development. In Afghanistan, she worked to help Afghan stakeholders explore options for an Afghan peace process.

Minna Jarvenpaa is a policy analyst who has worked in Afghanistan since late 2005. Most recently, she served as international advocacy director for the Open Society Foundation. She previously held senior roles with the European Stability Initiative and was the head of analysis and planning at the UN Assistance Mission in Afghanistan. In addition to Afghanistan, she worked in conflict and postconflict settings in Bosnia, Kosovo, Serbia, Macedonia, Northern Ireland, and Iraq. She is a founding member of two think tanks, the Afghanistan Analysts Network and the European Stability Initiative, and an associate of the Centre for International Studies at Oxford. She studied international relations at the London School of Economics and Slavic languages at Harvard University.

Hamish Nixon is an independent consultant who has most recently conducted research and assessments for the World Bank, the Asia Foundation, and the Hague Academy for Local Governance. His work focuses on decentralization and local governance issues, peace and conflict studies, and election monitoring and observation. From September 2010 through January 2012, he coordinated a joint project of the Chr. Michelsen Institute, the Peace Research Institute Oslo, and the U.S. Institute of Peace on durable peace in Afghanistan. He is a member of the advisory board for Afghanistan Watch and worked in Afghanistan for the World Bank and the Afghanistan Research and Evaluation Unit from 2005 to 2010. He holds a PhD in comparative politics from the University of Oxford and a bachelor's in political science from Stanford University.

Barnett Rubin is director of studies at the Center on International Cooperation of New York University. Currently, he is the senior adviser to the special representative of the president for Afghanistan and Pakistan in the U.S. Department of State. In 2001, Rubin served as special adviser to the UN special representative of the secretary-general for Afghanistan during the negotiations that produced the Bonn Agreement. He advised the United Nations on the drafting of the constitution of Afghanistan, the Afghanistan Compact, and the Afghanistan National Development Strategy. Rubin served as a fellow at the U.S. Institute of Peace and director at the Council on Foreign Relations in New York. He previously taught at Columbia University and Yale University and has authored multiple books on Afghanistan and Central Asia.

Lisa Schirch is director of 3P Human Security, a program of the Alliance for Peacebuilding, where she is also a policy advisor. She is a research professor at the Center for Justice and Peacebuilding at Eastern Mennonite University. A former Fulbright fellow in East and West Africa, Schirch has worked in over twenty countries in conflict prevention and peacebuilding. Her current research interests include civil-military dialogue, the design and structure of a comprehensive peace process in Afghanistan, conflict assessment and program design, and the role of the media in peacebuilding. She has written four books. Schirch holds a bachelor's in international relations from the University of Waterloo, Canada, and a master's and PhD in conflict analysis and resolution from George Mason University.

Abubakar Siddique is a senior correspondent covering Afghanistan and Pakistan for Radio Free Europe/Radio Liberty's central newsroom. Siddique has spent the past decade researching and writing about security, political, humanitarian, and cultural issues in Pakistan, Afghanistan, and the Pashtun heartland along the border region, where he was born. Siddique holds master's degrees in journalism and anthropology. He was a Fulbright scholar at New York University from 2005 to 2006 and, while at NYU, also worked at the Center on International Cooperation, a think tank that seeks to enhance coordination of international responses to humanitarian crises and global security threats.

Mohammad Masoom Stanekzai was a fellow at the U.S. Institute of Peace from 2007 to 2009. He currently serves as the head of the joint secretariat of Afghanistan's High Peace Council, which is tasked with leading Afghan government peace and reconciliation efforts. He previously served as the minister of telecommunications in Afghanistan's transitional government. Prior to that, he was director of the Agency for Rehabilitation and Energy Conservation in Afghanistan. Stanekzai earned a master's degree in philosophy of engineering for sustainable development from Cambridge University and a master's in business management from Preston University. He has a bachelor's from the Kabul Telecom Institute and is a graduate of the Kabul Military University.

Marvin G. Weinbaum is professor emeritus of political science at the University of Illinois at Urbana-Champaign and served as analyst for Pakistan and Afghanistan in the U.S. Department of State's Bureau of Intelligence and Research from 1999 to 2003. He is currently a scholar-in-residence at the Middle East Institute in Washington, DC. At Illinois, he served for fifteen years as the director of the Program in South Asian and Middle Eastern Studies. He is the author or editor of six books and has written more than one hundred journal articles and book chapters. Dr. Weinbaum was awarded Fulbright research fellowships for Egypt in 1981–82 and Afghanistan in 1989–90 and was a senior fellow at the U.S. Institute of Peace in 1996–97.

Matt Waldman was a Harvard Carr Center for Human Rights Policy fellow from 2009 to 2010 and is currently a research fellow with Harvard's Belfer Center international security program. He previously served as a senior UN official in Kabul, covering conflict resolution and reconciliation with the Taliban. He also worked as head of policy for Oxfam in Afghanistan from 2006 to 2009 and, prior to this, as a foreign affairs and defense adviser in the UK Parliament. At Harvard, his research focuses on the Afghanistan conflict, especially reconciliation, negotiations, and the role of misperceptions. He also conducts analysis of certain armed conflicts and is involved in, and advises on, mediation initiatives.

Huma Yusuf is a freelance journalist and columnist for the Pakistani newspaper *Dawn* and was the 2010–11 Pakistan Scholar at the Woodrow Wilson International Center for Scholars in Washington, DC. Her reporting on human rights and ethnic conflict in Pakistan won the European Commission's Prix Natali Lorenzo for Human Rights and Democracy Journalism (2006) and the UNESCO/Pakistan Press Foundation Gender in Journalism Award (2005).

Salman Zaidi is deputy director at the Jinnah Institute (JI) in Islamabad. Zaidi leads JI's Strategic Security Initiative and works on the Indo-Pak and Pak-Afghan Track II dialogues, in addition to its Water Security project. He has a background in conflict research and has written on resource conflicts in South Asia and the Middle East. Zaidi previously worked for the development sector in Pakistan, where he conducted monitoring and evaluation of governance and conflict resolution projects in interior Sindh, Punjab, and Balochistan. He holds a master's of science in violence, conflict, and development from the School of Oriental and African Studies and a bachelors of science in development studies from Iqra University in Karachi.

Board of Directors